Democracy Reloaded

Recent Titles in

OXFORD STUDIES IN CULTURE AND POLITICS
Clifford Bob and James M. Jasper, General Editors

Democracy Reloaded

Inside Spain's Political Laboratory
from 15-M to Podemos

CRISTINA FLESHER FOMINAYA

OXFORD
UNIVERSITY PRESS

OXFORD
UNIVERSITY PRESS

Oxford University Press is a department of the University of Oxford. It furthers
the University's objective of excellence in research, scholarship, and education
by publishing worldwide. Oxford is a registered trade mark of Oxford University
Press in the UK and certain other countries.

Published in the United States of America by Oxford University Press
198 Madison Avenue, New York, NY 10016, United States of America.

Library of Congress Cataloging-in-Publication Data
Names: Flesher Fominaya, Cristina, author.
Title: Democracy reloaded : inside Spain's political laboratory
from 15-M to Podemos / Cristina Flesher Fominaya.
Description: New York, NY : Oxford University Press, [2020] |
Series: Oxford studies in culture and politics |
Includes bibliographical references and index.
Identifiers: LCCN 2019047139 (print) | LCCN 2019047140 (ebook) |
ISBN 9780190099961 (hardback) | ISBN 9780190099978 (paperback) |
ISBN9780190099992 (epub) | ISBN 9780197500002 (online)
Subjects: LCSH: 15-M (Organization) | Protest movements—Spain—
History—21st century. | Social movements—Spain—History—21st century. |
Political participation—Spain—History—21st century. |
Democracy—Spain—History—21st century.
Classification: LCC HN583.5.F54 2020 (print) |
LCC HN583.5 (ebook) | DDC 303.48/40946—dc23
LC record available at https://lccn.loc.gov/2019047139
LC ebook record available at https://lccn.loc.gov/2019047140

9 8 7 6 5 4 3 2 1

Paperback printed by Marquis, Canada
Hardback printed by Bridgeport National Bindery, Inc., United States of America

A
Madrid
y
a mi madre
María del Sagrado Corazón de Jesús Fominaya Escrivá
de Romaní
(1932–2019)

Contents

PART III: *From Occupation to Movement: Inside the 15-M Network*

PART IV: *From 15-M to Podemos*

PART V: *Conclusions*

Maps and Figures

Tables

Images

Preface

OVER THE PAST several years, I have had the opportunity to talk about 15-M and the Spanish political laboratory to diverse audiences around the world, many of whom have expressed a fascination with the "Spanish revolution" and were eager to know more about it. This book tells the story of this remarkable movement from the inside. Throughout the book I engage with some core debates about the nature and significance of contemporary progressive social movements, but this book is also for people who might care little for such debates but want to understand what happened in Spain's 15-M movement, how it happened, and why.

When the Spanish "Indignados" burst onto the international scene by occupying Madrid's Central Plaza and, shortly thereafter, central squares across Spain, pundits and scholars immediately began to characterize what was happening as "spontaneous," "new," "unprecedented," and driven by social media. As someone who has participated and researched autonomous social movements in Madrid since the early 1990s, my own reaction was very different. While I had never seen such large, "open air" assemblies, I also knew that effectively running an assembly of that size requires people with very specific skills and experiences in assembly practices. Despite widespread claims that "no one in the square knew each other," I saw activists I knew had over 20 years of experience helping to facilitate the assemblies in the Puerta del Sol. As to what the people in the square were demanding, the core slogan, "We are not commodities in the hands of politicians and bankers," was very close to what activists were saying during the Global Justice Movement (GJM). After all, what was the GJM if not a movement that questioned the global political and economic order? Nevertheless, I also immediately noticed significant differences. The first was the central demand for "Real Democracy Now!" and a shift toward reclaiming democratic institutions, a process I have called "the democratic turn" (Flesher Fominaya 2014a, 2015b, 2015e, 2017). Another was a shift from the denunciation of global capitalism in the abstract to a specific targeting of *national* political elites for their role in the crisis and its aftermath (Flesher Fominaya 2017).

As to the role of digital tools, I wasn't sure. Was it true that they had radically transformed the organizing logics of collective action, as some claimed? What was really going on? In 2013, thanks to a two-year Marie Curie Fellowship, I endeavored to find out. I re-entered the field armed with a few key questions: How did the 15-M movement start? Why and how did it develop to become one of the most influential and sustained mass mobilizations in the world? What motivated its participants and what did they actually mean when they demanded "real democracy now"? What sustained the movement beyond the squares, in contrast to so many other "Occupy" movements that fizzled out? What impact and outcomes had the movement had? And what did all this tell us about the potential of contemporary progressive movements?

In 2014, Podemos appeared on the political scene, introducing a new and unexpected movement outcome that demanded analysis. From 2013 to 2015 I spent hundreds of hours in movement assemblies, protests, and squatted social centers, participating with activists and speaking to them in many different contexts, during assemblies and protests, but also over drinks and meals, at squat parties, film screenings, and social events. What I found was a laboratory of democratic experimentation that had transformed the lives of thousands of people and Spain's political landscape. I interviewed some 50 activists in the movement, some of whom I have known for over 15 years and with whom I share past activism, others who became politically active with 15-M. The youngest were in their late teens, the oldest in their late 70s. The long-term activists helped me understand what had really changed and what hadn't, and the new activists helped me see the movement through their eyes.

In Spain and in Madrid the activist/scholar/intellectual is a common figure, and many fellow activist/academics enriched my understanding and analysis of this movement immensely, through their formal writings, some included here, but also through many, many conversations over the past eight years that have contributed much to what you will read here. Although I include activists and cases in Barcelona (15MpaRato, Chapter 7, and the PAH, Chapter 8), this book is based primarily on Madrid's 15-M network, which is where the movement started, arguably its most influential node, and where I spent most of my time. There are other 15-M's, and no single book could ever capture the complexity and diversity of such a dynamic movement. I hope, though, that what I have written will resonate with those who have lived through the experience of the 15-M movement, as well as introducing it to people completely new to it. I have found "15-M" to be deeply provocative, illuminating, and inspiring, and I hope that through this book, you will too.

Acknowledgments

MY DEEPEST GRATITUDE to all the activists who trusted me with their stories, without which this book would not exist. I am so thankful to so many people who helped me with this book over the past years, but it would take me another year to thank all of you individually. Please know I am truly grateful. Special thanks to Celia Valiente, Ramón Feenstra, Andrea Teti, and Casilda Montgomery, critics and animators extraordinaire. Thanks also to Antonio Montañés Jimenez for all his help. Thanks also to Sofia/ "DJ" Eguiarte Flesher for help with the index. Thanks also to Jim Jasper and James Cook at OUP for their support. This work was supported by the Marie Sklodowska-Curie Fellowship [grant number 326712].

An Important Note about Names and Attribution

IN THIS BOOK, all interviewees identified by first name only (e.g., Blanca, Carlos) are pseudonyms. All sources identified by first and last names are real names. A few interviewees appear in some parts of the book with their real names and in other parts with pseudonyms. This is either to respect their wishes regarding attribution or in cases where the attributed quote comes from a public source and not a personal interview. Unless otherwise indicated, all interviews were conducted by me, face-to-face, in Madrid, Barcelona, or Dublin, between October 2013 and September 2015, with the exception of one Skype interview. All groups and organizations are real and identified by their actual names. Finally, the term "hacker" is used in the movement and in this book to denote someone with some IT skills who embraces a hacker ethos; it does not imply that they engage in any illegal activity.

Abbreviations

15-M	Movement named for May 15, 2011
AGSOL	Asamblea General de Sol (General Assembly of Sol)
ANOVA	Anova-Irmandade Nacionalista (A Galician Nationalist Party)
APM	Asamblea Popular de Madrid (Madrid Popular Assembly)
ATTAC	Association for a Tobin Tax to Aid the Citizens
CCOO	Comisiones Obreras (Workers Commissions)
CGT	Confederación General del Trabajo (General Worker Confederation)
CNT	Confederacion Nacional de Trabajadores (National Workers Confederation)
CNN	Cable News Network
CNMV	Comisión Nacional del Mercado de Valores (National Stock Exchange Commission)
CMI	Producciones Con Mano Izquierda (Left Handed Productions)
CSOA	Centro Social Okupado Autogestionado (Self-Managed Squatted Social Center)
CT	Cultura de la Transición (Culture of the Transition)
CUP	Candidatura d'Unitat Popular (Popular Unity Candidacy) (A Leftist Catalan Independence List)
DIY	Do It Yourself
DRY	Democracia Real Ya! (Real Democracy Now!)
EU	European Union
FRAVM	Federación Regional de Asociación de Vecinos de Madrid (Regional Federation of Madrid Neighborhood Associations)
FROB	Fondo de Reestructuración Bancaria (Bank Restructuring Fund)
GJM	Global Justice Movement
IA	Izquierda Anticapitalista (Anticapitalist Left)
ICTs	Information and Communication Technologies
ILP	Iniciativa Legislativa Popular (Popular Legislative Initiative)
IMF	International Monetary Fund
IU	Izqueirda Unida (United Left Coalition Party)
JSF	Juventud Sin Futuro (Youth without Future)

LGBTQ   Lesbian, Gay, Bisexual, Transgender, Queer
MEP   Member of the European Parliament
MLGM   Movimiento de Liberación Gráfica de Madrid (Madrid Graphic
            Liberation Movement)
MRG   Movimiento de Resistencia Global
OWS   Occupy Wall Street
PAH   Plataforma de Afectados por la Hipoteca (Platform for Those
            Affected by Mortgages)
PCE   Partido Comunista de España (Spanish Communist Party)
PP   Partido Popular (Popular Party—Right Wing Party)
PSOE   Partido Socialista Obrero Español (Spanish Socialist Workers Party)
SAREB   Sociedad de Gestión de Activos Procedentes de la Reestructuración
            Bancaria (Management Board of Assets from Banking
            Restructuring, or "Bad Bank")
SAT   Sindicato de Trabajadores de Andalucía (Andalusian
            Workers Union)
UGT   Unión General de Trabajadores (General Workers Union)
UPyD   Unión Progreso y Democracia (Union, Progress, and Democracy)

Introduction

IN MAY 2018 the Victoria and Albert Museum in London opened an exhibit called *The Future Starts Here*. Posters for the exhibit posed a series
of defining questions about the future. One such poster asked, DOES
DEMOCRACY STILL WORK? Such a question would have been bizarre
even a decade earlier, but today, it seems, everyone is debating the state of
democracy. The question was printed on an image of a woman with her
back turned wearing one of the pink "pussy hats" worn by protesters for
women's rights following the inauguration of Donald Trump as president
of the United States. The juxtaposition of the words in the image sum up
very well the ambiguous relationship between social movements and democracy in democratic states. While some point to mass mobilizations as
evidence that contemporary democracies are increasingly failing to satisfy
the demands of their citizens, for others mass mobilizations—or at least
those with a progressive or democratic agenda—are taken as a sign of
optimism for democracy's continued survival and potential renewal. The
reason everyone is debating democracy is precisely because of the wave of
mobilizations that filled the central squares across the world following the
global financial crisis of 2007–2008, in which demands for an end to austerity cuts, or for greater economic and social justice, were coupled with
demands for greater or "real" democracy.

The salience of the demand for greater or real democracy was a striking
feature of mobilizations across a range of political regimes, from authoritarian nations to liberal democracies. While the demand for democracy is
to be expected in those countries lacking democratic governments, more
surprising is the widespread demand for greater or "real" democracy in
countries understood to have consolidated democratic institutions. The intensity of mobilizations, their uneven extension across countries similarly

Democracy Reloaded. Cristina Flesher Fominaya, Oxford University Press (2020). © Oxford University Press.
DOI: 10.1093/oso/9780190099961.001.0001

impacted by the crisis and austerity measures, and their curious demand for democracy has thrown up a series of questions for scholars, observers, and even participants in these movements. In Europe, in a post-crisis scenario characterized by harsh austerity policies in many countries, a central concern with the state and nature of contemporary democracy has framed the debate. What does it mean to demand "real democracy" if you are living in a democratic society? How can we understand the apparent paradox of contemporary Western democracy whereby citizen dissatisfaction with really existing democracy is increasing, yet a commitment to democracy as a value is stronger than ever? What explains the emergence and resilience of these movements in some contexts and their transient or weak expressions in others? Are we in fact facing a crisis of democracy?

For those concerned about the erosion of democratic freedoms and the trend toward authoritarianism and far-right politics across countries long considered consolidated democracies, these scholarly questions are accompanied by questions of a more political nature. In times of financial and democratic crisis, what new challenges and opportunities open up? Is it possible to build resilient movements that contest the hegemonic logics of neoliberal capitalism and austerity politics? Is it possible to "save" democracy? If so, what role can progressive social movements play in contributing toward the regeneration of robust democracies?

In this book, I take on these large questions by delving deeply into Spain's 15-M movement. No single movement has the answer to the question "Can democracy be saved?" but as a democratic laboratory that mobilized millions in times of crisis, the 15-M movement provides some indications of how the neoliberal underpinnings of really existing democracy can be contested, and how new democratic imaginaries can emerge. As such, it can contribute to our knowledge of democratization and social movements, as well as to our understanding of contemporary Spanish and European politics.

15-M: Politics in times of crisis

On May 15, 2011, thousands of demonstrators took to the streets of Spain demanding "Real Democracy Now!" While the protest's organizers were delighted by the high level of participation, no one could have imagined they were taking part in the beginning of a social movement that would put some 3.5 million people on the street in 2011 alone. Originally dubbed the "Indignados" movement, in reference to the outrage or "indignation" expressed by the protesters, the movement became known in Spain simply as "15-M" in reference to that first protest on the 15th of May.

At the time of the protest, the unemployment rate in Spain had reached almost 21%, with youth unemployment at almost 50%. The risk of poverty was 26.7%, and the housing crash (with an almost 20% drop in housing prices by 2012) coupled with widespread unemployment meant that an astonishing 349,000 foreclosures were executed between 2007 and 2011 (Consejo General del Poder Judicial 2012). The Spanish "Indignados" protest was not the first of the European anti-austerity mobilizations, but rather forms part of the European wave of anti-austerity movements, which in turn are part of a global wave of protests following the global financial crisis.

Although the economic crisis and subsequent increases in socioeconomic inequality and hardship provide a crucial motivating factor for protests against austerity, in Europe, and especially in Spain, one of the most remarkable features of these protests was the centrality of the demands for greater democracy. It is significant that the central slogan of the 15-M protest was not "No More Cuts!" (as in the UK, for example); it was instead "Real Democracy Now! We are not commodities in the hands of politicians and bankers." The Spanish protesters' slogan highlighted that the financial crisis and austerity policies brought into sharp relief the longer-term crisis of legitimacy of representative democracy in Europe and in Spain. They were presenting a central claim that the origin of the crisis was *political*, and not the result of abstract economic processes outside of anyone's control. From their perspective, austerity policies weren't inevitable, but rather the result of collusion between financial and political elites, who not only failed to protect citizens against the worst effects of the crisis, but also forced citizens to assume the losses of private capital speculation. "We are not commodities" was the expression of a collective political subject that refused to be subsumed to the logic of austerity capitalism, and who was demanding a different relationship between the governed and the governors, one that placed the lives and welfare of citizens above the interests of economic elites.

Spain's 15-M movement, and particularly the experiences of its occupied squares, was a model for European anti-austerity movements, but its demands for "Real Democracy Now!" had a far-reaching influence on movements around the world (Accornero and Pinto 2015; Romanos 2016; Roos and Oikonomakis 2014). Despite being influenced by the Arab uprisings and Iceland "Saucepan Revolution," the protesters' demands were directed primarily at Spain's national political elites (Flesher Fominaya 2017). They insisted on their rights as "ordinary citizens" to occupy public space and to take part in politics without intermediaries and in complete autonomy from established parties and unions.

Spain's 15-M movement stands out as one of the most dynamic, sustained, influential, and transformative movements in the global and European wave of post-crisis protests. Castells (2015, 310) called it "the most potent networked social movement in Europe." It is worthy of careful analysis for a number of reasons. First, because of its ability to generate "consensual dissent": overcoming historic deep-seated socioeconomic and ideological cleavages in Spain and managing to garner an astonishing 80% support from Spaniards at the time of the mobilization, an approval rating that was still at 68% one year later (Sampedro and Lobera 2014). Second, 15-M stands out for its ability to maintain sustained levels of protest long after the squares were empty of their original occupations, and for the increasing development of the movement network following the initial mobilizations—in contrast to many experiences elsewhere that faded rapidly after the squares were emptied (Eschle 2018; Roberts 2012; Tufekci 2017). Third, the movement transformed Spanish public debate on key austerity issues such as housing, but more importantly engaged in a process of critique and resignification of the meaning of democracy itself. Fourth, the movement reconfigured Spain's political landscape and inspired a process of democratic experimentation that continues today, not only in non-institutional spheres and social movement networks, but also in the municipal movements that in 2015 won elections to govern Spain's major cities, and in the new political movement/party Podemos. Fifth, the movement was and continues to be an inspiration for movements elsewhere; it is certainly one of the most influential movements in the global wave of post-crisis "Occupy" movements. As such, 15-M offers insights and lessons not just for Spanish or European politics and society, but also for the future of progressive social movements throughout the world. It also throws up a series of compelling questions and puzzles for contemporary scholarship on democracy and social movements.

The first puzzle is why activists in consolidated democracies are demanding "Real Democracy Now!" Answering this question for the case of Spain's 15-M movement is a core task of this book. By excavating the meanings this demand has for activists in this mass movement, the book contributes to contemporary debates on the state and future of democracy in times of crisis (Brown 2015; Dahl 2015; della Porta 2013; Fernández-Savater

2015a; Flesher Fominaya 2017; Foa, Mounk, Dalton, and Welzel 2016; Iglesias 2015).

The second puzzle goes to the heart of core questions of concern for social movement scholars: What explains the emergence of this movement and its sustained mobilization over time? How can we understand its ability to have such a strong impact on the national political landscape when this was not the case in many other contexts where seemingly powerful movements dissipated following the emptying of the squares? By using a genealogical approach to trace the emergence and evolution of the movement—from protest, to occupation of the squares, to movement and beyond—I contribute to social movement scholarship in three core areas: (1) the process of movement formation (Freeman 1999; Snow and Benford 1992); (2) the elements that hold movements together generally (Diani 2015; Diani and McAdam 2003; McAdam, Tarrow, and Tilly 2003; Tarrow 2011), and, more specifically, the role of ideational frameworks, autonomous movement cultural logics, and collective identity formation in shaping and sustaining movements over time (Flesher Eguiarte 2005; Flesher Fominaya 2010a, 2010b; Juris 2008; Melucci 2003; Snow and Benford 1992; Tarrow 2013); and (3) the consequences and outcomes of social movements, a notoriously challenging area of research (Bosi and Uba 2009; Giugni 1998). One of the most notable unintended consequences of the 15-M movement and other "Occupy" movements has been the rise of hybrid parties, which attempt to bridge the gap between vertical and horizontal organizing logics, but which as political parties fundamentally differ from the autonomous movements that gave rise to them or fueled their resurgence.

The third puzzle that arises therefore for the case of Spain is: How could so many members of a movement that was radically committed to critiquing representative democracy, and so adamant about autonomy from parties and unions, less than three years later embrace the Podemos electoral initiative while still claiming allegiance to the spirit and identity of the 15-M movement? I show how early risers in the "electoral turn" engaged in extensive discursive work to enable 15-M activists to overcome their cognitive dissonance and realign their activist identities to embrace the electoral "parties and municipal movements for change," as they are known in Spain. Here I am contributing to emerging work on hybrid parties (Chironi and Fittipaldi 2017; della Porta et al. 2017) and the tensions between vertical and horizontal logics of collective action. Let's take these puzzles in turn.

"Real" democracy now?

Why demand real democracy if you are living in a democracy? The first puzzle revolves around the paradox of Western liberal democracies in which satisfaction with really existing democracy, with its representatives and its institutions, is declining, yet citizens are increasingly demanding greater democracy. A striking feature of contemporary liberal democracies is that the decline in trust in really existing democracy is *not* accompanied by a decline in support for the idea or value of democracy, but quite the contrary (della Porta 2013; Held 1995). For its part, Spain is held up as an exemplary case of a successful transition to democracy following the 36-year Franco dictatorship. In a post-crisis scenario, protesting austerity cuts makes sense, but after 40 years of stable democracy, what explains the 15-M movement's mass demand for "real democracy"? And what can this tell us about the state of contemporary democracy today?

As Dahl (2015, 2) point out, despite its 2,500-year history, there has never been "a tidy set of ideas on democracy on which everyone can agree." If it is true that some conception of democracy was central to "Occupy" mobilizations around the world, it is also true that the substantive content of the idea indicated by the signifier "democracy" varies from one context to the other. Democracy, in short, is a "floating signifier." If agreement is lacking on what exact form and content democracy should take, there is an emerging consensus, in European pro-democracy movements at least, around the need to contest the problems that Max Weber argued plagued modern society: the rise of a mass democracy that fails to address the substantive needs of the citizens even when complying with formal rules, and the development of a technocratic elite organized in a political power structure divorced from ordinary people. But if really existing democracy is to be contested as fraudulent or "fake" (or as the movement slogan puts it, "They call it democracy, but it isn't"), what alternative can be provided? What does "real democracy" look like?

Exploring the emergence of a new democratic imaginary, unearthing its core elements, and showing how it is manifested through activist narratives and embodied prefiguratively in activist practice forms a central goal of this book. At the same time, I want to show how these ideational frameworks profoundly inform the way new and renewed democratic imaginaries are transmitted to the broader society, through extensive symbolic and discursive work aimed at transforming the public narrative of democracy, on the one hand, and by directly engaging with institutional political parties and governing practices, on the other. In this way I show how social movements' internal cultures, practices, imaginaries, and collective identities can transform the wider political landscape symbolically and materially. In so doing, I contribute to one of the central and most difficult challenges of social movement studies: assessing the consequences and impact of social movements (Giugni 1998).

Twin legitimation crises

The second puzzle that arises from the case of Spain's 15-M movement is: What explains its emergence and sustained strength? Can it be explained by the severity of the impact of the financial crisis and the adoption of severe austerity policies by first the PSOE (Spanish Socialist Workers Party) and then the PP (Popular Party) governments? The post–global financial crisis and the Eurozone crisis created a political and economic context that has provided increased political opportunities for mobilization. In those countries most affected, the decrease in material conditions due to the impact of the crisis (e.g., rising unemployment and collapse of housing markets) have combined with austerity policies that have, inter alia, drastically cut welfare state measures to mitigate the effects of these consequences on citizens. This context has made possible a greater receptivity of the public toward anti-neoliberal capitalist critique and calls for greater democracy and socioeconomic justice, particularly where people have experienced strong effects of the crisis. It has also resulted in scholars calling for greater attention to the material bases of mobilization, or political economic opportunity structures (Císař and Navrátil 2017). Yet the countries most affected by the global crisis and the Troika's demands for economic adjustments (pejoratively denominated PIIGS, for Portugal, Ireland, Italy, Greece, and Spain) had strongly different mobilization responses: Spain and Greece having strong and sustained mobilizations, while Italy, Ireland, and Portugal having relatively moderate ones (see Baumgarten 2017; Kanellopoulos et al. 2017; and Zamponi and Fernández 2017). Clearly, therefore, the disparate mobilization responses across PIIGS countries call for a nuanced exploration of the relationship between different political-economic configurations and patterns of protest (Císař and Navrátil 2017; della Porta 2015).

Although the global economic crisis (and the related Eurozone crisis) is important, understanding this European wave of contention requires recognizing the central importance of the legitimation crisis of democracy (della Porta 2012; Flesher Fominaya 2017; Kaldor and Selchow 2013; Langman 2013). Economic/financial crises provoke legitimation crises when elites are perceived as having caused and benefitted from them, and having failed to protect citizens against their worst effects (della Porta 2012a, 2012b, 2015; Flesher Fominaya 2015e, 2017; Langman 2013). The financial crisis brought to a head a longer-term decline in trust, legitimacy, and satisfaction with democratic regimes, fueled by an increase in demands for democracy (rising public aspirations for democracy), an increase in negative news about government, and an analysis of the actual performance and structure of existing democratic regimes (Norris 2014). Economic crises and austerity policies reflect and contribute to the crisis of representative democracy (della Porta 2012a, 2015; Flesher Fominaya 2015e), in which the recent waves of movements of the squares "are just the most visible" manifestation (della Porta 2012a, 33). Political-economic legitimation crises also transform interpretive frameworks of meaning, "as people withdraw commitment to the social order—creating spaces for alternative views and understandings" (Langman, 2013, 159). The Spanish case undoubtedly opened up particular political opportunities, but so did other PIIGS countries with much weaker mobilization responses.

If the legitimacy of representative democracy is declining, what makes it so resilient? Badiou (2005), Mouffe (2005), Rancière (2004), and Žižek (2000) characterize the mechanisms that keep liberal democracies in place as the "post-political," or what Crouch (2004) terms "post-democracy." In the post-political sphere, representative democracy is closely tied to liberal economy, and is mobilized as a means of restricting or foreclosing public debate about the social and economic order. "Politics" is reduced to a form of social administration, organized around consensus about neoliberalism and the liberal state. Did the economic crisis and austerity policies then produce a rupture in the post-political consensus? Although mobilization is partly a response to the crisis, and increases potential receptivity to critique, grievances on their own will not automatically lead to mobilization (Langman 2013; Oliver 1989; Koopmans 2004). Channeling grievances into collective resistance requires activating networks of actors willing and able to make effective use of the political and economic opportunities opened up by these "twin" crises. Here the interplay between the particular strength and density of *local and national* activist networks (and their human, material, cultural, and ideological resources) and public perceptions of the crises (and who is responsible for them) is important. Public perception is itself partly affected by the mobilizations of critical social movements (e.g., disclosing and disseminating corruption scandals and counter-hegemonic narratives or slogans such as crisis/swindle), but also *countered* by viewpoints disseminated by mass media that support dominant narratives, (e.g., austerity is inevitable, banks are too big to fail). At the same time, *transnational* diffusion processes also significantly influence and contribute to mobilization processes, and here national and trans-national activist/critical citizen networks played a key role through whis-tleblowing and critical alternative media, and through the influence of groups such as Anonymous and WikiLeaks. I explore all of these factors throughout this book.

In the heady early days of protests and occupations, grievance theories were not the only explanations on offer. Pundits and scholars were quick to offer theories to explain what was happening, many of which centered around claims of newness, spontaneity, and the unprecedented (for a re-view, see Flesher Fominaya 2015b). Often those narratives were infused with optimism for progressive social change fueled by early victories in Iceland, Egypt, and Tunisia. This widespread feeling of excitement and possibility has been observed in previous waves of intense mobilization, described as "moments of madness" (Zolberg 1972) or the "eros effect" (Katsiaficas 1989). Once waves enter into inevitable subsidence or suffer reversals of early victories, we are able to better evaluate some of early explanations in light of their trajectories and outcomes.

Spontaneity arguments are often invoked in periods of sudden intense mobilization, including the Arab Spring and the Occupy movements (Flesher Fominaya 2015b). These arguments suggest protests spring from the ether, without the intervention of social movement actors and in the absence of organizing structures. In the digital age, spontaneity narra-tives are often coupled with narratives that posit a determining role for Information and Communication Technologies and digital media in mo-bilization (e.g., Twitter Revolutions), arguing that these can mobilize the power of weak ties and can replace organizing structures (Bennett and Segerberg 2012; Peña-López, Congosto, and Aragon 2014; Anduiza et al. 2014; Gerbaudo 2012). I argue that we cannot understand the emergence and strength of the 15-M mobilizations by recurring to spontaneity argu-ments, whether enabled by digital media or not, but must instead adopt a genealogical approach that enables us to understand the mechanisms through which the original mobilizations emerged. This enables us to address a key question for social movement scholars, which is not only *how* movements come to be in the first place, but, crucially, *why* they do (Freeman 1999; Melucci 1989).

Adopting a genealogical approach also allows for the evaluation of another characteristic frequently attributed to intense mobilizations—including Spain's 15-M movement—which is novelty (e.g., Baiocchi and Ganuza 2012; Néz 2012; Bennett and Segerberg 2012). This claim is made with regard to the use of social media, which *is* relatively new (e.g., Twitter dates from 2006, Facebook from 2004), but also for other distinguishing features of the movement, such as the insistence on autonomy from parties and unions, absence of programs and leaders, formal structures, and the central role of deliberation. As I show, far from being novel, these have been hallmarks and mainstays of Spanish autonomous movements since at least the 1980s (Botella Ordinas 2011; Flesher Fominaya 2005, 2007a, 2010b, 2015a; Juris 2008; Lorenzo Vila and Mártinez López 2001). Although I do not dispute the existence of novel elements, and indeed devote close attention to them, understanding the origins of the movement and the motivations and practices of those directly involved enables a more accurate evaluation of what is new and what is building on previous movement history and culture, and helps carefully distinguish between cause and novelty.

The power of autonomy

Within the global wave of protests, Spain's 15-M stands out for the strength of its mobilization, but also for its autonomous "horizontal" forms of organizing. In a scenario of mass mobilization, these autonomous forms of organizing have been become more visible and have captured attention because these seemingly spontaneous and unorganized movements defy common sense and scholarly understandings of what strong social movements look like. On the face of it, autonomous movements are unlikely candidates for "success," lacking the key elements that have so often been highlighted as requirements, such as formal bureaucratic organizations; centralized power; issue, identity, and ideological convergence; strong professionalized leadership; programmatic logics; access to or integration in institutional frameworks; and abundant resources (Badiou 2012; Gamson 1990; Katzenstein 1998; McCarthy and Zald 1977; McCarthy et al. 1996; Meyer and Staggenborg 1996; Morris and Staggenborg 2004; Staggenborg 1988; Zald and McCarthy 2017). Since building large movements requires creating networks and coalitions across heterogeneous actors, social movement scholars have long considered the contexts or circumstances within which diverse actors are likely to work together, focusing in particular on political opportunity structures (Eisinger 1974; McAdam 1982; Meyer 2003; Tarrow 2011; Tilly 1978).

In this book I tackle the problem of cohesion and network building in a different way. While recognizing the role of the economic and political context in movement formation, I argue that the internal processes of movement building, specifically the processes of political culture and collective identity development, provide a compelling answer to the question of how to build cohesion across diversity. In the literature on internal movement-building processes, key scholars have focused on the role of resources, effective recruitment, influencing authorities, and achieving new gains for group members as central movement tasks (Gamson 1990; McCarthy and Zald 1977; Meyer 2003; Piven and Cloward 1979), within a framework that sees movements as a series of alliances between discrete social movement organizations (SMOs), (e.g., Zald and McCarthy 2017). Here I am focusing on the role of political culture, collective identity, and praxis as crucial elements of movement building in prefigurative autonomous social movements, to argue that in a context of scarce resources, limited institutional opportunities for influence (i.e., lack of elite receptivity to movement demands), limited integration into safe spaces within mainstream institutions (Katzenstein 1998), and the absence of formal organizing structures or professionalized leaders, autonomous social movements can nevertheless exploit the opportunities offered by crisis contexts to build strong and sustained movements. How this is possible is a core contribution of this book.

Movement political culture, collective identity, prefiguration, and praxis

Culture is one of the most contested, elusive, and difficult concepts to specify (Lofland 1995, 190). Because political culture is central to my argument, it is worth spelling out up front what I mean by it. Culture encompasses the symbols, norms, beliefs, ideals, customs, myths, and rituals that are transmitted over generations and which shape the identities of a given community. Culture guides, orients, and gives meaning to social practice, as well as cohesion to a given community or society, to the extent to which it provides shared traditions, representations, and collective experiences that shape people's sense of belonging. Culture can be constraining as well as facilitating of creative agency (Bourdieu 1977; Flesher Fominaya 2016a; Jasper 2008). Politics, for its part, is that realm of society related to the organization of power, classically defined as who gets what, when, and how (Lasswell 1936). It's the space in which decisions are taken that affect the distribution of goods in any given society. Politics isn't limited to a set of procedures and mechanisms, however, but also refers to "the authoritative allocation of values" (Easton 1953), and to the *contestation and challenging of that authority and power*. The term *political culture* encompasses the values, conceptions, and behaviors that are oriented toward the political sphere, and which configure the subjective perception of a group of people toward the system of power (Peschard 1997). Almond and Verba's (1963) classic formulation includes two ideal types, which are most often found in combination: *subject* political culture, in which citizens feel subordinate to government, and *participant* political culture, in which citizens feel they can be involved in government decisions and policy. 15-M can be seen as attempting to shift Spanish political culture from the former to the latter.

The concept of political culture is most often applied to nations, and combines two elements: it is never circumstantial, since it is the result of shared ideas and experiences over time, but it also isn't fixed, as it is dynamic and changing. Although shifts in political culture can be initiated by elites (e.g., modernization processes), more often it changes when political and social movements provoke a rupture with a dominant political culture and manage to change the beliefs, expectations, and evaluations of a society toward its representatives, its institutions, and its political practices. This process may be gradual, or in periods of intense mobilization it may be accelerated. The agents of these changes (insofar as they are working together and see themselves as sharing a collective identity) also share what we can call *political subcultures*, which embody critical alternatives to the dominant political culture, but which (in the absence of a violent overthrow of existing power structures) in order to be successful, necessarily contain some elements or features of the dominant political culture that enable its demands, critiques, and proposals to be widely accepted (Snow and Benford 1992; Tarrow 2013). *Movement political cultures* are constructed but not arbitrary or endlessly flexible (Jasper 2008, 52), nor do they develop in isolation from the wider local, national, and transnational political cultures.

My approach to culture recognizes that struggles over meaning are important sites of contemporary protest (Touraine 1988). Creative agency and meaning-making are integral social movement practices, including the development of frames or interpretive schemata (Gamson et al. 1982; Snow et al. 1986) that seek to challenge hegemonic narratives and widespread common-sense understandings (in this case of austerity and democracy). However, I move beyond analyzing the reflexive strategic *externally* oriented activities of social movements to also interrogate the more submerged cultural elements that constitute "their whole way of struggle" (Thompson 1963). By movement culture, therefore, I am also referring to (a) the generalized *ideational frameworks* that motivate action and through which activists make sense of their collective action (by which I mean not just mobilization, but also the many activities that take place in the activist community milieus), and (b) widespread *forms of praxis* in which ideational frameworks are linked to practice.

Movement political culture is crucial for the development of *collective identity*, which emerges through a process in which movement participants create cohesion across diversity and mutually recognize each other, establishing the boundaries of social movement participation through a distinction between "us" and "them" (Flesher Fominaya 2010a, 2010b; Melucci 2003). The politically consequential nature of the distinctions between "us" and "them" has important implications for social movement strategy and internal cohesion processes. As I will show, 15-M collective identity was built primarily around movement political culture, that is, around a whole 15-M way of doing; and shared master frames about the twin crises of austerity and democracy, rather than around a shared commitment to particular austerity issues. This explains why, for example, 15-M activists and unions shared critiques of austerity but did not, for the most part, see each other as belonging to the same movement. I am drawing here, therefore, on insights from both the social constructionist tradition and the neo-Gramscian tradition (Errejón 2015; Errejón and Mouffe 2016), as well as the work on the importance of narrative (Polletta 1998a, 1998b) and cultural logics (Coleman 2013; Crossley 2003; Flesher Eguiarte 2005; Flesher Fominaya 2007a; Juris 2008; Maeckelbergh 2009) in social movements.

Prefiguration is crucial for pro-democracy movements that seek to align their internal practices with their political goals (Blee 2012; Maeckelbergh 2009; Polletta 2012), to embody in their own praxis the changes they seek in society. These movements are themselves laboratories of democratic experimentation in which shared understandings of democracy develop: what "good" or "real" democracy might look like, and what is required for it to work. By exploring the relation between ideational frameworks and praxis, or logics of movement practice, and not just analyzing the specific issues activists mobilize around (e.g., austerity cuts, post-crisis public debt burdens, housing, unemployment), we can understand why movements such as 15-M are demanding "Real Democracy Now!" and what they mean by it. In this I depart from treatments in the literature that posit a relation between individual core beliefs as an impetus for movement participation, or that take the alignment of individual beliefs and movement ideologies as a core task for movement emergence (Laraña et al. 2009; McAdam 1988; Meyer 2007; Muller and Opp 1986). Instead I show that participants develop their beliefs as a result of involvement (Munson 2008), and that social movements are themselves producers of knowledge and new ideas (Cox and Flesher Fominaya 2009; Eyerman and Jamison 1991). Attention to movement praxis and cultural logics illuminates the central puzzle of what it means to demand "Real Democracy Now," but also provides key and novel insights into what can build resilient and effective movements.

Contemporary radical politics and movement outcomes

Some members of the radical intelligentsia have reacted to the movements of the squares by interpreting them within their political theoretical frameworks, recognizing their historical relevance but either finding them lacking or seeing them as evidence for the revolutionary future they see ahead. Žižek (2012, 78) diagnoses "the fatal weakness of the current protests" as their inability to transform themselves into "even a minimal program for socio-political change." Badiou (2012, 5) for his part, recognizes the challenge posed to the power of "financial and imperial oligarchies" by this global wave of participatory egalitarian uprisings, but characterizes them as "blind, naïve, scattered and lacking a powerful concept of durable organization." Lapsing into the tired rhetoric of the old Left, Žižek (2012, 82) stands outside the fray and offers political solutions from above, arguing that what is needed is "a strong body able to reach quick decisions and realize them with whatever force may be necessary," and to forge "a new form of organization, discipline, and hard work."

As I will show, the actors discussed in this book demonstrate great capacity for discipline, hard work, and organization. It's just that their organization doesn't take the form of a "vanguard of the proletariat" party.

In the face of the many political reversals faced by many of these movements, some observers are quick to diagnose their faults as lying with the lack of "real" political capacity (by which they mean institutional politics) in social movements, and almost seem to blame the authoritarian reaction to progressive pro-democracy movements on the movements themselves. Here I argue that the impact of social movements can last much longer than visible mobilizations, and that we need to evaluate movement effects outside the binary of success and failure and beyond a linear conception of historical progression. We need to stop looking down on social movements from a great height and measuring their defeat or failure in short-term political gains. Their "afterlives" are complex and multidirectional, unexpected, and sometimes unintentional. Their effects should not be evaluated solely by short-term political gains or losses, but should include more widespread cultural and political shifts that can take many years to bear fruit. Even then, their gains can be reversed and are never fixed or final. In this book I build on my earlier work on the "logic of autonomy" (Flesher Eguiarte 2005) to explore the cultural logic that fueled the 15-M movement's capacity to enable mass participation in a process of democratic engagement in times of crisis, not in order to provide a prescription for action, but in order to contribute to knowledge about the challenges and possibilities engendered through this process.

Contemporary "radical" political theory is characterized broadly by a tension between those who view autonomous grassroots horizontal and nonhierarchical networked movements favorably (and here we could include Antonio Negri, Michael Hardt, Manuel Castells, Jacques Rancière, Donatella della Porta, and Amador Fernández-Savater), and those who are sympathetic but argue for the need for a construction of renewed political hegemony of the people (e.g., Chantal Mouffe, Ernesto Laclau). This theoretical tension is also reflected in practice throughout the history of European social movements (Flesher Fominaya 2007a, 2014, 2018). The 15-M movement has come close to successfully integrating these two positions, though not without tensions, into a shared collective identity that transcends its heterogeneous composition, integrating both autonomous and neo-Gramscian understandings of collective action—an ambiguous positionality best exemplified by Podemos, but already present in 15-M. As such, I argue that it represents a departure from previous waves of mobilization, where the cleavage between the two approaches was much more marked, and a shift toward more hybrid forms of autonomy (Fernández-Savater 2014; Martínez 2016).

I began this introduction by pointing to the ambiguous relationship between social movements and democracy and the way in which the recent global wave of post-crisis mass mobilization has been interpreted as either evidence of the crisis of democracy or hope for its salvation. Both of course are true. The rise of mass movements (whether progressive or regressive) in democratic states are manifesting the crisis of really existing democracy and its failure to adequately address the needs of significant numbers of citizens. The rise of mass movements that take democratic deficits and imaginaries as their central concern offer a source of potential democratic innovation in times of crisis.

Given the strength and influence of the 15-M movement, therefore, if pro-democracy social movements provide one possible hope for democracy's "salvation" through contesting the status quo and innovating in democratic regeneration, learning from this movement, both its strengths and limitations, provides a good place to start.

PART I

Democracy and 15-M

1

Spanish Democracy and 15-M

If 15-M did one thing, it was to challenge once and for all the idea that democracy means alternating power between two parties every four years. For so long we have accepted that that was the proof that we had had a successful transition from the dictatorship. 15-M finished with that idea once and for all, democracy has to mean so much more than that.

—MARTA (2013, 15-M and migrant rights activist)

IN THIS CHAPTER I provide a theoretical, analytical, and empirical framework within which to understand the emergence of the 15-M movement and its core challenge to dominant conceptions of Spanish democracy. I highlight the central importance of critique and resignification for social movements, showing that counter-hegemonic discursive work by the 15-M movement around "common sense" understandings of democracy and austerity was a distinguishing feature of the movement, and also one of its central tasks and achievements.

Real democracy?

What does it mean to demand "real democracy"? Despite wide disagreement on the precise definition of democracy (Dahl and Shapiro 2015), contemporary use of the term is often—or almost always—shorthand for liberal representative democracy.

There has been a dramatic increase in dissatisfaction with democracy in Europe since the 2007–2008 global financial crisis, due to a combination of citizen perception of loss of national sovereignty and economic deterioration. Armingeon and Guthman (2014, 426) argue that movements such as Spain's Indignados or the Occupy movements were "based on the idea that external actors have eroded national democracy." While certainly the role of the so-called Troika (the European Commission [EC], the European Central Bank [ECB], and the

Democracy Reloaded. Cristina Flesher Fominaya, Oxford University Press (2020). © Oxford University Press.
DOI: 10.1093/oso/9780190099961.001.0001

International Monetary Fund [IMF]) and the subservence of national governments to the dictates of these three organizations are crucial aspects of the critical response to austerity politics and the demands for greater democracy, it would be overstating the case greatly to understand these movements as primarily motivated by this preoccupation. In addition, as with all work based on aggregating data on individual citizens to illuminate macro processes, the role of social movements in shaping the debates around democracy, and in influencing both satisfaction with really existing democracy and what Norris (2014) refers to as "rising public aspirations for democracy," is a factor that needs to be taken into consideration, as Armingeon and Guthman recognize. In other words, we should not see movements like Spain's 15-M as an aggregation of individual sentiments that "spontaneously" find collective expression, but rather as collective actors that shape public opinion. Although, as I will show, what Spanish activists mean by "real democracy" requires careful unpacking, and encompasses multiple ideational frameworks and forms of praxis, what is clear is that these demands are based on contrasting an analysis of really existing democracy with their own understandings of what it *should* be, and this encompasses much more than a simple recognition that political and financial sovereignty has been transferred to the Troika, important as that fact might be. Instead, their demands are rooted in a rethinking of democracy in Spain following the Transition.

Yet as Touraine (1997, 8) argues, if democracy is primarily "a set of rules [. . .] which establish *who* is authorized to take collective decisions and *which* procedures are to be used," in which "large organizations such as parties and labor unions exert an increasing influence on political life," but where truly democratic processes do not actually penetrate most areas of social life, why should citizens actively defend it?

Why indeed? Spanish activists demanding "Real Democracy Now!" clearly had more in mind than a set of rules and procedures. Instead, they manifested democratic action in which citizens oppose "institutional practices and rules, which usually serve to protect the powers of the dominant," mobilize "the collective and personal will toward liberation, which is by no means synonymous with the rational pursuit of self-interest," and appeal to "universal cultural values in its struggle against the power that it accuses of serving particular interests" (Touraine 1997, 132). They brought together the two understandings of democracy that Castoriadis (1997) distinguishes as procedure and regime.

Democracy as procedure versus democracy as regime

Castoriadis's (1997) distinction between democracy as procedure and democracy as regime provides a useful point of departure for understanding 15-M activists' demand for "real democracy now." In classical political theory, democracy was understood as a regime that was inseparable from a substantive conception of the ends of political institutions and of a conception of human nature and the desirability of the ends that human beings seek to realize. In contrast, in contemporary political theory that draws on Schumpeter (1943), democracy is emptied of any consideration of substantive and normative elements and reduced to a set of procedures. One core element of the procedural understanding of democracy is the requirement for citizens to be able to participate in the democratic process. Yet even within a procedural view, movements and political theorists have often moved in opposite directions with regard to the desirability of the *degree* of participation in democracy, as Pateman (1970) and Rancière (2014) have argued. If citizen movements and even some governments have championed greater citizen input and engagement, there is a whole tradition of political theory that is hostile to active political participation. Schumpeter's influential analysis saw democracy as a method, not a commitment to political ideals. In Schumpeter's view, democracy is a mechanism for arriving at political decisions through a particular set of institutional arrangements. In this view, participation is only necessary to the extent that it enables control of political leadership through citizens' right to vote. As Pateman (1970, 7) shows, for Schumpeterian democratic theorists, "high levels of participation and interest are required from a minority of citizens only and, moreover, the apathy and disinterest of the majority play a valuable role in maintaining the stability of the system as a whole." Control of leaders by the electorate is considered essential, but only insofar as they replace one set of leaders with another set of leaders competing for the same top positions. Too much participation from citizens threatens the stability of the political system, and therefore "limited participation and apathy have a positive function for the whole system by cushioning the shock of disagreement, adjustment and change" (Pateman 1970, 7). Such "participation" rejectionists sought also to jettison values and normative elements from theory, reducing democracy to something procedural and representative.

Castoriadis (1997, 1), in contrast, argues that "whatever the philosophical window dressing, a purely procedural conception of 'democracy' itself originates in the crisis of the imaginary significations that concern the ultimate goals of collective life," and aims at obscuring this fact by dissociating all discussion of political goals from discussion of political forms. Castoriadis's understanding of *democracy as regime* encompasses many of the elements that 15-M activists embraced, and through which the movement represents a break from Marxist and anarchist rejections of formal institutions, on the one hand, and the simultaneous refusal to divorce substantive conceptions of democracy from demands for procedural reform, on the other. Several key elements of his formulation resonate with 15-M conceptions of democracy: (1) the notion that no one can be free as long as others are not free; (2) the understanding that the objective of politics is effective freedom, or what he calls *autonomy*, which can only be achieved through explicit self-institution and self-governance; (3) the understanding that whatever the different branches of power under consideration, no decisions can be conceived and adopted without taking into account considerations of a *substantive* character; (4) that democracy should be understood as "the regime in which the public sphere becomes truly and effectively public—it belongs to everyone, and is effectively open to the participation of all" (1997, 7); and (5) that there can be no democratic society without democratic *paideia*, or a broad cultural education that creates the democratic citizen. This last point is crucial to understand the role of prefiguration in the 15-M movement, not only in the squares, but in the development of 15-M political culture and collective identity as well.

Castoriadis (1997, 15) argues (and 15-M activists embraced this idea) that "for individuals to be capable of making democratic procedures function in accordance with their 'spirit,' a large part of the labor of society and of its institutions must be directed toward engendering individuals" who are able to critically think through what it means to achieve a democratic vision, and are capable therefore of creating institutions and carrying out procedures in accordance with this democratic spirit. Not only is the distinction between procedures and substantive values a mirage, he argues, but so is the idea that a democratic regime could be instituted through "representation" in the absence of a truly critical democratic citizenry and genuine participation. Democracy as a regime must do everything possible to create citizens who are capable of governing and being governed (as Aristotle said), and it must be predicated on a collective definition of shared substantive values and common social goods that make up an essential part of the social imaginary. This shared understanding has to result from reflective and deliberative action within a particular social historical moment and cannot be predetermined by a fixed political theory or philosophy.

Castoriadis's argument offers the possibility of transcending the duality between formal (institutional) and informal (extra-institutional) politics (and therefore between institutional politics and social movements), and of understanding better what was happening in the movements of the squares. There, activists were attempting to achieve *paideia* through the education of citizens (an education that could only come from collective participation and deliberation and not from a predetermined philosophy or authority), but at the same time demanding a reform of the formal institutional structures that prevent "real" democracy from existing—a reform that would require the integration of substantive and normative elements that would ensure greater equality and freedom (the common democratic good), as well as participation. The idea that the notion of the common good is not predetermined but emerges in the particular sociohistorical context in which it is actively deliberated enables us to understand the 15-M movement as being both anti-austerity and pro-democracy, not as two separate elements that are added together, but as two intertwined elements impossible to dissociate. It enables us to consider the movement not only from within, but also to place it in a specific politico-historical context that helps explains its emergence, development, and consequences.

While I have no idea how many 15-M activists have read Schumpeter, Castoriadis, or other democratic theorists, it is clear that in their demand for "Real Democracy Now!," 15-M activists are explicitly rejecting democracy as procedure and instead embracing the notion of democracy as regime. Understanding that most political leaders express what Rancière (2014) would call "hatred of democracy" in their disdain for citizen participation beyond voting every four years, 15-M activists instead call for what Castoriadis (1997) would call "autonomy" and Touraine (1988) would call "historicity," which encompasses a challenge to the way dominant norms shape the social order, but also a demand for social movement actors—and people in general—to be able to take part in the decisions that shape their lives. In contrast to Schumpeter's disdain for the electoral mass, which he argues is "incapable of action other than a stampede" (1943, 283), 15-M activists embrace the notion of collective intelligence, the possibilities for collective learning, and the desirability of a democratic *paideia*, which they attempted to enact prefiguratively in the squares of Spain and later in the neighborhood assemblies and other democratic spaces of experimentation.

As useful as Castoriadis's distinction is, 15-M activists are not caught up in a debate between political theorists. Rather, they are influenced by movement political traditions that nourish their conceptions of democracy, and they integrate insights from traditions that some mainstream political theorists are either ignorant of or hostile to. One central endeavor of this book, therefore, is to elucidate this democratic imaginary, arriving at a more synthetic, cohesive, and integrated ideational framework than would be found in any given activist or democratic space within the movement. And while the 15-M democratic imaginary does also contain procedural elements of the kind Keane (2011) calls "monitory democracy" (i.e., mechanisms to foster control, oversight, and transparency on democratic institutions and representatives), they are equally concerned with imbuing democracy with substantive normative elements without which democracy ceases to be worthy of its name; that is, it ceases to be "real" democracy.

Despite declining satisfaction with democracy in Europe, democratic legitimacy is supported by what Badiou (2005), Mouffe (2005), and Rancière (2004) have referred to as the "post-political," in which politics is reduced to a form of social administration, organized around widespread consensus about neoliberalism and the liberal state. In Spain, that consensus encompassed a series of narratives about the success of the Spanish Transition and democracy, known as the Culture of the Transition (*Cultura de la Transición*), or CT. 15-M attempted to rupture that consensus.

15-M: Breaking with the Culture of the Transition (CT)

Although a questioning of representative democracy is a characteristic feature of many of the anti-austerity and pro-democracy movements following the 2008 global crisis (Flesher Fominaya 2017), the particular form that the demand for "Real Democracy Now!" takes in Spain is shaped by the experience of Spain's democratic transition.

Historically, Spanish governments have remained somewhat impervious to the demands of mass mobilization, a legacy of a "pacted transition" between elites that did not rely on engagement with civil society, and its resulting institutional framework that isolates politicians from direct pressure from movements (Fishman 2019; della Porta et al. 2018). Fishman (2019) has shown how these transition legacies have shaped public understandings of the meaning of democracy. Della Porta et al. (2018) suggest that frustration at lack of access informed movement critique of democratic deficiency in post-transition Spain, and was also factor in the mass response to austerity politics. While autonomous social movements in Spain have long critiqued the democratic deficiencies of their government, organizing several illegal referendums to demand access to political decision-making, I do not think that the strong "democratic turn" (the centrality of democratic regeneration and the reclaiming of political institutions for citizens) taken by activists in 15-M in response to the twin economic and democratic crises is directly traceable to historic grievances about the particular institutional legacies of the Transition. However, activists and intelligentsia in 15-M *were* reflecting on the legacies of the Transition and developing an analysis that was directly influential in 15-M activist circles (see also Chapter 10). In contrast to the academic emphasis on the institutional legacies of the pacted Transition and the limited channels of public participation, these activists were much more interested in its effects on political *culture* and how it shaped the limits of the possible in the public political imaginary (see also Moreno Caballud 2015, trans. Grabner-Coronel).

In a provocative argument, numerous writers have developed the CT concept to delineate the key features of hegemonic political culture in Spain "born from the destruction of the radical movements of the 70s" (Fernández-Savater 2012b, 37) that characterizes the period from the Transition to the rupture of consensus represented by 15-M.

For Guillem Martínez (2012), who coined the term, CT represents a widespread and deeply depoliticizing consensus around the legitimacy of the Spanish Transition, and to a generalized political culture that actively avoids political conflict outside the confines of ritualistic rivalry between the dominant parties that alternate power every four to eight years (Fernández-Savater 2012b; Martínez 2012; Sampedro and Lobera 2014; Moreno Caballud 2015, trans. Grabner-Coronel). In contrast, for Martínez (2012, 23), the 15-M movement represents a fundamental "break" with the consensus of CT, a reappropriation of the critical function of culture, a new cultural paradigm not organized around guaranteeing the stability of the successful democratic state.

When compared with the Franco dictatorship, the Spanish Transition to democracy *is* a marvel of prosperity, freedom, and stability. 15-M, however, represents a fundamental generational shift that does not take the dictatorship or the civil war as its point of reference, and therefore evaluates Spanish democracy using different criteria, through the prism of the harsh economic realities of a post–boom-and-crash crisis scenario. It is not coincidental that 15-M starts with younger activists who contest the consensus embodied by the CT. What is remarkable is that this mobilization managed to convince so many people across demographic and ideological categories. Here corruption scandals and material deprivation provided a potential opportunity to break with the dominant narrative of Spain's exemplary democratic transition, but until they were joined together and articulated in a series of specific critiques and demands for "Real Democracy Now!," they did not galvanize public opinion.

The critique of CT is not limited to scholars but is shared by the 15-M activists involved in the origin of the movement. Carlos, a founding member of Youth Without Future (JSF), one of the organizations involved in the original 15-M protest, evaluates 15-M in relation to the legacy of the Transition on Spanish democracy. He understands the post-Transition scenario as being dominated by a discourse of democracy that upholds consensus, dialogue, and pacts between political elites as the maximum value of political culture. In contrast:

We conceive of democracy as conflict and not consensus. Conflict doesn't mean violence. Democracy is a rupture, it's a moment of political division. My conception comes from Rancière, politics as [. . .] ruptures in the structure of order that incorporate actors that were not previously part of the political community, and I think this has a lot to do with what happened in 15-M.

The balance between rupture and common sense around the notion of democracy is visible in 15-M. As Gramsci (1971, 333) argued, it is difficult to overcome the passivity generated by inherited consciousness, or to break free of the hold of its central discursive constructions. Carlos draws on Gramsci to explain the strategy developed in JSF and later expressed in 15-M:

If we want to transform common sense, we need to understand that we can't go in guns-a-blazing (*a saco*), that we need to generate mechanisms of seduction. [. . .] There is this phrase by Gramsci that's used incorrectly now to talk about institutional politics: "you have to have one foot in the streets and another in the institutions." Gramsci actually said that you have to have one foot in common sense and the other in rupture. If you have both feet in common sense you aren't transformative, but if you have both feet in rupture then you're just a fucking ghetto and you won't change anything. [. . .] You have got to permanently play with this unstable balance and ambivalence.

Carlos describes the enduring effects of CT on movement political culture and the challenges it poses for those seeking political change. He argues that for decades oligarchies and political elites have held the monopoly on politics in Spain, establishing the rules of the game that shape political interaction. The narratives that legitimize that monopoly have become "common sense" and therefore also influence 15-M activists who are seeking rupture. One core idea that Carlos considers "almost dangerous" is the fear of conflict:

> This idea that we all have to be together, that there can't be any serious disagreements [*broncas*]. Consensus and democracy have meant the exact same thing for 40 years in this country. [. . .] I mean it's fucking incredible! We have never valued a political figure for standing firm on their principles but rather for *not doing so*, [. . .] so the mainstream discourse is all about the pacts that led to the Constitution and the fucking consensus! [laughs], and that's what we need to break! But we can't break it by telling people "This is shit and we need conflict because democracy is conflict." If people hear you saying that they're going to flee, flee, flee, and you're going to be left alone preaching in the desert like a fucking moron [laughs].

Carlos is highlighting the difficulty of introducing a neo-Gramscian concept of democracy as conflict in a post-Transition political culture in which conflict is constructed as the *opposite* of democracy. Hence, JSF developed mechanisms of seduction to shift the narrative (see Chapter 2).

Carlos Taibo, a professor and libertarian activist involved in Spanish movements for global justice and 15-M, is not convinced that 15-M managed to break with the CT (despite titling one of his books on 15-M *Nothing Will Be as It Was Before*). Speaking in 2015, and in light of the "electoral turn" represented by Podemos and the municipal movements, he argued that the most that has happened is that there is some questioning of the electoral system, but not a widespread critical assessment of the Transition per se:

One of the collateral effects of 15-M has been the development of self-organized spaces, spaces that are de-commercialized, and within this world obviously there's a really vivid criticism of the current political system. That [. . .] wasn't there before to nearly the same extent. But I think that this needs to be put into perspective in terms of how widespread it is, because when I engage with my students in class, certainly there are complaints about corruption, criticisms of the bipartisan system, and even about the monarchy, but the debate is about the regime and not really a critique of the system that upholds it.

As someone committed to grassroots politics from below and outside state institutions, it is not surprising that he is less than sanguine about the impact of 15-M, given the decline in mobilization and the renewed interest in electoral politics (very notable by 2015). Despite his reservations, he later speaks to the longer-term and more widespread impact of 15-M on Spain's political culture:

A friend and I were debating recently about whether or not 15-M was still an active movement. The question merits a nuanced answer, because in some places it is and in other places it has literally disappeared. I said that I wasn't sure if it was still a movement, but I was sure that it was still a state of mind. And he said, astutely, that that was very interesting, because movements are easy to repress, but states of mind aren't. And I think that's what long-term movements generate: they provoke certain spasms in people's minds that weren't there before and that cause changes in their daily behavior. And if that's the legacy of 15-M, it's a fantastic one, because it's a legacy for the future. The other aspect [the movement per se] is more provisional, it's more ethereal: it comes, it is there, and it's gone.

However deep or long-lasting the critique, 15-M sparked a profound social debate over the nature of democracy that reflects the perceived decline in quality and satisfaction with democracy noted over the past few decades (della Porta 2013, 185). Taibo (2011, 33) notes that prior to 15-M, being anti-systemic and anti-capitalist were considered the worst thing you could be called in Spain, yet the slogans and chants of the first 15-M protest in 2011 were nothing if not a clear rejection of the system and its political and union representatives, which surprisingly *motivated* rather than discouraged public participation.

If CT depoliticized, 15-M repoliticized. Suddenly, it seemed, everyone was talking about politics: at work, on the street, in the squares, and at home. Carlos Taibo remembers:

> 15-M immediately became a topic of public discussion. You would go into a bar and ask for a coffee, and everybody was talking about it, and that . . . reflected . . . something fundamentally new.

15-M triggered a process of rethinking the nature and quality of Spanish democracy in ways that no established party or union could avoid engaging with. The search for alternatives to "really existing democracy" has spawned a process of democratic experimentation that encompasses everything from consensus decision-making in assemblies of 5,000 people in a central square, to municipal movements that use participatory movement methods to configure electoral lists and develop deliberative experiments within democratic institutions, to the emergence of a party claiming to be part movement/part party, Podemos. If the CT is no longer the dominant paradigm for interpreting Spanish democracy, 15-M has detonated what some believed was the beginning of Spain's *second* democratic transition.

Spain's anti-austerity mobilization in context

Grievance theory (Klandermans 1997; Kriesberg and Dayton 2012; LeFebvre and Armstrong 2018; McVeigh 1995) and common sense posit that the more people perceive themselves or others as victims of illegitimate inequality, or feel a moral indignation about social or political affairs, the more they are likely to protest. Unfortunately, social conditions such as poverty, exclusion, marginalization, exploitation, and oppression are widespread, yet often (indeed most of the time) they do not produce sustained collective action to protest or resist these conditions. Yet the global financial crisis, and particularly the political response to it centered on austerity policies, has facilitated the resonance of social movement frames critical of existing democratic political cultures and has spurred the commitment to action of a large number of people in Spain and across Europe.

The very different collective responses to austerity politics across Europe call for careful exploration of the various factors that can lead to a strong anti-austerity response. The varying mobilization responses in those hardest hit show that grievances alone cannot account for the emergence and strength of the 15-M movement. What is more, what we find is that even those countries *least* affected by the crisis, such as Germany, witnessed anti-austerity and pro-democracy mobilization. Clearly something else is needed to explain the anomalous strength of the Spanish case. Within classical social movement theory, the resource mobilization paradigm (RMT) would argue that what is needed to sustain effective mobilization are well-resourced, efficient, and effective organizations with clear chains of command and hierarchical professionalized structures with clear goals (Zald and McCarthy 2017). Yet the loose nonhierarchical networks of small groups of activists working on a wide range of issues that characterize the 15-M network hardly fulfil these criteria.

The political process model, which absorbed the RMT paradigm but attempted to correct some of its deficiencies, argued that movement participants can be aggrieved, organized, and strategically and effectively led, but in the absence of a favorable political context (or at least one that opens opportunities) they will not get far (Tarrow 1998; McAdam 1982; see also Edwards 2014). Two arguments could be put forward to support these claims: on the one hand, Spain had an aggrieved population and a relatively high propensity to protest (Christensen 2016; Torcal et al. 2015), and, on the other hand, Spain was rocked by corruption scandals. But as critics of grievance theory (Langman 2013; Oliver 1989; Koopmans 2004) argue, and as I show in this book, resilient social movements (those that do not dissipate after a protest event or a brief period) need to actually convert grievances into *sustained mobilization*. And as Jasper (2010b) compellingly argues, proponents of political process models have a tendency to find favorable political contexts for successful movements, and unfavorable ones for unsuccessful movements. What they fail to provide is a theory of action that actually delves into the motivations and internal experiences that social movement actors draw on to mobilize and that shape their interaction with their environment.

These critiques do not render the political context irrelevant, however. On the contrary, without the real suffering experienced by so many Spaniards in the post-crisis scenario, it is doubtful that the movement's claims would have found as much traction. In Europe, two key demands emerged: a demand for a need to address the democratic deficit (summed up in 15-M with the slogan "Real Democracy Now!"), and a rejection of the austerity measures that governments have put into place, intensely pressured by the Troika, and by other economic and political elites, encouraging a maintenance of the existing neoliberal order (della Porta 2012; Flesher Fominaya 2014a; Roos and Oikonomakis 2014; Shihade et al. 2012). In Spain, anti-austerity claims and pro-democracy claims are deeply intertwined. 15-M (and groups predating it like the Platform for those Affected by Mortgages, or PAH) sparked a fundamental struggle between political elites and citizens over the definition of the crisis (and thus the neoliberal model that underpins that definition) and the legitimacy of the existing model of democracy (Flesher Fominaya 2015e).

In this struggle, political elites not only fight to justify a neoliberal financialized capitalist economic model, with austerity cuts being presented as a necessary "unfortunate" consequence of that model, but they also defend a representative model of democracy that invests them with the legitimacy to make economic choices on behalf of citizens and for the greater good. In Spain, both of these arguments are tied to a refusal on the part of both majority parties (the governing Partido Popular, PP, and the main opposition party, the Partido Socialista Obrero Español, PSOE) to respond to the millions of people who have taken to the streets and squares to demand that the government not only provide more welfare and care for citizens in the face of the economic crisis, but also modify the existing democratic model to increase citizen participation and respect existing democratic institutions in letter, practice, and spirit.

As the 15-M slogan (channeling de Toqueville on the *Ancién Régime*) put it, "No one expected the Spanish Revolution." While no one could have foreseen the peculiar set of factors that came together in the precise time and space to produce 15-M, it is clear that the crisis context created receptivity among those suffering the consequences of the crisis and its (mis)management via austerity policies. In autumn of 2010, 22% of Spaniards felt that reducing public spending was the best way out of the crisis, with 35% thinking governments should first invest in measures to boost the economy, and 30% feeling both should be done simultaneously (Eurobarometer 74/2010).

The impact of the crisis on Spain was stark. Unemployment was already at 8% in 2007, but by May 2011, the time of the original 15-M protest, that figure had risen to 20.7% (Eurostat), rising to 26% by 2013. Youth unemployment was already at 18.1% in 2007, climbing to 46.2% in 2011 and a record 55.5% in 2013. This was accompanied by an increase in youth migration, at 44,853 in 2007 and climbing to 116,807 in 2011. While in terms of percentages of the total population (roughly 45 million) these emigration figures are not high, the connection between youth unemployment and migration was mobilized by groups like Juventud Sin Futuro (Youth Without Future), one of the original promoter groups behind 15-M (discussed in Chapter 9), and later by Marea Granate, the form 15-M took outside of Spain within émigré communities.

Austerity politics have led to an acute deterioration of living conditions for millions of Spanish residents (Sahuquillo 2013; Luna 2013), creating a public receptive to critiques of austerity politics. But grievances alone are not sufficient to explain high levels of mobilization (Langman 2013; Oliver 1989), as a comparison with other hard-hit countries with austerity cuts shows (Kaldor and Selchow 2013). Although the Spanish propensity to mobilize is higher than most (Christensen 2014; Torcal et al. 2015), comparative data shows that this is insufficient to explain the emergence of sustained high-level mobilization or the 15-M movement. Instead, we need to look deeper to find the origins of the movement, and I will turn to this in Part II. First, though, I want to show how Spanish activists discursively contested hegemonic narratives about the crisis and austerity, highlighting this as a distinguishing feature of the movement, and also one of its central tasks and achievements.

15-M: Contesting hegemonic narratives of the crisis and redefining democracy

Critique and resignification

Describing the post-crisis management by political elites, Colin Crouch (2011) notes that, paradoxically, the crisis was framed in such a way as to reinforce existing trends toward neoliberal, finance-driven, corporation-dominated public policy. As a result of elite framing, instead of *banks* being blamed for their irresponsible behavior, the welfare state and social policy—the clear *victims* of austerity politics—somehow became the scapegoats. This effective elite framing of public responsibility for the rescue of the banks, despite the banking sector's direct role in provoking the crisis, was difficult to contest and required a significant amount of discursive work on the part of social movements and other actors critical of the political management of the aftermath of the crisis. The capacity for critique becomes all the more challenging the further we move toward what Crouch (2004) terms a "post-democratic society." As Tarrow (2013) argues, contentious discursive work is a core activity for social movements. It not only involves the introduction of alternative language and meanings, but also requires the contestation, rearticulation, and—if successful—*resignification* of central terms. As Rancière (2011, 78) puts it, "Being fought over is what makes a political notion properly political [. . .], not the fact that it has multiple meanings. The political struggle is also the struggle for the appropriation of words."

In order for social movement claims to be taken up by the public and put on the political agenda, they must engage in substantial discursive work (Errejón 2011; Snow and Benford 1992; Tarrow 2013). An initial process of critique of the existing state of affairs (the status quo) is followed by the introduction of some alternative, often with *new* language (historical examples include "strike," "working class," "male chauvinist") (Tarrow 2013). If mobilizing new terms effectively is difficult, even *more* difficult is resignifying existing terms. This is because terms such as "democracy" already have deeply rooted historically and emotionally charged meanings with great cultural resonance that have been reinforced over time through myriad political and cultural discursive practices. Resignification depends on the concerted action of collective actors engaged in specific meaning-making and dissemination processes. If it is relatively simple—if not easy—to highlight the glaring democratic deficiencies of "really existing democracy" (corruption scandals, fraud, revolving doors, problems with electoral law, etc.), it is harder to actually resignify terms with alternative meanings. Throughout this book I will show how Spain's 15-M movement shifted from critique to resignification in their quest for a new democratic imaginary.

But the discursive realm cannot be divorced from the material one: as I am arguing throughout, the ideational democratic frameworks that provided a connecting element across diverse issues and groups are rooted in shared experiences of the crisis, and in substantive conceptions of the common good and how to realize it through democratic praxis. Recognizing the crucial importance of the *substantive* (and not just procedural) understanding of democracy enables us to understand the connection between the anti-austerity and pro-democracy elements that define the movement, and to take account of the social, economic, and political context in which the movement develops. The 15-M movement and related movement parties (e.g., Ahora Madrid, Barcelona en Comú, Podemos) are engaged in a process of democratic critique and resignification that first *delegitimizes* "really existing democracy" but holds on to the value of democracy as a guiding principle, and to its institutions as worthy of being reclaimed, which then *relegitimizes* democracy.

The realm of the cultural, and specifically the discursive, is often over-looked in explanations of mobilization, yet it is here, in the realm of the discourses that motivate practices, that we can discover some of the crucial differences in responses to similar material and political contexts. As the global crisis hit country after country, political and economic elites mobilized discourse that justified the necessity and the inevitability of implementing austerity politics as a response to it. The message was sometimes accompanied by a moralistic admonishment—not of the banks, whose actions had led to the crisis in the first place, but rather of ordinary citizens, who were told that they had lived above their means for too long and now had to pay the piper. The problem, according to this narrative, wasn't the easy credit that banks had aggressively marketed to people who did not have sufficient means to take on high-risk debt burdens, but rather the rampant consumerism of ordinary citizens, expressed in their desire for "second homes and plasma TVs," as President Mariano Rajoy stated in an interview (*eldiario.es* 2012). Such narratives blame individual behavior for the crisis, rather than the lack of regulation of the banking or financial sector. This message formed part of the elite narrative in both Ireland and Spain, two countries hard-hit by the crisis, and whose governments implemented harsh austerity measures and assumed massive public debts for bank bailouts. The response to these narratives, however, could not be more different in the two contexts. In Ireland, many people (at least initially) accepted this narrative and collectively assumed they should "reap what they sowed," and that following the boom of the Celtic Tiger, they needed to suffer the consequences, including seeing the mass migration of their youth as "a legitimate continuation of a historical response to hardship" (Power 2016, 1). In Spain, movements mobilized in myriad ways to contest this narrative. Whereas in Ireland, anti-austerity mobilization centered around specific material issues and some political responsibilities, in Spain this contestation combined two inextricably linked themes: a fundamental questioning of and demand for "real democracy," and a rejection of narratives suggesting that the crisis was the fault or responsibility of ordinary citizens. Instead, activists and critical journalists responded by disseminating a series of counter-hegemonic messages of their own, using banners, tweets, slogans, street theater, articles, and various media outlets (mass, alternative, and social) to do so. Analysis of slogans from the first 15-M protests reveals the main frames of contestation that characterize the movement. The crisis of representation is captured clearly in the slogan "They Don't Represent Us!" (*No nos representan*), whereas one of the main slogans of the original 15-M protest and DRY! (Real Democracy Now!)—"We are not commodities in the hands of bankers and politicians"—draws a clear connection between political and economic elites in their handling of the crisis.

Frame analysis of slogans collated from banners and chants at the June 19, 2011, protest in Barcelona (against the Euro Pact, austerity cuts, and political corruption) shows the clear connection between the demand for real democracy and a rejection of austerity in the face of the crisis. The demand for real democracy encompasses a critique of rampant corruption, the existing government, the current electoral system, the right to protest and occupy public space, and a combination of local, national, and transnational references. They also show that activists were not only indignant or outraged, but also hopeful and purposive. As one protester commented, being part of a contestation of dominant narratives was a clear goal: "We are changing the perception of reality. This is amazing!"

Of the 105 slogans analyzed (which is a comprehensive but not exhaustive list), the diversity of slogans is notable, as is the centrality of democracy, which is the most repeated word, but also the most dominant frame, as it is also referred to indirectly (e.g., idiocracy) (see Table 1.1).

One of the crucial features of 15-M discourse was the framing of a collective identity (a "we") that was elastic, ambiguous, open, and inclusive, constituted around notions of "we the people" and ordinary citizens. As Íñigo Errejón (2015, 124) argues, "a significant part of the 15-M political capacity relies on its discourse, characterized by broad, ambivalent and dichotomist interpellations." It is this aspect of the movement's discourse that has led it to be characterized (often pejoratively) as "populist." In addition, the movement played a crucial role in defining the "them" against which they mobilized, understood as an unholy alliance of political and economic elites that abused their power for self-interest and against the direct interest of the people, and, adding insult to injury, passing on the cost of their "crisis/swindle" to hardworking people. The frame analysis of the slogans from the June 11, 2011, protest shows that the construction of what the political party Podemos would later call *la casta*, or the political and economic elite caste, came much earlier. Through effective framing and discursive work, the movement was extremely successful in forcing the issue of corruption and the need for electoral reform, for greater institutional transparency, and for greater participation onto the political agenda: these issues became unavoidable, and a permanent thorn in the side of the governing parties. In addition, the already important issue of unemployment

Table 1.1 Frames of 15-M Slogans and Chants, Barcelona, June 2011

Frame/Target/Theme	Slogans (selected)	Slogans Original (Spanish/Catalan)	Frequency of frame in slogans (out of 105 total) Direct (Indirect)
Democracy	We want another democracy, No to the idiocracy	Queremos otra democracia, No a la memocracia	10 (12)
Politicians/Government	Politicians give me back my rights, don't take them from me	Políticos devolvedme mis derechos no me los quitéis	10 (4)
Banks/Bankers	My bank is robbing us; Bankers thieves you will fill the prisons	Mi banco nos roba; Banqueros ladrones llenareis las prisiones	4 (11)
Crisis/Austerity issues	When you cut, start with yourselves; We do not want to pay for your crisis	Para recortar empezad por vosotros mismos; No volems pagar la vostra crisis	14
Dreams/Waking/Another World/Future	Give me back my dreams and my future; Enough dreaming, we have awakened; If I don't dream you don't sleep; Failed system alarm, wake up!	Devolvedme mi futuro y mis sueños; Basta de soñar, hemos despertado; Si yo no sueño tú no duermes; Failed system alarm, despierta!	10
Violence/Repression	What a relief that when beaten, words don't die	Menos mal que a porrazos las palabras no mueren	8
Capitalism/Profit	Profits are privatized, losses are socialized	Los beneficios se privatizan las pérdidas se socializan	4 (1)
Self-reflexive/Political Subject ("We/I")	We are going slow (because) we are going far; We will not be silent in the face of injustice	Vamos lentos, vamos lejos; No callamos ante la injusticia	15

Table 1.1 Continued

Frame/Target/ Theme	Slogans (selected)	Slogans Original (Spanish/Catalan)	Frequency of frame in slogans (out of 105 total) Direct (Indirect)
Direct Appeal to citizens/people	Don't look at us join us, Join us, you are being robbed too	No nos mires únete***, Únete a ti también te roban *	7
Media	The reality of this revolution will be shown on TV, on Al-Jazeera, but not Channel 3; Television/ Manipulation	La realidad de esta revolución se verá en TV, en Al-Jazeera no en TV3; Televisión/ Manipulación	3
Global/ Transnational Reference	Iceland's dream	Islandia's dream	4
Bankers and Politicians	Politicians and bankers hand in hand make money; There is not enough bread for so much sausage (reference to thieves)	Politics y banquers de la má fan els calers; No hay pan pa tanto chorizo**	2 (11)

Slogans from 19 June 2011 protest, Barcelona. Originally in Catalan or Spanish. * sung or chanted, ** a common slogan that predates 15-M, *** both. Some slogans coded in more than one category. As some slogans are not fully translatable, the originals are in the right-hand column.

was further developed to highlight concerns about working conditions, precariousness, and migration.

As theories of frame resonance would lead us to expect, 15-M garnered support to the extent in which it was able to operate within and not against "common sense." 15-M activists resignified political and economic elites from being symbols of the legitimacy of the successful democratic transition to being symbols of corruption, responsible for the crisis. In so doing, they collapsed the partisan distinctions between political actors, "presenting them as united around their particular egotistical interests and their common subordination to private economic power. In this process 15-M points toward a populist rupture that dichotomizes the social space between 'the people,' [a concept] as broad as it is vaguely defined, and the elites or the 'regime'" (Errejón 2015, 145).

Resignification of existing terms is a difficult process that navigates between the need to deploy familiar and strongly valued referents (so that they resonate with the public) while at the same time *overcoming* their deeply rooted existing meaning in "common sense," converting common sense to "good sense" (i.e., the new democratic imaginary). When deployed by movements from below, these resignifications are designed to subvert the status quo or the established order of power, and in this sense are counter-hegemonic. Crucial here is the notion of *minimizing* differences between groups within the elite structure, something the 15-M movement did very effectively, encapsulating this idea within iconic symbols such as the hash tag #PPSOE and slogan *PPSOE la misma mierda es* (PP or PSOE is the same shit), challenging the idea that the socialist and right-wing parties were in fact different from each other (Flesher Fominaya 2015e). One of the key bases of legitimacy of representative democracy is precisely the idea that diverse opinions, ideologies, and constituencies are represented through a multiple party system and the alternation of governing political parties. Reconfiguring the political spectrum into an "us versus them" (as was later done by Occupy Wall Street with the very effective and iconic "We are the 99%") questions this fundamental claim to legitimacy. As with all successful progressive movements, crucial here too is the idea that the movement is mobilizing on behalf of universal or broad constituents, in this case one of the broadest of all political categories, "the people." This marks a rupture with the Global Justice Movement (GJM), where an "activist" identity was mobilized, despite the desire of many activists to find ways to break out of the "activist ghetto." This desire to connect with "ordinary people" and not just activists subcultural communities (i.e., the converted) formed a key part of debates in Madrid's autonomous political community[1] (and elsewhere in Spain and Europe), and finds expression in the 15-M movement and, later, in Podemos (formulated by Errejón, as lead political strategist for *the party*, whose campaigns constantly stressed the distinction between "the people" and "*la casta*"). The effectiveness of this strategy can be measured by the extent to which it was contested by political elites, and by the high levels of support for the movements' key demands (Sampedro and Lobera 2014), despite the strenuous attempts to delegitimize the movement by economic and political elites and associated media (Errejón 2015; Flesher Fominaya 2015e).

These counter-hegemonic messages formed part of a wider context of mobilization, declining standards of living, austerity politics, and corruption scandals that contributed to a drastic change in Spaniard's conception of and satisfaction with democracy.

Democratic decline and democratic regeneration

In 2008, Spain was the fifth *highest* of EU countries in satisfaction with the way democracy worked in their country (Eurobarometer 68/2008), with 77% of those polled responding they were either very satisfied or fairly satisfied. By 2012 that figure had dropped to 32%—now it was 66% of the population who were *not* very satisfied or *not at all* satisfied with the way democracy worked (Eurobarometer 78/2012). By 2013 the percentages had pretty much inverted, with 75% reporting *dissatisfaction* (Eurobarometer 2013), and Spain was now seventh from the *bottom* of EU countries in terms of satisfaction with democracy.

Marisa Revilla (Revilla et al. 2015) argues that long before Podemos, 15-M already represented not just the end of political bipartisanship but also social bipartisanship, due to the inability of the major parties to satisfy voter aspirations, or communicate effectively with them, particularly younger voters. She sees 15-M as reflecting a generational change in which young people mistrust politicians and no longer share the CT consensus about Spanish democracy. 15-M, therefore, is an expression of citizens who feel they do not have any viable political options. Revilla argues that the 2011 general election already provided clear evidence of this: the major parties (PP and PSOE) lost millions of votes, and the smaller parties (Izqueirda Unida [IU], Unión Progreso y Democracia [UPyD]) and abstention and null votes increased significantly. The cycle of mobilization characterized by 15-M issued forth an ideological reconfiguration that has transformed the political landscape in Spain.

Corruption scandals (e.g., illegal financing, slush fund payments to high-ranking members), involving primarily, but not only, the Popular Party, emerged throughout this period and are ongoing, which undoubtedly contributes to the decline in satisfaction with democracy (Norris 2014). But rather than being precursors, those scandals' emergence can be directly traced to the 15-M movement itself, with organizations like 15MpaRato exposing the Bankia fraud (see Chapter 7), the creation of Fíltrala ("leak it": an encrypted whistleblowing repository), and the emergence of new critical independent digital newspapers, collectively run by activist journalists, such as *eldiario.es* and *Infolibre* publishing exposés. Preexisting media like *Diagonal*, a nonhierarchical newspaper explicitly created in 2003 to provide service to progressive social movements, and *Público*, established in 2007, also developed a leftist/critical journalistic presence online that was strongly integrated into social media networks. Community radio, like Ágora Sol Radio, and television, like Tele K and *La Tuerka* (see Chapter 10), also contributed to a rich media ecology in which counter-hegemonic messages circulated through numerous platforms and outlets of social, mass, and alternative media. Spanish resistance movements in the context of the crisis have invigorated the public sphere. At their heart lies a profound contestation of the hegemonic narratives that justify crucial political decisions that shape citizens' lives. These resistance narratives call for an overturning of the economistic logics that drive dominant understandings of "crisis" and the justification of austerity measures.

15-M therefore had a crucial impact in simultaneously stimulating a decrease in satisfaction with *existing* democracy in Spain and a widespread clamor for a regeneration of democratic institutions. While a critique of political and economic elites has been at the heart of anti-capitalist and autonomous protest for decades, in 15-M we see a much more sustained, profound, and engaged critique of the democratic institutions put in place during the Spanish Transition, and of specific mechanisms that facilitate political corruption, lack of transparency, and lack of "real" democracy. This "democratic turn," with its emphasis on democratic reform and renewal and a reclaiming of the constitution, with its guarantees of basic social rights (housing, education), is a very notable feature of 15-M, and one that distinguishes it from some other anti-austerity mobilizations such as those in Ireland, where "real" democracy and anti-corruption were not core demands. Resistance to austerity narratives and the "democratic turn" does not rest solely on discourse, of course. As I will show, activists engaged in numerous forms of direct action—from blocking evictions, to disobeying unjust laws, to occupying not only plazas but also banks and buildings—using crowdfunding to bring court cases against bankers for fraud, and, of course, creating platforms, assemblies, ethical banks, food banks, municipal election platforms, Podemos "Circles," and much more. But within each one of these spaces, from each symbolic and material act, there has also been a constant effort to resignify the consensual "common sense" that was shared (prior to 15-M) by a great part of Spanish society about the meaning of democracy, the legitimacy of the pacts of the

Transition, the lack of viable alternatives to the bipartisan political system, and the desirability and necessity of neoliberal policies before and, above all, *after* the crisis.

Far from representing "anti-politics," as some observers have claimed, one of the key features of 15-M, and one of its most significant departures from previous autonomous movement politics in the GJM (where state institutions were shunned as illegitimate) is a re-engagement and reclaiming of the state and its institutions (Flesher Fominaya 2015b). Holding legislators accountable to their *own* laws is a different strategy than arguing that the laws themselves or the rules of the game are illegitimate. While some laws are contested as illegitimate (e.g., the current electoral laws that favor the large parties, the criminalization of protest, etc.), by and large 15-M mobilized to reclaim democracy for the people, not replace it with something else.

Errejón (2015) argues that one of the most overlooked aspects of 15-M (in favor of attention to the how and why) has been it's construction of a public discourse that has challenged hegemonic narratives of the crisis. Therefore, before I too embark on an exploration of the "how and why," I want to highlight that one of the movement's most significant achievements lies in introducing a rupture in the consensus around neoliberal capitalism and the need to orient all social life around its preservation as the ultimate good. Laying bare the human costs of the crisis and austerity politics (Stuckler and Basu 2013), challenging narratives about their inevitability, and arguing that their causes and effects should lead us to rethink the nature of democracy itself—this has been the major impact of 15-M, and one whose consequences, like the full impact of austerity policies, cannot be measured in the short term, but are likely to persist for some time.

Note

1. Debates both Errejón and I were participants in, as well as many others who appear in this book, including Pablo Iglesias.

PART II

15-M

From Protest to Occupation

Introduction

The stunning occupation of squares around the world has understandably attracted much attention, with less attention paid to what came before or what followed. This conflation has produced strong claims about the changing nature of social movement organizing more broadly, especially with regard to the use of digital technologies or the salience of "individuals" in the crowd (see e.g., Juris' "logic of aggregation" thesis, 2012; Bennet and Segerberg's "logic of connective action," 2012, or Milan's "crowd of individuals," 2015), that need to be calmly examined in the cold light of post-collective effervescence. 15-M and Occupy Wall Street are taken as exemplars of these new logics of mobilization. Each of these theses offers valuable insights into contemporary mobilization dynamics. But the overall vision they posit is that of a new form of collection action in which unaffiliated individuals with personalized action frames are aggregated together via digitally enabled means and through the physical proximity produced by the encampments. The analysis presented here problematizes these interpretations, which suffer from two main weaknesses: conflating protest events, protest encampments, and social movement communities; and lacking an awareness of the fundamental role that movement political cultures and legacies have in shaping movement dynamics.

The term 15-M is used to refer to (a) the original 15-M protests on May 15, 2011; (b) the month-long occupation that succeeded it, known in Spain as Acampada Sol when referring to the Madrid occupation; and (c) the movement that adopted this label following the original protests and the occupations. Although all three are connected through overlapping actors, themes, and movement cultural practices, it is important to distinguish clearly between the three phases, because each followed different dynamics and involved a different range of actors. By exploring the case of Madrid in detail, I hope to illuminate more clearly the different phases of the evolution of the 15-M movement, contributing analytical clarity for its analysis and social movement studies more broadly.

A *protest event* is contained in time and space. In the case of a march like the original 15-M protest, it follows certain patterns in its organization and development. Although it can deviate from its path, it has a planned route, with an origin and end point, and a set of objectives, previously defined (although not necessarily agreed upon or coordinated). Once underway and out in public space, however, no amount of planning or consensus can control what happens, although some contingencies can be mitigated. The participation of members of the public, counter-demonstrators, police or security forces, or even sympathetic protesters who differ in tactics or are not aware of the objectives, plans, or previous agreements all interact to make each protest a unique event.

A *protest camp/occupation* is a distinct phenomenon. Once underway, encampments depend upon a complex internal organization that seeks to satisfy the material and political needs and goals of the participants. The experience of communal living and communal action over time, and their containment in bounded physical space, makes them qualitatively different from protest marches. They are more clearly physically contained while still being public, visible, and open. At the same time, they are less constrained temporally, so that the porous margins or borders of the camp can be penetrated over time by a constantly shifting random, complex, and indeterminate set of actors. Despite this, within the camp, a shared spirit or ethos often takes hold, punctuated by moments of collective effervescence, which participants often refer to in emotionally charged terms (e.g., "it was the most powerful experience of my life").

All occupations eventually decline or decamp, but the dynamic of the camp before this happens, and the nature of the end of the camp, can have an important impact on what happens next, and this varies greatly from context to context (Eschle 2018). Some camps, like Acampada Sol, take a clear (if contested) decision to decamp before they are evicted, and develop an organizational strategy to continue the political work in different forms and venues. Others are violently evicted, or hang in there until only a few committed people are left, but the critical mass of participation has dissipated or re-aggregated elsewhere (Chabanet and Lacheret 2016; Eschle 2018; Hammond 2015; Roberts 2012; Tufekci 2017). Whatever the dynamic, even when the "objective" political goals have failed or been reversed (e.g., Tahrir), all occupations can have long-lasting impacts on political communities, either through affecting the activist biographies of individuals, influencing and transforming political perceptions in the wider population, transforming political cultures, forcing or influencing a change in electoral politics, or creating an iconic political milestone event that will later be referred to by historians, politicians, writers, and individuals (e.g., "I was there").

A *movement, movement community*, or *movement network* is again a different phenomenon, much more diffuse in time and space, whose precise boundaries are hotly debated among scholars.[1] Sometimes entirely new movement communities can be born from protest events and/or occupations. More often, however, previously existing movement networks and communities precede and continue after occupations, sometimes regenerated and increased in activity, or, conversely, winding down into periods of abeyance and latency (if, for example, the occupation has been brutally repressed, or if the internal dynamics worked to increase tensions or divisions). In other words, there is no formula or unidirectional relation between protest events, occupations, and movements, and each of these needs to be considered separately, but in relation to each other. All are shaped by movement political cultures, which include ideational frameworks (the understanding of collective action) and the collective action frames (practices, organizational forms, etc.) shaped by them.

In order to understand the democratic project at the heart of the 15-M movement, it is necessary to understand the logic of autonomous movements, because the influence of autonomous ideational frameworks shaped 15-M movement dynamics, including organizational forms, decision-making procedures, alliance structures, strategy, tactics, and collective identity.

The logic of autonomy

Autonomous social movement actors have played a key role in the genesis and self-definition of the 15-M movement. Autonomous movements can be understood as movements organized in horizontal networks, underlain by principles of self-organization, direct/participatory democracy, autonomy, diversity, and direct action. Historically, there have been many forms of autonomous movement, specific to the particular local and national contexts in which they develop. Autonomous actors distinguish themselves from the practices of the Institutional Left, rejecting representative democracy and majority rule, and instead defending more participatory models, based on direct democracy and self-governance, horizontal (nonhierarchical) structures, decision-making through consensus (if possible and necessary), in the forum of an assembly (usually open), and rarely with permanent delegations of responsibility (Flesher Eguiarte 2005; Flesher Fominaya 2007a, 2010e; 2013, 2015b; Katsiaficas 2006). Autonomy refers not only to internal organizing principles and structures, but also, crucially, to independence from established political parties and trade unions. This is manifested in the refusal to allow acronyms or party or union banners and flags at protest events (and sometimes heated altercations can break out around this issue). The distinction between autonomous and Institutional Left logics of collective action is often shorthanded as a difference between "horizontals and verticals."

A full analysis of the features of autonomous movements can be found elsewhere (Flesher Fominaya 2007a, 2015b). Here I will highlight five features particularly relevant to 15-M:

1. Autonomous political practice is prefigurative in that it attempts to create tools and practices today which foreshadow the future society that is aspired to. Organizational forms, decision-making processes, and forms of action are not just means to an end, but ends in themselves. Social transformation comes through the creation of alternatives, not through the existing institutional system. For 15-M, this is reflected in assembly practice that is inclusive, participatory, and nonhierarchical, and that eschews leader and representatives. In Spain this assembly-based organizing tradition is known as *asamblearismo*, and this term will appear numerous times in this book.

2. The ideological base of autonomous movements is heterogeneous and frequently not explicit. Ideologies are seen as frozen and prescriptive, with a tendency to divide and exclude rather than increase diversity and inclusivity. They are also identified with "old" leftist orthodoxies. Theory should arise from practice and should remain open to question, change, and modification (see McKay 1998; Plows 1998; Wall 1999; ULEX 2008).

3. Although the legitimate political actor is the autonomous individual, *acting collectively*, this does not mean collectives or affinity groups are rejected. Rather, the autonomous actor actively attempts to negate the isolationism created by capitalist consumer society through the nurturing of social relations that create community. Solidarity and collective

resolution of shared problems are key. The autonomous understanding of political legitimacy facilitates greatly the construction of the "ordinary citizen" as collective actor.

4. A rejection of assistentialism, clientelism, and charity models are another key feature. This is linked to a refusal to conceptualize problems such as homelessness and unemployment as individual problems. Instead, these are resolutely framed as systemic failures, which, within neoliberalism, are socially constructed as individual failures, leading to depression, self-blame, and guilt. In 15-M and related movements this aspect of autonomous political philosophy is a crucial organizing principle (see Chapter 8 on the PAH).

5. A DIY (do it yourself) philosophy is also crucial and encompasses various elements: the desire to work without intermediaries, the idea that pretty much anyone can learn how to do anything, and a commitment to sharing knowledge in an open way. This breaks down the notion of expertise associated with hierarchies, and is strongly connected to a philosophy of replicability: if you provide practical, technical, substantive information freely, then others can take that information and set up their own camp/working group/movement/workshop, etc. Freely sharing replicable information and models has strong synergies with hacker ethics, particularly its open software philosophy, but is not limited to digital or technical information or software. All of this is, therefore, connected to an idea of inclusivity and diversity: no matter what your initial skill level or experience, if you are willing to participate collaboratively, you are welcome.

Elements of the autonomous ethos stem from and share strong connections with anarchist traditions, but also feminist, queer, nonviolent civil disobedience, and hacker/technopolitical and free culture philosophies; the importance of these in 15-M will be developed further later on in the book.

Collective identity in autonomous movements

In the absence of formal organizational and institutional infrastructures, collective identity processes involving reciprocal ties between collective actors across informal, non-institutional, yet organized networks are crucial in maintaining internal coherence. This shared collective identity across movement networks, sustained and developed in movement subcultures such as urban and rural social centers, university student political groups, and other movement-related "scenes," enables rapid mobilization in new contexts (rather than the mobilization of formally organized membership structures, as in the case of more institutionally based movements) (see, e.g., Morris 1984).

Paradoxically, it is precisely its anti-identitarian orientation—that is, a refusal to visibly identify with any particular collective, acronym, or political symbol—that forms one of the bases of the autonomous collective identity (Flesher Fominaya 2015a). This has a double implication for understanding the discourse and collective identity of 15-M as a political actor. First, it helps explain the rejection of political parties and unions in the protest and the camp on ideological grounds in four senses:

1. as an evolution of autonomous thinking and practice in a specific movement subculture,
2. as a statement of principles (i.e., "we are autonomous from parties and unions and will not be subject to their control"),
3. as a desire to break out of the activist ghetto and to reach "ordinary people" (i.e., "we are ordinary citizens, just like you, not political experts"), and
4. as a rejection of representative politics ("They do not represent us!").

Second, it reflects a strategic principle, long deployed by autonomous movements, to prevent co-optation (*cooptación y fagocitación*) from established collectives, parties, and unions.

Despite long-standing cleavages between autonomous and Institutional Left logics and actors in Spanish (and European) progressive movements, actors from both sides of this divide do come together on specific campaigns, and the phenomenon of multiple militancy means some actors move between the two types of spaces (see Flesher Fominaya 2007a). The refusal to allow Institutional Left actors to participate (as representatives of organizations, not as individuals) in 15-M movement assemblies is well documented (Calvo 2013; DRY! 2011; Juventud Sin Futuro (JSF) 2011a; Martínez and García 2015; Romanos 2013). Autonomous movements in Spain have long rejected the participation of political parties and trade unions in their autonomous spaces (and refused also to participate in many "unitary" spaces dominated by Institutional Left actors), but this trend has evolved over time and become more marked as it became a more widespread feature of Madrid's and Spain's social movement culture.

Elements of these various facets of autonomous thinking, and their ascendance within the lead-up to 15-M in the original protest's preparatory spaces, will be apparent in the narratives that unfold in the next chapter.

Note

1. For an overview of definitions, see Flesher Fominaya 2014a, Chapter 1.

2

Origin Stories

From where do the people come who make up the initial, organizing cadre of a movement? How do they come together, and how do they come to share a similar view of the world in circumstances that compel them to political action? In what ways does the nature of its sources affect the future development of the movement?

—JO FREEMAN (1999, 7)

EPISODES OF INTENSE visible protest are often characterized by observers, journalists, scholars, and even participants as spontaneous. Movement outsiders and newcomers are often unaware of the behind-the-scenes organization involved, whereas movement insiders gain a number of benefits from "spontaneity narratives" (such as presenting their demands as the will of the people, or proving autonomy from the existing power structures they want to challenge) (Flesher Fominaya 2015e; Polletta 1998a, 1998b). As Polletta and I have shown, spontaneity arguments are rarely empirically verifiable for sustained mobilization processes (see also Zamponi and Fernández González 2017).

If intense sustained mobilizations are rarely spontaneous and rarely unprecedented, they are often unpredictable. Despite a temptation to recur to economic grievance theories as a means of explaining intense mobilizations in times of crisis, such theories are insufficient to account for the great variation in protest responses to austerity politics across countries with similar crisis/austerity impacts (Flesher Fominaya 2017). Instead, other factors need to be considered in addition to the real significance of material grievances.

As I show in this chapter, the 15-M protests were not a spontaneous collective response to precipitating events (Arab Spring, European anti-austerity, and student protests), or even to intermediate causes such as the

Democracy Reloaded. Cristina Flesher Fominaya, Oxford University Press (2020). © Oxford University Press.
DOI: 10.1093/oso/9780190099961.001.0001

global financial crisis (which started in 2008 and did not trigger a highly visible mass response in Spain until 2011), although these are important in understanding the timing and strength of the mobilizations.

More structural approaches to the study of social movements, such as the political process model, focus primarily on cycles of visible mobilization and perceive social movements primarily as political actors looking at political institutions from the outside in, attempting to achieve gains and recognition from the state (McAdam 1982; Tarrow 2011). Such approaches stress structural factors outside social movement control, with social movement actors responding to political opportunities, and depending on internal resources, to mobilize (Goodwin and Jasper 1999). In the ideal typical model of cycles of contention, movements *appear* in response to political opportunities, *consolidate* resources that they mobilize on behalf of their constituents, undergo *transformations* through the process of contention, and then *disappear* after mobilization. In contrast, a genealogical approach looks at social movements from the inside out, playing close attention to their latent, and not just visible, activity, and recognizing processes of movement continuity between peaks of visible mobilization. While movements undeniably pass through cycles of highly visible mobilization and sometimes disappear afterward, more often the periods between the cycles of contention are not marked by disappearance but by ongoing social movement activity in a variety of environments (Flesher Fominaya 2013, 2015; Melucci 1994; Taylor 1989; Polletta 2002).

A genealogical approach recognizes the role of preexisting trajectories of dissent on mobilization. It allows us to understand how emerging political opportunity structures are effectively exploited to produce mobilization, and also what is new and what is reproduced from the past in new episodes of intense and widespread mobilization. It enables us to see the direct role of precursor movement organizations in the genesis of 15-M. A genealogical approach also points to the significance of social movement learning processes in movement subcultures that explain, for example, the ability of 15-M activists to effectively manage participatory assemblies of 5,000 people.

15-M (the protest and the movement) cannot be understood without the context of the crisis, yet the crisis would not have produced 15-M without the existence of precursor critical social movements. The changing political climate and the crisis opened up significant political opportunities that were exploited by movement actors. These actors were influenced by events elsewhere, such as the Icelandic Saucepan Revolution that had ushered in a change of government, and the mass mobilizations in Tunisia and Egypt in January 2011, which shook seemingly unmovable authoritarian regimes, facilitating a process of "cognitive liberation" in which the previously impossible suddenly seems possible. WikiLeaks, Anonymous, and more local struggles around intellectual property laws and Internet freedom, were also influential. The confluence of all these elements, plus the sustained collective efforts of activists in Spain, produced the original 15-M protest.

Carlos Taibo understands the origins of 15-M as lying in a crisis that particularly affects youth; the increased chaos in the universities caused by the Bologna reforms; the symbolic influence of the Arab revolts, which "the media portrayed as proof that it's possible to bring down dictatorships that seemed to be solidly grounded"; and "the preparation of the terrain by critical social movements during a long period of time." In his view, "this previous work by critical social movements is insufficient to explain 15-M, but 15-M can't be explained without it." I concur. One such immediate precursor was Youth without Future (JSF).

Juventud Sin Futuro (JSF)

The role of the university as a context for the development of student activism that later developed and expanded into the 15-M movement is important, particularly the connection with GJM activism, which provided a line of continuity with a legacy of student activism but also with faculty in the Politics, Sociology, and other departments, who were themselves active in the GJM.[1] This was not only the case in Madrid, but also in Barcelona (see Fernández-Planells 2015) and in the Basque Country (Fernández 2014; Zamponi and Fernández 2017).

One of the groups that participated in the original 15-M call to protest was JSF, who joined the wider coordinating platform, called Democracia Real Ya! (Real Democracy Now!), commonly referred to by its acronym, DRY! Before Youth Without Future (Juventud Sin Futuro, or JSF) was called Youth Without Future, it was a student platform that had already been mobilizing around student issues, but with a keen desire to transcend the student milieu and reach out to youth who weren't integrated into student networks. As JSF cofounder Verónica explains:

> After years of fighting against Bolonia,[2] the student movement was really exhausted and those of us who had been involved came to

the conclusion that we really needed to focus on a much broader struggle and that we were in the midst of a crisis. We saw [our key issues] as basically "no home, no job, and no pension" (*sin casa, sin curro, sin pensión*) and so we founded JSF [in fall 2010] On April 7, 2011, we held the first protest that really led to the whole 15-M.

The process leading up to the April 7 protest was complicated:

(Verónica) It was really difficult because there were people from every political stripe: from the Madrid autonomous movements, Stalinists, from the Communist Party of the Pueblos of Spain (*Partido Comunista de los Pueblos de España*), from Communist Youth (*Juventudes Comunistas*), there were also anarchists and a little bit of everything, so it was really hard to come to any kind of agreement. . . . We did manage to agree on the slogan but . . . [. . .] once we began to delve deeper into our objectives, lots of people left.

Cofounder Carlos noted that these early defectors opened the space up: "Loads of people left and it was very funny because the fewer *collectives* there were, the more *people* came to the assemblies." JSF cofounder Javier remembers this in a similar way, stressing the tensions between classical or Institutional Left positions and autonomous *asambleario* approaches, seeing the former as "old and outdated" and the latter as "new":

Interminable assemblies that reproduce the worst habits and practices of the classical left. Dirty tricks . . . I think that that the two different organizational models, discourses, aesthetics and political practices that divided the student movement in Madrid revolved around two ideas . . . those who want to appeal to the converted, and those who want to reach out to those that aren't converted.

Developing a new language to reach people who were outside existing movement circles but that would be effective in countering the hegemonic narratives of the crisis and neoliberal austerity politics was a central political concern for the autonomous/*asambleario* sector of JSF, prior to 15-M:

(Javier) There were also problems [in the assemblies] when we used the word "citizens" (*ciudadanos*) because there were people wanted to spend all their time talking about the proletariat, the working-class, and capitalism and we would say "we have to try something new because we have already talked and talked about how bad capitalism is, how bad commodification is, how bad privatization is, and we're not getting very far in terms of convincing people." [. . .] [We wanted] to break with the hegemonic discourse that says "this is how things are, there's no alternative and there's no point in protesting."

Carlos also highlights the active construction of a new political subject and language that they were trying to achieve:

A lot of us decided that "the student" is a political subject that was very difficult to mobilize after [the Bolonia] defeat, but young people were a collective that were particularly hit by the crisis. This doesn't mean that we thought that the crisis could be read in terms of young people and old people, that's idiotic. [But] we felt there was a real need to work on politicizing the [extremely depoliticized] youth. The real core of people in JSF were very closely tied to the assemblies of the Carlos III University and "Contrapoder" in the Complutense University of Madrid, but the reason people joined wasn't so much where they came from. The core shared an analysis that I think really connected later with 15-M: that we really needed a [new] political language [to] reach people and [. . .] we needed to stop talking like that and start talking a different way.

Carlos recounted the reflexive process through which JSF members recognized their desire to break with "an extreme leftist" political tradition that starts from a sophisticated theoretical analysis into which people's problems are then inserted, "so then you can tell them about it." Instead:

We [. . .] began to see that some problems we were facing could lead us to very similar conclusions that reading books had led us to, and it worked better when we worked from the problems to the theory, rather than from the theory to the problems. So, what we tried to do was to politicize the *problems* and not to problematize the ideological framework that we were bringing with us.

This very reflexive and active break with classical leftist ideological traditions prompted an effort to rethink political praxis and discourse. The decision to "stop talking like that and start talking a different way" was not just a vague intention; JSF made it a rule never to use certain "trigger" words (such as capitalism) in public discourse. Reaching people through shared problems/problematics rather than through proselytizing was core to their approach (and became widespread in 15-M). Although consensus between all the political orientations in JSF was achieved for the April 7 protest, the *asambleario* approach was clearly "carrying the day," as Javier's narrative shows:

> For April 7 we put the call out for the protest, as JSF, copying the black and yellow aesthetic from the *V for Vivienda* movement, using the same font and just changing the letters—a contribution of my political family, the autonomous *asambleario* tradition—[. . .] but we really wanted to reach people who didn't use those labels.

In terms of movement influences, Verónica stresses the influence of both local and Italian autonomous movements in JSF, but sees the Spanish student movements as key, arguing that Spanish activists involved in international mobilizations felt there are "big differences" between Spanish and other European student movement organizing practices. Javier, in contrast, draws a clear line of influence from other European student movements, in that it made young student activists in Spain feel like they too should be "doing something," but he also highlights that the internal organizational practices of *asamblearismo* follow locally rooted patterns.

As April 7 drew near, some activists began to notice a change in the political climate. Many of them speak of this as "smelling" a change in the air, sensing a hope or possibility that something new might be afoot.

April 7, 2011: The protest

When the members of JSF showed up for the protest, they couldn't believe the response, as Javier recalls:

> I was one of the people—and there were a bunch of us—who had argued that we shouldn't do a protest march, we should just do a *concentración* (a gathering in one spot) with the truck and the music, so that it wouldn't be obvious that there were so few of us [. . .]. We thought at the most we would be 700, and we found 5,000 to 7,000 people there. So, we do the whole route, and we end up at

the Reina Sofia, and the newspaper *El País* had a headline that said "The JSF Protest Ends in Disturbances," which I thought was hilarious. For the umpteenth time they were characterizing us as the anti-systemic youth who tear up the streets and so on. But I think what people were beginning to see was that we weren't just the four usual scruffy (*perroflauta*) suspects, because there were a lot of people there with a really different aesthetic and of all ages. It wasn't just a youth protest, there were a lot of parents there too. So for us that was like our founding moment, and in fact on our banner for the protest we had written "This Is Only the Beginning," because by then we were already attending all the preparatory meetings for the 15-M protest, and we wanted to sort of mark it out as the beginning of a new cycle of mobilization.

Laura, a journalist and activist who was not directly involved in JSF but participated in the April 7 protest, recalls:

> I remember it being like a little thermometer, like taking the temperature of the hopes people had around the 15th of May. And it was really great, it was a success and it wasn't even big.

Both Carlos and Javier highlight the failure of the established unions or parties to respond effectively to the needs of youth in the midst of the crisis and the desire to engage in politics with no intermediaries as motivating factors for JSF. When in 2011 the unions formed a pact with the government instead of refusing to go along with austerity politics and the labor reform, the activists in JSF decided it was time to pick up the gauntlet. The April 7 protest focused on key areas of concern for youth that were later central in 15-M as well: *labor*, specifically the issue of precarious labor, a rejection of the government labor reform and pension reform, the establishment of a maximum salary and an increase to the minimum wage, and gender equality (equal pay for equal work); *housing*, including the demand for social rent and the introduction of *dación en pago* (cancellation of mortgage debt on return of property); and *education*, including a stop to cuts, a reduction in fees and opposition to private financing of the universities (issues already important in the anti-Bolonia protests that brought many JSFers together in university activism).

Although the April 7 protest still included various political families within JSF, shortly afterward, continued internal tensions meant that most people left. Verónica explains the fault lines as lying between

> the people who were more from parties and from a more workerist (*obrerista*) tradition [and] the people who ended up in JSF at the end, who were interested in trying to reach out to social majorities [. . .] but it's also true that the more radical anarchists also left . . . they felt like the demands were too reformist.

The excision (on ideological and strategic lines) left only a core of activists who had a strong autonomous *asambleario* orientation but didn't share a radical anarchist ideology. This defined the character of the JSF members that participated in the DRY! 15-M preparatory assemblies along with members of ATTAC (more Institutional Left) and other nonaffiliated actors. This deradicalization of JSF prior to 15-M also facilitated the inclusion of a wider range of participants later on. The influence of the autonomous housing movement *V de Vivienda* ("H for housing," but in Spanish a play on *V for Vendetta*) in the aesthetic JSF adopted would also be reproduced by DRY! for the 15-M protest aesthetic (later adopted around the world for the "Global Days of Action") (see Figure 2.1). *V de Vivienda* was also one of movements in which Ada Colau, one of the founders of the PAH (see Chapter 8) and later mayor of Barcelona, was very active.

What is striking, particularly in light of spontaneity arguments about 15-M that argue for a sort of explosion of sentiment and indignation that coalesced into a movement, is how clearly defined the political objective to reach out to wide social majorities and project a broad, inclusive, autonomous collective identity was for these JSF activists, and the high degree of strategic reflexivity they showed in their attention to developing a language that did not rely on Marxist/Leftist "trigger" words like "capitalism," but at the same time could rupture hegemonic discourse about capitalism and the crisis. This desire was carried over from the autonomous movements of the 2000s to reach beyond the "activist ghetto" to non-self-identified activists (Flesher Fominaya 2015a). What is new in this context is the constitution of "youth" as a political subject, and the deliberate shifting away from an activist identity frame to the frame of "ordinary citizens" to whom they appeal for participation, with whom they identify as actors, and on whose behalf they mobilize (see also Gerbaudo 2017).

As is also clear from these testimonies, members of JSF had already been participating in the assemblies that were planning the 15-M protest,

FIGURE 2.1 JSF poster for April 7, 2011, protest, which is identical to the 15-M 2011 poster except for the date and place.
Source: Juventud sin Futuro (CC).

under the name/demand of *Real Democracy Now!* or DRY!, prior to the April 7 protest.

Democracia Real Ya! (DRY!)

DRY! began as a Facebook group that connected people around Spain wishing to organize a protest event to critique the crisis, austerity politics, and, crucially, the lack of citizen input into the decisions that were affecting the life of millions of people in a dramatic and negative way, as described by Verónica:

> In the beginning DRY! wasn't an organization or anything, it was just a page that somebody created on Facebook that decided to promote the 15th of May as this date—you know the craziness of social media networks [. . .] but a lot of different collectives started joining in—not to call for the protest, but to actually commit to going to the protest.

Despite starting (and continuing) online, it quickly moved to face-to-face assemblies that brought together individuals active in existing groups and unaffiliated individuals. This is a typical feature of autonomous preparatory assemblies in Madrid at times of increasing mobilization. These assemblies are known as either *plataformas* (specific campaign platforms) or *coordinadoras* (when they coordinate the activities of various organizations or collectives). Alberto, who had been active in autonomous spaces in the university but had dropped out of the activist scene, joined DRY! a month and a half before the protest. He explains that he became involved through Facebook, and after watching a video that confirmed that the people "behind it" shared "how I was feeling and thinking," he wrote to find out when and where the meetings were, and began to attend the preparatory assemblies in the squatted social center Patio Maravillas. But he stresses:

> It all started on the Net [. . .] with *The Platform pro-groups pro-citizen's mobilization* [sic], and it had around 400 associations apart from citizens that signed onto it. . . . It was a secret, closed group, and everything was written there, the whole communiqué, and it is true that it was all done really horizontally and in a participatory way.

Given the original name of the platform (which was actually *Plataforma de coordinación de grupos pro-movilización ciudadana*, or Coordinating Platform of Pro-citizen Mobilization Groups), it is little wonder people opted for DRY! instead, as even Alberto couldn't remember its name! Notice that the first thing Alberto does is request to find out where the meetings are held. His point of entry comes through "the Net" but quickly moves offline to participation in the face-to-face meetings, and his participation is maintained in both arenas simultaneously. The "Net" was also used for the collaborative development of the communiqué. Yet this online process was "fed" by the discussions taking place in the face-to-face assemblies around the country. The interaction between on- and offline activity was crucial, but the "behind-the-scenes" activity was the central arena for negotiating conflict and tensions away from public scrutiny. This negotiation of differences behind-the-scenes was one of the most crucial roles that the DRY! Platform performed, as Carlos of JSF describes:

> The 15-M protest is fundamentally organized by DRY! and sort of one step below, by us (JSF), and by ATTAC. So, some of us were participating in the DRY! preparatory meetings from the beginning, but not that consistently or constantly because those meetings were like a cage full of crickets. I think we (JSF) were able to connect with the political climate that was developing before anybody else. In that original coordinating body there were a lot of people who were involved in what is now the PAH, people from IU, people from Anticapitalist Left (*Izquierda Anticapitalista*), people who are now in the X Party (Partido X) and people who nobody knew what the hell they were doing there and who were really out of place in a leftist environment.

Carlos draws a clear line of demarcation between the 15-M protest and the camp, but also the strong connection between them:

> [DRY! was a coordinator set up by leftist activists to do a specific task: organize the 15-M protest]. But what happens later completely surpasses and overflows everything that came before. Everything that happened in the protest creates a political opportunity for what happened later in the camp, but what happened in the camp is another world. But since politics is always about process, it obviously has clear connections with what happened before.

The explicit framing of the DRY! Communiqué in terms that were inclusive of non-leftist participants prefigured the inclusive nature of the camp, and the wording, which included the phrase "some of us are more conservative and some of us are more progressive," "would have been unthinkable three years before, but nevertheless was agreed," according to

Carlos. Laura, a 15-M activist and journalist, also speaks about the key role that DRY! had in the lead-up to the protest:

> DRY! really took care of a lot of the planning production—as in organizing the lawyers, contacting with different groups, contacting with different neighborhood associations, really doing that behind-the-scenes person-to-person networking activity.

At the same time, online participation was also growing:

> (Laura) Social media networks really have a super important role because you can share information in a free way, outside the control of the media, the markets, or political control. Obviously, it's been a really key tool but it's not the only one. Come off it—if only! (*Ojalá*).

Daniel, an activist still very active in the Madrid DRY! Assembly, came to DRY! via the Internet, rather than direct involvement in the Madrid networks. His narrative also highlights the flow between online and offline spaces in the lead-up to 15-M and how the Internet enabled "contamination" by the outside world:

> I was really involved in what was happening in the Arab Spring and I was very connected to blogging networks in Tunisia and in Egypt. A lot of my political activity at the time was in getting that information from Arab Spring out to the Spanish networks [. . .] I started to connect with different bloggers here in Spain [. . .] and we started to form a network, so I got connected on Twitter, and it really activated me. [. . .] Since I was connected with everybody online, when DRY! began to organize as a citizen pro-protest organization, I also started getting information from JSF which I thought was really good. Although for me the real point of interest was the international dimension, from that point on I began to really get involved with what was actually happening in Madrid. At first, I didn't go to the meetings because I live far out here [but I was very active online]. There were loads of people who really wanted to *do* something.

Daniel began to connect people across issues and interests (Arab Spring, antiwar, followers of the Iceland Revolution) to develop a "general map" of the diversity of people ripe for action and to connect the virtual with the offline, "but primarily organized around [. . .] Arab Spring, the actual practices, occupying public space, protesting in the squares, and I was also writing about doing those kinds of occupations in Madrid." Daniel's story highlights the important role of online networks, including blogger networks (also important in the Arab Spring) in connecting people, and as with Alberto, enabling the shift from online to offline activism. The influence of the Arab Spring, which he experienced through his online connections, inspired him to reflect on the situation in Spain:

> We were in the same situation as the people in the Arab Spring. They were demanding liberty and we were demanding something else—we were demanding action. [. . .] So I could see a clear connection between what was happening there and here and the discourse and the demands of DRY! made perfect sense to me, even though I'm much more radical in every single point of that original manifesto.

Despite his own interest in the Arab Spring, Daniel feels that there was relatively little international inspiration within DRY! at the time. Like Laura, he stresses the important role that DRY! had in connecting different political actors in Madrid:

> Once the camp got underway it wasn't necessarily the people who had been most involved in DRY! who stayed in the plaza. But all those networks had already been created, because DRY! really did an incredible job [of that] seeking out organizations like ATTAC, organizations like *Ecologistas*,[3] just connecting all the groups.

Daniel also highlights the role of more experienced activists in integrating newcomers and shaping the planning of the protest, stressing the role of continuity between previous periods of mobilization and the transmission of practical knowledge to new generations, as well as the importance of locally rooted-on-the-ground networking practices:

> There were people of different ages and political sensibilities within DRY! At first there were people who didn't have an activist trajectory, who didn't even have a *political* trajectory. What they did have was common sense [. . .] But the logic of the platform and the people

who were really carrying it forward here in Madrid were a very heterogeneous group of experienced activists, that as we saw later didn't have that much in common, but who really united around this idea of getting people out to the streets on May 15, and creating contacts and networks between different political actors and people.

DRY!'s behind-the-scenes ability to connect people across issue areas, organizational forms, and ideological orientations was widely considered to be the most important factor that enabled the original 15-M protest to come off. In this they drew on the strength of groups with experienced local activists like ATTAC, Ecologistas en Acción, and JSF in pulling a wide range of actors together around a common call, strategically and effectively using social media and digital tools to develop the manifesto in a participatory way, but modifying the documents in accordance with internal "backstage" negotiations between participants.

Estado del Malestar: "A State of Ill-Being"

DRY! wasn't the only precursor to 15-M, despite ultimately managing to pull together the key actors involved in coordinating the original protest. The journalist/activist Laura described some of the different initiatives taking place in Madrid, prior to the 15-M protest around the time DRY! was formed. One was a group called Estado del Malestar,[4] which also started on Facebook and decentralized in about 50 different cities:

> In the beginning we used to meet up in the Puerta del Sol every Friday, and there were just like four of us who would get together and talk about why we were fed up. Each one of us would tell a little bit about our personal story: "I'm really sick of this," "I'm really sick of that," and we started to do a little bit of group therapy in the square.

Initially, very few people paid them any attention, so they began to "organize political performances about the bankers to wake people up. We tried to say 'Wake up! They are robbing us! We have to do something!' and we were doing that right up to 13 May [. . .] At the time I really had the feeling that something was finally going on." Laura highlighted the "buzz" around the planned May 15 protest in political intellectual circles, and then reflected on the political climate and the influence of events happening outside Spain and her hopes and fears, which she felt were widespread:

> 2010 was a moment of really low mobilization, of apathy, of lack of trust. People felt it was really difficult to connect with others. [. . .] You could see that things were getting worse, that the country was sinking, but you also started to smell that feeling of "they don't represent us" and things started happening. I remember there was a general strike in September 2010 and my God it was really a failure—mostly because you could *feel* that people didn't want to march behind the flags of the unions, to play the game of the unions who were responsible for allowing this horrible situation of unemployment, etc. I did go to the protest march for the general strike, but I was like holding my nose.

This generalized feeling of "ill-being" (*malestar*) motivated others in the aptly named organization. Veronica Antolín, one of the founders of Estado del Malestar, describes its evolution and relevance to 15-M:

> 15-M really is not a social movement in and of itself but comes from the union of many smaller movements that emerged and came together, [. . .] as a result of a call to protest. After the first meeting [of Estado del Malestar] we established the [. . .] principles of the group that are basically the same ones that you can see later in 15-M: not to be aligned with any political party; to promote protesting/mobilization; citizens as the principal objective of the group; and the responsibility of each one of the members. I think this is really important.

The principles of Estado del Malestar are classic autonomous organizing principles, applied in the context of widespread social media use, which, as Antolín notes, are the same essential principles that fueled the 15-M movement. Antolín, who is also a media/movement analyst, also highlights the complex multidirectional relation between on- and offline participation, and how getting out on the streets was a key goal:

> The social network of "Estado del Malestar" was born on Facebook from ties created between three people who did not know each other previously, not even online, but were connected with each

other through a fourth person on Facebook, who had put out a call to protest. So we began to chat on this Facebook feed about the need to express all of that bad feeling about how the government was handling the crisis, social policy and economic policy, and not only our government but also what was happening in Europe, and just really getting out on the streets to manifest our nonconformity with that and to do that in a way that was maintained over time.

So, we decided [. . .] to get together in the Puerta del Sol every Friday at 7 o'clock in the evening. Our objective was to turn our small initial protest into a social outcry. All of this is happening three months before 15-M. There were about 15 of us on February 11, 2011, and everybody had brought along either family members or other people who were interested [. . .] We decided to name the group "Estado del Malestar" and we created a Facebook page [. . .] and within two days [. . .] we had about 300 members [. . .] 24 hours later we jumped from 300 to 3,000 and it didn't stop growing.

After a Twitter follower who had organized a 26,000-strong petition against the *Ley Sinde* anti-digital-piracy bill, they linked all the signees to the Estado de Malestar Facebook page, and the page took off.

As with Alberto and Daniel, Verónica's narrative shows how fortuitous and spontaneous online connections led to offline face-to-face action to create a call to action. The online discussions were crucial in generating a climate of political critique and a feeling for many that "something should be done" in the face of what Laura, Verónica, and the members of JSF perceived as widespread political apathy. If online connections were spontaneous, the immediate move to face-to-face organizing shows that, for these activists at least, there was no sense that it was sufficient as a form of political action, but rather a useful tool to connect people and share information. Estado del Malestar wanted above all to prompt the Spanish people to rise up and take action, to organize against the crisis and austerity politics. Video footage of the Estado del Malestar protests in the Puerta del Sol shows a man speaking into a microphone trying to convince people that real change would not come "spontaneously":

We can see what is happening in Tunisia, in Algeria, in Egypt, in Libya, in Yemen, and to this long list Portugal is being added, and Iceland has already been on the list for a long time. These states are witnessing what have been called "spontaneous revolutions." They are not spontaneous!" (cited in Grueso 2012)[5]

The zeitgeist was channeled by activists in JSF, DRY!, and Estado de Malestar into a language and organizational form that would fit their autonomous tendencies, and represent something new (for them) with respect to "old politics." The similarity between Estado del Malestar and Real Democracy Now! is clear from the former's self-description:

> Estado del Malestar is a citizen movement made up of "members of all ages with a diverse ideology but with a common denominator: indignation and anger in the face of a political and financial system that we feel betrayed by, and that in our opinion has reached its limits.

Miguel Arana, one of the people who decided to stay in the Puerta del Sol after the original 15-M protest, also spoke about the political climate, the organizing efforts, and the false starts leading up to 15-M, first trying out ATTAC, then Anonymous and WikiLeaks, which were important reference points. He also was influenced by the *No Les Votes* campaign (calling for a boycott of all parties who supported the Sinde Law):

> *No Les Votes* was really horizontal and participatory and everybody contributed their little bit and it seemed to me that it had a lot of strength and power behind it, and it seemed like the right approach. It wasn't about the Left or the Right, it was something else. . . . When the whole Arab Spring happened, I followed that really closely with my friends, because we never imagined that that would happen there. We really hoped that it would spread to other countries. (Interview with Stéphane Grueso for 15m CC)

Some analysts, such as Postill (2014b, 156), who argues that "*No Les Votes* marked a radical break, a schism, between Spain's netizens and its political class that would shape subsequent events," have stressed the importance of technopolitics in the origins of 15-M (see also Fuster Morell 2012). Clearly, they form an important strand of influence within movement networks, and places like Media Lab Prado in Madrid was and continues to be an important space for technopolitical initiatives. The struggle against the Sinde Law, WikiLeaks, and *No Les Votes* are all mentioned in numerous interview accounts as points of reference (see also Monterde and Postill 2014). The role of Facebook and the Internet as a route to activism and participation is also clearly important for some of the activists involved in the lead-up to 15-M, and absolutely *crucial* in the origins of groups like Estado del Malestar and DRY!. However, I was struck, given some narratives that privilege the importance of the Ley Sinde, *No Les Votes* campaign, and free culture movements in 15-M's origins (e.g., Fuster Morell 2012), that relatively few people referred to technopolitics or free software as a significant influence or precursor in interviews.

What this suggests is that we need to distinguish between cyberactivism as a practice (i.e., using digital tools to organize online) and technopolitics or hacktivism as an ideational framework (i.e., a commitment to free software/culture, etc.) that motivates movement practice. The latter is always accompanied by the former, but not vice versa. In the case of 15-M, technopolitics *has* influenced the movement (and the previous GJM movement) and this influence grew through the experience of Acampada Sol (see Chapter 4). But it was not a widespread influence on participants at the time. David Aristégui, himself a long-term free software activist and developer, addresses this:

> There is this whole argument that one of the most important origins of 15-M was the fight against the Ley Sinde and hacktivism and so on. . . . It makes no sense. . . . The hacktivist movement had very few people who made a lot of noise because they used [online] social networks very effectively, but here in Madrid there were very few people that actually mobilized against [the Sinde law] . . . and for starters, it was a campaign that failed.

One key precursor movement noted by activists was *V de Vivienda* (see also Haro Barba and Sampedro Blanco 2011). JSF activists clearly reference the key importance of the *V de Vivienda* movement on the discourse and aesthetics of the JSF, DRY!, and the 15-M movement, but its influence did not only "travel" via JSF. Blanca, a journalist active in community and alternative radio, also discusses the connection between *V de Vivienda* and 15-M:

> I was involved in *V de Vivienda* in 2007. [. . .] The movement was calling attention to housing speculation and the fact that the housing bubble was going to blow up in all of our faces. [. . .]

So a camp was established at the University [Complutense] and I went over just to do a radio program on it, and [. . .] without even meaning to suddenly I was part of it. [. . .] [The] camp lasted four months and then in the end it kind of lost its way. Our inspiration for the camp was the Sintel workers[6]—remember when they occupied? So we did two live radio programs with them [. . .] so that they could share their experiences with us. [. . .] [The camps purpose was] to call attention to the [housing crisis] [. . .], but it also had a really 15-M vibe: we had all these workshops, sewing workshops, meetings. . . . There were a lot of people there from El Labo, the [squatted] social center . . . and they brought us these super hacker things, and all the really *asambleario* techniques, and all those online tools that we are using now.

Although much has been made of the uniqueness or unprecedented nature of occupations before 15-M, Blanca's narrative clearly shows not only the importance of the four-month-long *V de Vivienda* encampment, with what she retrospectively calls "a really 15-M vibe," but also how they were inspired by the six-month-long Sintel workers camp, showing the influence of labor movements as well. Madrid had witnessed mass camps in occupied public space before: Adell (2011) documents at least 42 encampments in Madrid prior to Acampada Sol, organized around a wide range of movement issues. While none of these camps had the impact and scope of 15-M's Acampada Sol, the practice of occupied camping was not a new political tactic for Madrid, and was being used in anti-austerity protests before the strong inspiration of Tahrir. Blanca's narrative also highlights the connection between El Labo, one of Madrid's squatted social centers, and *V de Vivienda*, tracing another line of influence and continuity, bringing specific *asambleario* practices and "superhacker" tools.

As we can see also with the example of Estado del Malestar, the 15-M protest was also by no means the first or only anti-austerity protest that was organized, but it was the one that turned into a sustained and dynamic movement, through a series of factors and confluences that I will describe in the following chapters. As Stephane Grueso shows in his film on 15-M (2012), the day before the 15-M protest in the very same Puerta del Sol, a totally unrelated group had organized a "Laugh-in against the Crisis," under the slogan "We will laugh at you until you take us seriously" (*Nos reiremos de vosotros hasta que nos toméis en serio*).

Continuity and change

The roots of any powerful and sustained movement usually run deep, and 15-M is no exception. Narratives from previously politically active participants about how they arrived at 15-M, or later tell their 15-M story, make frequent reference to the influence and importance of numerous precursor movements and specific struggles, including the GJM, the antiwar protests of 2003, the political flash mob of 13-M in 2004, protests after the *Prestige* disaster off the coast of Galicia, and student/squatting/housing and technopolitical activism. The inspiration of key transnational protests such as the Arab Spring, WikiLeaks, and the Icelandic Revolution facilitated a process of cognitive liberation, where suddenly the impossible seemed possible.

These "origin stories" provide insight not only into the specific planning process behind the 15-M protest, but also a picture of the broader political climate and influences that inspired the enthusiasm and commitment to the protest and its forms and content. What is clear from these narratives is that far from being a spontaneous coming together, a natural collective expression of indignation, or a magical connection of people on Facebook or Twitter, both the April 7, 2011, protest and the 15-M protest, as well as other initiatives at the time, like Estado del Malestar, or the earlier *V de Vivienda* movement, were the fruit of a lot of difficult political work in preparatory assemblies that navigated between a diverse set of political actors to reach a unified position around specific calls to protest. That consensus did not last beyond the protest events, which were followed by mass excisions that were rearticulated along more Institutional Left (vertical or more formally organized) and autonomous lines (horizontal and nonpartisan), in JSF's case after April 7 and before 15-M, and in DRY!'s case after 15-M (see Flesher Fominaya 2014a, Chapter 7).

Despite these challenges, they created, through a lengthy process of hard work and negotiation, a political opportunity for the 15-M camp to develop. The role of online political action was also crucial in establishing a point of connection for all those who were not directly involved in the preparatory assemblies but who were interested in or committed to supporting the protest. Social media also acted as a facilitator and creator of opportunities: both DRY! and Estado del Malestar started on Facebook, although they almost immediately moved to offline assemblies and encounters around Spain, while maintaining an online presence as an important part of their activity and development. In the case of Estado del Malestar, the role of Facebook was essential in keeping the offline protests going. Antolin's (2015) research shows that once the interactive discussion on the Facebook group was closed down, the offline presence of the group also disappeared. These narratives make clear that, for the case of 15-M at least, online networks are insufficient to explain the emergence and organization of the 15-M mobilization, and, contra Bennett and Segerberg (2012), therefore, 15-M does not provide an example of the capacity for social media to produce networks that can take the place of social movement groups "on the ground." Likewise, 15-M does not reflect a connective logic whereby individual personal action frames are exchanged online, but rather a collective action logic whereby the connective capabilities and affordances of digital connectivity are strategically and effectively integrated into existing movement political cultures that rest primarily on face-to-face interactions.

It is clear there that at the time of the 15-M protest, there was a political climate of people who wanted to take action around the crisis and austerity politics, but not yet a "15-M" collective identity, which would develop in and beyond the occupation of Acampada Sol (and other occupations around Spain). Acampada Sol for its part, happened as a direct outcome of the 15-M protest, which was the unexpected detonator of the 15-M movement, and the subject of the next chapter.

Notes

1. To name just a few professors actively involved in the GJM in Madrid, Victor Sampedro (UNED), Pablo Iglesias, Juan Carlos Monedero, Ariel Jerez, Sara López, Íñigo Errejón (Complutense), Ígor Sádaba, and myself (Universidad Carlos III).

2. Bolonia was a European University Reform rejected by student protesters, who saw it as increasing the neoliberal nature of the university, youth precariousness, and student fees, among other critiques.

3. Ecologistas en Acción (Environmentalists in Action), a long-standing activist group in Madrid, whose locale and resources have supported many activist projects.

4. In Spanish this expression is used for when people are feeling anxious or ill, but it's also a play of words on the term for the welfare state, *Estado del Bienestar*.

5. Available in Stéphane Grueso's film: https://www.youtube.com/watch?v=cBouuM-64Ik.

6. In 2001, 1,500 Sintel workers established a Camp of Hope for 187 days on Madrid's Castellana Avenue to demand fair severance packages following mass layoffs. See http://www.lavanguardia.com/economia/20130822/54379643230/empleados-sintel-cobran-indemnizacion.html.

3

May 15, 2011

AN UNEXPECTED DETONATOR

Real Democracy Now! We are not commodities in the hands of politicians and bankers.

—15-M protest banner

THE ORIGINAL "15-M" protest —held on May 15, 2011—was the outcome of months of preparation that involved not only bringing a multitude of heterogeneous actors together, but also developing a clear critique that tied together the twin pillars of the movement: anti-austerity and democracy. The demand for "Real Democracy Now!" stemmed from a wish to highlight the democratic deficit that had allowed austerity policies to devastate so many people's lives. According to this critique, deficient democracy rested on its reduction to "democracy as procedure" (see Chapter 1), and a gesture toward the substantive basis upon which a new "real" "democracy as regime" might be built was set forth in the demands of the DRY! manifesto. The twin elements of austerity and democracy were brought together in the conjoined targets of indignation: politicians and bankers.

Despite hopes for the success of the protest, no one planning it expected it to be a launching pad for an occupation, nor did they anticipate the strength of mobilization it attracted. Although the media paid little attention to the 15-M call to protest, there was a feeling of expectation in activist circles as the day approached. DRY! had developed a call to protest via a carefully designed media campaign, centered on a series of posters that highlighted the key concerns of the platform (note the aesthetic similarity with the JSF poster in Chapter 2, which reflects the direct influence of JSF in DRY!). Each poster declared "Take the Streets (*Toma la Calle*)

Democracy Reloaded. Cristina Flesher Fominaya, Oxford University Press (2020). © Oxford University Press.
DOI: 10.1093/oso/9780190099961.001.0001

Table 3.1 Real Democracy Now 15-M Call for Protest Poster Slogans[7]

TAKE THE STREETS

- Because while you pay taxes, the super wealthy avoid taxes in offshore tax shelters.
- Because you won't get a pension unless you have worked continuously for 35 years.
- Because the minimum wage for a congressman is 3.996 euros a month.
- Because almost 50% of Spanish youth are unemployed.
- Because we are not commodities in the hands of politicians and bankers
- Because while your social rights (benefits) are being cut, they are giving banks public subsidies.
- Because our politicians govern for the markets and not for the citizens.
- Because our current electoral law benefits the major parties who have over 700 lawsuits for corruption.
- [Because] when you don't have a job, your parents have no pension, your mortgage goes up, they take your house, and you still owe the banks.
- Because Spain's five largest banks posted 14 billion euros profit in 2010.
- Because now corporate profits are an excuse for layoffs.

15.05.11" and offered people different reasons to "Become Indignant!" (see Table 3.1).

On the day, thousands of activists gathered in central Madrid behind a large banner that read "REAL DEMOCRACY NOW! We are not commodities in the hands of politicians and bankers!" and began their planned route through the city center. The march was peppered with hand-painted signs with slogans such as "We are not anti-system, the system is anti-us!" and "System error 404—Democracy Not Found."[1] At the top of Madrid's iconic "Tío Pepe" building, conveniently clad in scaffolding, a small group of JSF activists unfurled a huge banner that read, in part, "They are not bailouts. It is blackmail. We won't pay for your crisis." The crowd below, meanwhile, cheered enthusiastically.

The main column of the protest eventually wound its way to Sol (Madrid's central plaza) for the reading of the manifestos and speeches. The DRY! platform's desire to signal its independence from parties and unions was reflected in the choice of the anarchist/libertarian Carlos Taibo as the closing speaker. He remembers his involvement in the protest this way:

FIGURE 3.1 Original poster for 15-M.

This poster says only: "Take the Streets 15-05-11. Become Indignant!" and provides the website for DRY! The poster's aesthetic reproduces that of JSF, which in turn deliberately references that of the earlier *V de Vivienda* housing movement, providing a visual representation of movement genealogies.

I was asked to speak at the end of that protest, and I asked them to send me the manifesto. It seemed really ill-defined, but because of the people who were sending it I cut them some slack and agreed to speak. [. . .] When I got to Cibeles (the starting point for the demonstration) my fear was that what I was going to say in Sol (the end point) was going to be too radical. But when I heard the messages that were coming off the truck at the head of the demonstration, [and the crowd] I was worried what I was going to say was going to be too moderate!

Here Taibo is highlighting three sets of discourse: those captured in the DRY! manifesto, those coming from the JSF truck, and those coming from the crowd. Each reflects a different process of production. The DRY! manifesto was the result of negotiations between a specific set of actors in a platform, and was the distillation of a series of encounters often fraught with debates, shifting alliances, and power struggles (lending it a certain incoherence). JSF's more radical narratives come from a particular group with a more consolidated collective identity, coherent narrative, and critique. Finally, the crowd, which included many people not involved in the planning, offers an insight into the zeitgeist, less mediated by specific organizational political settings, with their slogans, chants, and home-made signs. Each of them reflects a series of political processes involving different sets of actors, who to outside observers can become indistinguishable from each other, especially in the absence of acronyms, flags, and other identifiers typically absent in autonomous movements.

Autonomy, emotions, and something "new"

For Taibo, the fact that the crowd was full of people he didn't know, and that bystanders seemed to be strongly identifying with the slogans and chants, was an important indication that something "new" was underway.

The emotional investment in the protest was high, and activists felt a lot was riding on it. Laura recalls arriving at the protest after months of anticipation:

During the previous months through my involvement in Estado del Malestar and a bit in DRY! I was super excited and full of hope about what 15-M could be. I could also see that a lot of people around me were recovering hope and emotion, but also feeling like if it came out badly it was going to just be like "let's just forget about it." . . . 15-M finally arrived I remember thinking "God this is so cool!" and not seeing any kind of political acronyms or banners except those of DRY!, none of that political party stuff, [. . .] seeing people of all ages, children, old people. . .

Her delight that political parties had been prevented from co-opting the protest was widespread, and was a principle people were committed to defending, both in the original protest and later in the camp. Alberto of DRY! also recalls his emotion arriving at the protest:

> We could tell it was going to be something really big, but we didn't want to let ourselves think that, in case we were going to be disappointed. I remember the emotion that we felt . . . above all being able to break through the apathy! That was the most important feeling. To be able to get together and to say that we were not in agreement with the way things were, and it was such a strong feeling that it made people want to stay. I was crying, and speaking to so many people, and we were all saying, "Finally, we managed to get all these different people out into the streets!"

Verónica's (JSF) experience was very different. She tells how JSF led the march with symbolic book shields and a bit of smoke:

> So people started following us and it was incredible, because I've never been in a demonstration that was that big [. . .] we started going up toward Callao, and we did a sit in there and then the police started to charge. Really hard charges given that what people were doing was completely peaceful. I remember those police charges going on and on for hours.

Their experience of repression through police charges highlights how a single protest event can encompass a wealth of diverse experiences, depending on what happens in "your" part of the march and who you go with.

Real Democracy Now!

In Sol, the DRY! manifesto was read:

DRY! Manifesto[2]

We are ordinary people. We are like you: people, who get up every morning to study, work, or find a job, people who have family and friends. People, who work hard every day to provide a better future for those around us.

Some of us consider ourselves progressive, others conservative. Some of us are believers, some not. Some of us have clearly defined ideologies, others are apolitical, but we are all concerned and angry about the political, economic, and social outlook which we see around us: corruption among politicians, businessmen, bankers, leaving us helpless, without a voice. This situation has become normal, a daily suffering, without hope. But if we join forces, we can change it. It's time to change things, time to build a better society together. Therefore, we strongly argue that:

- The priorities of any advanced society must be equality, progress, solidarity, freedom of culture, sustainability and development, welfare and people's happiness.
- These are inalienable truths that we should abide by in our society: the right to housing, employment, culture, health, education, political participation, free personal development, and consumer rights for a healthy and happy life.
- The current status of our government and economic system does not take care of these rights, and in many ways is an obstacle to human progress.
- Democracy belongs to the people (demos = people, krátos = government), which means that government is made of every one of us. However, in Spain most of the political class does not even listen to us. Politicians should be bringing our voice to the institutions, facilitating the political participation of citizens through direct channels that provide the greatest benefit to the wider society, not to get rich and prosper at our expense, attending only to the dictatorship of major economic powers and holding them in power through a bipartidism headed by the immovable acronyms PP and PSOE.
- Lust for power and its accumulation in only a few create inequality, tension, and injustice, which leads to violence, which we reject. The obsolete and unnatural economic model fuels the social machinery in a growing spiral that consumes itself by enriching a few and sends the rest into poverty. Until the collapse.
- The will and purpose of the current system is the accumulation of money, not regarding efficiency and the welfare of society. Wasting resources, destroying the planet, creating unemployment and unhappy consumers.

- Citizens are the gears of a machine designed to enrich a minority which does not regard our needs. We are anonymous, but without us none of this would exist, because we move the world.
- If as a society we learn to not trust our future to an abstract economy, which never returns benefits for the most, we can eliminate the abuse that we are all suffering.
- We need an ethical revolution. Instead of placing money above human beings, we shall put it back to our service. We are people, not products. I am not a product of what I buy, why I buy, and who I buy from.

> For all of the above, I am outraged.
> I think I can change it.
> I think I can help.
> I know that together we can.

The manifesto bears the hallmarks of a collaboratively written negotiated text between a series of collective actors with differing political priorities (the list of bullet points feels summative rather than coherent), but it also reflects the effort to frame the protest within an elastic collective identity that would encompass the widest range of people possible and, as the JSF activists in the last chapter highlighted, move away from exclusionary ideological identifications (i.e., Left or Right), and break out of the activist ghetto with an "ordinary citizen" frame ("We are ordinary people, we are like you").

The JSF logic of reaching out to people through shared problems and presenting the solution through a collective action frame based on autonomous principles (i.e., "no-one will do this for us, we need to work together to change it") and a cognitive liberation frame ("I think I can change it. I know that together we can") is also in clear evidence, as is the damning critique of neoliberal capitalism, but note the avoidance of the JSF-prohibited "trigger words" *capital* and *capitalism*, and instead a discussion of "the current status of our government and economic system," "a machine designed to enrich a minority which does not regard our needs." Throughout, the democracy is center stage through a critique of the democratic deficit, and a demand to reform "democracy as procedure," and to implement the monitory democratic mechanisms needed for this to happen ("corruption among politicians, businessmen, bankers, leaving us helpless, without a voice"), as well as to transform "democracy as regime"—the substantive basis upon which political priorities are determined. In this case, this vision centers around an ethical revolution in which life is placed above "money" ("equality, progress, solidarity, freedom of culture, sustainability and development, welfare and people's happiness"). The desire to break the bipartisanship of the PP and PSOE is also a break with the Culture of the Transition (CT) and its fundamental claim that "politics" means alternating between these parties once every four to eight years, and that political conflict should be limited to a performance enacted by politicians on the stage of parliament.

After the manifesto and several speeches, an open letter from then 94-year-old José Luis Sampedro, a writer, economist, and inspiration to austerity critics, was read aloud. It expressed his adherence to the DRY! initiative, summed up the spirit that motivated the movement, and captured the solidarity between young and old that characterized it, despite its primarily youth-oriented origins:

> It makes me happy that [you] have understood that it is not enough to become indignant, that it is necessary to convert our outrage and resistance and to take a step further. This historical moment demands action, mobilization, protest, peaceful rebellion. [. . .] I express my solidarity with you and I wish you a clamorous 15-M. But above all, I encourage you to advance in the struggle toward a more humane life. The official media is not going to pay attention to you and you will find many obstacles in your way, but your future is at stake. 15-M should be something more than an oasis in the desert; it should be the beginning of an arduous struggle, until we achieve [the result that] we are not nor will we be "commodities in the hands of politicians and bankers." Let's say NO to financial tyranny and its devastating consequences.
>
> —José Luis Sampedro[3]

For the organizers, the 15-M protest was a great success. It broke through a widespread feeling of apathy and resignation. It made manifest a widespread sense of indignation around core demands. The development of DRY!'s discursive and aesthetic framework had proved to have a capacity for mobilization that far surpassed expectations, reaching out beyond the initial organizing groups and networks. The influence of JSF on the manifesto is evident. Through a strategic and reflexive use of discourse that emphasized the shared problems and grievances of citizens affected by the crisis and austerity politics, and that squarely placed responsibility for this on political elites, they had managed to frame the protest in such a way as to bridge historic and deep cleavages between left and right and encompass a wide range of participants, also transcending generation gaps. Later, the movement clearly shifted to the left, but initially this framing was effective. This emerging collective identity created a clear distinction between "us," ordinary hard-working people, and "them," (corrupt) bankers and politicians, who saw citizens as mere consumers of politics and commodities, and who attempted to convert them into "commodities." It defined the protesters (and later the movement) as being autonomous from formally organized parties and unions, but committed to active and engaged participation in the democratic process. In a process I have described elsewhere as "the democratic turn" (Flesher Fominaya 2015b), it carried on a long-standing claim by autonomous movements that Spanish democracy was a "fake," but that differed from earlier claims in that it that sought to actively reclaim democracy *and its institutions* for the citizens (as opposed to seeking to only create autonomous spaces free from institutional contamination). In this way, the protest claims simultaneously delegitimized really existing "fake" democracy (by condemning corruption, mismanagement, and greed), but relegitimized democratic values by demanding "real" democracy.

Sampedro's hope that through concerted action and effort indignation would become "the beginning of an arduous struggle" came true, but the protest alone was not enough. First, the protest needed to become an occupation. As the 15-M meme put it "No one expects the Spanish Revolution."[4] The "Spanish Revolution" would need an additional impetus, and here, the actions of both protesters and police would play a part.

From protest march to Acampada

After the protest wound down, most people went home, even after they found out some people were planning to stay on. This is the point at which many of the actors who were most closely involved in the planning of the demo were replaced by others who took the initial decision to camp. So even though the camp came as a direct result of the protest, the driving core of actors shifted from protest to occupation, as various narratives from JSF and DRY! participants show. Laura of Ágora Sol Radio, for example, recalls:

I remember that my friends and I just hung out afterwards drinking beer in the Plaza and then went home. It wasn't until the next day that I realized that something different was happening. I got on Twitter and everybody was talking about "What's happening in Sol? People are being evicted and there's violence"—that was Monday, and then on Tuesday again—and people saying, "Be there at 8 o'clock."

The buzz about the evictions and violence attracted a lot of attention and outrage, as had the arrests during the protests. Laura's story also illustrates how the core set of actors shifted overnight from the JSF/DRY! nexus to a (mostly) different set of people. Carlos (JSF) and Verónica (JSF) tell similar stories that also poke fun at their inability to foresee (and therefore miss out on) the historical moment of foundation of the camp:

(Carlos) When the protest ended we came back here to the Patio (the social center) to leave all the gear. We had taken shields and signs and we were totally loaded down with different stuff, [. . .] So we go back down to the Square to see what kind of vibe there was, and at around one in the morning I was on my way home with a bunch of people when I bump into two mates from JSF, and one of them says to me, "Hey! We have to camp over tonight!" And I said to him, "What are you talking about? I spent the whole afternoon carrying around all this gear and I'm totally exhausted!" And he's like, "Yeah, yeah! We have to camp here! This is going to be the Spanish Tahrir!" And I said, "You're crazy, man!" and I took off. So, the next day I wake up, I head down to Sol, and I say to him, "Well, you were right, but who the hell could have foreseen this?" It was like 9 or 10 in the morning and the camp was just beginning to grow. There were like 50 or 60 of us there.

(Verónica) It was late at night when we found out that there were people who decided to camp in Sol [. . .] So, we went down to check it out, and to be honest, we didn't really pay much attention to it because there were only like 15 people there and we thought, "These are four crazies and this isn't even going to last a day." The rumors were spreading that more people were going to come, but we went home because there weren't that many people there, and there was nobody really there from JSF or anybody who was very organized at that time.

The "four crazies" (who were eventually about 40 people) weren't ready to go home yet. Miguel Arana, who was not a part of planning the protest, but who was one of the originators of the camp, explains:

> To be honest I wasn't actually going to go to the 15-M protest. The whole thing about going to protests—I was just sick of it. Protest after protest and nothing ever changes, [. . .] but I started hearing about it from a lot of different people and a lot of different networks that weren't usually the ones that would be involved with political stuff. [. . .] So I thought, "Well, maybe this protest is going to be something different. Something is going on." [After the protest] people started to leave and we were sitting there looking at each other, like "No way! This can't be over. We can't just end like this once again!" So we [thought], "What would happen if we just stayed here? What if we just stay and sleep here until Election Day?" So first it was kind of a crazy idea and people were kind of laughing it off. But once people realized that we were actually serious [. . .] people's faces suddenly started changing and they said, "Okay let's do it!" So the more people joined in and agreed, the better the idea seemed, so we formed this little group and that's how it all started. Because from that moment on, once we decided it was a good idea, we immediately began to organize: "How can we organize sleeping here overnight? How can we contact people?" [. . .]
>
> I don't think we imagined that anything that big would happen, but having seen what happened in the Arab Spring, we did imagine that it might be possible. It seemed a bit far-fetched, but [. . .] there are those moments where ideas can see the future, the possibility of it becoming real. (Grueso 2011)

A number of participants mention the inspiration of Tahrir as offering a sort of "cognitive liberation" (McAdam 1982) whereby the seemingly impossible suddenly seems possible. But the way the Spanish activists thought about their collective action drew heavily on previous local movement cultures. Dani Vázquez was among those who decided to stay. His story attests to the influence of hacker ethics (*tecno-política*) in the original Acampada, an influence that would become a key strand of "15-M" political culture. It also shows how experienced activists played a crucial role in setting up the communication infrastructure of the camp, drawing on preexisting networks. After the police desisted from attempting to clear the square, the first assembly got underway. The synergy between autonomous *asambleario* and hacker traditions is clear in the way activists approached the task at hand:

So [the police] retreated [. . .] and this buoyed us. We thought: "Well, they've gone. We've kicked them out, we can stay." This is how ideas like "Why don't we just stay?" or "Look, this is what they did in Egypt" or "We, too, need a square" started to circulate. Someone grabbed a mike and said, "Listen, some people here are saying that we're staying. What shall we do?"

That is how the first assembly came to happen. Someone called out: "Assembly!," people sat down and the 15-M format began to take shape. [. . .]

I said: "If I have your permission to announce this and we form a small communication group and come up with a strategy, this could make a lot of other people feel the way we are feeling. They may see possibilities in our action and decide to take their own squares."

[. . .]

Vázquez immediately opened a Twitter account, @acampadasol:

In the scene I come from, the way we usually communicate is to copy other people's best practices, mix them, combine them, and then offer them freely so that others can do the same. [. . .] I decided that the first task was to communicate what had already happened, even if nobody read it at first. After all, we had no followers yet. The first tweet said something along the lines of: "We've camped at Puerta del Sol and are not leaving until we reach an agreement." With hindsight, this may look as if it referred to an agreement with the town hall or the government, but in fact I was aiming lower. The idea was to agree among ourselves whether we should stay or go.

As a "hacktivist" committed to free software, Vázquez and other hackers, including some members of the Isaac Hacksimov collective,[5] began to use their networks and tools to spread the word about what was happening, drawing other people down to the plaza with sleeping bags, and asking them to bring hot coffee: "I had a great deal of confidence in the networks we'd been weaving all those years. I knew I could count on them to pass on the news." At 4:30 a.m. he sent e-mails to his contacts with the subject "In Madrid as in Egypt?," explaining they were camping in Sol:

> When I got up in the morning the Twitter account already had around 1,500 followers. It was incredible. [. . .] The hours went by and it kept growing by the hundreds. More and more people arrived [. . .] and you could see the conflict was getting more and more interesting.

Vázquez and the other hackers got together to discuss security issues and other practicalities (e.g., choosing names, a server, setting up a website, mailing lists), drawing on previous experience of best practices to communicate effectively. In the spirit of generosity and replicability that characterizes hacker ethics (and later characterized the camp as a whole), they set as their goal lending assistance to everyone who also wanted to use free software, but hyperlink to others who used commercial platforms such as Gmail or Facebook to make sure their content was also visible. They were clear, however, that "[o]ur own tools have to be in line with how we do things: they have to run on free software and be as self-managed and horizontal as possible." They also took inspiration from across the Mediterranean to internationalize the struggle:

> We created *takethesquare* for a host of reasons. First, to tap into the solidarity and support of a global network. Second, so that people could connect with other struggles. Finally, it is much harder to repress and criminalize your conflict if it's playing out on an international stage. (Interview in Grueso 2012)[6]

Vázquez's narrative shows how the *asambleario* tradition was present from the very beginning in the square (note that he addresses "the assembly," despite this being a somewhat random group of activists who had decided to take a decision as to whether or not to stay on an ad hoc basis), and how he immediately mobilizes preexisting networks he has faith in. His narrative shows how activists drew on their *habitus*, those internalized routines of behavior that shape action in particular movement milieux, and also on more explicit and reflexive ideational frameworks and rules that guide action ("our own tools have to be in line with how we do things"). His language is rich with technopolitical frames, the belief in the power of collective intelligence, networked collective action, and digital imaginaries:

> For me 15-M was the crystallization of a long struggle to create new networks and develop more open, integrative ways of doing politics, as well as new forms of aggregation that allowed many different groups to join together. I see 15-M as a network of interlinked swarms, of different groups and persons with the capacity to come together and carry out a common action. In the early hours of May 16 a new political actor was born, and not only locally, in Madrid, but also at the national and global levels. (Ibid.)

Continuity and change

The 15-M protest and the camp played different yet crucial roles in the emergence of the 15-M movement. The 15-M protest was not a spontaneous event, but a planned demonstration that took months of planning. But the camp was something different. The decision to camp was spontaneous, taken in an ad-hoc post-protest assembly. Unlike the protest, the camp was not authorized, and thus was born as an act of civil disobedience—an aspect that would become more marked as protesters were evicted in the early hours of the following morning, creating a tipping point that would result in thousands of people joining the occupation. Although a different "animal," the camp was also a continuation of the 15-M protest, sharing the critiques and a commitment to *asambleario* orientation and practice. The narratives of Miguel Arana and Dani Vázquez belie the idea that 15-M began spontaneously by a group of previously nonpoliticized actors. The fact that the participants in the demonstration who remained in the square called for an assembly to decide whether to stay or not shows that they were used to operating with an *asambleario* repertoire of decision-making. The presence from the beginning of activists from Isaac Hacksimov (a "hacker" collective) as well as the past trajectories of the people there show that the original nucleus were drawing on their collective experience and skills. As María Bilbao, who was one of the people who set up the Feminismos Sol committee, said, "We had a lot to offer that space, because we had a lot of experience in associational politics and collective action, and in the politics of care (*cuidados*)." Members of the activist legal support team on duty for the 15-M protest were also present at the first assembly and negotiated with the police to stay overnight. As Miguel Arana recalls:

> That police officer must be driving himself crazy now because letting us stay the night really set the whole thing going, and of course by the next night the whole thing just exploded.

Explode it did. If the protest was the unexpected detonator, in which core demands and principles for a pro-democracy movement were put forward, the occupation of the Puerta del Sol provided the crucible and the chrysalis from which a 15-M political subject would emerge. Because of its persistence in space and time, Acampada Sol provided the opportunity for experimentation with *paideia*—a democratic education that could only come from collective participation and deliberation, and not from a predetermined philosophy—that Castoriadis (1997) argues is necessary for real democracy.

Notes

1. There is a wealth of slogans and images available online. See, for example, http://nosinmibici.com/2011/05/25/las-mejores-pancartas-del-15m/ and http://www.mensajedepublicidad.com/blog/carteles-del-15m/.
2. Available online: http://democraciarealyatoledo.blogspot.com/p/manifiesto-democracia-real-ya.html.
3. Republished by DRY! upon Sampedro's death (at 96), April 9, 2013.
4. A play on the Monty Python sketch "No one expects the Spanish Inquisition."
5. An anonymous collective named with a pseudonym, in the tradition of guerrilla communication.
6. Original translation by John Postill (2014a), adapted.
7. Translated by author from the Spanish originals, which can be viewed on http://www.democraciarealya.es/promocion/material-oficial/.

4

Acampada Sol

THE CHRYSALIS AND THE CRUCIBLE

Acampada Sol is a whole adventure to try to understand. I'm still coming across people who to this day don't understand how it worked—and they were there.

—JULIÁN, camp participant (2013)

ACAMPADA SOL, THE month-long occupation of Madrid's central plaza, the Puerta del Sol, was not just a highly visible and effective tactic of mass mobilization, it was the *sine qua non* of the 15-M movement. It was a *chrysalis*, a protected stage of development within which the 15-M movement was born, and a *crucible*, in that it served as a container into which old and new elements fused together under an exceptional situation of close proximity and intensity to create something new. This "something new" was a consolidated ethos and political culture, as well as new sets of relations that would go on to generate a broad network of interrelated assemblies, collectives, events, and political projects, organized around a reciprocal identification as a collective political actor referred to in Spain simply as "15-M."

The role of the originators: Establishing the camp's autonomy

The originators of the camp set their stamp on it from the beginning, stressing the *asambleario* nature of its political orientation and the importance that digital communication and a hacker ethos had for the first people directly involved. The first tweet from @Acampada Sol (sent at 3:55 a.m. on the 16th)—"We have just camped in the Puerta del Sol. We are not leaving until we come to an agreement"—highlighted the emphasis on democratic prefiguration: it makes no demand but focuses on

Democracy Reloaded. Cristina Flesher Fominaya, Oxford University Press (2020). © Oxford University Press.
DOI: 10.1093/oso/9780190099961.001.0001

IMAGE 4.1 Protesters wearing Anonymous masks, Madrid 2013.

the *process* of reaching a decision. It is *asamblearismo puro* (pure assembly-style politics).

The morning of May 16, the first very small assembly set up the infrastructure and information points of the camp. Stéphane Grueso's photos of that morning (Grueso 2012) and later images from the first press conference show a very empty square, where members of the camp are working in small groups, as people wander through the plaza as they normally would. For the afternoon assembly, participation increased to only about 50 people.

The campers, however, were already working on a manifesto to present themselves to the world that drew its spirit directly from the 15-M protest, clearly defining it as nonpartisan and anti-austerity. At 8 p.m. they held their first general assembly, now with several hundred people, livestreamed by the hacker contingent that had been working nonstop since the night before:

Who are we? We are people who have come freely and voluntarily. After the first protest we wanted to continue to demand dignity, and social and political consciousness. We do not represent any political party or association. We are united by our desire for change. We are here because we want a new society that gives life priority over economic and political interests! [applause from the assembly]

After the general assembly, working groups got underway, in assemblies of 5–15 people. The establishment of *grupos de trabajo temáticos* (thematic working groups) is a typical feature of Madrid's *asambleario* politics.

Scale shift: The role of repression

By the following evening, thousands had joined the camp. But what led to the sharp increase in participation? While some narratives stress the role of communication via digital media, as we have seen, that was already in operation from the very beginning (only attracting a few hundred people by the end of the first day), and while people were becoming aware of what was happening in Sol, they had not necessarily decided to join in. One factor that clearly had an effect on decisions to join the camp initially was the order by the Government Delegate (*Delegada del Gobierno*) to evict the camp by force. Numerous testimonies (in my interviews and in documentaries on the camp) allege that that was the point at which people felt it was necessary to go down, support the campers, and defend the camp, and it was a turning point in terms of the camp's scale shift.

The role of police repression is often overlooked in accounts of the origins of Acampada Sol, but is absolutely crucial. It turned the camp from something novel and moderately interesting into a massive explosion of citizen participation. According to David Aristégui:

> One thing that is never told about the whole origin of 15-M is that the [original] leitmotif of the Acampada is "we aren't leaving until the people who are arrested are set free." It was about fighting against repression [. . .] the whole thing really explodes very quickly when they try to evict the people from the Plaza and then they began to address other themes, but in the beginning it was anti-repressive.

At 5 a.m. on May 17, police evicted some 150–200 people from the Puerta del Sol, and some 200 people protested in front of the courthouse in Plaza de Castilla (on the other side of Madrid) over the arrest of 19 people during the 15-M protest. If several dozen people were in the Puerta del Sol on the morning of the 16th, reaching several hundred by that evening, after the campers were evicted by the police in the small hours of the

17th, word spread rapidly, and by that evening thousands had come down to the Puerta del Sol to retake the square, despite police orders to decamp. The visual contrast between participation before and after is stunning. As activist/filmmaker Stéphane Grueso quipped, "Many say that the *Delegada de Gobierno* was the movement's strongest asset," because had it not been for her decision to evict the Puerta del Sol, it is unlikely so many people would have been motivated to take part.

Once in the plaza, many more people decided to stay overnight, and by May 18 the more complex internal shape of the camp began to take place. Camps began to spring up all over Spain. In Madrid, the camp applied for permission for a protest (*concentración*) at 8 p.m., which was not granted. In response, thousands more joined the camp. Once again, it was the resistance to political control of public space that triggered increased indignation.[1] Police set up barriers to prevent more people from joining. By the 19th, the Central Electoral Junta declared all concentrations and assemblies (*concentraciones y reuniones*) illegal on the "day of reflection" (the day before elections, when political campaigning is unlawful). Despite the prohibition and the rain, the 8 p.m. assembly filled the square, and some 400 people decided to stay overnight.

Aristégui reflects on the importance of civil disobedience to the growth of camp, juxtaposing it to narratives that attribute growth (scale shift) to the power of social media:

> The crucial factor was the number of people who are willing to put their bodies there, even in the rain, even with police evictions and [stay overnight]. When there's repression, it's recorded on cell phones, and therefore, the next day more people come. . . . So there's a dialectic between what's happening in physical space and what's happening on [digital] social networks, but the determinant factor, just as with the plaza of Tahrir, wasn't Twitter—in fact most people didn't even have Twitter [. . .] so therefore it's impossible that they could have found out about it by Twitter. The important thing is that people went out on the streets and practiced civil disobedience.

Civil disobedience in the face of repression, combined with a savvy use of social media and the activation of existing movement networks, transformed the camp into a major protest event that spread quickly across Spain and claimed international attention. Infamously, the national mass media largely ignored the mass occupation of Madrid's central square, not running any cover stories until the *Washington Post* ran a cover story with a picture of the packed plaza on May 19, 2011.

Civil disobedience in an electoral context

In their quest to manifest "Real Democracy Now!," campers were rejecting the idea that democracy meant voting every four years, and instead embraced the notion of a collective democratic *paideia*. Therefore, it was fitting that the general assembly decided to engage in civil disobedience on the day of reflection. Under Spanish electoral law, the "day of reflection" is set aside as a day for each individual citizen to contemplate their vote in the absence of outside pressures and distractions, and all campaign activity must be suspended. The general assembly decided to deliberately violate the prohibition with a silent scream, called for 12:05 a.m. on the 21st, and instead initiate a process of public "*collective* reflection": an act of civil disobedience that is the antithesis of "political participation as individual voting," and is a manifestation of the camp's prefigurative challenge to really existing democracy.

Despite some observer's belief that the violation of the day of reflection was born in the 15-M Acampada (see, for example, Grueso 2012), in fact the illegal political flash mob known as "13-M" in 2004 was an important precursor event (Flesher Fominaya 2012; Iglesias 2015). However, the context, meaning, and outcome in 2011 were very different. The 2004 violation had been triggered by outrage at the PP government for what protesters perceived to be a deliberate misleading of the public about the perpetrators of the Madrid bombings. The result was a last-minute mobilization of the youth and abstentionist vote, resulting in an unexpected victory for the PSOE. In the case of 15-M, the camp, in line with one of 15-M's precursor movements, "Don't vote for them" (*No Les Votes*), appealed to people *not* to vote for any party that supported the Ley Sinde, which effectively meant calling for a boycott of all the major parties.

Despite mass mobilization around Spain against austerity following the 15-M protest, Election Day (May 22) ushered in a sweeping majority for the right-wing Popular Party, and despite the resolutely *nonpartisan* character of the camp, this outcome was hardly seen as an improvement. For the majority it only renewed their commitment to a grassroots struggle. A few, however, were angry that the call for a PSOE boycott could have helped usher in an absolute majority for the Popular Party. The newspaper *Público* (a critical pro-movement paper) referred to the camp as "avoiding its responsibility for the election outcome" (*Público.es* 2011). In response, a spokesperson from Acampada Sol replied that it was "unfair to lay the responsibility for the election results on the campers. It is the political parties who need to look to themselves for that" (Rusiñol 2011). Whatever the impact on the vote, Acampada Sol and the Indignados's demands had already unleashed a debate over democracy that no party could avoid. While the PSOE made some noises about listening to the protesters (despite ordering them to be evicted), the Popular Party closed its campaign by declaring, "*This* [the election] is democracy and not what's happening in Sol!" (Rusiñol 2011). On Election Day, the camp assembly decided to stay on in the square until the May 29.

Defining an autonomous camp collective identity: "We, the people"

Despite the rapid scale shift, the *asambleario* tone set by the original campers resisted modification by the influx of newcomers. Lidia Posada, a member of DRY! and one of the organizers of the 15-M protest, recalls the first massive assembly:

> When Miguel got up and said, "This is an assembly and the assembly is going to begin now" and everyone sat down and was quiet, and the whole plaza was completely full, I said this is impossible. I am dreaming. It was very beautiful. (Grueso 2012)

Miguel, for his part, addressing the crowd of thousands, stressed that the camp was not a concentration (protest), it was an *assembly*:

> This is much more than a protest (*concentración*), this is an *assembly*. We are going to take care of organizing and coordinating things a bit, but the assembly is ALL OF US!

A woman then took the mike:

> As we have always said, we are not any group, not any association, we do not take orders from any union, we are PE-O-PLE!

Miguel continued:

> Up to now we have been holding on here in Sol, we have been meeting in assemblies, creating working committees, and we have

two key questions that we want to ask everyone here, OK? The first one is: Do we want to stay here overnight tonight? [Mass applause and shouts of Yes!]

The crowd chanted things like "The revolution has started" and "It's the system not the crisis!" The feeling of collective effervescence that can only be transmitted in a crowd was very powerful, and over the following days those involved later admitted to feeling that "anything was possible." One participant later recalled, "The government could have fallen, the revolution could have started, really we felt like anything was possible, and all we knew was we had to be there."

Raquel, a participant in DRY! and JSF, describes the moment when the tents went up: "We all hugged each other and started to cry, we couldn't believe it, seeing all those people there."

Carmen, a political activist from Italy, who prior to 15-M had been struggling with political crises in the European Social Forum and considered Spanish politics to be "really boring," describes her abrupt change of heart when she arrived at Sol:

From the moment that first sofa goes over my head and reaches the middle of the square and people start the Acampada, a really beautiful moment begins. Because I see myself from one moment to the next—one moment in crisis and suddenly I see myself in this square and I can see the political practice that has been my ideal for the past 10 years right before my eyes: the discourse around horizontality, the principle of consensus and not of majority voting, the occupation of the Plaza, to be out in a square where people can pass by and participate, the plurality, the diversity that is being expressed in that square, with a new modality of life, of practice, of being—from the spiritual group that practices meditation to the most radical Leninists—you see everything there.

Another long-term fellow activist in Madrid's GJM scene, Nacho, who did not go down to the square for personal reasons, describes his sense of the Acampada being the manifestation of long-held horizontal political ideals: "Cristina, I did not even *have* to go down there. I recognized them as our children" (by which he means inheritors of Madrid's autonomous GJM activism).

Variations on the theme of a beautiful life-changing experience characterize the testimonies of all the participants I interviewed. The feelings of hope, possibility, and joy were as much in evidence as the feelings of in-dignation and rage at the system that had produced the crisis and passed its costs to society's most vulnerable. Carmen's and Nacho's words also echo a feeling common to many long-term activists at seeing the reality of their autonomous ideals of political practice finally materialized in a mass experience, an event they were aware might only happen once in a lifetime.

The role of preexisting networks

A camp as complex and large as Acampada Sol requires significant sup-port to keep going. While, of course, much support is inherent to the camp itself, and to the people within it, resources and support also came from many preexisting organizations and collectives in Madrid's network. Such resources provided the means to satisfy material, organizational, communicative, political, and legal needs. One key resource was the cul-tural knowledge necessary to organize the self-governance of the camp along *asambleario* lines.

The autonomous legacy at work: Transmitting asamblearismo

Raquel, who despite being in her 20s had been active in the GJM, the CNT, JSF, and DRY!, explains how the emergence of *asambleario* practice took place in the plaza:

> I was completely used to all that [assembly practice], but really, these were *way* bigger assemblies and we started to use sign language in them. [. . .] So many people had shown up and the idea was for them not to leave, and everything happened pretty spontaneously. We said, "Well, we need to form some groups and get organized." And since the only thing we knew how to do was *asamblearismo*, well, we started to do it like that. So first we needed an info point [. . .] and we needed to address the basic needs, food and all that, and once we had the info point and the basic needs covered, be-cause a lot of people started camping, then everything else followed. First the basics, then the [thematic assemblies].

Although many people involved in the camp from the beginning were fully familiar with *asambleario* practice, they were nevertheless amazed at seeing it implemented in public in assemblies of thousands of people, which was unprecedented in their experience. Verónica's recollection echoes that of Lidia Posada:

In JSF, and in all of the Madrid movements we have ever been in, we always worked with an assembly practice, but what was remarkable was to see assemblies with so many people. [. . .] And it really highlighted the problems that you can encounter in an assembly sometimes, because in an assembly of 20 people you can work it out, but when you've got 1,000 people everything is *much* more complicated.

Carlos Taibo, who has been working in *asamblearios* spaces for decades, also reflects on his reaction to the assemblies in the Puerta del Sol:

I was astounded by the capacity to draw people into that space (*poder de convocatoria*) and the effort to run everything along *asambleario* lines. At first we just looked at each other in disbelief, when we saw 5,000 people in front of us, and they said, "We're going to start the assembly." We thought to ourselves, "This is a joke! How the hell are they going to organize an assembly with 5,000 people?" But they did it, and [. . .] the scope transcended everything that had come before, and it reflected an effort to stand for the assembly and for horizontality.

Raquel explains how *asamblearismo* was transmitted by experienced activists to the newcomers in a collective and challenging learning process:

First we devoted ourselves to learning about the language and what an assembly was, because 70% of the people there had no idea what an assembly was and they didn't know how to participate, and they found it odd that there was no one there telling them what to do, and guiding their participation. Suddenly they can speak, they have a voice (*voz y voto*), and what is more, their opinion counts as much as the person's next to them, independently of their education, their position. The only thing that mattered was their experience. So, just like that, older people began telling us about their experiences of the war, and the Transition in Spain. Since it was all a horizontal movement, from the very beginning the first general assemblies that lasted eight or nine hours were devoted to assemblies, what they are, how to participate, time and space. Second were the principles, and from there emerged the working groups.

Raquel's account is interesting because she positions herself as a learner ("we devoted ourselves to learning"), despite being an experienced activist and transmitter of practice. She spent part of her time manning the info point (Punto Sol), and describes the constant pedagogical practice of the camp, which included online dissemination of informational pamphlets about assembly process and a lot of face-to-face tutelage:

> People would come to the info point and we would explain to them what an assembly was, and we would help each other out during the assemblies, too. We explained that people had to respect the *turno de palabra* [taking turns to speak in order], that you can't speak loudly, that you should moderate your language and tone, that your opinion is as important as the person next to you, that we have to reach consensus. And people would say "But aren't there votes?," and we would say "No, this is horizontal," and to be honest, it was really hard.

Squatted social centers

The autonomous legacy that nourished the camp from the beginning had been kept alive in myriad *asambleario* movements, and in the squatted social centers that provided the camp with essential material resources. Social centers play a crucial supporting role in Madrid's movement network, as well as being political actors in their own right.

Patio Maravillas and other social centers, such as Casablanca, which was very close to Sol, provided resources and space, as Miguel Martínez, a long-term squatter active in the Madrid social center scene, describes:

> [Casablanca immediately provided] tarps, chairs, and physical infrastructure. Later they opened the center to campers for all kinds of emergency situations. [. . .] Not only Casablanca, also Tabacalera and Patio Maravillas. A triangle of three active affinity spaces was created, all of which were willing to intensely collaborate with the camp.

Martínez remarked on the cross-contamination between campers and members of the squatter collective, forcing them to rethink their political praxis. People tend to see camps as self-contained spaces, but in fact they are porous and elastic, and not always neatly physically delimited. Acampada Sol was surrounded by a network that supported it, and traversed it, not only through social centers, but also via the camp's communication infrastructure.

Communication networks in a complex media ecology

The camp evolved within a rich and complex media ecology that combined social media (e.g., Twitter and Facebook), web pages (e.g., tomalaplaza), and media such as radio and newspapers, on- and offline. The communication infrastructure was crucial, and it was nourished not only by "hackers," but also activist-journalists active before 15-M, and individual "power" tweeters and bloggers.

Laura of Ágora Sol Radio describes her role in the communications working group:

> By the third day I said, "OK! Enough of being a spectator, I want to contribute. Because I'm a journalist and that's what I love to do. Part of my specialization is public opinion and the public sphere. [. . .] I got to communication and said, "Hi, I want to collaborate." This guy [gives me some options] and I said, "Okay, I'll be a spokesperson."

Despite the frenetic pace, the autonomous/hacker commitment to replicability and knowledge transfer prevailed, and spokespeople took time to get training in public speaking. Communication networks were mobilized not just to reach outside audiences, but also to coordinate *internal* communication within the camp. This is often overlooked in narratives that privilege the role of online digital media in camp communications. Activists show that analogue media and cell phones in fact played an even larger role in internal communication, which Laura explained was mostly managed "face to face in the plaza." "Communication assemblies were announced via a sign hung on the booth. [. . .] There was an email list for communication coordination, but we didn't use it much. We just connected there in constant assemblies in the square and in the side streets" and "constant telephone communication." The 20 members of the spokespeople commission worked on a rota system, giving interviews to "a lot of international media, Al Jazeera, CNN, Russian television, Mexican television, German,

French, from everywhere." Although frenetic, their system developed very well over time, and some of the groups created, such as Difusión en Red (Dissemination via the network), lasted well beyond the camp.

Julián, who provided technical support for communications, also recalls the limited reliance on the Internet:

> I know people who donated electronic generators [. . .] but we almost never had Internet in the camp. We worked with paper and cell phones. [. . .] Ágora Sol Radio was set up on Montera Street, the locale belongs to the Association for the Convergence of Cultures (Asociación Convergencia de las Culturas) and they shared the costs.

The communication committee was also committed to getting the message of the camp out to a wider audience. Diverse media practices, including live tweeting and live streaming, press releases, interviews, and radio and TV broadcasts, all served to transmit specific political messages, but also to generate a collective self-representation of the camp, which was retransmitted back to the camp participants, and worked toward creating its collective identity. Laura sums up what she, as a spokesperson for the camp, was trying to convey:

> The idea was that the citizens, instead of being infantilized, were taking their place in the public sphere, having a voice in the decisions that affect all of us, becoming actors not puppets and [. . .] not allowing those decisions to be taken by other people. [. . .] Participation needs to be a reflection of what people are asking for in the streets, of their desires, their needs [. . .].

The revitalization of the public sphere to create spaces of encounters, debate, understanding, and creating a life in common was a crucial idea:

> That's really what we were trying to do, and not what had been happening under this aggressive capitalism, that was really fomenting individualism, the depoliticization of society and converting citizens into consumers and not really into people, which is what we are.

The collective identity of the camp was also nourished by the hacker/ technopolitical contingent, who transmitted a hacker ethic on the camps' communication system, including a commitment to free software, open access and encryption/security. As Marta G. Franco, one of the original participants in the camp, put it, they were experienced in movement political communication and were committed to having maximum respect for collective assembly processes (Grueso 2012). Ensuring that communications were not hijacked to promote particular interests and reflected the spirit and message of the camp as defined by the assemblies avoided the problems often associated with the power of a few tech-savvy people to disseminate (and control) movement messages.[2] The communications teams in Sol were remarkable in their ability to manage communications in a consensual way, despite the chaotic environment. Crucial here is not just the technology per se (any political group can use technology to transmit political messages), but rather the particular hacker ethos of the activists in Madrid, which reflected a commitment to key principles that shaped, in a meaningful way, how those messages were transmitted, which in turn increased the feeling of trust and inclusivity of those participating in the camp. This is another example of how the ideational frameworks and core values that underlie practices matter, and how praxis contributes actively to collective identity.

Media communication is another way that the camp extended beyond its physical boundaries—and it did not flow in only one direction, but out, back, and through the camp. Raquel highlights the role of the communications group in sharing knowledge, and how the process of learning about *asamblearismo* worked in a combination of on- and offline forms:

> From the beginning the communication assembly worked on getting [all the knowledge about *asamblearismo*] online, the online networks were just incredible, because the 15-M hackers, as they were called, managed to reach something like 15,000 and 30,000 people in the first couple of days online. So using technological communication, they began to publish informational pamphlets on the language, on what an assembly is, and then they set up the pages tomalosbarrios and tomaMadrid ["take the neighborhoods" and "take Madrid"] putting everything up on the Web so that people could see it, and for those who couldn't, well, they would come down to the information point and we would explain it to them.

As important as the communication infrastructure was, David Aristegui (himself a free software activist) argues strongly against technopolitical narratives that overstress the importance of a free software, free culture, or hacker movement in the origins or evolution of 15-M or in Acampada Sol:

> Sure there are a lot of free software *frikis* (geeks/freaks), but that doesn't make a free culture movement, as in an actual movement of people that is self-referential, has important points of reference, different collectives, and engages in campaigns and mobilizations. Apart from the virtual campaigns that they do once in a while, there really is nothing. It's been an enormous bluff, statewide and in Madrid.

I agree with Aristégui about the need to guard against fetishizing technopolitics, believing activists' self-hype, and the absurd but persistently stubborn technodeterminist idea that the availability of certain technological tools, in this case digital and social media, somehow plays a causal role in mobilization. However, the importance of cyber/activist hackers in the camp and in 15-M is greater than what a simple head count of "hackers" reveals. A hacker ethos and what I call a "digital democratic imaginary" did and does play an important role in the political culture of 15-M, and the camp(s) were an important source of this influence. As important as communication technology is, so are other factors that are often overlooked, such as the legal context in which movements operate. The availability of legal expertise can have a crucial impact in sustaining social movements, and this was the case in 15-M and the Acampada.

Legal support

The legal committee was a key actor, already active in the 15-M protest and supporting those arrested, but continuing their support work in Acampada Sol. As Paula, a lawyer in Legal Sol, recalls:

> We set up "Legal Sol" the first day. It brought together people with a judicial background, lawyers, law students, and interested parties [. . .] to provide a juridical service for the camp, for all the many doubts that would arise. For example, I stick up a poster and they come and ask me for ID—what do I do? What can happen to me

with this tent or this booth that I'm manning? When the camp decided to stay on the day of reflection, there was also a whole issue about what could happen to people as a result of that.

Karry, another member of Legal Sol, highlights its transition from a more practical to a more political role in the camp:

Legal Sol arises from a practical need in the first instance, addressing the anti-repressive aspects, but then begins to engender a more political debate around questions like: Why does repression happen? Why is there police harassment of the citizens when the citizens are exercising their right to participate in politics? (cited in Grueso 2012)

This shift is indicative of the ways that the practical aspects of a protest camp (legal, physical, self-care) take on a political and reflexive role in a community that is questioning and posing an alternative to the status quo. That political reflexivity—be it a questioning of state repression and the rights to assembly and occupation of public space, or a feminist critique of social reproduction or fostering reflexivity around self-care and solidarity— was nourished by activists who had spent many years thinking and mobilizing around these issues, and found in the camp a means of putting that experience at the service of a collective endeavor that was taking shape as a political actor. At the same time, the experience of Acampada Sol was also provoking experienced activists to reflect on their own political practice, in some cases changing it in profound ways. But not everyone in the camp was politically experienced or *au fait* with autonomous practice, and the newcomers brought energy and enthusiasm as well as multiple forms of expertise and resources.

The camp takes on a life of its own
Newcomers, young and old

The first day I didn't understand anything that was happening. But I loved it. And like everyone, I began to help out in any way I could.
—STÉPHANE GRUESO, filmmaker (2012)

Despite the important activist DNA of the original protest and camp, it immediately drew in people who had little or no previous experience with political activism, and this influx not only changed the internal dynamic of the camp, but was also a crucial factor in expanding its scope. As with any protest cycle upswing, the influx of previously nonmobilized people is essential, bringing fresh ideas and energy, but also challenges that come from integrating people into movement practices without reinventing the wheel.

One newcomer was Julián:

> I am part of the generation who became politically active with the Acampada in Sol. Prior to that I had never done anything that could be considered activism. [. . .] I was at work and I saw on the Internet and in the newspapers that there were a lot of people in Sol, and you could see them from above and I said, "Wow! They put up tents!" That same afternoon I went down there. [. . .] As soon as I got out of the Metro I saw this huge multitude sitting down with megaphones. . . . They were taking turns participating, making proposals, people were communicating with each other, they raised their hands, they intervened, and I said, "Wow! This is even more interesting than it looked."

If Julián represents the newly politicized indignant youth, Rubén, who is in his 70s, represents someone who became politicized by the camp after a lifetime of avoiding politics as much as possible, since, as he explained, during his youth all political options came via the dictatorship's union and associations, demanding allegiance to either state or church. A former communication technician, Rubén also arrived at the camp with no previous contact with anyone there:

> 15-M for me was like a political awakening. I saw what was happening on TV and I went down to the Plaza to see what was going on. I got there and people were saying, "Hey, we are collecting signatures against the privatization of water in Madrid, we are gathering signatures to protect our health services, we are gathering signatures for I don't know what" [. . .] and I said, "Yeah, I'll sign, I'll sign everything." It was like suddenly all of these issues were made visible in the square, and up to that point I wasn't aware that all of those struggles were happening in Madrid.

Rubén was so impressed with the camp that he began to participate actively, slowly gaining confidence in his abilities to speak up in assembly, and eventually becoming a committed activist at 71 years of age.

Juan, who is in his late 50s, also describes his political awakening through the camp:

> I had been in Catholic Youth as a youngster, but it wasn't for me. I got to the camp and said: Parties? No. Unions? No. This? Yes, this is for me.

Like Rubén, Juan's previous political experiences had been channeled through the church or state under Franco. All three of these "newbies" would go on to actively shape the 15-M network: Julián through online archiving and providing IT and communication support to numerous groups, projects and campaigns; Juan through an active communication and organization role in the anti-Gag Law group No Somos Delito; and Rubén as one of the founding members of 15-M Mayores, a post-Acampada assembly bringing together pension-age activists, and as a 15-M "keeper of the flame" who kept the weekly public AGSOL (General Assembly of Sol) meetings going in Sol long after the camp had lifted. Rubén also managed communication and internal organization for those collectives through e-mail list serves and telephone support. All of them became committed to *asambleario*-style politics in the square, despite never having directly experienced them before.

For those who had never experienced *asamblearismo* before, 15-M became the term with which they referred to horizontal assembly-style practice, and in a departure from autonomous practice previously, which eschewed any particular label, even that of "autonomous," "15-M" became an important political identity marker. People, projects, assemblies and ways of doing things became 15-M or *15mayista*. This was also the case for some people who had been very active prior to 15-M, such as Carmen, who nevertheless embraced the 15-M identity as a result of her experience in Acampada Sol. As Karry of Legal Sol said when asked "What is 15-M?":

> Above all it is a collective identity. . . . Even though the label is first of all imposed by the media, calling them "indignant" (Indignados) after Hessel's book, and later 15-M, which is just the protest date, later on many people who participated [. . .] in those mobilizations came to identify with that label of 15-M, and from the minute we

took on that identity, we began to construct and build a movement around it.

That collective identity was incubated in the preparation to the protest event on May 15, 2011 (with the poster campaign around 15-M), but it was born in Acampada Sol.

Shifting identities

However integral a role played by preexisting networks, the camp itself was a moment of chaos and catharsis that could not be directed or controlled by anyone. It had its own dynamic. Even those involved in planning the 15-M demo who hoped to influence its political outcome rapidly realized that was not in line with the spirit of the camp, which resisted any attempt to be defined by a collective identity that was not completely open and inclusive.

Carlos of JSF recalls the way the urgency and exceptionalism of the camp experience lent an ad-hoc quality to his involvement, and how the JSF collective "dissolved" into the camp:

> People in JSF took the decision that we needed to bring down our flags. JSF had played its role, it had done everything possible to get the protest organized and now it was time for us to be there like everybody else. My activism during the Acampada had little to do with JSF. I was in the Economy Sol working group, and afterward I disappeared and I've never been in that group again in my life.

The strong nonpartisan stance established by the originators did not only apply to political parties or unions, but to *any* collective identity marker (such as the name of a collective) that was distinct from the whole. Speaking almost four years later, Carlos (JSF) is not so sure that dissolving JSF during the Acampada was the right decision:

> Why do I think it was a mistake? Because I think that we were the closest thing [. . .] to the spirit of the camp. At the same time, we were already a collective that was cohesive and homogenous with a lot of potential to keep working. I get the sense—seeing it from here now—that it would've been good if JSF could have become in that moment something bigger if possible, instead of just a collective of 60 or 70 people.

He feels that the social movement scene has been reduced to "small islands," and given the fate of DRY! (which split acrimoniously), JSF could have played a cohesive role. Yet he recognizes it may have been the only possible decision at the time:

> So that's how I feel now, but it's more personal anger than anything else, because [. . .] in that moment, with that climate of lowering the flags, and nobody trying to make a country out of their own collective or party, I'm not sure we could have done anything else. I don't know if we did it because we thought it was the best thing to do, or if we thought it was the *only* possible thing to do.

Carlos's narrative highlights the intense energy that lent the camp its exceptional emotional charge, but which is perhaps impossible to channel or maintain over time, as well as the strong anti-identitarian ethos that characterized its collective identity (Flesher Fominaya 2015a).

If some groups were dissolving themselves within the camp, others were finding themselves as new collective actors within the chaos. One such nucleus that coalesced from fragmented elements within the Madrid scene was the Feminismos Sol group, whose members rapidly realized that it was vitally necessary to engage in feminist pedagogy in this new environment, one that despite holding some horizontal principles, had also been imbued with the everyday sexism that plagues contemporary society.

María Bilbao of Feminismos Sol was involved in the creation of the feminism committee from the beginning of the camp. She explains the rationale for setting it up:[3]

> [Despite coming from different collectives] we decided that we needed to create a committee with one mind [. . .] and the need to process everything through a feminist lens. Our logic was if this is going to be a revolution we have to be here. [. . .] I think we really surprised ourselves because the different strands of feminism were capable of understanding each other. [. . .] We made a kind of pact to set aside all the things that didn't unite us—for example, the whole issue of prostitution—and we really fostered the whole theme of caring for each other, of getting to know each other and working as a group. That's why we decided to call ourselves Feminisms Sol, plural, so that it was clear that we had different collectives and different types of feminism within the group.

As a camp full of "ordinary citizens," the camp reflected many of the problems found in the wider society, but also the persistent sexism encountered in activist spaces:

> (María) The camp was a sort of microcosm in which all the defects of the social system were reproduced, and we encountered a lot of resistance too. A lot of everyday sexism started to appear, hierarchies between people, hierarchy between committees, power struggles, paternalistic attitudes, and all of that. So what we did was to try to develop pedagogical strategies, we did a *lot* of pedagogy. [. . .] All of the groups started to collectively empower themselves and others within the assemblies and within the groups. So within the general assemblies, and also within the camp, through this pedagogical work, little by little the feminist committees started to spread through the different cities.

Gracia Trujillo of trans/queer Transmaricabollo recalls some of the problems feminists encountered:

> There was that whole incident with the feminist banner [being ripped down] . . . and then some of the women who were sleeping in the camp at night [. . .] were very uncomfortable with some of the behaviors and it was super unpleasant [. . .] and they decided to stop sleeping in the camp and they wrote a communiqué to explain their decision [. . .] so these kind of incidents which are things that those of us who have been in activism for a long time know about, but maybe some of the younger women knew less about, the whole issue of women being marginalized within activist spaces and the demand that we need to have a voice and we need to be here, and all of this needs to have an important place.

The value of "lowering the flags" was taken to extremes and adopted as a sort of unreflexive orthodoxy by some, as is illustrated by the ripping down of a banner that said "The revolution will be feminist or it will not be" to cheers and applause by bystanders. People operating with lay misdefinitions of feminism had understood the flag to be divisive and establishing a hierarchy of women over men, as opposed to embracing a universal value of fighting sexism and patriarchy. The incident was a wake-up call for many feminists in the camp regarding the pressing need for pedagogy, a need they addressed remarkably well, given the hostility and negative media attention they received (see Ezquerra 2012; Gámez Fuentes 2015).

This incident shows the limitations of a collective identity framed in terms of the "citizens" against the "caste" (political and economic elites), which can easily obscure the many forms of hierarchy and oppression that traverse the 99%, including sexism, classism, racism, homo- and transphobia (Calvo and Álvarez López 2015; Flesher Fominaya 2015c). Groups like Feminismos Sol and Transmaricabollo Sol work to navigate these tensions by showing the myriad ways the struggle against austerity and for democracy are entwined with struggles against sexism and heteronormativity. The incident also highlights the need to guard against fetishizing ideational frameworks (i.e., autonomy, horizontality) and turning them into new forms of orthodoxy rather than seeing them as guiding principles that should be adopted reflexively.

Paradoxically, it was the camp's *failure* to adequately create a safe space for all of its participants, along with its manifestations of sexism, that prompted feminists to come together around a shared project to ensure 15-M became a feminist movement.

The camp experience prompted preexisting groups like JSF and feminist and social center collectives to re-examine their own political practices and identities in relation to this new phenomenon, while at the same time putting themselves at its service. Without losing their core activist identities and affiliations, they were realigning them with a broader 15-M collective identity.

Organized chaos and the challenges of horizontalism

Despite the early internal organization of the camp, video footage reveals the chaos, noise, and multitude of the environment. On the May 17, at 9:20 p.m., Juan Luis Sánchez (2011) recorded the plaza from a bird's-eye view. A woman trying to make herself heard through a megaphone competes with the roar of the crowd and the background noise of a batucada, while she explains the internal infrastructure of the camp:

Silence please! Silence! Silence please! [. . .] We have organized the camp into different working groups (*comisiones de trabajo*) that relate to the different components of the camp, including infrastructure, communication, and a whole series of things that we need to move forward. All of us (feminine plural and masculine plural) are super important, please this is not going to happen again in our country for a very long time. We have the power now and the world is watching!

Her intervention was followed by huge cheers from the crowd, who started to chant camp slogans (e.g., "The revolution has begun!") followed by repetitive chanting of "We are not afraid!" with different overlapping chants coming from diverse areas of the crowd.

The chaotic nature of the camp is also captured in other videos (Linegraphics 2011). At one point a young man is shown shouting into a megaphone:

"I need help to gather proposals! I have no paper! I have no pens! I only have a box and a megaphone!"

Julián recalls the chaos and frenetic pace of the camp, which was nevertheless organized:

When I first got there, what really caught my attention was all of the people [. . .] and you couldn't even walk. It was really hard for me to get through that big mass of people, because it seemed like the people who wanted to get across the square had to follow this circular path that went in two different directions. Some of them walked in one direction and on the right side there was a whole other line that seemed to be going in the other direction, and you had to kind of switch lines back and forth to get in and out. It was completely crazy!

It wasn't until he reached a booth with a large color-coded map of the camp and its commissions that he made a realization:

"Wow, this is really organized!" Right next to me was the action committee, and they were taking all the proposals that people had made and entering them into the computer, and I said, "Hey look! Here is something that I can do!" and that is how I really started.

Campers found that normal life was suspended and replaced by a new intense reality where days and nights blurred into one another:

(Julián) From that moment I entered into a phase in my life in which every day was like an episode from a TV series. Lots of things happened from one day to another, from one week to another, and it's really hard to remember it in order [. . .] because it was so chaotic. [. . .] From the very first night of the camp, when the people who decided to stay realized that in order to be able to stay they really had to cover certain material needs, they set up the committees. The creative infrastructure committee that brought cardboard and blankets, the food committee that brought water and some food, the legal committee that began to investigate everything that happened with all the people who had gotten arrested and who figured out a strategy for how we could defend our right to stay in the Plaza. The communication committee that started the Twitter account of #Acampadasol. . . . And when it started to rain a bit and [they put up the tarps] you could see that there were tons of people in different committees that became permanent "booth" fixtures within the camp.

Julián told me a story about a man who set up an art committee to help people who needed signs. After a long day of camp work, he left,

and when he came back the next day, he bumped into this other guy, who said to him, "Hi! Do you want to participate in the art committee? We are here organizing with cardboard, and if you're an artist, you can help us out" and it was like, "This guy is explaining to me what I started yesterday!" And that's how it was. That kind of constant rotation that gave the whole camp so much life.

In a document he later wrote called "15-M Conspiracy Theories" (*conspiranoias 15-M*) Julián responded to a claim that the camp was "clearly orchestrated, as could be seen by its quasi-military organization":

HA HA HA! The camp was totally chaotic! Some areas were very organized but only as long as someone maintained them. The tendency was much more toward disorder. The maps and signs helped a lot . . . if that is what you think "quasi-military organization" is!

Meeting material needs wasn't the only form of organization that was taking place in the square. Meeting the political needs of the participants was also a key part of the organizing committees. But even that had a chaotic element to it, as Julián explained, with the original organizational design (which would pass action points to an action committee) mutating into a division of labor between intellectual work, such as research and developing ideas around different thematic areas, and committees addressing more practical needs:

> For example, say the environment group wanted to do a performance at 7 p.m. next to the statue of the bear (*el oso y el madroño*). Someone would go to the action committee and stick up a post-it that put what time the performance was going to be. . . . But it was complete chaos and it never actually worked. We did everything we could, but at one point the action committee just became so saturated that what happened is that those groups broke off and became independent and formed themselves into working groups.

Personal affinities (and antipathies) also affected the evolution of the camp's internal structure, as Julián explains:

> The communication group, for example, split into various different subgroups—social networking, coordination, and so on—it just evolved depending on the needs of every moment, the tasks building up and all the work that was still left to do, but also along personal lines [. . .]. Affinities, falling outs, miscommunications, all of that really influenced the genealogical line of the groups that developed. In the end it was a working solution.

Raquel gives an example of the organic growth of new groups from previous ones:

> When Feminismos Sol started [. . .] I remember the first assemblies were about women in the workplace and the importance of equal rights [. . .] then they moved to the importance of female energy, and from that idea a new group, "Spirituality Sol," emerged and set up right next to them [laughs].

The desire to organize within a chaotic environment led to some compromises on the original "open" model, as well as sacrificing efficiency to constant modifications made by the shifting influx of people, as Julián explains:

> Sometimes, of course, work was duplicated. You could be working on one side of the camp and on the other side something completely different might be going on, or they might be doing the same thing you were. Because when you are inside one of the booths it was like being in a little building. For example, when we were working on the action committee on all the proposals, in order to be able to work we actually had to close the booth! Because if we didn't, we were constantly being interrupted by people who would come up to the booth, ask you a question, talk to you about something, and of course you're all excited and you want to engage with them, but you just mess everything up, and of course you can't focus on the work that you're supposed to be doing in the committee. So in the end it was like one of those bureaucratic windows (*ventanillas*). We would take turns attending to people while other people would sit at a table and actually get work done. But the next day you'd show up and find out that everything was completely different. You would hold an assembly; you would define how everything was going to work, and two days later somebody else would have convinced everybody to change everything. [. . .] So it was like that: you had to adapt yourself constantly to new flows of people and new ideas.

Despite the chaos and the challenges, the internal organization of the camp was remarkable as the map below shows.

This complexity and diversity also means that it is difficult to speak of the Acampada Sol in general terms, as David Aristégui stresses:

> There were so many different committees in the camp. Some worked really well and others didn't. [. . .] That's why we have to really be careful when people say Acampada Sol was, did, or said this or that. [. . .] One thing is the dynamic that was generated in the general assembly, another thing is the dynamics that were related to the working groups, some things were tremendously consensual and others not so much.

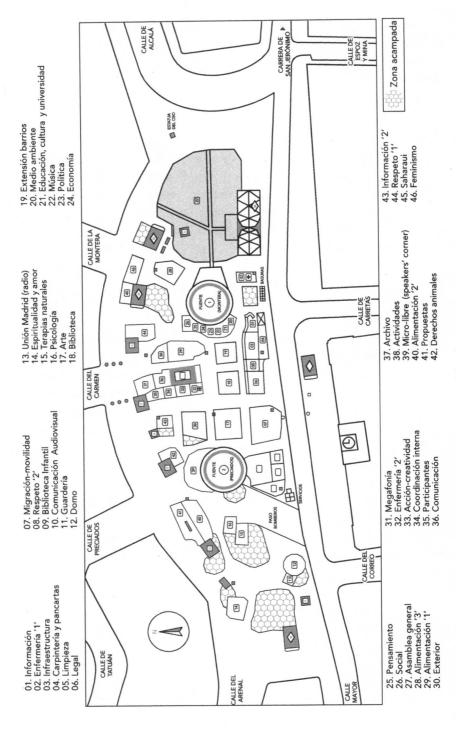

01. Información
02. Enfermería '1'
03. Infraestructura
04. Carpintería y pancartas
05. Limpieza
06. Legal

07. Migración-movilidad
08. Respeto '2'
09. Biblioteca Infantil
10. Comunicación Audiovisual
11. Guardería
12. Domo

13. Unión Madrid (radio)
14. Espiritualidad y amor
15. Terapias naturales
16. Psicología
17. Arte
18. Biblioteca

19. Extensión barrios
20. Medio ambiente
21. Educación, cultura y universidad
22. Música
23. Política
24. Economía

25. Pensamiento
26. Social
27. Asamblea general
28. Alimentación '3'
29. Alimentación '1'
30. Exterior

31. Megafonía
32. Enfermería '2'
33. Acción-creatividad
34. Coordinación interna
35. Participantes
36. Comunicación

37. Archivo
38. Actividades
39. Micro-libre (speakers' corner)
40. Alimentación '2'
41. Propuestas
42. Derechos animales

43. Información '2'
44. Respeto '1'
45. Saharaui
46. Feminismo

MAP 4.1 Map of Acampada Sol that was available in the Puerta del Sol.

Unsurprisingly, some of the assemblies reproduced the long-standing differences between Institutional Left and autonomous approaches, as Aristégui recalls:

[A lot of] the dynamics in the camp were old, previous to the camp. Fortunately, the majority did manage to generate good new dynamics or dynamics that were farther away from classical platform-isms. The committees that had fewer people with previous experience or people aligned with parties worked relatively better, those with older people who were linked to previously existing leftist organizations were similar to those classic left platforms.

Aristégui highlights the way these "old Left" vs. "autonomous" differences intersected within the assemblies and working groups, crosscut by the pros and cons of newcomers and experienced activist involvement:

The people who tended to have a more classical leftist approach curiously were also the people who didn't sleep there overnight. They would only go down to the camp to do politics and later would leave, those people were the least respectful with the exhausting and long assembly practices.

Those committed to *asambleario* practice also ran into one of the classic problems associated with it:

[There were] problems. They did a lot of things right; they were incredible facilitators. From the very beginning there were experienced facilitators that enabled people to participate to the max, to make sure that people wouldn't use abusive language, that there wouldn't be aggressive tones in the interventions, that language would be inclusive, that there would be use of sign language, all of that was done really, really well, and in record time. The facilitation committee worked perfectly. Unfortunately, they failed in one crucial, crucial point. They confused consensus with unanimity. One thing is consensus and another thing is that every single person out of 2,000 people in the assembly have to be in agreement and say the same thing. They wanted, for example, to take a resolution on secular education, and there was one person who was in favor of having religious classes—one single person blocked the whole decision when it was a clear consensus.

I suggested this was likely due to a lack of experience, but Aristégui pointed out another reason:

There was also a lot of fear that the camp would produce some kind of political program or some kind of electoral program. [So] they felt that if there was nothing tangible in the camp that was a good thing, because that was the way to be more inclusive.[4] The minute that you show your cards and start making concrete demands you're not that inclusive anymore.

Although some more experienced activists did try to explain the crucial distinction between consensus and unanimity, it was lost on many who adopted "consensus" as an orthodoxy, a common problem among people new to *asamblearismo* (although some people are ideologically committed to pure consensus).[5] Another problem (but one I witnessed only once in 15-M assemblies) was the confusion between blocking and dissensus, as Aristégui recounts:

Something that they used in Acampada Sol that we have never used in Madrid, or I never remember it anyway, is the blocking symbol. People didn't express their dissensus, instead they just systematically blocked things. [. . .] If that person who blocked the decision on the resolution in favor of secular education had simply expressed their dissensus and hadn't blocked, there wouldn't have been any problems, they would've integrated their dissensus and approved the proposal. [. . .] Over time I think it got a little better, but it was used in a very undisciplined way. People blocked when in reality what they wanted to do was say "no."

Like Aristégui, in my experience in Madrid's autonomous scene prior to 15-M, blocking was hardly ever invoked, as it runs counter to one key aspect of *asambleario* culture, which is that if you do not want to do something, that shouldn't stop others from doing it if enough people are willing and able. In fact, prior to 15-M I had never seen *anyone* block something in an assembly. Blocking is reserved for deep ethical, moral, or legal/

security/logistical reasons, and its facile use is one of the major stumbling blocks to collective action, and—just as with confusing consensus with unanimity—it can demobilize very quickly, since stopping action can cause frustration, burnout, and exit. The necessary use of hand signals in such large assemblies and their introduction to newcomers may have inadvertently created this problem, since blocking (holding up crossed arms with closed fists) is one of the signs taught. Since the use of hand signs was not widespread in Madrid assemblies, but had been used in large statewide assemblies during the GJM, I asked Aristégui where he thought they came from:

> I think the student movements have kept that alive, [. . .] because I've seen that they've always used them in their assemblies. If you have an assembly with 10 people you don't need them, if you have 100 people you absolutely need them, with 1,000 people, you have no other choice.

In addition to distinctions between newcomers and old-timers, and people with a greater or lesser commitment to Institutional Left or *asambleario* practices, there were also differences between those who camped overnight and those who came and went. Although Aristégui links these primarily to differences in political orientation, one has to consider that not very many people are free to suddenly stop their personal and work commitments to stay in a camp overnight. That level of commitment is the result of a combination of biographical availability and political desire, and numerous interviewees who were strongly committed to the camp made huge sacrifices to juggle studies, work, and family demands to devote themselves as much as possible to the camp, often at the cost of sleep. Carmen shows the high level of commitment and the physical exhaustion involved in sustaining camp life, even for those who did not sleep there:

> It was a strong and generous movement. I spent a great part of the day and the night there although I didn't ever camp overnight. I would come home for two or three hours and then I would go right back to the camp, and I would take food and things that could be useful. Since my home was really nearby, a lot of people would come over to have a shower or to stay and rest for two or three hours, because it was really difficult.

What comes through in participants' narratives is the way that various strands of influence and political cultures came together to shape the dynamic of the camp, and how a combination of experience and inexperience intersected to create the strengths and limitations of the camp's internal functioning. Some elements are common to all urban occupations (e.g., distinctions between people with and without time available; problems integrating people in the urban environment who normally occupy those spaces, especially at night, such as homeless people or sex workers; and so on). Others are challenges and limitations inherent to assembly-style processes (e.g., assembly fatigue, consensus orthodoxies), and others reflect the unique and unpredictable confluence of heterogeneous groups of actors in a given space and time. Acampada Sol reflected Madrid's movement political culture but managed to transcend and transform elements of it, as I will discuss below.

Within the organized chaos, there was also *catharsis*, as over time, person after person took the microphone to narrate their experience of the crisis and their reasons for being in the plaza. Carlos (JSF) recalls his reaction:

> There is also a part of 15-M in the camps that has to do with impotence. [. . .] There were a lot of assemblies that were exasperating because they were only expressive. There were people who would take the microphone and start to cry because they would just tell you about their lives. And you'd say to yourself "Mother of God! What a drag!" The first time it was very moving, the third time it was very moving, but by the fifth time you felt like slitting your wrists. It was terrible. So the assemblies reflected various tendencies. On the one hand, the fact that people were fed up with those who were supposed to be our representatives in the institutions [. . .]. On the other, a certain inability to give that some kind of form. And another tendency, which was a political will in some sectors that *wanted* that organization to take some kind of political form.

Carlos is highlighting here the fact that despite the nonpartisan nature of the camp's collective identity, there were those who wanted the energy of the plaza to be not merely expressive but channeled into some specific political form, institutional or otherwise. This aspect of the camp shouldn't be overlooked when exploring the rise of Podemos and the municipal movements. A commitment to autonomous nonpartisan practice in the camp did not preclude wishing for a reform in institutional politics, and indeed multi-militancy across autonomous and alternative party affiliations has long been a feature of Madrid's autonomous scene.

The camp was also characterized from the beginning by a resolutely nonviolent orientation, an aspect that Carlos (JSF) sees connected unhelpfully to a lasting, unwelcome effect of the Culture of the Transition (CT): the avoidance of conflict and desire for everyone to be united in their decisions (which Aristégui attributes to a fear of not being seen as inclusive). I would also attribute this classic problem to the presence of many people who did not have experience in *asamblearismo*. What is remarkable is how many decisions actually *were* taken rather than the fact that many people were frustrated at times by the lack of ability to move forward and give the camp more "political shape." The constant flow of people in and out of the public space meant that assemblies would repeat the same themes again and again, causing assembly fatigue for those who were spending more time there (a common problem for autonomous *asambleario* movements). For "cathartic" or "therapeutic" assemblies, repetition is not a problem, but for operational assemblies, revisiting the same decisions and discussions over time leads to burnout. Managing emotions in activist spaces is an important task (Goodwin, Jasper, and Polletta 2001). While catharsis is important, repetition of tragic stories can work against the motivating power of hope and optimism, of the "Sí se puede!" energy that the movement worked so hard to promote. Of course, assemblies can have elements of both, but sustaining them over time requires tremendous collective self-care and a very high level of reflexivity about methodology, as well as a shared commitment to following it.

Acampada Sol was remarkable in its ability to sustain so many assemblies and such a complex internal structure over time. This was due not only to the previous experience of many of the participants, but also to the inclusivity of the camp, one of whose basic principles (announced by megaphone to the general assembly the first evening and repeated thereafter) was that *anyone* with *any* skills, in *any* degree, who was willing to *participate* was welcome in the camp. People who were feeling lonely, disconnected, useless, or depressed about being unemployed could feel useful in a shared, exciting, and, for the most part, caring environment. The commitment to solidarity, caring, and nonviolence had both ideological and strategic roots. The presence of anti-militarist, conscientious objector, ecologist, and feminist currents meant that a politics of nonviolence and collective self-care was already strongly represented, as was a culture of civil disobedience committed to nonviolence as a strategic means of juxtaposing the violence of the state (police) with peaceful protesters.

Real democracy now!

In the course of the camp's life, democracy was the interpretive master frame through which anti-austerity demands were made. Despite the camp's complex and ever shifting nature, its political demands began to take greater form by the May 20, when the general assembly agreed on a manifesto that incorporated the following key elements[6]:

- Political reform with an emphasis on eliminating the privileges of the political class and changing electoral law, which favors large parties.
- Reducing unemployment.
- The right to housing.
- The right to high-quality public services, including healthcare, education, and public transportation.
- Regulation of banks and financial institutions, and nationalization of the banks that have been bailed out with public funds.
- Fiscal reform, including eliminating tax benefits for corporations and the super wealthy.
- Citizen freedom and the right to political participation, including the abolition of the Sinde Law (anti-piracy), mandatory public referenda on EU directives imposed on nation state members, and separation of powers between the legislative, judicial, and executive branches of the state.
- Decrease in military spending, defining the movement in pacifist terms.

There were also calls for renewable energy, closing nuclear installations, the separation of church and state, and a reference to the Movement for the Recovery of Historical Memory (which seeks reparations from the Franco dictatorship). Most of these demands have remained at the heart of 15-M.

Handmade signs on cardboard also expressed the different demands of those assembled. The rejection of repression and criminalization is clear from the repeated chanting of "these are our weapons" as the protesters raised their hands in the air, and signs such as "The Voice of the people (pueblo) will never be illegal." Another sign expressed the rejection of party and union politics that characterized the camp: "We don't need acronyms to struggle."

In an electoral context, anti-partisan sentiments did not preclude demands for political reform. One sign read simply "Electoral Reform Now!" The democratic reform and critique at the heart of the camp did not only manifest in prefigurative *asambleario* practices, but also in demands that existing institutions work for, not against, citizens. Taibo (2011) distinguishes the twin souls of 15-M as experienced activists with a strong anti-capitalist orientation, on the one hand, and the younger activists fed up with the lack of opportunities, widespread corruption, high price of housing, and usury of banks, who demanded political reform, on the other. What his characterization misses, I think, is the profound influence of feminist discourse and its emphasis on the need to redefine the central task of politics as primarily caring for citizens and placing the interests of life before capital. This shifted the earlier radical/reform cleavage significantly toward a demand for democratic renewal resolutely oriented toward the common good, an argument that in its essence challenges the promotion of individual self-interest that underlies neoliberal capitalist ideology.

By constantly connecting the disinterest of political elites in citizen welfare to their role in colluding with economic elites to pass the costs of the crisis-swindle to citizens, 15-M protesters were implicitly and explicitly critiquing the capitalist system. But by reclaiming democratic institutions for the "citizens," they were also venturing into territory long considered the exclusive domain of the Right and preparing the terrain for the later rise of the municipal movements and Podemos. Direct appeals to the "nation" (*la patria*) later became a core discursive strategy of Podemos. While it rubbed some Leftists the wrong way, it made sense as an extension of the framework of 15-M narratives.

Leaving the square

Unlike some camps that hold on till the bitter end, converting the occupation into an end in itself (Chabanet and Royall 2015; Hammond 2015), Acampada Sol took the collective decision to decamp to the neighborhood assemblies before the camp fell into further decline or was evicted. The debate was not new: on May 29 the general assembly had debated for four hours whether to stay or go, and eventually decided to remain. So the final decision to leave the square was a difficult and contested one, but ultimately consensual. None of the people I interviewed felt it was the wrong decision, and some felt it was one of the best decisions the camp had ever taken. The camp had already put into place a post-camp infrastructure, by establishing the neighborhood assemblies some weeks *before* leaving the plaza—another key difference between it and other Occupy camps (Chabanet and Royall 2015; Eschle 2018; Roberts 2012; Tufekci 2017; Uitermark and Nicholls 2012) that attests to the importance of a network infrastructure in enabling the movement to continue. These assemblies were already up and running in some cases by May 28. The campers felt it was important to leave on their own terms and with their own agenda in place. As the woman who announced the decision through the megaphone put it:

> We came when we wanted, freely. We leave freely and because we want to, not because we have internal divisions or external coercion.

Maintaining an occupied space in the center of a major urban area is challenging and exhausting, and Acampada Sol was no exception. In Javier's (JSF) view, issues with sharing space with other city occupiers at night (sex workers, drug addicts, and homeless people); sexist aggressions; and police infiltrators made the assembly really difficult to manage:

> There were a lot of internal discussions [. . .] because there were people who were clearly in favor of an eternal camp in Sol, "The objective is Sol, the objective is Sol" and then there were those of us who said, "Please, let's leave Sol!" I'm talking about at the end, of course. It wasn't hygienic, I mean it actually was starting to give a really poor image to the outside. Rather than an image of citizens who were empowering themselves, it was more the lumpen.

David Aristégui agrees that the decision was very astute:

> The general assembly was inoperative by then. [The idea] wasn't to abandon the camp but to have the neighborhood assemblies taking their own decisions, without everything passing through the general assembly. Then the neighborhoods can come and tell us what is going on, and we can support that and give it visibility and coverage. Decamping helped a lot [because it revitalized the neighborhood assemblies].

On June 12 the camp was lifted under the slogan "We aren't leaving, we are expanding" (*No nos vamos, nos expandimos*). Another simply said, "We'll see each other in the neighborhoods" (*Nos vemos en los barrios*). Another offered an existentialist touch: "We are not leaving, we are moving to your conscience/consciousness" (*No nos vamos, Nos mudamos a tu conciencia*). One sign tied to the central "horse statue" promised more to come: "Today we are decamping. We are not leaving, and we are not shutting up. We are continuing to make noise" (*Hoy levantamos el campamento, ni nos vamos, ni nos callamos, seguimos haciendo ruido*). The participants decided to leave the Puerta del Sol cleaner than they found it, by organizing cleaning committees. Many of the proposals, banners, slogans, and other material were archived in the 3peces3 Social Centre, although many others have been lost or dispersed. Only an info point was left in the square, which was removed by the city on August 2.

But leaving the square didn't really mean leaving the square. Over the next years the Puerta del Sol, always a focal point of protest in Madrid, took on a new symbolic association, and witnessed thousands of protests, many directly related to or identified with 15-M. In addition, a general assembly continued to be held in the square every Sunday, albeit with dwindling numbers of people, for the following four years, and multitudinous 15-M anniversary protests have also been held there. Hunger strikers against the crisis took up residence, as did other shorter-lived occupations and performances against austerity, the crisis, sexist violence, and repression. Reclaiming the symbolic and physical control of the space became part of the repertoire of engagement between activists and police at certain key moments, the physical space around "the whale" (one of the metro entrances) being considered particularly significant, as this extract from my fieldnotes shows:

Puerta del Sol, close to midnight, May 22, 2015
On the eve of the day of reflection (May 23), a group of people involved in the 15-M network decided to meet in the Puerta del Sol to carry out a silent scream, consisting only of raising hands in the air and holding them there for one minute. When they arrive, police squads are everywhere, and prevent anyone from walking close to the whale. The activists circle the plaza arm in arm, casually mixing with other people out for a stroll. When they got near the whale, the police randomly stop people to check for identification and to ask them what they are doing (in a public square!). Tourists and

passersby are baffled: they cannot understand why police do not want to allow people to walk through that bit of empty space. They do not understand that for those involved (protesters and police), 15-M redefined the symbolic meaning of the square, even when there is no material representation of the movement in it, even when it is, effectively, empty space. This is the intangible yet visible impact of the occupation and its legacy, this is what it means to declare "Take the Square" (Toma la Plaza), this is what it means to declare, once occupied, as 15-M did, "Plaza Tomada" (Square Taken). Once occupied for a sustained and meaningful period, it leaves an imprint that cannot be "evicted," because how can you evict a collective experience that lives in the minds of thousands of people? You can't, no matter how many IDs you check, or how much you try to make people afraid to do something as simple as silently wave their hands in the air for a minute, no matter how hard you try to retake control of the space once the occupiers have left. *Plaza tomada.*

Notes

1. This wasn't exclusive to Madrid. An activist from León told me about middle aged participants who decided to support the camp there primarily because they felt indignation about the restriction of public space: "What do you mean I can't be in the public square of my city?"
2. See Juris et al. 2013 and Pickerill 2004 for a discussion of this in other movements. In Madrid, cyberactivists in the GJM experienced related disputes in the Indymedia project.
3. At a talk in Madrid on 15-M outcomes, May 9, 2014, Jornadas UNED.
4. This was a crucial problem in the European Social Consulta that I analyze in depth in Flesher Eguiarte 2005.
5. See Flesher Eguiarte 2005 for a discussion on this in Madrid and Barcelona's GJM networks.
6. Acampada Sol (2011), *Propuestas aprobadas en la Asamblea de hoy día 20 de mayo de 2011 en Acampada Sol*, May 20.

5

Assessing the Significance of Acampada Sol

We want a new society that places life above economic and political interests
—First Communiqué of Acampada Sol (2011)

ACAMPADA SOL WAS one of many "occupation" camps that combined a pro-democracy and anti-austerity orientation. Demands for greater democracy form a central shared theme across a wide range of protest sites and forms of protest (Dekker and Feenstra, 2015) within and beyond Europe. But not all of these resulted in strong and sustained movements afterward (Fernández-Savater and Flesher Fominaya 2017; Tufekci 2017), and not all mass mobilizations in times of crisis result in the emergence of social movements (Freeman 1999). The experience of Acampada Sol had two crucial impacts that served to fuel and sustain the 15-M movement. The first was to establish democracy as the central problematic around which the movement cohered. The second was to consolidate a political culture and a collective identity that would sustain the movement, enabling it to expand and evolve. Autonomous, feminist, and hacker ethics forged a political culture that would strengthen the movement's political identity and efficacy.

Democracy Central

The critique of really existing democracy and the development of alternative democratic imaginaries manifested in Acampada Sol in six key ways. First, the camp enabled the construction of citizens as a collective political subject that could and should play an active part in democracy and demand democratic reform. During the camp, over 15,000 proposals to improve democracy were gathered. Activists identified deficient democracy

Democracy Reloaded. Cristina Flesher Fominaya, Oxford University Press (2020). © Oxford University Press.
DOI: 10.1093/oso/9780190099961.001.0001

and its agents as the problem ("They do not represent us!" "We have a right to be indignant"), and expanded the frame of who could be an agent of change, identifying themselves and appealing to others, not as activists, but as "citizens" and "ordinary people" rightfully occupying public space in the name of "real democracy." The insistence on nonpartisan and nonrepresentational participation (no flags, acronyms, parties, or unions) enabled an elastic collective identity that allowed for the integration of a wide range of people. Collective identity formation involved framing the crisis as a shared problem. The camp allowed many people to shift from individual despair ("What can I do?") to a feeling of hope and indignation ("What can we do?"). It enabled a positive channeling of the emotional energy and cognitive liberation needed to fuel social movements (Goodwin et al. 2001; McAdam 2013).

Second, the camp was a laboratory of civil disobedience that, in an electoral context, directly engaged with politicians and agents of the state, posing a challenge that political elites were unable to ignore.

Third, the camp prefiguratively experimented with deliberative participatory processes organized around commitment to nonhierarchy (horizontalism), inclusivity, and the creation of a *res publica*. Throughout, campers developed and disseminated shared "democracy" master frames, including diagnostic and prognostic frames (Snow et al. 1986) about who was to blame for the crisis, how existing democracy enabled it, how austerity issues were connected to the democratic deficit, and what could be done about it.

Fourth, the camp brought people together who would not ordinarily engage with each other in urban settings, across age, class, and ethnic divides, defying social conventions and providing a new model for democratic civil-social interaction. It crowdsourced resources and expertise, fostering a sense of democracy as potentially being collectively self-empowered rather than dependent on elites or "experts" to resolve collective problems and promote the common good.

Fifth, democracy was not limited to the rational discursive sphere of the general assemblies. The need to organize the material aspects of the campus life in common provided numerous opportunities to politicize the normally mundane, from rethinking child care and feeding people to interactions with police.

Sixth, and crucially, the camp brought diverse preexisting networks of activists together around a shared problematic of democracy, allowing them to cross-contaminate through synergy, reciprocity, and contestation, thus lending specific *substantive* content to the new democratic imaginary.

Acampada Sol as incubator of 15-M political culture and collective identity

The camp existed as a physical space that brought people together, regenerated existing movements, and incorporated a large number of actors new to political action. Campers developed bonds of solidarity through a shared experience that was focused on concrete collective tasks, but which was also emotionally and politically charged. Meeting the material and social reproductive needs of the camp—*working* together, as opposed to just talking—played a role in solidarity building, an important factor in collective identity formation (Flesher Fominaya 2010a, 2010b; Melucci 1996).

Although nourished by preexisting networks and shaped by long-standing traditions such as *asamblearismo*, the experience of the camp prompted reflexivity about political practice and served to realign previous political orientations to encompass the lessons and insights from the occupation. In this way, individuals and groups redefined their collective

IMAGE 5.1 15-M protesters in the Puerta del Sol, Madrid 2013.

identities to fit a new 15-M movement identity. Verónica reflects on how the Acampada experience affected JSF:

> [It] altered our understanding of political conflict. Before we were very fixated on trying to wage war and push for greater conflicts, and I think later we understood that the struggle needs to be waged differently. [. . .] Benedetti said "defend happiness and organize anger" . . . before it seemed that people on the left were always angry and that we wanted "the struggle," and now we've understood that it's got to be more enjoyable, to try to make people see that there really is an alternative and that it is a *better* alternative. [Laughs]

Miguel Martínez explained the positive impact of the Acampada Sol on his social center's inability to connect with people in the neighborhood prior to 15-M: "We just didn't seem capable of overcoming certain barriers. With 15-M, those barriers are overcome."

Acampada Sol revitalized the network, increased the visibility of existing projects and created many new ones, some directly tied to the infrastructure of the camp via coordinating structures (Popular Assembly of Madrid [APM]) and the General Assembly of Sol [AGSOL]), the neighborhood assemblies, and working groups:

> So many things were happening . . . a feminism group, an urban garden group . . . a communication group, a million things. And [while] they are developing [in Sol] they are in contact with and feed into many other spaces. . . . The bike people hold a workshop in Sol, and puts people in touch from all the different bike workshops around the city, and new people.

The Acampada broke activists out of the "activist ghetto" and the "academic ghetto" and put them in contact with people in the street in a political context, often for the first time. This is the element of the plaza occupations that participants relate to the creation of a new ágora. As María Bilbao says in relation to feminism,

> What did 15-M bring to feminism? I think it revitalized it. It put different kinds of feminism and different generations in contact

with each other. [. . .] In 15-M we found a way to understand each other.

One of the most remarkable subcultural changes introduced was the widespread adoption of the feminine plural (e.g., *todas, nosotras*) as the universal plural (replacing the male universal plural used in general speech (e.g., *todos, nosotros*). Although when the camp started, activists were still using feminine plural and masculine plural together (e.g., *todas y todos*) to critique the universal male subject, soon the masculine plural was dropped altogether and replaced by a feminine plural universal, a feminist gesture designed to subvert everyday sexism as expressed linguistically. Gracia Trujillo explains:

> One of the important contributions of Feminismos Sol to 15-M was to question the language the movement was using, a sexist language that makes invisible everything that is not the universal male subject. So, everyone started speaking in feminine, which was a political and pedagogical strategy to say, hey, things need to change, and one of those things is our language.

This linguistic change had a lasting impact in Madrid's movement scene and is standard usage to this day in many movement spaces.

As a newcomer to activism, Julián describes how the Acampada Sol experience altered his conception of politics:

> Politics for me up to that point was a television screen, where you could change the channel according to what you liked more or what you liked less, because the representative system allows you to choose between different people that are going to make decisions for you about your life. And when you realize that *you* can construct those decisions—that was completely new for me.

Julián and María Bilbao's words evoke one of the most radical impacts of Acampada Sol, and one that I was to hear in different forms from dozens of people: it gave politics "back to the people." What that actually means differs across individuals, but a feeling that politics was something everyone could and should be involved in, and not the purview of a select group of "expert" people who "do politics" on others' behalf, signified a rupture with the Culture of the Transition (CT), at least for participants.

For journalist Juan Luís Sánchez,

> 15-M is a diagnosis, a state of mind, an inspiration. People are still not fully aware of the huge number of projects that were born in May 2011. Neurons have been activated within groups of friends as well as with strangers. A whole new field of audiovisual and other projects has emerged, inspired by 15-M. It is these projects that will lead the future evolution of the movement—more so than the assemblies or the street protests. (Grueso 2012)

Acampada Sol was not a utopia, but a biopolitical *heterotopia*, characterized by bringing together different elements in an alternative form to existing spaces (Foucault and Miskowiec 1986). It expressed a rejection of dominant forms of social relations (violence, hierarchies, inequalities, exclusion, marginalization) and tried to embody an alternative to these forms: caring, solidarity, collective empowerment and endeavor, horizontalism. These were framed clearly in relation to the specific crisis/austerity context. If austerity policies neglect people's material needs, placing capital before life, as some activists succinctly put it, the camp inverted that formula, putting life before capital. The camp provided a model for meeting people's material needs in a way that respected, engaged, and empowered them, drawing on, inter alia, feminist, autonomous, pro-commons, DIY, and anti-charity models. This commitment to life and to the commons, especially in an urban context, was fundamental later in the rise of the municipal movements (electoral initiatives made up of different collectives and parties). Collective practices that began as a way to meet practical first-order needs (e.g., food, shelter, infrastructure, legal assistance, child care) gradually took on a political character in the context of collective reflection about how things were normally done, how they could be done differently, and why they should be.

Analytical exposition inevitably imposes coherence on complexity in order to unearth meaningful explanations. Acampada Sol was a heterotopic incubator in the 15-M political laboratory, but it wasn't hermetically sealed. It was traversed by outside influences and forces it could not control, and by internal contradictions and conflicts.

Core ideational frameworks: Forging movement culture in the crucible

If anti-austerity and democratic regeneration were the key substantive demands that fueled mobilization, the political culture of the camp (and later of the 15-M movement), emerged from the cross-contamination of the different movements that were present and influential in the square, resulting in key ideational orientations, issues, and ways of doing things that activists identified as "15-M."

15-M culture was clearly shaped by the legacy of the GJM and autonomous movements, including *asamblearismo*, commitment to diversity, horizontality, inclusivity, anti-identitarian collective identity, consensus decision-making, a DIY ethos, and a rejection of mediation and representation. New here was the framing of the political subject as "citizens" and "pueblo."

The term "autonomous movements" encompasses many movement traditions. The camp was founded on a mass act of *nonviolent civil disobedience*, a feature of many previous movements (e.g., conscientious objector, environmental, and squatter). The claiming of public space for political and social purposes is closely tied to the long tradition of *urban squatting*, which holds within it a strong belief in *"the commons"* and the *"right to the city."*

Feminist, anti-militarist, and *environmentalist* epistemologies and methodologies that promote the self-care of the collective were an active part of camp culture, despite some problems with sexism and sexist violence. The commitment to "life over capital" involved reflexivity about breaking down the individualism fostered by competitive capitalist society and actively encouraging collective solutions predicated on solidarity. The camp ethos also reflected a sense of *collective self-empowerment and a belief in the possibility of change.* Believing change is possible (cognitive liberation) is a crucial "victory" over fear, apathy, and the belief that there is no alternative to the status quo (i.e., crisis, austerity, capitalist consumer society, deficient representative democracy).

The presence of activists imbued in a *hacker ethos* also influenced the camp, not only in the communication infrastructure, but especially in the desire to share information globally from the very beginning in order to facilitate the replicability of the camp model, in line with free software and DIY philosophy. The experience with and commitment to *asamblearismo* practices shaped the way information was packaged and shared. A digital democratic imaginary fueled the commitment to the use of digital media and open, transparent, and secure information sharing. This hacker ethos influenced the broader 15-M democratic imaginary far beyond those who actually had "hacker" skills.

A belief in the *power of collective intelligence* (also a core part of hacker philosophy) also emerged from an experience where all skills and knowledge were put at the service of the camp. Participants speak of their sense of unity (*todos a uno*) and a sort of "group mind" that took hold of the crowd during critical moments: confrontation with police, and during important decisions in the general assembly, which were characterized as a mass exercise in active listening.

An overview of core principles and salient traditions is seen in Table 5.1. Note the synergy and overlap of some core ideas across traditions and how they work together to contribute a substantive and normative underpinning to a "real" democratic imaginary. All of them are also united in an implicit or explicit critique of neoliberal capitalism. These core ideas were later expressed in the political narratives of Podemos and the municipal movements (see Part IV).

Although many movement traditions nourished 15-M, the core ideas embodied in these three frameworks emerged as a salient matrix

Table 5.1 Core Ideational Frameworks of 15-M

- **Autonomy:** commitment to deliberative/participatory/direct democracy, horizontality, inclusivity and diversity, DIY and direct action, social transformation through resistance and creating alternatives, unmediated politics, prefiguration, consensus/common minimums, assembly based, nonpermanent or fixed delegations of responsibility, leaderful/leaderless
- **Feminism:** overturning patriarchy, highlighting the gendered nature of austerity; focus on care, solidarity, and collective self-empowerment; nonviolence; redefining citizen security as being that which guarantees the individual and social welfare of citizens (as opposed to guarding them from external threats); expertise as including shared knowledge from below; consciousness-raising; prefiguration
- **Hacker Ethics and Technopolitical Imaginaries:** commitment to open source/transparency, commons, collective intelligence, crowdsourcing, replicability, participation, and horizontal information/knowledge sharing; hacking (finding better solutions to problems by collectively building on existing knowledge); anonymity; right to privacy; contesting surveillance; harnessing the power of the digital; DIY

following Acampada Sol. This is an analytical construct rather than an empirical representation (as the map of the movement network in the Part III shows). All of these elements (in various combinations and to various degrees) would later be shorthanded as 15-M or *15mayista*, when people would refer to political initiatives or groups they felt reflected this orientation. Identifying with core elements of this political culture and engaging in collective action based on it formed the 15-M collective identity that lived on beyond the camp. Collective identities are not coherent or fixed (Melucci 2003) and are constantly negotiated and renegotiated through interactions, but they establish a series of criteria and a habitus that activists use to determine if other people, groups, ideas, and ways of action belong to the movement or don't, and if they are authentic or not. These criteria are invoked during boundary work within and across movement groups and spaces (i.e., us versus them; who is in or out of the community) (Flesher Fominaya 2010b, 2016a, 2019).

In general, activists with an autonomous political identity prior to 15-M did not embrace the 15-M label so tightly, whereas those politicized through the Acampada or the movement assemblies did and invoked it as a way to claim the legitimacy of certain political spaces (or conversely. saying something *wasn't* 15-M to delegitimize them). In the afterglow of the Acampada Sol, "hacker" Marga Padillo emphasized the hegemony of a 15-M "style of doing politics": "Nothing that is not 15-M matters anymore" (Grueso 2012).

A camp ethos predicated on inclusivity and consensus facilitated its sustenance by effectively navigating conflict, but also limited the creation of more formalized political organization, frustrating some. Instead, it led to a multitude of experiments around Madrid and Spain encompassing a diversity of specific issues, but connected through a reciprocal collective identification as being part of "15-M." Acampada Sol, therefore, established a shared problematic of democracy and shared master frames around which that problematic could be mobilized by the movement. It created a co-optable communications network (Freeman 1999) and a renewed movement network that could be mobilized, as well as an emergent political culture and collective identity around which activists could mobilize. It provided, in short, the key elements that are needed for a social movement to emerge and flourish in times of crisis.

IMAGE 5.2 15M assemblies in a *batucada*, Madrid 2014.

Making movements

What led to 15-M? In a comparative analysis of four major US movements, Freeman (1999) identified recurrent elements involved in movement formation that, when they interact in a sufficiently grievance-laden context, support three key propositions. The first is that no amount of discontent will produce a new movement. Small groups may form spontaneously but they must be linked through a preexisting communications network or infrastructure for the protest to become generalized. Second, this network must be co-optable to the new ideas of the movement and composed of people whose backgrounds, experiences, or locations in the social structure makes them receptive to these ideas. Third, precipitation occurs either through a galvanizing crisis or through the organized action of committed activists "who are skilled and have a fertile terrain in which to work."

Freeman's propositions hold for the formation of 15-M. The original 15-M protest and Acampada Sol emerged in the context of a crisis, engendering a wide range of people who find themselves in a similar structural location, suffering from the effects of the crisis, and crucially sharing a perception of its (mis)handling by political representatives through austerity policies and an erosion of the welfare state. The movement has at its disposal both highly organized activists operating in a fertile terrain and a highly developed preexisting communication network and infrastructure that continues to develop and expand beyond the Acampada. The camp served to break the barrier between a self-referential group of critical movement groups (the activist ghetto) and the wider group of receptive participants suffering an active grievance. As I have shown, in the case of Acampada Sol, a whole range of resources sustained it, including the activation of autonomous, feminist, squatter, hacker, and civil disobedience legacies. But it is the context of the crisis and the experience of the camp itself that enabled something *new* to emerge.

Unlike the movement's Freeman studied, which each mobilized around different core themes, 15-M initially managed to generate a very wide and elastic "container" within which many issues, interests, and orientations could mobilize (over time it fell back to a more clearly leftist orientation). Freeman's schema allows us to bring together a number of competing arguments around the causes of the recent wave of anti-austerity protests that are better understood as acting synergistically. Common sense and evidence show that austerity/crisis was a crucial factor enabling mobilization, but cannot explain mobilization on its own, evident in the uneven strength of post-crisis anti-austerity mobilization in those countries hardest hit. Arguments that stress the importance of technopolitics, digital media, or communication infrastructures in protest emergence and expansion are again supported by common sense and evidence, but insufficient to explain different levels of mobilization across contexts with similar access to digital tools and expertise. In 15-M all of these factors come together, but they are *organized* by a specific set of actors who channel grievances and exploit opportunities and resources to create effective collective action frames.

Spontaneity arguments (i.e., people suddenly became aware of their shared grievances and took to the streets) are not supported. The 15-M protest was not spontaneous, but carefully planned. The decision to camp *was* spontaneous, but grew directly out of the protest event, and the camp did not increase to a critical mass nor spread to other cities until repressive state action and the mobilization of *preexisting communication networks* kicked in.

In the wake of the global wave of occupation-style movements, theorists such as Juris (2012) and Bennett and Segerberg (2012, 2013) have proposed an emergent and fundamental shift in organizing forms, whereas

Gerbaudo (2012) privileges the communication infrastructure of the "Occupy movements," in which soft leaders exploit social media's affordances to choreograph and orchestrate assemblages of people in public space. Juris (2012, 260) argues that the occupations of the squares show that social media have enabled movements to shift from a network logic to an aggregation logic "that involves the assembling of masses of individuals from diverse backgrounds within physical spaces." For Juris, "[a] logic of aggregation is an alternative cultural framework that is *shaped by our interactions with social media* [emphasis mine] and generates particular patterns of social and political interaction that involve the viral flow of information and subsequent aggregations of large numbers of individuals in concrete physical spaces" (266). He contrasts this with a networking logic in which "a praxis of communication and coordination on the part of collective actors that are already constituted— including particular organizations, networks, and coalitions" operates (266). He argues that these aggregation logics emerge alongside, rather than replacing, decentralized network logics, which may "help to ensure the sustainability of the #Occupy movements in a post-eviction phase."

Juris's argument is useful in explaining the rise and subsequent dissipation of some of the Occupy-style movements (see also Tufekci 2017). But reading it through the lens of 15-M reveals some problems, as well as helping to clarify its strengths. The first problem is that it conflates "protest camp" with "social movement." Separating the two, and seeing the protest camp as a distinct spatially and temporally bounded phenomenon that can, *in some cases*, give rise to a movement, enables us to tease out the different logics at work in each. Juris' own formulation intimates this, but by linking aggregation logic to the emergence of social media it establishes a diachronic/chronological development from one form to the other.

Protest camps, which existed *prior* to social media, by *definition* follow an aggregation logic, if by that we mean the joining together of individuals in space and time. This space of aggregation can generate an agglutination of individuals, where even collectives (such as JSF) *temporarily* dissolve their identifying features and their organizational practice in the face of the magnitude and imperatives of a historical event. The aggregation of bodies in space and the fast pace and chaotic nature of urban camp life make an emphasis on "individuals moving in a collective space" an appealing metaphor or thesis. But as we saw in Acampada Sol, the complex internal organization of the camp still revolved around *networked* assemblies, working groups, and affinity groups, with their own collective identities and priorities within the larger camp, despite the dominant feeling of being one with the whole and having an *esprit de corps* (*todas a uno*) and an experience of collective effervescence. It followed a commons logic, not an aggregation of individuals logic.

As for the communications networks, even they were in large measure coordinated by a group of hackers and *frikis* who shared a commitment to a distinct hacker ethos that they propagated throughout the camp. While social media played an important role, and certainly a massive increase in Twitter use was observed during the period of the camp (Fernández-Planells et al. 2014; Monterde 2015; Monterde and Postill 2014), narratives from people deeply immersed in the communication assemblies of the Acampada show that they were operating in a complex media ecology in which social media played only one part. Narratives that take Twitter and social media as the movement starting point, and then develop an argument about the evolution of mobilization from the *assumption* that social media provides the starting point, generate tautological technopolitical causality narratives that fail to interrogate alternative mechanisms and explanations.

Acampada Sol did not represent "an alternative cultural framework" predicated on "interaction with social media." As we have seen, it drew from the first on established cultural logics of *asamblearismo* and was deeply influenced and sustained by other preexisting actors in the network. Although it did draw in many new individuals, so does *any* period of mass mobilization (if they did not, we would see constant membership between mobilizations, with mass mobilization reflecting a reactivation of previously mobilized people). Privileging social media, as important as it was, simply does not stand up to the narratives of dozens of people who were directly involved in the preparation of the 15-M protest, nor of establishing the Acampada Sol, nor to pre-social media experiences of camp occupations that followed similar logics. The work of Ariadna Fernández-Planells et al. (2014) on the Acampada in Barcelona shows that initial involvement in the camp came via personal contacts, but *later* led many people to open new social media accounts, especially Twitter, which then became an important means of keeping up with what was happening.

As free culture activist David Aristégui argues:

Those arguments are completely backward. Movements use the tools they have available. No tool generates a movement . . . [People don't say] Oh! Finally! Let's mobilize now because we have a tool now that we didn't have before! No . . . the problem with that "individual actor who mobilizes" thesis is that there are a lot of people who ratify that discourse, like [names a power tweeter]. He loves to say it was all about "individuals" who got coordinated. That is *not* what happened. You are forgetting DRY!, you are forgetting organized civil society, you are forgetting *a lot* of things.

While the role of social media in movement emergence and transforming logics of collective action has been overstated, social media *has* enabled new forms of mobilization and communication. This has opened new opportunities, challenges and contradictions for social movements, especially those that purport to be leaderless and "led by the base." One new phenomenon visible in 15-M was the emergence of "power tweeters"—individuals with large Twitter followings who are taken by many to be the voice of the movement (and in a sense they are when reaching so many people). As Gitlin (2003 [1980]) pointed out with regard to the movements of the 1960s and 1970s, mass media outlets love to baptize leaders, even in leaderless movements. Today, public social media means that power tweeters can emerge as movement spokespeople without being given that role in any movement communication assembly. Neither protest camps nor movements operate in a vacuum. Heterotopias like Acampada Sol are "other spaces" precisely because they attempt to represent an alternative to the status quo. Yet a free market logic interpenetrates a collective movement logic in certain spaces within cyberspace, Twitter being one of them, and this cannot be controlled by any camp or movement protocols.

A protest camp is not a "crowd," even if it generates moments of crowd euphoria and "group mind" behavior (such as silent screams). Despite a concerted effort to define the camp in one sense as a largely undifferentiated mass of individual citizens (a representation of the "people" or *pueblo*), at the same time it is actively mobilized as a shared collective identity and a defined political actor. The porous and elastic boundaries of the camp, the constant influx of passersby and newcomers, meant that new and previously non-networked people arrived at the camp, some to pass a brief time with no lasting impact or commitment, and others to stay. Those who did stay were initiated into camp culture through the myriad pedagogical practices I have described, and the camp ethos, strongly shaped by the originators, imposed itself even on seasoned activists, despite some efforts to channel the camp in one direction or another (e.g., toward more Institutional Left or electoral avenues).

Juris (2012) is right to argue that networking logics are needed to sustain the camps after they are lifted or evicted, and that the absence of such networks dissipates the mobilizing energy accumulated in a camp (Flesher Fominaya 2015e; Tufekci 2014; Tufekci 2017). A 15-M collective identity, which included, above all, a 15-M *way of doing things*, as well as a set of broadly defined political priorities (against austerity and for democratic renewal), emerged to generate a 15-M movement, which was very much organized in network form, as I show in Part III. Once the camp was lifted and "went back to the neighborhoods," despite valiant attempts to keep the Acampada Sol collective/shared experience going, the camp fragmented back into component parts that made up a newly reconfigured 15-M movement network. For some, that identity marker became their new "flag," for others, adopting *any* new flag, even one that says "15-M" misses the entire point of the experience.

Protest camps and the politics of life in common

In assessing the significance of "the movements of the squares," much attention has been devoted to the important role of deliberation in the public assemblies. Scholars have noted the importance of autonomous deliberative discursive arenas for the development of counter-discourses through which collective identities, interests, and new needs can developed (della Porta 2005; Fraser 1997; Mansbridge 1994). In this vein, Habermas's (1981) stress on communicative rationality has been critiqued for failing to recognize the important role of passion, emotions, and storytelling in public deliberation (Polletta 2006, della Porta 2013), including social movements and protest actions. Central critiques of the deliberative conception of democracy in the public sphere characterize it as exclusionary, institutionally biased, overly concerned with reason, and failing to recognize the importance of deliberation from below (della Porta 2013). I want to suggest that this critique can also be extended to assessments of social movements (and the movements of the squares in particular) that privilege public deliberation in assemblies and protest actions over other forms of social movement praxis that take place "offstage" and outside the explicitly deliberative or communicative realm.

Although the assemblies of the movements of the squares are taken as the most emblematic form of democratic prefigurative practice, the most influential process of politicization resulted *not* from Habermasian exchanges of rational arguments extolling the virtues or challenges of democracy in the general assemblies, nor even from the passionate storytelling about the effects of austerity politics (themselves evidence of deficient democracy), but rather from the shared experience of resolving the *practical* organization of life in common. Protest camps are spaces of material reproduction of life, organized collectively around a *commons* logic (which is fundamentally different from an aggregation of individuals logic). As Fernández-Savater (2016) argues, the material aspects are often made invisible, while the overtly "political" are celebrated and not subjected to reflexive critique. For Fernández-Savater, it is the material or practical aspects of the camp that provide the more radical political possibilities for transformation of the status quo, as it is rooted in daily life in common, and makes difference, decentralization, and the corporeal into key political components, whereas the general assembly (seen as the emblematic representation of camp politics) still reproduces the notion of a central vertical masculinized public space organized in line with classical and sovereign political imaginaries.

As I have shown, what began in many cases as a means to satisfy first-order needs, such as organizing food, shelter, legal support, and communications, quickly became the basis for political reflexivity around diverse questions and issues that have long been the concern of movement activists and theorists, such as the politics of care, the role of repression in modern states, the daily violence to which women are subjected when occupying public space, the right to the city and its implications when displacing the homeless or sex workers, the role of mass media and its relation to the political apparatus, and so on. In other words, the experiential aspect of decision-making, of living and thinking through camp life, can be deeply politicizing in itself (Eschle 2016), in addition to the discursive aspects of "politics" that come through making demands for democratic regeneration in the general assemblies or in the manifestos and communiqués. In Acampada Sol, camp life allowed for collective identities, affective ties, conflicts, and new ideas to develop through shared experiences in spaces free of the pressures brought forth by the nature of deliberative public space (e.g., the performative nature of public speaking, the pressure to be articulate and knowledgeable) that even the most well-facilitated, open, horizontal assemblies engender.[1]

If "politics" to many conjures up the vision of a performative conflict between parties who fight against each other, the plaza showed politics could be something else entirely: working together to solve shared problems, starting with the most essential, those that address life, where even keeping the camp clean was an exercise in reflexivity about the shared use of urban space. Privileging the camp's discursive politics and its communicative infrastructure (such as Gerbaudo's 2012 distinction between communication activist "choreographers" and participant "dancers") therefore misses out on the profoundly politicizing aspects of life in common, and reproduces some of the flaws critics have pointed to in Habermas, even when recognizing the importance of emotions and storytelling in the camp's assemblies.

At the same time, people were not occupying the camp for its own sake: they had a political purpose centered around a contestation of austerity and a demand for democratic renewal. The camp itself was an exercise in mass civil disobedience and disruption that *delegitimized* "really existing democracy" through a process of critique and contestation that worked to break down post-political consensus around neoliberalism and representative democracy, and then *relegitimized* democracy through attempted resignification that involved discursive and practical work (praxis). The campers manifested their demand for a politics of life above capital, for the commons over individual interest, in an emotionally charged shared experience that forged a collective political subject based on the idea that politics could and should be the domain of "ordinary citizens," and should and could mean much more than voting every four years.

This collective political identity built around the shared experience of the Acampada, core ideational frameworks, a whole way of doing politics, and shared master narratives about the crisis, democracy, and austerity became known simply as "15-M" and fueled a dense and vibrant movement network, renewing and transforming preexisting projects and inspiring the creation of many new ones. As Silvia Nanclares and Patricia Horrillo (in Fernández-Savater and Flesher Fominaya 2017) put it:

> What happened after the end of the camp at Puerta del Sol is described by many of us as the transformation of the spirit of 15-M into a sort of "virus" [that spread]despite the system's defense mechanisms [. . .] and like every good virus, it hasn't stopped mutating and becoming more resilient.

"Occupation" protest camps are unique sites that can foster cross-contamination between different ideational frameworks to create new synergies and substantive content to democratic imaginaries. I have argued for protest camps to be understood as distinct from protest marches or demonstrations, and distinct again from social movements. The 15-M protest, the Acampada Sol, and the 15-M movement network can and should be analyzed separately, as they have distinct features, actors, and impacts. At the same time, I have shown how these distinct phenomena can be, and in this case *are*, connected to each other and help explain the emergence of the 15-M movement. There was no Acampada Sol protest camp without the 15-M protest, and there would be no 15-M movement without the Acampada Sol occupation of the Puerta del Sol.

If the 15-M protest, and especially the 15-M occupations of the squares, acted as a sort of starting pistol in bringing critiques and demands about Spanish democracy to a wide audience, it has been the sustained actions of networked groups engaging in daily forms of resistance to austerity that have maintained this critique and its visibility, forcing a response from political elites. They have highlighted mechanisms of power and exclusion, bringing them into the sphere of public contestation. They have challenged and destabilized the legitimacy of key political and economic actors, as seen by the increasing number of anti-corruption cases and the unprecedented shift from a primarily bipartisan to a multiparty system. Once the Puerta del Sol was decamped, myriad assemblies went back to the neighborhoods and the social centers that have long nourished cultures of resistance in Madrid, but they did so with renewed vigor and initially with greatly increased numbers of participants. Over time, that initial participation waned substantially, but many smaller core projects remained, connected in a network that continued to actively resist austerity politics, pushed for a deeper and more responsive democracy, and eventually produced new electoral initiatives in the form of Podemos and the different municipal movements around Spain.

Note

1. See Eschle 2018 for a very different experience in Occupy Glasgow.

PART III

From Occupation to Movement

Inside the 15-M Network

Introduction

The 15-M protest and Acampada Sol had their own life cycles, each with a clear end. What happened next, however, is much harder to define. The experience of the camp revitalized and transformed existing projects and groups, and led to many new initiatives, often, but not always, labeled "15-M." The crowdsourced map shown below, coordinated by https://archive.org/details/MapaNuevo, gives a good if not exhaustive indication of the complexity and scope of the 15-M network created post–Acampada Sol. As such, it provides a visual representation of the parameters of the 15-M network, albeit from a Madrid-centric perspective (it does include some Catalán initiatives). The map is color-coded thematically, with each theme flowing from the central icon, which represents "15-M Mutations, Projections, Alternatives, and Convergences." The color-coded themes are represented as: #Acampada Sol, Culture, Economy, Politics, Civil Disobedience, Anti-Repression, Democracy, Transparency, Justice, Old Age (Third Age), Science, Education, Energy, Self-Management (Autogestión), Ecology, Water, Housing, Health, and Labor. Each of these has numerous projects, assemblies, organizations, or mobilizations flowing from them. The map is organized by theme and does not show connections between organizations within the network.

It would be impossible to cover each of these many initiatives in a single book. Instead, I will analyze some of the most emblematic, showing how they resist austerity, work for democratic renewal, and manifest 15-M political culture. First, however, it makes sense to think about the 15-M network itself. I have shown how the occupied space of Acampada Sol lay

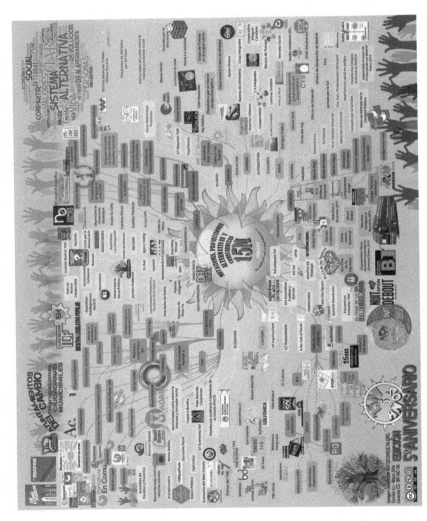

MAP III.I 15-M network map.

Source: https://archive.org/details/MapaNuevo.

at the heart of Madrid's preexisting progressive movement network. Once Acampada Sol was lifted, the movement reverted to a more complex networked community. A network has multiple nodes of coordination and influence, with multiple points of contact between different actors within it. The size of nodes and groups does not necessarily correlate with influence or power within the network. Diani (1992) placed the concept of network at the center of his definition of social movements:

> Social movements are defined as networks of informal interactions between a plurality of individuals, groups and/or organizations, engaged in political or cultural conflicts, on the basis of shared collective identities.

The inclusion of a reference to a collective identity might seem to suggest the existence of a community, and not just a network. But collective identities can function at a high level of abstraction quite removed from primary personal identities and activities, whereas the term "community" suggests a shared set of social relations, resources, and conjoint actions. Not all social movement networks are communities, and not all social movement communities are networks, but 15-M is both.

The 15-M network map raises some questions: What holds all of these initiatives together? Why do they all belong on the same map? Is there any mechanism of coordination between the various initiatives?

The simplest answer is that as a collectively produced network map, the fact that different groups included themselves shows that they see themselves as part of the 15-M movement, and therefore share a 15-M collective identity. As Castells (2010, 73) argues, in one sense, "social movements must be understood in their own terms: namely, they are what they say they are." On the other hand, anyone can claim a label, sometimes to capitalize on its legitimacy, to co-opt it, or to sabotage it. Social movement analysis requires going further than taking movements' self-expressions at face value. The actors on the map are connected to each other in a collective effort to resist austerity policies and regenerate democracy. In so doing they share resources, frames, discourse, actions, strategies and tactics, commitment, and solidarity. They are also in conflict, tension, and disagreement with each other over political practices, priorities, and ideological orientations. But all strive to act in a way that is true to their interpretation of 15-M principles. By experimenting with different forms of assembly practice and coordination, they strive to reach toward the elusive goal of "real democracy" while directly contesting the matrix of austerity politics.

In aftermath of Acampada Sol, there were two main competing efforts to give organizational form and continuity to the emerging movement, each representing a different trend within the movement. One was AGSOL (Asamblea General de Sol), which attempted to maintain the Acampada's General Assembly (GA) in Sol despite the camp being lifted. The idea was to maintain the GA as a coordinating space across all working groups and neighborhood assemblies, as well as keep a weekly presence in Sol to maintain contact with the public. AGSOL tried to keep the spirit of the camp alive through an open assembly that would continue to serve as a mouthpiece and decision-making space for the movement. The assemblies were held in the Puerta del Sol (by the horse statue), where a banner reading *Movimiento 15-M Asamblea General de Sol* (15-M Movement General Assembly of Sol) was attached to the iron bars surrounding the statue and a megaphone and a microphone were available for people wishing to speak, supported by the Assembly of Sign Language Interpreters. Weekly topics varied but a typical range of topics can be seen in the June 8, 2014, assembly, which included a call to action on the TTIP (Transatlantic Trade and Investment Partnership), including specifics on planned protest activities and details of the next assembly involving Ecologistas en Acción, Podemos Circulo de Lavapiés, 15M Plaza de los Pueblos, Medioambiente Sol, Economía del Bien Común, and ATTAC; an action against human rights violations in Mexico; a planned 15-M "statewide assembly"; a call for solidarity with Palestine and a boycott against Israel; and a lengthy intervention about the citizen's referendum on the monarchy (*referendum-realya*), along with various opinions on the questions it should include. Prepared informational interventions were followed by an open mike session, wherein a range of people discussed: (a) financial genocide (intervention by a 60 year old Ecuadorian woman), (b) opposition to the armed forces (Spanish Civil War, military propaganda, military expenditure), and (c) recycling oil to make soap. As usual, all of this was typed up and published on the web.

AGSOL assemblies often numbered 10 or fewer participants and struggled to maintain AGSOL's relevance. A particularly poignant moment came one Sunday during an assembly of seven people. Suddenly the Marea Blanca (White Tide) came marching into the square with hundreds of people chanting for public healthcare. The AGSOL speaker struggled to be heard over the noise of the protest march, to little avail.

It was a good indication of the way the movement had moved on from the Acampada.

The organizers of the AGSOL assemblies were under no illusions about its representative nature. Carmen was one of the primary "keepers of the flame" of the AGSOL, and she spoke of her motivations:

> We need to create a space that people feel they can trust, but that doesn't exist right now. AGSOL or Acampada Sol tries to be a space of coordination, but not all the assemblies recognize it as their space of coordination. We also have the APM, which is presumably the popular assembly of the neighborhoods but really isn't because only some of the neighborhoods see it as their point of reference. Then we have other kinds of platforms, like Citizens Tide, that not everybody recognizes either. In all these political spaces the problem isn't personal, its actually differences in political practice.

The attempts at coordination took three different forms once the Acampada rules of engagement (no parties, unions, or representation) no longer applied. These forms reflect the different tendencies in movement networks in Madrid before and after 15-M. AGSOL is modeled on more autonomous *asamblearismo*, with an insistence on any individual's right to participate, whereas the APM is based more on a *coordinadora* model of *asamblearismo* that allows representation only for coordinating bodies. The Marea Ciudadana's decision to allow parties and unions representation crosses the "red line" of pure autonomous *asamblearismo*, but is used for larger alliances around specific issues or coordinating bodies. These tensions between forms of *asamblearismo* and between Institutional Left (more vertical) and autonomous (more horizontal) approaches is also crosscut by a tension between the emphasis on "local realities" common in the neighborhood assemblies and many social centers, and the desire to create spaces that are open to all. The latter desire reaches its apotheosis in the technopolitical imaginary, which sees cyberspace and digital tools as liberating activists from geographical confines and bringing them together from any point on the globe. AGSOL attempted to use Mumble to achieve this goal for "state-wide coordination," given the difficulties of bringing people together physically from across Spain, but very few people attended the meetings, and the dream of digitally enabled participation fell short of the organizing ability needed to guarantee participation.

AGSOL also had a Web presence in the Madrid section of Tomalaplaza. net (Take the square.net), which hosted a calendar of diverse working groups and assemblies that were not organized by neighborhood but by theme or issue (e.g., 15-M Citizen's Justice Tribunal, Assembly on Electoral Reform, Office of Economic Disobedience, Economy Sol, Transmaricabollo Sol, etc.). While the number of active working groups meeting regularly and advertising on the web page dropped significantly after 2011, there were still a number of groups using the page to advertise their meetings until about 2015 (and several more that meet but no longer post notices in this calendar). While the Puerta del Sol has continued to fill with protest events of all types since 2011, the fate of AGSOL has been to fade away almost entirely, as the movement spread into other areas of the city, and as the once seemingly undifferentiated mass of people in the square regrouped into myriad projects and initiatives.

AGSOL's aspiration to bring people together into a nonrepresentative common decision-making space embodying the 15-M spirit contrasts sharply with the approach of the other coordinating body that emerged after 15-M, the APM (Asamblea Popular de Madrid), which functions in the tradition of the neighborhood assemblies (*asambleas vecinales*) predating 15-M that were revitalized by the sudden influx of activists returning from Sol to the "barrios." This tradition is very strong in Madrid and has diverse representations: the more traditional popular neighborhood assemblies coordinated by the FRAVM (Federación de Asambleas de Vecinos de Madrid), and the network of more "radical" squatted social centers. The APM is a coordinating group that meets with representatives of each neighborhood assembly and takes decisions as a body. In contrast to AGSOL, APM meetings are only open to representatives from neighborhood assemblies and invited guests, in order to avoid being hijacked by particular interests and to represent the "local realities" of the neighborhood assemblies. Like AGSOL, the APM initially had a great deal of participation at the local level, with certain neighborhoods, such as Carabanchel, having particularly strong and vibrant assemblies. Over time, however, most dwindled, falling victim to a number of problems typical of horizontal assemblies, including the following:

• Lack of a clear agenda or concrete problems or issues to address, leading to frustration or seeing the assembly as irrelevant in solving pressing issues.

- Lack of reflexivity about methodology, and an absence of effective moderation, leading to aimless or very long meetings, and burnout and decline.
- Co-optation by members of parties, unions, or other interests who want to use the assemblies for their end ends. (This is a recurrent theme in interviews and discussions, with IU the most notable "offender." This has not changed since the 1990s).
- Lack of response by local authorities, and lack of effective strategies of intervention with local authorities.
- Influx of enthusiastic but inexperienced activists who unwittingly exacerbate some of the issues above.

The APM tried to avoid some of the problems faced by "open assemblies" by creating a higher level of coordination that did not open discussion up to a general assembly, as Reyna explained:

> The APM is much bigger than AGSOL and is more representative and connected to the base. [. . .] It is deliberately set up to make it impossible [for individuals to bypass their local assemblies and try to hijack decision making by showing up at the APM assemblies], so only people in the APM are actually representing their local assemblies, and coming with consensus already agreed, unless their local assembly has given them express permission to make decisions on their behalf.

The competition between the two coordinators led to frustration at their role in dividing the dwindling energy in the movement, leading to competing parallel anniversary events in 2014:

> (Reyna) So this whole ridiculous situation has arisen whereby the APM is organizing one Mayo Global [15-M anniversary event], and AGSOL is organizing another one!

Reyna is critical of both coordinators contrasting them with DRY! Madrid:

> In relation to this whole proposal for the Open Days (May 17 and 18, 2014) DRY! Madrid really worked hard, going from one assembly to the other with their proposal and getting people on board. They

put in the work. Whereas AGSOL just put out this call saying "we are the statewide 15-M movement and everybody has to come to us to make a space of coordination," but those people don't work, they don't actually connect with any of the local assemblies. But the APM, who knows that it's a bigger fish, doesn't try to build a project in common with them either.

Interestingly, both coordinating spaces are mostly populated by older activists (40s, 50s, 60s, 70s). Each also created websites with domains reflecting their different emphases: AGSOL's is "take the square," the central, public space; APM's is "take the neighborhoods," the decentralized, local-level assemblies with a representative coordinating structure. Their websites are hyperlinked, but the two organisms have competed for representation of the post-Acampada scenario.

Despite the criticism of activists like Reyna, I was struck by the high degree of reflexivity in both groups as to what constituted behaving in a legitimate "15-M" way, and the lengthy debates grappling around this issue in their respective internal (not public/open air) assemblies. In one of the first attempts to create a "common space" organized by AGSOL, held in the Quimera social center in Lavapiés (February 2, 2014),[1] discussion went on for over an hour around how the space could be articulated in such a way as to not represent the movement yet serve as a common coordinating space. Participants would frequently intervene with comments like "that would not be 15-M," or "that would be 15-M." During one of the APM assemblies in preparation for the 15-M anniversary of 2014, discussion also turned repeatedly to the issue of representation, which came up at different points on the agenda (in relation to media interviews, signing their documents, and even if the Twitter logo had been agreed by consensus!). Activists in both groups cared deeply about staying true to what they saw as the spirit of the 15-M movement, even if they differed about what that was and how was best achieved. The differences were not just between groups, but within groups, reflecting a collective struggle to define what the movement actually is, which is itself a core process of collective identity formation in horizontal networked movements.

What many activists perceived to be sterile feuding between the two organisms rendered both spaces largely irrelevant as a point of reference within the network. Other coordinating attempts have been made, but none have gelled. After one frustrated attempt to coordinate various groups rendered almost inoperable by continual disruptions by members of leftist coalition party IU, some of the participants gathered in the plaza in Lavapiés for the "postmortem." Discussion turned to coordinating attempts in Madrid. A member of Short Term Politics Sol (Política a corto plazo Sol) mentioned that he and a number of other people from 15-M groups with the tag "Sol" (e.g., Economía Sol) were keen to create a third coordinating node that bypassed both AGSOL and APM. A member of the Debt Observatory (Observatorio de la Deuda) chimed in philosophically:

> It's always the same. Everybody wants to just work on their own thing in their own space. For example, I support everything *No Somos Delito* (a platform against the Gag Laws) stands for, but my thing isn't messing with the Minister of Justice, I want to mess with the Finance Minister. The assembly approach means we have to deal with [trolls and difficult people] and it slows things down, but it's beautiful because we actually think about things. The party people don't want us to think for ourselves, they want to think for us—we vote for them, and they think for us. So they come and try to take over the assemblies, but it will never work, because we think for ourselves.

Not everyone sees coordinating 15-M as necessary or desirable given the diversity of issues, preferences, and priorities in the network, as well as the risk of co-optation or hijacking (especially by parties and unions). Yet despite their limitations, the AGSOL, the APM, and the Mareas have all contributed to maintaining the network, organizing actions, and sharing information in a systematic way. The compilation of minutes of hundreds of assemblies, as well as the Titan Pads and chats used to prepare and document them, is itself an important archive that reflects many debates, concerns, and actions of the movement since 2011. But because all the actors are connected in a network, the actions of some can affect the others and cause *desgaste* or unnecessary and costly energy expenditure. The difference of opinion between the AGSOL and the APM on how to celebrate the 2014 15-M anniversary not only split the movement (people had to decide whether to support the protest ending in Sol (the AGSOL option) or show up to the open days (the APM option), but also meant that Legal Sol had to provide legal support in both places, stretching its limited resources.

The 15-M network cannot be contained in any single organizing body. Instead, like any living community, it comes together periodically in myriad configurations that connect discrete elements in different combinations depending on the issue, time, and mode of action. So if we cannot "find" the movement in specific coordinating or organizing bodies, where is it? What does it mean to say there is a 15-M movement, and what holds its diverse elements together? Classical social movement scholarship, influenced strongly by organizational theory, prioritizes formal visible social movement organizations, or "SMOs," as the units of analysis within social movements (e.g., Hensmans 2003; Jenkins and Eckert 1986; McCarthy and Zald 1977; Staggenborg 1988; Zald and McCarthy 2017). But for autonomous networks, with informally constituted, often ephemeral assemblies with no fixed membership or structure, recurring to self-declared coordinating bodies or SMOs will not reveal the configuration of the movement. Instead, we need to dig deep into the social fabric of the movement community to find the movement and what holds it together. In the following chapters I explore diverse initiatives in the movement, showing how shared master frames about democracy, the crisis, and austerity; 15-M political culture and collective identity; and an autonomous cultural networking logic (Flesher Eguiarte 2005; Juris 2008) serve to define the movement's boundaries and hold it together.

Note

1. The full minutes can be seen here, although obviously not all of the discussion is documented: http://actasmadrid.tomalaplaza.net/?p=6998.

6

"It's Not a Crisis, It's a Swindle"

INDIGNANT AND PRECARIOUS PENSIONERS

It was something to help with my pension, so that in the last years of my life . . . but I retired, and they scammed me [. . .] and now I find each day with my pension I can buy fewer things

—RAMÓN, *preferentes* victim

I FIRST MET Mari Rubia in the Puerta del Sol at the "5-O" (October 5, 2013) protest, "Goodbye Mafia, Hello Democracy." A petite woman in her 60s with short, blonde hair, she was dressed as an elf, with a little 15-M felt sunflower button pinned to her green cone hat. The frivolity of her outfit contrasted with her solemn, determined expression. She was holding a sign that said "Preferential shares. WE WANT OUR MONEY. Caja Madrid-2009." It was the first time I had heard the term *preferentes*, but not the last.

Preferentes is one of the most infamous terms associated with the financial crisis in Spain, known as a "complex financial product" that was aggressively marketed to society's most vulnerable: old age pensioners with long-standing relationships with their banks or savings and loans, little formal education, and lifetime savings in the bank. Preferential shares are high-risk products that are perpetual (not fixed). Following mass actions and protests, and a complaint submitted to the National Stock Exchange Commission (Comisión Nacional del Mercado de Valores, or CNMV), investigations were opened into Spanish banks and savings and loans that offered preferential shares (Calleja 2013). According to numerous investigations and testimonies, salespeople were told to offer these high-risk products as a safe, limited-time investment

Democracy Reloaded. Cristina Flesher Fominaya, Oxford University Press (2020). © Oxford University Press.
DOI: 10.1093/oso/9780190099961.001.0001

IMAGE 6.1 *Preferentes* protest in front of Bankia, Madrid 2013.

and aggressively pursued potential clients, leaving some 700,000 people affected (El País 2014). Leaked documents show the directions sales-people were given, with the indication "Do Not Show to Clients" (see these at https://xnet-x.net/docs/15MpaRato-dossier-english.pdf). Caixa Catalunya, for example, lied about the conditions of these controversial products, trapping thousands of small savers in this way (*El País* 2014). Industry-wide, the practice was a "mass fraud" that the government rec-ognizes was "a mistake" that should have been prohibited or regulated (*El País* 2012). When Bankia and other entities failed, many pensioners lost their lifetime savings.

Preferentes has come to symbolize the fraud and corruption that led 15-M activists to argue that the crisis was in fact a "swindle," as the sales of *preferentes* reached their peak in 2008–2009, and cynically and aggres-sively targeted the most vulnerable. Although it was initially argued that these products were widely sold as investment opportunities, 15MpaRato (see Chapter 7), using anonymously submitted documentation, pre-sented evidence to the courts that in the case of Bankia (potentially one of the largest cases of banking fraud in Spain's history), the products were sold only to small savers, and not a single share was sold to other banks or any large financial companies. According to this evidence, the money taken from these small savers was then used to pay off the banks' large debts.[1]

Mari Rubia explained her reason for being in the Puerta del Sol:

> I have always been a fighter, ever since I left to work in Australia with my husband many years ago. They took all our money and said they were moving it from a fixed rate to a preferential rate because we were such good clients and had been with the bank for so many years. Then Bankia went under and all our savings are gone. But Bankia belongs to the state now, and they won't give us our money back. They don't want to hear us. We have made these costumes to be seen, because we are invisible. But I don't just come to the protest today for this reason. I go to all the 15-M protests, because all of it concerns me.

IMAGE 6.2 *Preferentes* protester in the Puerta del Sol, Madrid 2013.

As we finished our chat, Mari Rubia told me that a group of people affected by Bankia's fraud meet twice a week in front of the Bankia branch on Alcalá (right next to the Puerta del Sol), and that I should come by.

A few days later I arrived at the Bankia branch office on Alcalá, where a group of old-age pensioners were making a racket with whistles and chants, holding signs with slogans such as "Bankia steals from its clients" and "PP + Bankia = Stealing from Old People. Give us back our money." There I met three pensioners who explained to me why they were there and would keep going there as long as they could manage it. Felipe, Juan, and Iván told me their stories:

(Felipe) It is obvious that it was a total scam, a total scam! And so many people were taken in by it. . . . We've been through so much, so much, so that in the future we wouldn't have to go through hardships. And because of the trust that we had in the banks, they said "Hey! We've got this product" . . . and they call you one day and then they call you another day and then they call you again until finally you went down there . . .

(Juan) They got me in May 2009 . . .

(Felipe) I had these things called Caja Madrid Bonds, and I was getting 3% and they had €60,000 of mine, which is what they scammed off me, you know? The branch director of the branch on Marqués de Corbera 59 called me, saying, "Felipe! There's this really great thing that's come out and we're going to give you 7%, and listen this is something that's really good and really safe, come down here and we are going to fix it up for you. All these little words, everything was fantastic, just like in Wonderland you know? And then look what it was. My wife and I went down. I'm blind and I can hardly see, just enough to get around [. . .] imagine for me to read all those papers that they gave us. My wife doesn't understand anything about these things, she only understands saving. In her whole life, if she had to buy something that cost five, well she'd get by with something that cost three, always, always saving so that—

(Iván)—denying yourself so many things because you think after 30 years—and you say to yourself, our life is coming to an end, and then you find yourself like this, being deceived in this way—

(Felipe) I came to Madrid in 1960 when I was 26, I got married in 63, and I started off with this account in 1965, and each month 100 pesetas would go in it, and the next month another 100, and the next month I'd have to take them out again, and so on, you know?

(Iván) Life was very hard in the 60s here in Madrid. I started working in 1962 and I earned 250 pesetas a month and I had to make a lot of sacrifices. . . we gave up so many things in our youth to save for our old age, and now . . .

All the *preferentes* victims I spoke to were very clear about the fact that they were specifically targeted. As Felipe explained:

I never went to anybody asking whether they could give me higher interests. I think that, as you can see, all you can see around you here are old people. People who had been saving for their retirement, for their old age and with their savings in the same account all that time. [. . .] It was a total scam . . . [. . .]

(Iván) They would call up and talk to my wife and ask her when I would be home. They would call and call.

(Felipe) The Spanish government tried to tell the European Union that we weren't savers, we were investors—they actually called us investors! "Yes, yes, they are not savers, they are investors and the stock market has dropped! When the stocks rise again, they'll be able to make back what they lost!" We are not investors, we are savers! I don't think that there will ever again be savers like the ones they scammed, because there are millions in the bank from all these old savers—

(Iván) No there never will be, first of all because people have a different mentality today and their life is different—people can't save! They don't even have enough to eat!

Despite their own losses, they immediately turned to their concern for the younger generation:

(Iván) If they make €500–€600, they don't even make enough to eat, and a lot of people would be happy with those salaries, because they are unemployed [. . .] people used to work long hours and they'd say "Well, I'm going to save for tomorrow" and now they can't say that, they cannot save.

From victims to activists

Felipe discovered the *preferentes* protest group when he went to get new eyeglasses, whereas Juan found out about them by watching TV. The group has no weekly assembly, nor do they communicate online, they just show up once or twice a week at the agreed time. As Iván explained:

> On Thursdays we go around protesting. We just decide on the fly what we are going to do, whoever is here just says OK let's go down Gran Vía, or around Sol, or wherever; we meet and whatever needs to happen happens, there is no one who leads anyone else—well, you can see what we look like, we are not people who look like leaders of anything.

Felipe's outrage doesn't only relate to his own situation, which is why he, like Mari Rubia, doesn't only protest against *preferentes* and Bankia:

> I go to all the 15-M protests because I think it's outrageous what they're doing—all the crap with housing that's so expensive, but people have to have somewhere to live! People will never be able to pay that in their whole lives, and the minute one or the other loses their job, then the whole family goes under, because it's not just them, they drag their parents down with them, because how could any parent leave their kids in that situation?

Both Felipe and Iván are aware of the cases brought against Rodrigo Rato, former director of Bankia, and demonstrate their disgust at the revolving door between economic and political elites in Spain:

> (Iván) There's a son of a whore if ever there was one! The 15-M people went against him, saying that he couldn't get away with it, mentioning the *preferentes* case, and there he was making a big celebration with the bells [Rato sounded the bell for trading to open when Bankia went public],[2] and it turns out that he had a humongous hole in the banks accounts, you know? It was this huge fraud! [. . .] But then, of course, he gets out of that and he goes

over to Telefónica! Turns out some people can have really amazing careers—

(Felipe)—and now they're offering him a position at Santander!

(Iván) It is a total outrage, they have no shame.

(Felipe) It's all a mockery. It's a mockery of the people what these scum (*gentuza*) are doing, [. . .] they just look out for their own. Everybody else can just go die. . . and all of this with the consent of the Bank of Spain, they authorized this!

I later met Ramón, another victim of *preferentes*, who told me,

I was scammed by Rato, "the guy with the bell," only in my case it wasn't much, 3,000 euros. But you know, why did they promise me anything? I will never forget it. The sub-director of the bank called me! I don't know why. So, I went down there and she said, "Why do you have this money sitting here if it isn't doing anything?" And I said, "Well, we might need it for a vacation." And she said, "Well, you won't need all of it, at least put two or three thousand in here" and me, who hasn't got a fucking clue, believed her. She said, "This gives dividends every year!" and I never saw my money again.

As we were speaking, a truck full of people with union banners from CCOO (Comisiones Obreras, or Workers Commissions) and UGT (Unión General de Trabajadores, or General Union of Workers) pulled up and began protesting against pension cuts. Ramón told me he quit the union after 45 in disgust at their lack of support for the workers, and criticizes them for showing up to protest without joining the *preferentes* demands on the pension issue: "Why don't they [say] something like "Give back the money!" or "Pay me my pension and give us back our savings." He broke off and joins the crowd yelling "Chorizos!" (Sausages, slang for thieves) as a black limousine pulls up to the ministry, after which he continued his story:

It was something to help with my pension, so that in the last years of my life . . . but I retired, and they scammed me [. . .] and now I find each day with my pension I can buy less food and fewer things. And it comes to a point where . . . when winter comes what will we do about heating? We are going to have to stay in bed to keep warm because we won't be able to pay the heating, look what they have brought us to. If they stole our savings, [it's because] they allow it (indicating the ministry), the same people in there cutting our pensions, they allow it [. . .] They have no shame and there is no name for them.

After the pension protest died down, the *preferentes* regrouped further down the street. I saw Mari Rubia chatting calmly to the Channel 4 journalist and news anchor on the monitor while she waited to go live. As she spoke, she radiated dignity and the force of her convictions. In this leaderless group, she speaks for all the pensioners who surround her, demanding reparations and bearing witness against those who, as the evidence presented to court suggests, cynically colluded to rob them of their life savings.

Two weeks later, Mari Rubia welcomed me into her home, inviting me into the kitchen, where her husband Federico joined us. Mari Rubia started working at age 14, Federico at 11. Their *preferentes* story is the same as the others: aggressive targeting, false claims, and the loss of a lifetime's savings. Mari Rubia's political awakening did not come through 15-M, but as a union organizer for immigrant workers, where she advocated for women workers' rights and fair treatment within the union, as well as leading the first strike of catering workers in the Royal Melbourne Hospital. When she returned to Spain in the late 1970s, she was eager to put her skills to use, but found it very difficult to participate in the unions and parties of the time:

We came with really high hopes [. . .] but we came up against the bureaucracy of the unions, the political parties [. . .] I consider myself a worker of the world. [. . .] When we were mobilizing in the unions in Australia, we did it in everybody's name, and that's something I will never forgive the Communist Party of Spain, because for them we had to be exclusively fighting for Spanish people and only addressing Spanish people's problems.

The open and anti-identitarian spirit of 15-M embodies more closely her approach to a politics based on mutual solidarity and a recognition of crosscutting systemic problems. They see the current evolution of the 15-M and particularly the Citizen Tides (*Mareas Ciudadanas*) as reflecting

some of the earlier barriers to participation and change by being too focused on sectorial groups and issues:

> The Citizen Tides divide people. Take the example of *preferentes*.
> We get together in Sol every Tuesday and Thursday and we make as
> much of a ruckus as we possibly can. We cut traffic because it's the
> only form of protest that we have. Because we have already written
> to the prime minister, to the king, to the European Economic
> Community, to the public defenders, and all of them admit that
> it's a scam, but there it is. The banks are the banks. And they put
> the banks before people. And imagine if I thought, "Oh *preferentes*
> is our issue," and education, healthcare and all the rest weren't our
> concern. [. . .] Let's make a circle where we all can form part of it!
> Let's more of us take to the streets.

Mari Rubia's analysis of the impact of the crisis and austerity demonstrates comprehensive insight and compassion for those hit even harder
than her family, highlighting the connections between housing evictions,
government cuts, and human suffering:

> The *preferentes* has hurt me badly, you know? Because that was
> our life savings. But I don't think that is as horrible as having your
> home taken away, to be thrown out onto the streets with your chil-
> dren, and not know where to go. You become completely uprooted,
> you can't even put your children in school because you don't have
> a home.

For Mari Rubia the strength of 15-M lay in the united front it presents and
its cross-generational solidarity:

> Before 15-M we would always complain at all the protests that
> we organized—where are all the youth? And this time the youth
> responded, "Here we are." For me that was wonderful.

Mari Rubia thinks the return to the neighborhoods after Acampada Sol
hasn't stopped people mobilizing in 15-M assemblies, but it has been difficult to coordinate, due to the size of the city and the inability of the APM
to coordinate. Nevertheless, she feels it is still going strong, especially

the connections between 15-M and the PAH (Chapter 8) which has transformed the latter:

> The (local) PAH is working really well, and that is thanks to the 15-M here in Vallecas. Whenever there are evictions, most of the people who go are members of the PAH who have been affected (by mortgage debt), but there are also a lot of people from 15-M, young people who confront the police.

Mari Rubia and her husband came into contact with the *preferentes* protests through their involvement with the Association to Reclaim Historical Memory (reparations for Franco's victims), and she describes their action repertoire, which they share with the PAH:

> We made those little green outfits to call attention to ourselves, and then we decided to go and occupy banks and close down the branch offices. We divided up into groups and would go around closing down the branch offices so that they would suffer losses and wouldn't be able to work in the mornings. So that they would take us into consideration. One person goes in first and everybody else waits outside. Then everybody goes in together. We do the same things to protest the evictions. If the bank director doesn't want to pay attention to somebody, then lots of people from the platform go together and we make them listen to that person.

The *preferentes* group works very spontaneously, never planning what they will do ahead of time, just deciding once they are together:

> When we found out Rato had to declare at the National High Court we all went down there. And Blesa, they put them in jail and then they forced the judge to set them free. That's how justice works here. . . . So, we find things out on TV or on the Internet or whatever and we go. We stand in front of the National High Court and we blow whistles, or we throw things at them, whatever we can think of in that moment. A little while ago one of the ones who has been charged left the High Court on foot and we followed him and he tried to take a taxi and we opened the door of the taxi and we wouldn't let him get in and the police came right away. They are the people the police protect. They don't understand the drama

that we're living through, because we have families . . . I mean *blind* people, how could they possibly have read and signed those contracts if they weren't given to them in braille? People who don't even know how to read or write and have even signed with their fingerprints! I mean really cruel cases. . . . People who are 90 years old! Some of the *preferentes* protesters have to walk with canes!

Their belief in the need for solidarity (ethically and strategically) leads them to try to influence other protesters affected by *preferentes*, as Federico explains:

Some of the *preferentes* are only there because of their own case, they don't have a consciousness of struggle and of defending pensions, schools, healthcare and so on—they're not used to that. So, they think that their problem is the only one that they need to fight for. [. . .] And they even think "nobody helps us." You know what? What you have to do is help yourself, and if you want solidarity what you have to do is show solidarity, understand? And then you will have help and solidarity from other movements [. . .] but we tell them every time, there is a protest about healthcare, there is a protest about education, and bit by bit, some of them are starting to go.

Their belief in the crosscutting nature of issues has led them to be highly active in diverse spaces within the movement. Federico was attending the preparatory meetings for the 23N 2013 protest against the bank bailouts, which was meeting in the locale of Ecologistas en Acción, and regularly supports the PAH eviction-blocking actions (STOP Desahucios), and both of them also attend their local 15-M assembly, as well as participating in multiple protest events across the city. As *Yayos* (grandparents), they also discuss *Yayoflautas* with me, a group they support but do not actively participate in given time constraints and health issues, although they stress that the *Yayoflautas*'s "door is always open, they don't turn anyone away":

The *Yayoflautas* protest because they don't have enough money from their pensions to maintain their unemployed children and their grandchildren and they connect that to all kinds of social issues, health, education—which is relevant to them for their grandchildren. In other words, they protest about everything. All of those things that concern them from the perspective of older people.

The way Mari Rubia frames the *Yayoflautas*'s demand for pensions is very revealing: they're not asking for the pensions for themselves, but rather demanding pensions so that they can take care of their children and their grandchildren, and then broadening that demand to wider social issues. The support of *Yayoflautas* for the youth is reciprocated: as a popular activist youth slogan puts it, "When I grow up, I want to be a *Yayoflauta*."

Their commitment to the movement, however, does not preclude believing in an electoral option, which they feel is needed for system change. At the time of the interview (2013), neither Podemos nor Ahora Madrid had yet emerged, and they believed that the best existing option was to support was IU, though with little enthusiasm, because "[t]his government will go and another government will come, but this unjust system will continue." Mari Rubia summed up her attitude:

> I don't think the people in 15-M are really up for creating a political party. But I also think that if we don't have a party within the institutions to defend us and to try to transmit what people on the street think, then how are we going to do it? We can have 50,000 protests, we can read 50,000 manifestos, but it won't change.

Mari Rubia laments the "eternal division" in the Left: "Federico and I squeeze our brains dry trying to figure out how we can get all the different groups together," and she contrasts it with the party discipline of the Right, "who always vote," before turning to her negative opinion of the majority unions and parties:

> Yesterday CCOO and UGT were at the protest, but they've never come to stand with us when we are protesting against Bankia, even though we have asked them to do so repeatedly. And the only thing that the Socialist Party has ever done is to get us passes to enter into Congress on the day that they were debating our cause. IU is with us 100%, they argued that we should be reimbursed directly, and all the parties voted in favor except for the Popular Party. And when the guy from the Popular Party came out to try to defend their position, you should've seen us! They threw us out immediately because the guy couldn't even speak. They are allowed to say all the outrageous things they want, but the citizens can't even open their mouths. And the PSOE was in government

when the *preferentes* were sold. The Bank of Spain is the biggest guilty party of all. Because they needed to be vigilant. They knew that that product was not for small savers. There are [loads of] documents that state clearly that [*preferentes*] was only for investors. Investors were given three days to get all their money out before the crash, but nobody told us anything.

Mari Rubia ties the revolving door to the democratic deficit (the citizens who have no voice), and connects the legitimation crisis of representative democracy to the priorities of neoliberal capitalism (i.e., the banks). She and her husband reflect much of the spirit and practice of 15-M: a commitment to protest; participation in multiple movement spaces; solidarity with and support of others who are suffering, as opposed to exclusively focusing on their personal issue; cross-generational concern for the future; a critical and comprehensive analysis of the crisis and its political consequences; and critical reflection about existing democratic institutions, their limitations, and the need to reclaim and regenerate them.

In 2018, Judge Andreu determined that there was insufficient evidence to demonstrate intent to defraud by Caja Madrid/Bankia and closed the criminal case of the *preferentes* (Pérez 2018). However, there is a widespread understanding that fraud and deceit lay at the heart of the case (El País 2012), and many of the *preferentes* have managed to recover some or all of their money through the civil courts (Europa Press 2018).

At the time of the interview (2013), Mari Rubia and her husband were pursuing their case with the help of a pro bono lawyer who met regularly with them and others affected by the *preferentes* scheme in a local café. They were aware of and grateful for the work of "15MpaRato," which has done so much to further their cause and bring those responsible to account. I turn to this remarkable collective in the next chapter.

The *preferentes* pensioner activists are far from the tech-savvy youth commonly associated with 15-M. Yet they embody key elements of 15-M political culture. They share the same critique of austerity and democracy, and are integrated into the movement network. They build the movement by protesting issues beyond *preferentes*, and actively working to convince other pensioners to do the same. They are "analog activists" who manage to disrupt, make noise, and break through the mass media barrier without using digital tools. They too are 15-M.

Notes

1. Court cases against Bankia were presented by UPyD (Unión Progreso y Democracia), a centrist-right political party, and by 15MpaRato, and involve fraud and corruption beyond *preferentes*. The documentation related to *preferentes* can be seen here: https://15mparato.wordpress.com/2014/05/20/pruebas-estafa-preferentes/.

2. The report submitted to the courts by two auditing investigators (*peritos*) of the Bank of Spain stated, "According to the documents examined it is not possible to allege lack of knowledge, because Bankia had the necessary information, or was able to access such information to accurately value its stock" before going public (Otero 2014).

7

"The Citizens Did It"

15MPARATO, AUTONOMOUS HACKER ETHICS IN ACTION

We are going after the bankers.

—Xnet

ON MAY 12, 2012, close to the first anniversary of 15-M, Xnet published an anonymous post that was the germ of what would become 15MpaRato. It read in part:

> . . . Last year we created a cathartic [global]movement, an absolute scream that brought together all of our energies [. . .] Last year was the year of indignation.
>
> What we need now is something different. Our clear demands have not been heard. [. . .] dialogue is impossible. [. . .] Those on top are there to protect their privileges and destroy us. If we want this to change, we need to do it ourselves [. . .].
>
> How? By appropriating our life spaces and creating new ones. [. . .] The virtual world has created new forms of organization, of information, of learning and participating . . . in a decentralized way, in which by supporting each other, we can create a democracy in which we can carry out projects in a collaborative way. [. . .]
>
> Last year our strength came from moving like a herd. [. . .] The time has come to adopt a new form. The term *catalyst* in chemistry refers to small combinations of molecules that alter the speed of a reaction [. . .] catalysts amplify potency. They are an infinite number of small and agile groups that channel collective attention.

Democracy Reloaded. Cristina Flesher Fominaya, Oxford University Press (2020). © Oxford University Press.
DOI: 10.1093/oso/9780190099961.001.0001

There are historical periods that ask us to behave like a herd and periods where we need to behave like catalysts. [. . .]

We are going after the bankers. [. . .] None of those who govern us [. . .] are going to ask Rodrigo Rato to assume responsibility for the plundering that is taking place, whereas there are people in jail simply for trying to find a way out of a life of slavery . . .

Our weapons are our intelligence, affection, and the solidarity between all of those who have suffered the abuse of privilege of the infinitely rich, of the politicians and bankers. Our weapons are the transparency of the evidence [. . .] their acts will be revealed by citizens on the Internet, through social networks that constantly uncover what they are up to.

[. . .]

Greetings to the whole movement from the neighborhood of the Internet.

Free Internet or Barbarism! (https://xnet-x.net/para-12m15m/).

This dramatic philosophical call to action is an unexpected beginning for one of the most dynamic, practical, and sustained initiatives emerging from the 15-M movement. It combines Habermasian allusions to the colonization of life spaces and Deleuzian references to the multitude with a technopolitical vision of democracy based on networked collaboration, inspired by WikiLeaks and hacker ethics. It contains an implicit criticism of the localism of the geographically rooted neighborhood assemblies by saluting the movement from the "neighborhood of the Internet" and encourages people to embrace smaller guerilla type political actions that serve the common good, and which, when multiplied, will be more effective than the mass gatherings of the "herd" (which was useful "last year," but not anymore).

In this way, this call to arms contrasts with *preferentes* activist Mari Rubia's (Chapter 6) vision, whose ultimate aspiration was to get everyone out on the streets together, and also with the coordinator of assemblies approach of the APM (see Introduction to Part III).

This initial text reflects the political influences of those behind the 15MpaRato project in a way that the campaigns themselves, which are crystal clear, practical, and written in accessible and often very humorous language, do not. My discussions with Bea and later with Manuel, two core activists in 15MpaRato, reveal how this philosophical orientation manifests in a very pragmatic political practice.

As I reached the address in Barcelona I was given for my interview with Manuel, I pressed a buzzer and asked to be let in. A weary voice answered, "Next door." Next door was an unlikely looking rundown locale called "Conservas" (Canned Goods), which turned out to be a longtime activist establishment in Barcelona. Inside, a group of mostly anonymous activists[1] coordinate an initiative that has exposed some of the most significant political and economic corruption scandals in Spain after the crash. 15MpaRato's genius starts with the name, which is a clever play on former IMF and Bankia director Rodrigo Rato's last name, which means "a while." 15MpaRato means "15M going after Rato," but it also means "15M is going for a long while." So far 15MpaRato has not slowed in its intent to bring first Rato, and then other bankers, to justice for banking fraud and crimes against the citizens who have subsidized this fraud with public money and without their consent. 15MpaRato wants the money to be paid back, and in 2012 it laid out a five-year plan for achieving this goal.

Manuel showed me around the locale. The space has a backroom large enough for theater presentations, screenings, and assemblies, and upstairs there is a loft where someone is working at a bank of computers. We settled at a table in the front room, getting up often to let people in and out. I was put in touch with Manuel by Bea, a member of Xnet (a precursor sister of 15MpaRato), whom I had interviewed the year before. I had been following 15MpaRato since 2012 and was eager to discover their ideational motivation and modus operandi. What I found was that 15MpaRato comes out of an autonomous, free software/free culture project for net neutrality and against copyright monopolies called Xnet (previously exS-GAE) that predates 15-M by a number of years. Xnet was involved in the anti-Sinde Law mobilizations (a precursor of 15-M), and found renewed impetus in 15-M, particularly in the specific project of 15MpaRato. Manuel explained this history:

> What brings us together is that we share a certain way of working. One of the things that we really like to play with is anonymity, from the strictest anonymity which means that when people leak information nobody knows who did it so they can't be charged with cybercrime, to the idea of anonymity that fights against personalism[2] in politics, so that everybody more or less knows who's behind a

particular project, but that the project itself isn't based around a particular person or a spokesperson.

Xnet's idea of what they needed to do during 15-M's initial phase, namely dissolve their organizational identity into the crowd, echoes the words of Carlos in JSF (see Chapter 4) almost exactly:

> During the first year of 15-M, we were like "What do we do?" Well, we do what the situation dictates, which is to dissolve ourselves completely within this torrent and just be more bodies in this crowd; it's not the time to be here as Xnet. By the second year of 15-M, we felt it was the moment to try to set up more complex projects with a clear logic and very defined objectives, and we were kind of anticipating what eventually happened: that bifurcation of the 15-M [. . .] into different concrete projects. Because hey, 15-M is a political logic that is sufficiently potent to be applied to almost any area of politics, from the way water resources are managed, to pensioners, to housing, to everything [We discovered a project that was auditing the debt and wanted to complement it from 15-M], and we thought, "Hey, let's get right up into Rodrigo Rato's face."

Manuel echoed *preferentes* activist Mari Rubia's rejection of Institutional Left politics in his discussion of Xnet's political approach, and the strong affinity they felt for 15-M:

> One thing about our political culture is that we don't have that 1970s leftist militancy of the Communist Party type, where you're born into the party, you get married in the party, you go to the movies in the party, you have a son and you baptize it and you die in the party, and if you ever leave the party, it's this huge terrible drama. No, for us there will be 100 flowers of dissidence of little importance that enter and exit, that's what net politics is.

Xnet organizes around specific projects with a small core of people supported by the wider network:

> We don't believe in membership [. . .] The thing is to have a really concrete objective, and a very, very detailed plan—and certain people who take responsibility for making it happen, while at the same time opening it up to other collectives and other people to help out from time to time.

Manuel's description of their praxis combines the core elements of autonomous and hacker ethics: networked activism based on the collective intelligence and skills of autonomous participants pursuing action based primarily on the practicality principle (i.e., clearly defined objectives). Like most of the people I spoke with in 15-M, Manuel's activism predates 15-M and has its roots in the GJM, specifically the *Prestige* disaster mobilization in Galicia. That experience taught him that an initial explosion of mobilization based on "self-organized collective action" can give away over time to decline and burnout. 15MpaRato is fueled by a group of five or six people who are committed to seeing the five-year plan through to the end.

Bea described 15MpaRato as a networked node, a catalyst group that works "on the basis of distributed networks and federated skills":

We have people who are specialized in law, others in communication. . . . And they take the decisions on what they are experts in. Others might comment, add, or even have a different opinion, which might be discussed, but there is confidence that people are skilled, and they can work without having to go through assemblies and consensus constantly, so it makes groups much faster. [Assemblies] are slower, but they do have different benefits to them . . .and they all add up at the end of the day.

In the absence of a regular assembly, work is coordinated via "online calls, or face to face meetings, or work on the pads (Titan Pads). It's very organic."

Bea highlights the need for a rapid reaction unit with activists with specialized skills when the political objective is a legal proceeding that you don't control the timing of. She contrasts this form of organization with the PAH (Platform for those Affected by Mortgages) which relies more on an assembly approach:

The PAH would be an example of mid-long-term work. It's not so fast and it doesn't have to be, it doesn't have to be a small catalyst group, but [we definitely do]. After 15-M we decided we needed to create a separate satellite that is faster to attack the bankers, which would go straight to the chosen objective, which was Rodrigo Rato, and rescuing the money they had stolen from us.

Trust enables their work to be carried out autonomously along specialist areas and coordinated as and when needed. Bea explained:

> It's the work over time and the results achieved that is the basis for that trust, as well as the emotional connection that you feel. It's the respect for the work, and what you learn from others.

Manuel highlighted another element of hacker ethics that distinguishes it from "old leftist politics," but also from the logic that fuels some 15-M spaces like AGSOL and the APM:

> Internet culture has the 1% rule, which is something that is really very clear to us. You can see it on *Wikipedia*, it's kind of like the power law: in all projects, like *Wikipedia*, 1% edits, 9% collaborate at any given moment, and 90% use it. So that's another thing about leftist political culture that I just can't handle, this idea that democracy is everybody deciding everything all the time. And it's like, no, if that's democracy, a permanent Residents Association meeting, then I'm going as fast as I can to Vox (a right-wing party) to see if they'll let me in. [. . .] Or this business of "everybody's opinions are equally valuable." Our vision of democracy is based on a community where democracy is pragmatic. It's like with Linux: opinions are free, show me the code. Opinions aren't worth anything. If I take your code and it works much better than mine, automatically I will remove my code and use your code instead, and it will be the best news ever for me, because I'll have a much better way of working. [. . .] In 15mpaRato [. . .] we follow the *quien propone se lo come* philosophy (literally "who proposes, eats it," an autonomous maxim that means if you make a proposal you must be willing to follow it through with action).

Manuel's and Bea's commitment to collective intelligence and knowledge-sharing is not at odds with recognizing the value of expertise.

15paRato is the brainchild of Simona Levi, the most visible face of the group. Manuel described his reaction when she first explained her idea:

> I said to her, "Let me see if I've got this right. You're telling me that we're going to take on the president of the International Monetary Fund, ex-vice president of the Spanish government, ex-minister of

the economy, ex, ex . . . [. . .] one of the most powerful people in Spain . . ."

It was complete madness, but [. . .] fit within our political logic, which is based on scalability and which draws on a hacker mentality and not on a leftist mentality. Because the leftist mentality says, "What we need to do is do away with capitalism." Yes, but how do you actually do away with capitalism? [You need a more specific target]. [The plan was to go] after Rodrigo Rato over a five-year period with a super robust protocol, with each step paying for itself in the event that we would be able to progress. [. . .] We really had it all worked out in our heads, down to the last detail.

15MpaRato thought it would take them a year to gather the evidence they needed to bring Rato to trial. They launched a campaign on May 23, 2012, asking citizens to provide any evidence that would serve to put Rato in jail, using their secure Xmailbox (known in English as Xleaks, in Spanish as BuzónX). BuzónX is a secure way for anyone with information about corruption to make it available to journalists, lawyers, activists, and auditors. They use a Tor network to conceal whistleblowers' IP addresses. Only accredited journalists can read the e-mails in the Xbox, because under Spanish law journalists have the right to withhold informers' identities in court.[3]

After the journalists filter the messages, they draw up a fully anonymized report containing the information considered worthy of follow-up, which is then sent to a second mailbox that other Xnet members can access (Sainz 2014). Leaked documents submitted through BuzónX enabled them to gather the necessary evidence within two weeks. Their initiative was widely reported in the media, and with this another key motivation of 15MpaRato was also achieved: the spreading of the idea that ordinary citizens could take action and use existing institutions, even if those institutions were failing to carry out their civic duty.

By June 4, 2012, thanks to citizen input, the draft of the lawsuit was almost complete, but they needed to cover legal fees. Using another net politics tool (goteo.org) they launched an online crowdfunding campaign, reaching 130% of their target in 24 hours. When the original 15,000 euros ran out, they once again turned to the public for help, as Manuel explained:

We thought it was going to be more difficult, but in 24 hours we had another €15,000. But another thing that we did that was quite historic was to justify the expense of the original €15,000. [We put all the bills and receipts on the web, removing all the personal information]. That's not just so people can see it, but so people can actually audit it, because that's what transparency needs to be about.

Manuel is an IT expert, but not a coder or a "hacker" strictly speaking. Nevertheless, his political logic and networked political practice is influenced by the hacker ethic, which infuses a broader autonomous approach to collective political action. This is common in 15-M: people don't have to have any particular IT skills to be inspired by a technopolitical imaginary and infused with a hacker ethic and logic in their political practice.

15MpaRato's campaigns are not just about the technicalities of political action such as raising money or bringing a lawsuit. Like so many groups within 15-M, first and foremost they are interested in contesting hegemonic narratives about the causes and consequences of the crisis. Their objective has always been to transform the public's view of the Spanish crisis. The very first campaign "objectives" (and principles) that they published publicly made this clear, and the language picks up directly from 15-M slogans:

- This is not a crisis; it is not a divine punishment but an organized scam, and as such it has people who are responsible [for it] who have names and surnames.
- To put an end to impunity and plots involving governments and corporations.
- We will bail ourselves out with money recovered from the corrupt: the bailout must be paid for with the money they have stolen, our money. [. . .] (Xnet 2015, 7)

Their ability to break the mass media grip and shift public perception motivated them to keep going:

(Manuel) On TV the reporters would portray Rato as a victim of all this, but then in the bar, we would hear people watching the TV and saying, "He is a thief." That's when we realized we were working effectively as catalysts to change this perception. [. . .] They told us the banks were too big to fail, and so the bankers are too big to fail . . . but there is no legal impunity for bankers, only for the king.

Uncovering corruption

Ultimately, 15MpaRato uncovered a remarkable amount of corruption that went far beyond Rato and the fraud at Bankia. The lawsuit's intent was to demonstrate that Bankia was engaged in a scam, including forgery, manipulation of documents, and misleading advertising with the intention to defraud. *Público*'s headline put it succinctly: "The Bankia case was a massive fraud, Rato knew it, and hid it" (Otero 2014).

The lawsuit's intention was also to recover the money for those who were sold shares in a bankrupt entity that was later bailed out with public money, and for those responsible, starting with Rato, to be put in jail. Later, the lawsuit integrated the issue of the *preferentes* (see Chapter 6) and those who had lost their money due to Bankia's bankruptcy on the grounds that they were not informed, misinformed, or lied to. Leaked documents provided a key piece of evidence: an internal Caja Madrid sales-pitch document marked "do not leave this document in view of the clients" that demonstrated that small savers and not investors had been targeted.

Other documents requested by the judge revealed, after a tangled and complicated search, that according to the court-appointed experts' report, the financial statements included in the prospectus used to advertise Bankia shares did not reflect the true state of the savings and loan bank and the value of its shares, and that the banks knowingly did so (a criminal offense). In addition, the report from the Comisión Nacional de Mercado de Valores (National Stock Exchange Commission, or CNMV) proved that the savings banks involved in the *preferentes* scheme did not comply with Security Market Laws. According to the complaint, Bankia was already bankrupt when it was floated on the stock exchange, and those responsible knew it at the time (*El Boletin*, July 31, 2015).

In December 2014, Instructing Judge Andreu decided that there was sufficient evidence to proceed with a criminal case against Rato, leading to his arrest on April 16, 2015 (Badcock 2015). That night 15MpaRAto tweeted: "Once more to all of you who have helped us over these past 3 years: Thanks! #TheCitizensDidIt! Goodnight!" (*Mucha*, April 26, 2015).

According to two investigators from the Bank of Spain, in March 2011, Bankia's accounts (used to calculate share value when it was floated on the stock exchange) should have reflected a deficit of 864.67 million euros instead of the 64.16 million printed on the commercial prospectus used to promote the shares (Segovia 2015). On June 27, 2012, El País reported that Bankia was worthless—in fact, worse than worthless, as it was valued at—13,635 million euros according to the valuation carried out prior to its nationalization (El País 2012), which cost Spanish taxpayers 22 billion euros (Badcock 2015). Rato's defense team and the FROB[4] dispute these figures (Segovia 2015). On June 16, 2017, Spain's National Bank admitted that 66 billion euros of the bailout would not be recovered, a news item that failed to feature as a headline in any of the major newspapers on that or the following day (*El País, ABC, La Vanguardia, La Razón, El Mundo, El Periódico*). The court case brought by 15MpaRato led to the historic posting of bail by the instructing magistrate for Rato and Blesa (the former president of Caja Madrid) at 800 million euros (later reduced to 34 million by the High Court). The link between the floating of Bankia and the *preferentes* scheme was also established during the investigation for the lawsuit, as Manuel explained:

> When we first started the lawsuit about Bankia being floated on the stock exchange, when they knew they were bankrupt, we suddenly came across all these people who had not bought Bankia shares but who had been scammed by the *preferentes* shares from Caja Madrid (later part of Bankia), and when they asked for their money and couldn't get it, the bank said they would exchange them for Bankia shares, which they had valued at 300 euros and which of course immediately dropped to zero. I mean, it's like some kind of macabre joke. [. . .]

> At first, when we became aware of the *preferentes*, we couldn't make head or tail of what it was. We had a meeting in Madrid and there were about 12 of us trying to explain it to each other and we couldn't understand it. It was like, "well this is a really complicated financial product and because we're idiots we can't understand it." Yet some of us had an understanding of finances, of microeconomics. [. . .] It began to dawn on us, "either we are really stupid, or this is a scam." So we went directly to the CNMV (National Stock Exchange Commission), because if they authorized them they should know what they are. We asked two investigators from the CNMV for documentation, and [informed the judge].We got the report back, and basically, to summarize, it's a classic Ponzi scheme, there was no internal market, they just looked for people they could scam and with that money paid interest to other people. The minute people try to take their money out, everything collapses. That report was historic, because although it didn't allow us to advance the criminal case, it did allow for hundreds of civil cases to be put forward.

According to 15MpaRato, over 100 bankers and politicians have been taken to court as a result of the lawsuit, supported by citizen collaboration and leaks (Xnet 2015). But their work did not stop with the Bankia/ Rato lawsuit. An even greater scandal known as "Tarjetas Black" was yet to be uncovered. It began with the receipt of an anonymous e-mail stating that the sender "had a very important volume of information that would reveal a clear picture of institutional corruption in Spain." That it did. BuzónX, working with the X Party's Anti-corruption Commission, worked with journalists from *eldiario.es*, *El Mundo*, and *Infolibre* who analyzed 8,000 of these leaked e-mails and documents sent from Caja Madrid's corporate accounts. 15MpaRato managed to have some of the e-mails admitted as evidence (once they were requested by the judge through official channels). What the e-mails revealed, among other things, was the existence of "black" or opaque Visa Cards with which bank managers charged hundreds of thousands of euros for luxury goods and vacations, against the accounts of the savings banks without declaring it to the Treasury, thereby evading 15.5 million euros in taxes. But that wasn't all. The e-mails also revealed that 58 members of the major political parties and trade unions also had these black Caja Madrid credit cards: 28 from the PP, 15 from the PSOE, 4 from IU, and 10 from CCOO and UGT (one had a card but did not use it). The scandal revealed complicity between the banks and political elites to "loot Bankia in exchange for credits to parties and trade unions" (Xnet 2015). Deloitte, the auditor that "miraculously" never noticed anything suspicious in Bankia's accounts, has also been fined 12 million euros, but Bankia continued to use Deloitte as its auditor. In a communiqué to the judge explaining why it would be impossible to comply with a court order to produce evidence in 15 days, the chief inspector of the National Fraud Investigation Office explained that the Rato lawsuit included money laundering, fraud, and corruption, involved 48 companies, and required the analysis of 40,000 signed and stamped documents (Europa Press 2016).

The Tarjetas Black scandal also revealed that corruption in the political classes went beyond any left-right divide and encompassed *all* the major parties, including the left-wing IU Madrid and the two major trade unions, CCOO and UGT. This scandal in particular laid some groundwork for Podemos's later framing of the political class as "the casta," a corrupt elite that served their own interests at the expense of the public, regardless of ideological affiliation. (When Podemos later joined forces with IU, they were criticized by activists who were reminded of the Tarjetas Black scandal).

15MpaRato managed to maintain an important media presence that was fueled by the cleverness of their campaigns (with, e.g., photo shopped images of Rato mug shots with "Alcatraz 2015 11 23 59" beneath them), the strength of their evidence, and the support of the network of critical newspapers (such as *Infolibre*, *Público* and *eldiario.es*) that were the first to publish the evidence, later picked up by all the major national papers regardless of political affiliation, as the news was simply too big to ignore.

The challenges of transforming common sense into good sense

In its quest to convey wider political messages to the public, 15MpaRato, like all activist groups, ran up against deeply rooted common-sense arguments that sustain the status quo and contribute to political apathy. To combat this, 15MpaRato insisted on the slogan, "The citizens did it." Transmitting this message was the most difficult challenge, according to Manuel, and ran up against media conventions that want to attribute actions to established institutions or particular individuals:

> You know, if you asked me, "What stumbling blocks have you come across along the way?," I'd say that in fact everything has been really straightforward, because the logic of guerrilla communication is to flip things on their head, to change the field of engagement so that weaknesses become strengths. So we take their impunity, which is something really bad that has fucked us all over, let's take that and use it in our favor. [. . .] Because they put it in writing, they wrote about it in their e-mails, so their impunity becomes an advantage, because they've done such a botched job that in fact it's made our job easy, once we decided to do it. [. . .]
>
> We are not as defenseless as we lead ourselves to believe, and as they would like us to think. You know, this idea that we are never going to be able to touch them, because they always get away with everything.
>
> But what has *really* been the big stumbling block is getting people to recognize that ordinary citizens have done this, *that's* what's really complicated. The black cards were the scoop of the year, Blesa's e-mails were the scoop of the year, and the news media presents it like it's something that Rajoy, Montoro, or Rosa Díez did [PP and UPyD politicians]. Part of hacker culture is to get people to

copy you, and recognize you, and if they do, they double the value of what you are doing, but the media presents it like it has been done by [these politicians]. What we want people to do is to use this technique against lots of different targets. If we manage to [put Rato] in jail, but the message that people get is that this was something done by [politicians]—in that sense it will be a failure, because what we want is for people to know that unless *the people* do it, no one is going to do it. And what's more, we want them to know that it *can* be done. So this is the most difficult stumbling block that we've come across and what's hardest to take.

Manuel contrasts 15MpaRato's activist logic with the sexist personalism of mainstream media logic, and how this affects their ability to raise public awareness about people power and the crisis:

You know it's amazing; somehow, whatever happens, it was always done by a heterosexual male from Madrid! We are tired of playing that game—when it comes to the six most active people in 15MpaRato, right now you're speaking to the only male! That media logic that always wants to attribute things to an individual person is really perverse. . . . But our logic is not a media logic, it is an activist logic. . . . [. . .] What I want is for citizens to be able to have a comprehensive understanding of what actually happened with this crisis. I want them to know that collectively we can work together, and that by using the Web we can publish useful information that will help people understand.

Given how endemic it is, another difficulty lies in conveying to the Spanish public that impunity can be overcome: when Judge Elpidio Silva put Miguel Blesa in jail, not only was Blesa set free almost immediately, but the judge who incarcerated him was stripped of his office for 17.5 years and charged with "prevarication" by the Madrid High Court (Tribunal Superior de Justicia de Madrid).[5] Silva later went on to create a party against corruption and for democratic renewal called Renovación Democrática Ciudadana (RED).

Another widespread "common sense" argument that these activists are trying to dismantle is the idea that while corruption is morally wrong, economically it doesn't do much damage in the scheme of things, and after all, it has always existed.[6] Manuel points out that the real cost of corruption is not what is actually embezzled or creamed off the top:

> The best thing these people could do is just take from the public treasury directly, because that would be much less expensive. We should just turn our backs and say, "Please go ahead, just take your 3%." Because the real cost is not that 3%, it is that in order to get that 3% what they do is build a 500 million [euro] sports center no one needs or can use, and build it on land that is not habilitated for that sports center, and that is where the real cost is, in those 500 million that they spent of public money to be able to cream the 3% off the top. Generalized corruption also acts as a strong disincentive for investment, because investors are looking for judicial security, for courts that actually work.

As hard as it is to transmit the possibility of citizen action to effect change, they have succeeded in their goal to strip Rato and his colleagues of their impunity, and to reverse the mystique of the Spanish economic miracle, replacing it with an understanding that "the crisis is a swindle." In December 2015, the Rey Juan Carlos University stripped Rato of his *honoris causa* doctorate. A spokesperson from the student body said, "We are very satisfied and happy about this decision, because someone who has stolen from all of us can't hold an honor from this university" (El País 2015).

Manuel reflected on their trajectory (at time of this interview, Rato was still free):

> We've actually achieved everything we set out to do, and it kind of freaks us out. And people say to us, "Yes, but he is still free and he still has his money," but the thing is, in 2012 he was an untouchable that nobody said a bad thing about in the press. [. . .] Today he's a national joke and the Spanish economic miracle has been revealed to be a series of *chanchullos* (shady/shoddy deals). According to our roadmap, he's not supposed to go to jail until 2017, so we're not doing badly within our own plan.

15MpaRato and its sister organizations Xnet, Partido X (X Party), and the Anti-corruption Commission are proof that a few dedicated citizens, drawing on a savvy use of technological political tools and citizen support, can indeed change things. But their success was built on the fertile terrain created by the wider 15-M movement that they form a part of. The widespread support for the central 15-M demands provided the base for the 15MpaRato initiative, and the wider 15-M network supported them with important resources, including the critical alternative media network that broke the original stories into the mainstream. They drew on preexisting organizational and political cultural resources (Xnet, WikiLeaks, autonomous hacker ethics) to make an important contribution to 15-M's efforts to contest austerity politics, shift the public narrative about the crisis, and provide a model for democratic collective action that they hope will be a source of inspiration for others—not only in Spain, but around the world. In a reflexive distancing from 15-M's assembly-itis and "herd" mass gatherings, they embrace autonomous principles but dispense with the *asamblearismo* so influential in Madrid's autonomous politics, while still embracing the 15-M collective identity, which they see as an inspiration and source of strength. Like many other collectives in 15-M, they directly engage with state institutions to work on behalf of "ordinary citizens" who have been saddled with the billions of euros of debt that the bailout cost them. In the face of the inaction of political representatives to investigate the fraud and corruption associated with the financial crisis and the bailouts, they reclaimed the courts for justice rather than impunity. 15MpaRato mixed autonomy, hacker/technopolitics, culture jamming, and guerrilla communication to combat dominant narratives about the crisis—a mix reflected in the play *Hazte banquero* (Become a banker), directed by Simona Levi. The play tells the story of the cupola of Caja Madrid and dismantles the "rotten apple" by revealing the systemic nature of what took place:

> The plot that we reveal with the Blesa e-mails that led to the Black Cards (scandal) is the story of how what they call the "crisis" was created. (https://xnet-x.net/hazte-banquero/)

Their work continues, not only in the specific lawsuits they have brought against those they hold responsible for the crisis, but through Xnet, which holds training sessions on networked politics, among many other activities; the whistleblowing tool BuzónX; and the X Party's Anti-corruption Commission, which includes international anti-corruption campaigners and whistleblowers, including Hervé Falciani (the HSBC whistleblower), and hopes to fuel anti-corruption action around the world. They also played a role in bringing to light the financial corruption of the Pujol family, one of Cataluña's most powerful political families, another huge scandal in Spanish politics. The collective that rejects "personalisms" and embraces anonymity has succeeded in part due to their decision to personalize their 15MpaRato campaign around the figure of Rato, although for them he has always been simply an iconic representative of a systemic problem. As they themselves say, "Rato is a scapegoat. We want them all to fall" (Mucha 2015).

In 2017 Rato was sentenced to four years in prison and appealed to the Supreme Court. Blesa was sentenced to six years, but his criminal responsibilities ended when he took his life in July 2017. After losing his appeal, Rato finally entered prison in October 2018, one of the only bankers to do so, and only one year off 15MpaRato's target. International coverage made no mention of their role in bringing him to justice, but 15MpaRato has earned a place in the pantheon of 15-M legacies.

Notes

1. Except for a few spokespeople they remained anonymous until agreeing to a newspaper interview in *El Mundo* in 2015 (Mucha 2015).
2. *Personalismo*, highly criticized by autonomous actors, is a form of politics centered around a charismatic leader, and based on loyalty and commitment to that individual, rather than to a collective political project.
3. BuzónX works with some 50 journalists from the following newspapers: *Antena3*, *Cadena Ser*, *Café amb Llet*, *Cinco Días*, *Cuartopoder*, *Cuatro*, *Diario Crítico*, *EFE*, *El Confidencial*, *El Mundo*, *EL País*, *El Proceso*, *Europa Press*, *Gara*, *Huffington Post*, *Infolibre*, *La directa*, *La Sexta*, *Mongolia*, *Opengov.cat*, *Periodico de Catalunya*, *Playground*, *Público*, *Sentic Critic*, *Tercera Información*, *The Guardian*, *The Wall Street Journal*, *Tiempo*, *TV3*, *TVE*, *Vox Pópuli*, *WDR*, and *20minutos*.
4. The Fondo de Reestructuración Ordenada Bancaria, or Fund for Orderly Bank Restructuring, a banking bailout and reconstruction program initiated by the Spanish government in June 2009 that nationalized Bankia.
5. According to a lawyer I interviewed in Madrid in 2015, the political use of "prevarication" to neutralize judges who try to go after corruption cases is a recent but increasingly common phenomenon, and a symptom of widespread political interference in the Spanish justice system.
6. In this context, my mother told me a story of the early years of the dictatorship. The ministers' cars had special license plates reading "PMM" (*Parque Movíl del Ministerio*, or Ministerial Fleet), but since the ministers' wives used them for shopping excursions, everyone said the PMM stood for *Para mi mujer*, "For my wife."

8

The PAH

BUILDING A MOVEMENT WITHIN A MOVEMENT

I rob you. I bail out a bank with your money. You are left with no job and no unemployment benefit. That bank evicts you from your home. You video the police who carry out the eviction. They beat you and they give you a 30,000 euro fine for recording them and another 30,000 euro fine for trying to prevent your eviction. Demo-what?

—15-M meme

IN THE HIERARCHY of issues with the highest economic, social, and personal impact in the Spanish crisis, housing lies right at the top. After all, the collapse of the housing bubble lies at the root of the Spanish financial crisis, and at the core of its most significant consequences, including the bailout of banks sitting on millions of euros of toxic housing debt, and the mass foreclosures and evictions that have left so many thousands of Spaniards drastically affected. In the hierarchy of most universally admired and positively evaluated organizations associated with the 15-M movement, the Platform for those Affected by Mortgages (Plataforma de Afectados por la Hipoteca, or PAH) would also lie right at the top.

By 2008, housing was a key issue of concern for Spaniards (CIS Barómetro 2008). According to the Bank of Spain, the average price of housing increased by 180% between 2000 and 2005, with homes overvalued by 24–35%. Housing speculation, and the overdependence of the Spanish economy on construction, contributed to recession and deflation, which increased sharply after the 2008 crisis (Aguilar and Fernández Gibaja 2010).

Like a number of movements and organizations now widely considered to form part of the 15-M network,[1] the housing movement predates 15-M, but it was dramatically revitalized as a result of it. Concern for housing also predates the 2008 survey. Activists concerned about the

Democracy Reloaded. Cristina Flesher Fominaya, Oxford University Press (2020). © Oxford University Press.
DOI: 10.1093/oso/9780190099961.001.0001

over-reliance of the Spanish economy on housing, and the effect that property speculation was having socially, formed a protest movement for the Right to Decent Housing (*Movimiento por una Vivienda Digna*) in 2003. The movement initially consisted of a platform composed of numerous groups, unions, and left-wing political parties across Spanish cities. In 2005 a mass protest was organized with the slogan "For the Right to Housing. Stop Speculation" (*Por el derecho a techo. Stop especulación*). What was initially quite a conventional social movement took a significant turn in 2006 with the incorporation of youth activists who brought unconventional tactics and a more radical set of claims and demands. According to Aguilar and Fernández (2010), while this raised the movement's profile, the radical turn also increased internal tensions, reduced the possibility for institutional alliances, and alienated potential sympathizers through the use of provocative slogans such as "You will never have a house in your fucking life." Housing movement groups like *V de Vivienda* (a precursor to the PAH) consistently connected issues of youth precariousness with housing speculation, urban corruption, and the impossibility of home ownership for millions of Spaniards, thus beginning to link the matrix of issues that would fuel the 15-M movement. As we saw in Chapter 2, *V de Vivienda* strongly influenced the youth activist group JSF's aesthetic, slogans, and forms of action.

In the aftermath of the global financial crisis of 2008, the housing issue in Spain acquired tragic dimensions, in part due to the peculiar legal situation that regulates mortgages in Spain, a system that has not been significantly reformed since 1909. Unlike in many countries, bank repossession of a mortgaged property does not satisfy the debt of the mortgage holder. Instead, any difference between the value the lender receives for the property and the original debt is still the responsibility of the defaulter, meaning that people are not only losing their homes (after most likely losing their employment[2]), but also continue to be crippled by debt, significantly reducing their prospects of ever owning another home or recovering financially. However, this feature of Spanish mortgage law is not one that many people were aware of when they signed their mortgages, but only became known when the crisis hit and people began to face foreclosure and lose their homes en masse. In a context of easy credit, not only were people not informed of the consequences of nonpayment, but in many cases these were not even specified in the mortgage contracts (Colau and Alemany 2013, 15).

In the aftermath of the crisis, the key demand of the housing movement shifted: now access to homeownership was not the burning issue, but rather the inability of many who had purchased a home with the easy credit of the boom years to pay their mortgages, and for renters to pay their rent. Mortgages acquired in the context of the speculation fueled a housing bubble that had led to significant individual and family debt, which left thousands of people unable to meet their mortgage payments as unemployment skyrocketed.

It is difficult to get exact figures to measure the social magnitude of the housing crisis in Spain. The official entity that manages data on orders for foreclosures and evictions is the General Council of the Judicial Authority (Consejo General del Poder Judicial), which publishes reports on legal proceedings initiated each trimester, but only began to publish the number of foreclosures ordered by judges in 2012. These numbers fail to include evictions carried out without a judicial order, cases where homes have been repossessed in lieu of payment, and cases where families have abandoned the home from fear or shame prior to judicial proceedings being initiated (PAH 2012). Nevertheless, the official numbers are stark: Between 2007 and 2011 there were 349,438 foreclosures, and from 2008 to 2011, there were 166,716 evictions. In the first two trimesters of 2012, 126,426 foreclosures were initiated (Consejo General del Poder Judicial 2012). According to a United Nations report, in 2011 there were approximately 212 foreclosures and 159 evictions a day in Spain (United Nations 2012, 11). As Colau and Alemany (2012) document in their book on the mortgage crisis, these cold statistics reveal nothing about the human drama that accompanies each of the foreclosures that lead to the loss of a family residence, and from there in many cases to the prospect of a lifetime of insurmountable debt, social ostracism, and other mental health and social consequences.

In October 2012, 46 senior judges (*jueces decanos*) declared their unconditional support for a report presented to the General Council of Judicial Authority by seven judges critiquing current mortgage legislation, highlighting the abuses it allows financial lenders and the profound social cost generated by foreclosures. That same month, a highly publicized United Nations report on the right to decent housing was published (United Nations Document A/67/286 2012). The report condemned austerity policies for putting populations at risk and threatening further the right to decent housing, while simultaneously using enormous amounts of public resources to rescue financial institutions (United Nations 2012, 12). In

March 2013, the European Court of Justice decreed that Spanish eviction laws do not guarantee citizens sufficient protection against abusive clauses in mortgages, and therefore violate European Union law (European Council 1993). As the social drama of the housing crisis unfolded, newspapers reported on eviction-related suicides spanning all ages.

In contradiction with existing mortgage laws and practice under both PSOE (Socialist) and Popular Party (Conservative) governments, the Spanish Constitution (1978) guarantees the right to decent and adequate housing. Article 47 of the Spanish Constitution states, "Public authorities will promote the necessary conditions and will establish the norms to make this right effective, regulating the use of land in accordance with the general interest to prevent speculation." Yet there is an enormous gap between constitutional right and social reality.

As the housing crisis became increasingly visible, the PAH emerged as a movement that not only demanded the right to housing, but also radically contested the narrative of the crisis and questioned a democracy unable to care for its citizens. The discourse and actions of the PAH have been crucial in transforming the awareness and attitudes of the Spanish public towards the causes and consequences of the housing issue, the injustice of the existing mortgage law, the crisis, and even the legitimacy of squatting. By 2013, public opinion polls revealed that 95% of those surveyed felt that changes to the existing mortgage laws were urgent and necessary, and 91% felt that financial institutions had abused the good faith and lack of knowledge of home buyers by making them sign mortgage contracts with abusive clauses (Toharia 2013).

Like JSF and 15MpaRato, the PAH has paid careful attention to dismantling hegemonic narratives about the crisis and austerity and developing discursive strategies that foster a belief in "people power," encapsulated in the PAH slogan "*Sí se puede, pero no quieren*" ("Yes, it can be done, but they don't want to," referring to government inaction on housing and mortgage law and policy). The Spanish public became aware of the PAH through a video of the parliamentary testimony of PAH cofounder and spokesperson, Ada Colau, which was not initially covered by mass media but went viral on social media. Colau (2013) tells the story:

[O]n 5 February 2013 we arrived at the Congress[3] building, [. . .] to appear before the economics commission [on] urgent measures to protect mortgage debtors. We hadn't really prepared anything in particular because essentially we were just there to repeat what we've been denouncing and proposing for years. Nevertheless, something unexpected happened: we got there early and were able to listen to the previous speaker, the general vice-secretary of the Spanish Association of Banks, Javier Rodriguez Pellitero, [who] praised the financial institutions, declaring that their behavior had been exemplary, and giving assurances that they did everything possible to resolve all of the cases, including stopping evictions, and he concluded his speech characterizing Spanish mortgage law as one of the best in the world.

Obviously, words like that were going to inflame our passions. Our reaction was natural and intuitive. You have to be so far from reality not to become outraged in the face of such lies and offenses against the thousands of people affected.

When it was her turn to speak, Colau spoke the words that would catapult her to national celebrity:

To say these words when there are people who are taking their own lives as a consequence of this criminal law, I assure you . . . I assure you that I haven't thrown my shoe at this man because I thought it was important to stay here so that I could tell you what I'm telling you now. But this man is a criminal and that's how he should be treated.

As Colau says, "Who could have imagined that these words would leave the confines of this anodyne room in Congress?" Despite the late hour of her intervention (8 p.m.), the video testimony was picked up on social media networks, which were soon "smoking." The Parliament website crashed several times due to the number of people trying to access the testimony, and once the video got to YouTube it became a Twitter Trending Topic for 48 hours, managing to break through the mass media barrier and forcing the issue onto the national agenda.

As Colau notes (2013), her direct language contrasted with the language used by politicians to justify austerity politics and political inaction:

The worn out, empty, politically correct language used by the majority of our political representatives [. . .] used more to deafen than to communicate. [. . .] that hides more than it shows. A language that dresses up in technicisms to conceal a lack of courage and political commitment.

In addition to highlighting the power of social media to bypass and then influence mass media routines, Colau's story contains one of the key frames that the PAH has promoted, in line with the idea of citizen power promoted by 15MpaRato: that expert technical language is a powerful smokescreen to obfuscate concepts that can be clearly expressed, elevate the legitimacy and prestige of "experts" who hide behind that language, and make technical what is in fact political. Mortgages are a prime example of this. As Colau argues in the documentary *Yes, We Can! 7 Days in the PAH Barcelona* (Comando Video 2014),

> Presumably mortgages are very complicated, something only technical people or experts can deal with. That is not true. In fact, a mortgage contract is very simple: I give you money under these conditions and the house serves as a guarantee: if you don't pay me, this or that can happen to you. [. . .] "Technifying" political issues helps to depoliticize issues that are ideological. Should housing be a right or a commodity? This is not a technical question, it is question that as a society we need to be able to decide. [. . .] And for that we don't need a professional degree.

Colau and Alemany (2013) provide a damning analysis of the causes and consequences of the housing crisis in Spain that goes a long way to furthering the idea that the crisis was in fact a swindle, one of the central, recurring, and widely shared narratives within the 15-M movement. The system of experts acts as a strategic mechanism to elude democratic control, mobilized by certain political actors in order to distance debate from the citizenry. In this way, Colau links the economic crisis to the responsibility of political parties as well as economic elites. Characterizing bank representatives as financial experts without revealing their vested interests and their links to political parties is another way to confuse the citizenry. As Colau stated in her congressional intervention,

> We need to question the voices of supposed experts, who are getting too much credit today, if you'll pardon the irony, such as these representatives of the financial institutions. . . . They caused the problem; these are the same people who have ruined the entire

economy of this country . . . and you keep characterizing them as experts.

Colau and Alemany (2013, 15–16, 22) argue that the banks played an active role in creating the housing crisis, and that the "expertise" of the banking sector was accompanied by criminal policies, highlighting collusion between political and economic elites:

> The banks would never have been able to do what they did without the absolute complicity of the public administration. It wasn't simply a case of the state looking the other way or allowing systematic bank malpractice without any kind of control. It's not even a question of the revolving door between boards of directors and government ministries. The extent of the housing bubble in Spain can only be explained through aggressive public policies that fueled speculation far above our means.

Colau and Alemany provide a blow-by-blow description of the specific policies (deregulation, liberalization of markets, lowering of the Euribor, easy credit, etc.) accompanied by aggressive public campaigning in favor of mortgage debt acquisition that not only fueled the housing bubble, but also provided the fragile bases for the Spanish economic miracle that would come crashing down.

In their argumentation, Colau and Alemany manifest the discursive strategy widely used in 15-M to shift discourse from capitalism in the abstract to the concrete actions and responsibilities of specific actors, who have "names and surnames" (as 15MpaRato puts it), and can therefore be held responsible for those actions. They also link those actions to a deliberate democratic deficit that serves to place democratic institutions (through policy) at the service of elites rather than the people. They stress that, adding insult to injury, the failed banking sector has been bailed out with millions of euros of public money, which will be paid for by this and future generations, who will get nothing in exchange. Meanwhile, "the experts don't become scandalized by the *dación en pago* (write-offs) that are applied across the board to the real estate companies that made huge profits from the housing bubble and that now file for bankruptcy" (Colau and Alemany 2013, 25).

Colau and Alemany (2012, 2013) systematically show the discrepancy between policies applied to the financial institutions and those denied to individuals who have lost their homes in the crisis, continually tying their critique to a crisis of democracy. They argue that the consistent refusal of the Popular Party to change existing law to allow *dación en pago* has critical social consequences and an extremely high economic cost. Refusing to give families a second chance pushes them into the submerged economy and condemns them to "social death," violating human rights and increasing the strain on welfare services, making it "unsurprising" that 400 different city councils have supported the PAH motions for the government to change the law so as to stop the evictions and allow payment in lieu. Consigning more than half a million families to the rubbish heap and denying them the opportunity to participate in the economy also damages the credibility of the public institutions and makes social peace unlikely. In short, this refusal to change the law "undermines the very concept of democracy" (2013, 28).

From critique to movement

It is one thing to have a compelling analysis, and quite another to build a powerful movement around it. The PAH's organizational structure and philosophy are deeply rooted in autonomous networking logics, but they manifest the "democratic turn" (Flesher Fominaya 2015b) in their direct engagement with political, economic, and social institutions. PAH founders Colau, Alemany, and others come from the autonomous squatter movement in Barcelona and were active in the GJM, which has influenced and shaped their activism profoundly. Two key tenets of autonomy are a commitment to direct action and the idea that no one is going to do your activism for you, necessitating a DIY ("do it yourself, or better yet do it with friends") philosophy. For the PAH, this DIY principle is much more than a slogan, it is a core "rule" of the organization, as some of those approaching the PAH for help discover to their initial dismay. A woman who works in PAH Barcelona explains:

> I have spent a lot of hours manning the phones, and people will call in a state of distress, and say "I am losing my home, I need help, what should I do?" And I say what we always say, "Come down to the assembly on Monday and we will collectively address this issue." "No, no, but can't you just tell me what to do?" "That is not how we work. If you want to join us, our assembly is open on Monday and you are welcome to come by." They come to the PAH

just wanting someone else to sort out their issue for them, but that is not how we work at all.

The "rule" to refuse to act according to a logic based on *asistencialismo* (i.e., a logic based on service provision, rather than collective self-empowerment), is not only ideological, but also profoundly strategic, and it is key to the movement's phenomenal growth. When people do come to the assemblies, often extremely emotionally affected by their situation, a number of things happen. First, experienced members of the assembly, many but not all of whom have experienced foreclosure and/or evictions themselves, let them know three key things. The first is that what is happening to them is not their fault, not the result of an individual failing, but of a deeply flawed and unjust system that benefits others at their expense. As Colau (Comando Video 2014) has stated, addressing the deep shame and sense of guilt that many of those who have lost their jobs feel is a crucial first step in helping people face their situation:

> In the PAH one of the most difficult things we have had to address is solitude and fear, we live in a sick society, and one of its pathologies, and surely one of the most terrible, is the stigmatization of poverty. Those most vulnerable, those who have lost everything, on top of that need to feel ashamed for being poor. When the crisis started, the first thing we began to hear everywhere is that the crisis was the fault of people who had wanted to live beyond their means, that everyone here wanted to vacation in the Caribbean, that everyone wanted plasma TVs. [. . .] So of course we come up against thousands of physical and psychological pathologies, and suicides directly related to this fraud called the crisis. And fortunately the PAH has managed to begin to break with this, which has undoubtedly been one of its greatest and most beautiful victories.

The second key message is that if they are willing to participate in the PAH, they will never be alone in the face of their problem, and they will never find themselves out on the streets. And third, no one else will solve their problem for them or be as invested in doing so.

These three messages establish a commitment to the assembly that integrates people into the PAH not only for the course of their own personal experience with the banks and their home, but beyond. In this way the movement keeps reproducing itself, as those who have been supported by the PAH then go on to support others. Without this strategy, the movement would never have grown to over 200 chapters across Spain. It also de-individualizes the problem and establishes an alternative to the welfare/charity model based on horizontal collective self-empowerment. As Colau explains (Comando Video 2014):

> We generate [. . .] collective advice sessions. [. . .] We never see people individually. When people arrive at a collective space, [. . .] where there is no one up on a stage, but we are all sitting in a circle and people start talking, everyone realizes that what they thought was the complexity of their own case is in fact shared by others, and indeed that others are even worse off, this immediately has a therapeutic effect.

For the PAH, horizontal organizing forms serve strategic, organizational, and ideological purposes. As a member of the PAH Vallecas (Madrid) put it,

> The PAH has taught us that we have to reject welfarist models [. . .] we have to be conscious of the fact that the moment we delegate responsibility to others we become very vulnerable. The PAH doesn't delegate. You need to become an expert, you need to tell your lawyer what he or she needs to do, and in this sense you will never lose because the big change that you go through when you go back to your bank after being in the PAH is that you can look them in the eyes and say, "No, no, I know that this is a lie and I know that you can't do this." Knowledge gives you power that enables you to [. . .] negotiate in a much more agreeable way.

The PAH's motto that "you can't delegate in politics" (in other words, you can't leave it to others to represent you or solve your problems) later became one of the key reasons given by Ada Colau (and others) to shift from movements into the electoral sphere (see Chapter 10). The socialization of knowledge in the assemblies, normally the realm of individual "experts" or "specialists," is another way of implementing the logic of autonomy and hacker ethics, while transforming *afectados* into creative, empowered political subjects.

In contrast to the small catalyst group model of 15MpaRato, assemblies are essential to the way the PAH works. PAH assemblies are primary spaces for decision-making, the development of solidarity, collective identity, commitment to the movement, and transmission of the PAH's political culture and practice. Understanding the psychological trauma that accompanies home loss or the threat of it has led the PAH to also hold smaller group sessions with psychologists where people can forget about strategies and tactics and simply unburden their emotional distress about what is happening to them in a safe and supportive environment. In Spain's tightly knit families, the loss of a home often affects every generation. Many pensioners served as guarantors on their children's mortgages, and when the children lose their homes, not only do they and their children often have to move in with their parents, but their parents also face the threat of losing *their* homes to pay the banks. As Colau and Alemany (2013,13) point out, one foreclosure can drag up to three homes in its wake. And in contrast to the crimes of embezzling public funds or corruption, housing debt has no statute of limitations.

Key campaigns
Popular Legislative Initiatives (ILPs)

The PAH developed clear strategies to grow the movement before 15-M, drawing on their activist backgrounds and experience to do so. One of first crucial campaigns was to present an ILP (La Iniciativa Legislativa Popular, or Popular Legislative Initiative) in Congress. ILPs are one of the few legal participatory mechanisms available in Spain. They require great effort (half a million citizen signatures) for little return (consideration by Congress to debate the proposal or not). The PAH never considered getting the ILP debated as the key goal of the campaign, as they already had political parties willing to put it on the agenda (Colau and Alemany 2013, 33). Instead, they saw it as a means of making the issues visible to the public and of generating a shared timetable and consensus around the movement's key goals and demands. When they began to develop the idea, they had only 12 chapters, all concentrated in greater Barcelona. When they initiated the process in October 2010, they were searching for a means of forging alliances with unions, human rights organizations, and neighborhood associations, while maintaining autonomy from any political party. By the time they finished their campaign in February 2013, they had collected almost 1.5 million signatures and had grown to over 200 chapters across Spain. Setting out their tables in public squares brought the movement into contact with the people, following a Zapatista inspired *consulta* process that was used to great effect in the early 2000s by RCADE (Citizen's Network to Abolish External Debt) to build alliances and raise public awareness. It also gave affected people a way of telling their stories to sympathetic members of the PAH. Above all, the campaign was an effective way to mobilize members of the PAH, and to strengthen the movement from the inside, providing ways for people to become involved:

> It became the perfect opportunity to give talks, set up a booth in the local *fiestas*, or to visit the markets, the squares. [. . .] The affected began to organize themselves. Some prepared sandwiches, others took tables and folding chairs. In this way, little by little, the assemblies left the closed spaces and conquered the streets. [. . .] In this way, the movement became consolidated with each passing day. Each signature was a small victory. The movement grew. [. . .] It also served as a mechanism to form alliances with neighborhood associations, and the many neighborhood assemblies that emerged after 15-M. Along the way, a multitude of assemblies of *Indignados* ended up becoming parts of Stop Eviction! platforms or groups. (Colau and Alemany 2013, 34–35).

The ILP campaign was a key means of integration between 15-M and the PAH. It focused on the three key demands: (1) *dación en pago* (allowing mortgage debt to be cancelled by bank repossession), (2) stopping evictions, and (3) the development of social rent regimes (e.g., rent control and council housing). The ILP was submitted twice in 2011 (coinciding with the general election campaign), but it was rejected by the PSOE government, which alleged that the week before a similar ILP had been submitted by the "Ecopacifist Greens," a group that allegedly had never worked on housing issues and whose ILP was poorly written. In response, the PAH publicly called for a voter boycott of the PSOE and the PP, accusing them of bowing down to the banks.

This call for a boycott of the two major parties was framed as a rejection of the two-party system in which the Popular Party and the PSOE alternate power in government, and served to close the ideological gap between them as being two sides of the same coin, a key trope of the 15-M movement and later Podemos.

Following another lengthy process, in February 2013 the PAH presented another ILP to parliament with almost 1.5 million signatures, and this time it was the governing PP who refused to admit it for debate. Thousands of people gathered to protest in front of the PP headquarters, and the PAH launched a platform called Hear me.com (oigame.com), along with a mass e-mail campaign to PP members of parliament that they claim generated over a million e-mails. After intense pressure from the streets, the PP finally reconsidered and accepted the proposal for debate (they still did not move forward with the legislative reform, however). Members of the PAH in Congress chanted "Sí se puede!" (Yes, it can be done) while the Popular Party president of Congress screamed "Get them the fuck out of here!" ("Expúlsenlos coño!"). Colau and Alemany (2013, 43) affirm that "that night millions of Spaniards went to bed convinced that it was possible to reclaim democracy."

Escraches

The ILP was but one campaign within a series of actions undertaken by the PAH that combined engagement with banks and political parties with direct actions, including stopping evictions, occupying banks, occupying publicly owned buildings (repossessed by the SAREB "bad bank"; see below), and their controversial *escrache* campaign. The day after the PP rejected all of the ILP central demands in parliament, the PAH kicked off their back-up plan: the *escrache* campaign (PAH 2013a, 2013b). An *escrache* is a strategically high-risk form of direct action that involves a collective, public, and peaceful act of moral repudiation of individuals accused of perpetrating, participating in, or allowing an injustice. It is used as a last resort (when formal justice fails), and if framed in an effective campaign can be a powerful weapon of the weak against inaccessible and hegemonic power. *Escraches* are legitimized by the moral worth of the victims, who are juxtaposed with the moral corruption of the target of the *escrache*, in this case framed as uncaring politicians who refused to act on behalf of the citizens they purportedly represented (for a detailed analysis, see Flesher Fominaya 2015e).

Like 15MpaRato, this campaign personalized politics by putting names to the politicians who refused to act on behalf of citizens who were living through intense personal dramas. PAH activists would go to politicians' homes, blow whistles, and tell their eviction stories. Going directly to the politicians' homes transcended the boundaries of conventional political action and highlighted the discrepancy between the politicians' housing reality and that of those affected. The *escrache* campaign shifted social debate from the housing issue to a wider debate on democracy, with the PAH intent on highlighting the profound democratic deficit of the Spanish political system and representative democracies in general.

The campaign was effective in broadening the debate on Spanish democracy, but it came at a cost for the PAH, opening up a crack in their up-to-then irreproachable moral legitimacy, which members of the political establishment (with the support of the police) penetrated with a sustained attack against the collective, arguing that their "violent" form of action was illegitimate in democracy and even likening the PAH to the Nazis in Germany. Such was the legitimacy of the PAH, however, that despite the controversial tactic and virulent counterattack in mass media, they still retained a remarkable level of public support, dropping from 89% support in March to 78% in April[4] (Toharia 2013a, 2013b; Flesher Fominaya 2015d).

Escrache campaigns are risky because they can shift attention away from the issue to the tactic: in the wake of the rejected ILP, instead of talking about Spain's housing crisis, politicians and media focused on the legitimacy or illegitimacy of the *escrache* itself. Although the PAH lost some moral ground and focus on the housing issue, the campaign furthered the 15-M movement's challenge to the idea that representative democracy represented the will of the people, while strengthening the critique of the interpretation of the "crisis" put forward by political and economic elites to justify austerity policies. It also forged alliances with other actors in the 15-M movement.

The intense debate over the *escrache* reflects a broader social debate over the nature of democracy and the Culture of the Transition (CT) that fits with the decline in quality and satisfaction with democracy noted by a number of scholars over the past few decades (della Porta 2013; Feenstra and Keane 2014). The *escrache*, with its elements of bearing witness, highlighting politician's moral responsibility for the crisis and its effects, and demanding greater responsiveness to and participation of citizens in politics, is an emblematic expression of the wider call for democratic renewal, and the laying to rest of the CT (see Chapter 1).

Direct action campaigns

As with 15MpaRato (Chapter 7), in a context where neoliberal capitalism has devoted advocates with a guaranteed presence in mass media, "conquering the citizen's common sense" is an explicit and difficult task for the PAH. Contesting dominant narratives about the crisis, exposing the way the system works and why, highlighting the failures and complicity of the state, campaigning relentlessly for the right to housing, and finding solutions for those affected have been the hallmarks of the PAH's modus operandi. Each campaign slogan has focused on a particular facet of this complex task:

The campaign "*This bank cheats, swindles, and throws people out of their homes,*" involves putting posters and stickers with this slogan on banks that have refused to negotiate with clients having difficulty meeting their mortgage payments. The campaign has two goals: pressuring the banks to negotiate, and signaling that the banks are directly responsible for people's suffering.

"*Stop Evictions!*" involves a group of people physically blocking access to the homes of those who are being forcibly evicted. The most directly confrontational form of action, it managed to stop 600 evictions between November 2010 and March 2013, a number that increased to 2,045 by August 2016.[5]

When stopping evictions fails, the PAH resorts to what it humorously dubs *La Obra Social de la PAH* (The PAH's Social Work), a play on the term used by major Spanish banks that were bailed out for their charitable work. Now that some of these banks have disappeared, leaving devastation in their wake, it is the PAH who carries out the "social work." The PAH also contrasts its "social work" with the state's failure to offer families a solution to their housing crisis.

"The PAH's Social Work" (PAH 2016) involves individuals reoccupying the homes from which people have been evicted, and groups of families reoccupying entire buildings that are owned by banks that have acquired the buildings as a result of the bankruptcy of a real estate company. In both cases the goal is to negotiate with the banks and the administration to enable the legalization of the situation via a social rent contract (never more than 30% of total income, following UN guidelines). Targeted buildings are those owned by the "bad bank" or "toxic bank," the SAREB (Sociedad de Gestión de Activos Procedentes de la Reestructuración Bancaria), which consolidated assets from the savings and loans nationalized by the FROB (with public and EU funds), and whose purpose is to then sell these assets to investors seeking a profit, thereby socializing private debt and then privatizing profits from public expenditure. Under the circumstances, "occupation," formerly a term associated with squatting and widely seen as opprobrious, became, in the view of the PAH and its supporters, a legitimate reappropriation of public funds for public (citizen) use. By 2016 the PAH had occupied 43 buildings (although a few have been repossessed).

As a member of PAH Vallecas (Madrid 2015) put it,

> The point is to recover buildings and flats from the banks. [Since] all Spaniards have paid for them, and since we have the right to decent housing, well, we reoccupy them.

Building the movement

Sustaining a movement composed primarily of people who are going through an extremely difficult and precarious life situation is a remarkable feat in and of itself. Storytelling and *comradery* are a key part of fueling the movement in the face of small victories, but also many obstacles and defeats, including the suicides of fellow PAH members (and other people facing eviction) who have felt unable to keep fighting. The coining of the term *austericides* has been another way to challenge the language about these suicides, shifting the responsibility for them from the individual to the unjust and inhumane system that provoked them.

Storytelling to build the movement was a core goal of the three filmmakers who made the documentary *Yes, We Can! 7 Days in the PAH Barcelona*. As Silvi González-Laá, one of the filmmakers states,[6] "One of our slogans is that it isn't only important to *fight* battles but also to *tell* them because otherwise people won't be aware of what is happening." The film was designed to act as a tool that shows the PAH from the inside, offering a resource for others hoping to understand what makes the organization tick, rather than creating a documentary that makes an argument about the nature of the crisis or the housing issue. Pau Faus, another of the filmmakers, explains:

> After a year in the PAH we realized that what really defines it is the day to day way that thousands of difficult situations are handled, from preparing things the day before, to planning strategies two or three months ahead of time. This level of strategizing is what best defines the PAH, but what people see least.

The film doesn't focus on the human drama of evictions, save for a short opening sequence. As Silvi explains, the witnessing of an eviction provokes negative emotional energy. It is one of the reasons people come to the PAH, but also one of the most exhausting aspects of being in the movement. Pau explains that what they wanted to do was not only show others ways to mobilize, but also make a film for those already within the PAH, to celebrate its history and achievements, and to show that it can be done ("Sí se puede!").

The film is freely available, following a creative commons approach that is "very much in line with the PAH, which is all about replicability" (as another member of PAH Vallecas put it). Silvi adds,

> There are more than 200 PAHs in the whole country. How did they do that? By doing everything openly. If you go to the website you will find all the useful documents that have been prepared by the lawyers who are experts in mortgages, you will find the forms you need to request the *dación en pago*, and everything is shared openly. So this documentary is a useful tool for the movement that is open code, but what is *really* open code is the movement itself.

Silvi and Pau contrast the film, which was initially released for collective viewings followed by debate, with the shorter videos often circulated on social media. As Silvi says, "Sometimes viral videos on social media are very effective, other times they burn out. We think the film format [means] people should talk about it, often times when you just release something on the web, it creates a boom that disappears after two days." Pau adds:

> The idea of authorship in a documentary is absurd, we provided the cameras, (but) we are a mechanism of transmission . . . I think our merit has been to win the trust of the PAH day by day [. . .] We gave it our stamp and told it the way we wanted to, but we watch the film and still become emotionally moved by it, because we know everything that lays behind it.

Despite having a very different organizational form than 15MpaRato, the discussion of open code, replicability, and providing tools so that others can also mobilize in a DIY way, becoming their own experts, are all hallmarks of autonomous/hacker ethic politics that penetrate even a decidedly geographically rooted and assembly-based movement like the PAH. The PAH's organizational logic and political orientations draws on autonomous movements, squatters movements, right to the city movements, feminist movements, and the GJM, while developing a unique set of strategies and organizational forms that have inspired activists across Spain and beyond.

Critique and resignification

While the PAH is an important and exemplary case study within the 15-M movement, the privatization and speculation of essential human needs is not unique to housing but extends to the struggles against the privatization of, inter alia, healthcare, education, and water. The PAH's critique encompasses elements that are integrated in the discursive framing of numerous other issues addressed by 15-M. Note, for example, the similarity of key discursive claims in the argumentation of the Blue Tide (*Marea Azul*) platform against the privatization of Madrid's water supply (Canal de Isabel II), with that of the PAH: *Marea Azul* claims that water is a basic human *need* and *right*, a public good that has been turned into a *commodity* that creates *clear winners and clear losers*. The privatization of water has led to devastating environmental effects, and the *people have the right to decide* how a public good of first necessity should be administrated. *Collective action is necessary* and is at the root of citizen resistance to privatization. Finally, the platform provides a manifesto for a *democratic* management of water services in the Autonomous Community of Madrid (Marea Azul 2014).

The matrix of argumentation that connects multiple austerity issues across the movement connects these discursive elements: (1) a declaration of a good or right as a human right, (2) denouncing the commodification and privatization of the public good serving primary public functions, which (3) benefit a few at the expense of the many, requires (4) the active complicity between economic and political elites (democratic deficit), and therefore also requires (5) collective citizen resistance/mobilization and (6) democratic regeneration. In this way, anti-austerity and pro-democracy are not two separate components of mobilization, but rather the double helixes of the movement's discursive DNA.

Given its use of direct action and controversial tactics, perhaps the PAH's biggest challenge has been to combat media characterization of the organization as violent, radical, and anti-democratic. PAH spokespeople seek media engagement while maintaining that mass media "don't represent us." Despite the hostile mass media environment, the ability of the PAH to maintain the moral high ground, shift public awareness and debate, and force the housing issue onto the agenda has been remarkable.

The almost universal admiration for the organization within the 15-M movement (even among those who may disagree with the political orientation and strategy of the organization),[7] and the movement's embracing of the PAH as a central "15-M" actor, demonstrates the astuteness with which the PAH has built up its legitimacy as it has grown the movement. Like 15MpaRato and the 15-M movement as a whole, by refusing to see the human drama of those losing their homes to foreclosures and evictions as inevitable, and therefore acceptable, costs of the crisis, it wants to transmit a message that it is up to organized citizens, working collectively, to reclaim democratic rights and put public institutions at the service of the citizens who have paid for the "crisis/swindle."

Notes

1. When I asked interviewees to list which members of the 15-M network were points of reference, the PAH was consistently listed first.
2. According to the United Nations report on the right to decent housing, recent research estimates approximately 70% of foreclosures in Spain are related to the employment crisis (United Nations 2012, 11).
3. Congress is the most important and powerful legislative body under the Spanish system, not the Senate.
4. The wording of the question was: "Do you agree with these types of campaigns as long as they are peaceful, to try to get politicians to vote for certain issues according to their own values even if they go against the opinion of their party?" Popular Party voters dropped from 87% support in March to 68% in April.
5. Figures are updated and can be consulted at http://afectadosporlahipoteca.com/category/propuestas-pah/obra_social_la_pah/.
6. This discussion with the filmmakers and members of the PAH Vallecas took place in the context of an assembly and screening of the film in the PAH Vallecas (Madrid) locale, on January 31, 2015.
7. Some more "radical" squatters who reject negotiation with the banks and administration are not in favor of the PAH, and some feel that addressing people's individual housing needs as a priority dilutes the potency of political squatting as a mechanism of reclaiming property for public communal use. Others criticize the PAH for channelling people's desperation, arguing that they serve as a shock absorber for the system that enables it to reproduce itself (as opposed to provoking a revolutionary movement).

9

Indignant and Precarious Youth

No home, no job, no pension, no fear.

—JSF (Youth Without Future)

INITIALLY, 15-M WAS a mostly youth-led movement that had been mobilizing around youth precariousness. Their reflection on their own crisis situation led to the development of the analysis of a matrix of austerity issues that they viewed through the lens of democracy and connected to a wider 15-M collective identity across generations and issues. In this chapter I look at three different initiatives that mobilized around youth as a political subject: hunger strikers against austerity, Youth Without Future (JSF), and Oficina Precaria. Although three distinct projects, they are also connected through overlapping actors, issues, alliances, shared critiques of the crisis and democracy, and, above all, a shared sense of belonging in the 15-M movement.

Hunger strikers in the Puerta del Sol

On October 17, 2013, I went to the Puerta del Sol and discovered several mattresses placed next to the railings of "the horse" statue, a common meeting place for many protest groups. The mattresses were occupied by a young man, Jorge,[1] who was on a hunger strike against austerity and corruption and planned to remain until the government resigned. He was surrounded by a circle of people, some wearing PAH t-shirts. Others (members of different collectives) had clipboards and were speaking to members of the crowd about different social issues. As people approached Jorge one by one, and crouched down to speak with him, I felt I was witnessing a sort of religious ritual, where a holy man receives believers for a private audience. There was something beatific and otherworldly about

Democracy Reloaded. Cristina Flesher Fominaya, Oxford University Press (2020). © Oxford University Press.
DOI: 10.1093/oso/9780190099961.001.0001

IMAGE 9.1 Jorge, hunger striker in Puerta del Sol, Madrid 2013.

Jorge's countenance, his serenity contrasting with the severity of the slo-gans on the signs behind him:

Rajoy, making the people starve is genocide.

#Jorge's Motives: **Who am I?** An ordinary citizen. **What I am doing?** A Hunger Strike **Why?** For you. For me. Unemployment, Corruption, Evictions, Healthcare. Education . . .

Why am I on a hunger strike? Because I refuse to accept the current situation.

PSOE + PP = Savings thieves—Bankia Thieves.

Give us back our money.

Preferentes '09.

What achieves nothing is doing nothing.

A flyer with contact information and advertising a speech event the fol-lowing night read, "Jorge's motives are everyone's motives." Jorge spoke to me about his reasons for being in the plaza:

This is a drastic measure in the face of the drastic situation in the country, it's a desperate cry to try to make people react. . . .

There are many ways of fighting, of protesting, and the most common are the protest marches, but after so much time going to protest marches and seeing that the government doesn't listen to our voices, I thought that maybe it was necessary to go a step further, and this is the method that I've chosen to try to struggle.

Jorge tells me that he's originally from Bilbao but studied at the University of Burgos, where he was active in the 15-M movement and volunteered in various social projects. It was the Bárcenas (PP) corruption case that compelled him to come to Madrid:

I'm hoping this will serve as a sort of social detonator so that people will react once and for all, that we can all get together and simply ask for what is just, and for this government to fulfill the electoral program that it promised people. We all know that it's more of a mafia than a government, that they've received black money, that they've stolen public money, and they need to resign. I want people to leave aside the path of resignation and to take the path of rebellion in the face of the situation.

Like Carmen of AGSOL, for Jorge the post 15-M scenario is one that has divided into different sectors:

I'm not sure what the ideal solution is to get everybody to join together, but I thought I would try to come here to raise people's consciousness and to call for unity, to stop looking at what divides us and to focus on what unites us and to work together toward that common objective.

For Jorge, the decision to lift the camps and go back to neighborhood assemblies was a useful tool, but he also feels that 15-M needs to learn from its mistakes, which he identifies primarily as being overly concerned with leftist ideologies, people searching for leadership for egotistical reasons, and wanting to impose their vision on others. While he thinks that horizontal organizing is a good thing, he also thinks that the movement should have produced a political party that would have taken some power away from the Popular Party, noting,

"It would have had so much strength." He described the problem as he saw it:

> It's very difficult to unite all the different ideological currents within the Left, and a lot of the Left don't want to have any kind of relationship with power and are never going to support any political party. That's why it was impossible for an electoral option to come out of a consensus decision making process (like the 15-M general assemblies).

His position prefigured the appetite for the municipal movements and the rise of Podemos in the face of the continued refusal of the government to listen or respond to the demands of the millions of people who took to the streets after 15-M (see Chapter 10).

Alex, who had participated in JSF prior to 15-M, but had not been active in the movement since then, joined Jorge in his strike. He was inspired by Jorge's commitment, and also by a refusal to accept the abuse of the democratic system by the establishment political parties. For Alex, electoral

IMAGE 9.2 Alex, hunger striker in Puerta del Sol, Madrid 2013.

reform that would hold parties accountable to their election promises and guarantee transparency is his top priority:

> I don't belong to any particular ideology or movement or political party. I'm just an individual that supports other citizens. I feel close to the 15-M movement and to the Citizen Tide movements in certain respects, but not in all. I feel very close to the idea of a more horizontal way of government, [but] there are other things that I don't share. For example, a certain tendency to identify with the Left, the whole issue of the republic, I just think those are secondary things, because what citizens today care about—they don't care about what flag you're waving—they care about how much salary they are taking home, the education of their children, the quality of their healthcare, and I think these are much more concrete things that we should be talking about instead of flags and ideologies.

Alex is raising an issue that is one of the "eternal problems" in progressive social movements in Spain, a point of tension between autonomous and Institutional Left actors that the 15-M initially tried to avoid by rejecting all flags and partisan banners. Many people, like Alex, feel that reclaiming the Second Republic is a backward-looking, divisive issue, even if they support reparations and justice for victims of the dictatorship. In their quest for building a wide movement that will attract and encompass people across the Right-Left divide, opening the wounds of the civil war is seen as an ineffective strategy. Yet others deeply committed to republicanism see it as a central part of their political identity, and one that needs to be present as a crosscutting theme across all other issues.

In the absence of consensus, all it takes is a small minority to appear with their flags (of a party, union, or, most often, the Republic) to alienate potential supporters who might feel the crisis is a fraud, or be against austerity politics and corruption, but see the Republican flag as a "red flag" (pardon the irony) or a red line they will not cross.

The Acampada Sol and the early marches initially exerted sufficient pressure for Republican supporters to leave their flags at home, and in 2013 I witnessed a very heated confrontation between two men at a protest, with one insisting the other take his "damn flag and put it away (or else!)"—which he did. As time passed, the Republican flags crept back into myriad marches, offering a more classical leftist profile to outside observers and shifting the all-inclusive nature of the original 15-M decidedly to the left in the public imagination, reinforcing the old Left-Right cleavages the movement had managed to transcend in its earlier incarnation. As Alex argues,

> I am sure there are people who have distanced themselves from this movement because there's been a tendency to orient it towards a certain type of ideology, [. . .] and there are people who have other ways of thinking but are just as worried about the same issues, about healthcare, education, the minimum wage, etc., but when they see that [it is leftist] I'm sure it's made them decide not to participate.

While the Acampada provided a strong reference group and feeling of unitary action, once it was lifted the movement reconfigured into many different groups, often pulling in the same direction, but not always. While in many cases differences do not have any major ramifications, the issue of the Republican flags is one area that is still divisive and alienating for many people (on the left and the right). At the same time, those strongly committed to it have a right to mobilize around it. Alex's feelings about Republican flags didn't keep him from supporting the victims of the Franco dictatorship who were protesting on the other side of the "horse statue" a few feet from where he and Jorge were camped. Later that evening Jorge took the microphone during the Historical Memory rally and said a few words about the shame of living in a country where the victims of the dictatorship were still lying buried in unmarked graves. He finished his intervention with, "Long live the Republic," while Alex looked solemnly on, Republican flags waving. The wounds of the civil war still manage to cut through politics in contemporary Spain, a lingering effect of the refusal of successive post-transitional governments to address the brutality and injustices of the dictatorship, and instead to maintain the deliberate political pacts of amnesia that were agreed upon during the Transition (see Aguilar Fernández 2002).

Like Jorge, Alex sees his action, and that of other youth around the country who followed Jorge's hunger strike example, as a means of trying to reunite a 15-M movement that he feels has fragmented:

> We need to reunite around those common objectives that in the end form the basis of everything. We are the people, *they* are the Left and the Right. We are one and they are many. So we need

to act as a nexus and to show people that people with different ideologies, backgrounds, educational levels, like even Jorge and I have, that we can still fight together for a common goal. He might be closer to 15-M than I am, but we both share things like being unemployed and not being able to see a dignified future for us.

Alex's framing of "we are the people, they are the Left and Right," sums up the 15-M movement's transcendence of ideological cleavages through a populist discursive frame (Errejón 2015), as well as a distinction between the people and the political elite that would later form the backbone of Podemos's initial discursive strategy as an anti-party party (see Chapter 10).

Juventud Sin Futuro (JSF)

Seven months later, I found myself walking through the throng celebrating one of Madrid's most popular fiestas, San Isidro, which also happens to occur on May 15. Juventud Sin Futuro had invited me to meet them in the park for their direct action, the second in a year-long campaign called "Madrid Is Not a City for Young People." Antonio, my research assistant, former student, and activist in anti-Bolonia and JSF protests, was liaising with JSF members by phone so we could find them among the massive crowds. When we arrived, a journalist from Channel 4, which JSF has good connections with, was already there, chatting with some of them. Some of the JSF members dressed in traditional San Isidro costumes, the men adding a twist by wearing their carnations behind their ears (which women do) instead of on their lapels (as men do). Almost all of them were also wearing JSF T-shirts that read, "Youth Without Future: No Home, No Job, No Pension, No Fear." A huge knotted pile of painted fabric lay at their feet, and several of them were holding long wooden stakes. As they organized themselves, they began to spread out across the wide walkway on the hill in front of the Hermitage, impeding foot traffic. They slowly began to unfurl a very tall 35-meter banner that read, "Madrid Is No City for Young People." It takes eight of them with wooden stakes standing behind the banner to hold it upright. Meanwhile the remaining 12 begin to spread out around the front of the banner, handing out flyers and stickers that read "Never again a city without us" (in feminine plural) and "Madrid is no city for young people," and explaining the action to passers-by. They stopped to listen to their *compañera*, who took a megaphone and read out their manifesto:

> Juventud Sin Futuro wants to celebrate and demand that this is our city, the place where we grow up and live our lives, sometimes proud and sometimes full of anger. We think that what they have called a crisis is a massive fraud [. . .] Madrid is home to the largest corporations [. . .] and at the same time a city in which half a million jobs have been destroyed in the last five years. It's the city of unaffordable transportation, houses without people and people without houses, with a mayor and a president of the community suspected of corruption who have turned Madrid into the capital of the privatization of healthcare and education. But thanks to decent people, it's also the capital of the Green Tide (*Marea Verde*) and the White Tide (*Marea Blanca*) and the thousand social movements that have decided to say, "Enough!" and to reclaim their lives through democracy, and to exercise all rights through participation that goes beyond voting every four years. From Juventud Sin Futuro we want to make our small contribution to build a more democratic city and to put it at the service of its citizens. It's the city of the people (*el pueblo*) and not the oligarchs (*la casta*) [. . .].

The speech had all the major frames of the 15-M movement, but also incorporated terms such as *la casta* later widely popularized by Podemos. This was not a coincidence, as many active participants in JSF are very close to some of the founders of Podemos, and a number of them would subsequently go on to join the party and serve in parliament. Once the speeches had been read, the activists continued to work the crowd, cheerfully and courteously explaining their action: "Hi there! We're trying to raise awareness about the difficulties that youth are facing in the city, such as access to transportation, housing, and employment, so we are doing a year of actions around these core demands with different collectives to try and offer an alternative view of Madrid." People for the most part were very receptive to the action, often responding with phrases like, "No city for young people or for anyone else! No one can live here!" A woman in her 60s asked for a sticker to put on her car, and a man shared his disgust at the political priorities of the city, who "spend money on large football stadiums and big projects but don't take care of people." A young woman went by and said to them, "and then people get upset because we young people complain! Thank you, thank you so much for this." I asked Sonia, who had read the speech, how the campaign was going, and how they saw their current relationship with the rest of the 15-M movement,

> This is a long-term campaign that we launched on April 7 in the Puerta de Alcalá, and people have received it really well. We have had a few shouts today because, after all, we are sitting in front of one of the icons of the old Right in Spain! But were not going to stop making the issues and problems that young people are facing in the city visible and the lack of opportunities that we have.

One police officer who was speaking to Sonia as I was filming flashed me a peace sign, but was later joined by another officer who told me to stop filming. Since May 15 is the date of the anniversary celebrations of the birth of the movement, I asked Sonia what their plans were for the two competing AGSOL/APM 15-M anniversary events organized on May 17:

> We have very little time, some of us are going into our exams, and others have shitty jobs with irregular hours. So we really only have time to devote ourselves to JSF. At the same time, we have a lot of impact on social media, so we help promote 15-M, because all of those groups in 15-M are *compañeras*, and we have to support them. Some of us will go along to the protest or to the open days as individuals, but we won't be there as JSF.

JSF's decision to "dissolve themselves into the Acampada" during its month was time-limited. After the camp lifted, it reconstituted itself as a collective with its own identity, trying to use the momentum provided by the Acampada to recruit new members, who they personally greeted at the café of the Patio Maravillas squatted social center before each assembly, to explain the way the collective worked and make new members feel welcome. JSF used assembly meetings to debate, develop action strategies, and take consensus on their campaigns. The campaigns are developed once a year in a special all-day session that they call "refresh." In these assemblies they take stock of where they are as a collective, their strengths and limitations, and their goals and strategies, and, to a highly detailed and carefully planned degree, they plan their yearly campaigns. These campaigns include a central slogan;

a set of messages or frames; the aesthetic design of the slogans used on the posters, stickers, flyers, etc.; and a series of direct actions and how they will be integrated into their media strategy, which includes self-produced videos (sometimes with interviews, testimonials, or direct actions), Twitter and Facebook campaigns, appearances on television talk shows (usually on Channel 4's *Las Mañanas de Cuatro*), and articles published in the critical online newspaper *eldiario.es*. All of these campaigns are carefully scheduled ahead of time, and because of the limited time and resources of the group, they are not easily changed midstream. JSF's campaigns are the *opposite* of spontaneous—in other words, and they reveal the complex organization that lies behind a relatively small collective that manages to have an influence and media presence that does not rely on large numbers of activists. They work smart, plan carefully, and have focused and clear goals. The campaigns follow a Gramsci-inspired logic that has influenced the collective from the beginning, that of opening up gaps in the existing system and introducing counter-hegemonic narratives in a communicative "war," rather than attempting a revolutionary overthrow that will inevitably end in defeat.

JSF also integrates a strong commitment to feminism into its politics, following the 15-M practice of using the feminine plural, producing videos on sexual harassment and other gender-related issues, creating an online feminist map of Madrid highlighting all street names of women workers, and highlighting the gendered nature of austerity policies and their impacts.

The core of activists are university educated at Madrid's public universities (Universidad Complutense and Universidad Carlos III de Madrid), some in political and social sciences. In 2011 they wrote a book, *Juventud Sin Futuro*, published by Icaria. In it they explain the importance of their slogan (Juventud Sin Futuro 2011a, 25):

The slogans we chose "without housing, without jobs, without pension" defined the core demands of our manifesto, but we were looking for something more that could express [. . .] the right to dissent [so we chose] "without fear." [. . .]

On this point the influence of the *V de Vivienda* movement was very important. In a totally intentional way we wanted to recover their style and fuse it with our own [. . .] because [they] established a precedent in youth struggles for access to social housing and [. . .] began to point out the contradictions of the Spanish economic model.

In a chapter titled "Without Fear!" written by Rita Maestre (later spokesperson for the Ahora Madrid City of Madrid government) and Carmen Aldama, they develop further the notion of conquering fear and the right to live without fear as a demand (Juventud Sin Futuro 2011a, 59–61):

> The fear, the disillusionment, the malaise provoked by a shitty present and an even blacker future, can provoke rage and indignation, but can also generate apathy and egocentrism. [. . .] If to that we add the many years of ideological defeat and defense of individualism, the outlook was even bleaker.
>
> But it turns out that something was starting to change; [. . .] little by little, thanks to the work of the grassroots, thanks to an effective mobilization and communication campaign by JSF, directed to normal youth, those who still can't figure out why, but feel that their right to the present and to the future is being robbed from them.

JSF drew a clear line between *us*, precarious youth suffering the effects of the crisis they didn't create, and *them*, "the bankers, the speculators, the politicians who have lost their democratic legitimacy because they don't govern for the citizens, they govern for the markets." Against this "collective aggression" they offered a collective response on May 15, 2011:

> Together with tens of thousands of people we began to leave behind the lethargy caused by disillusionment and confusion, we spilled over the boundaries of the Puerta del Sol, and we left our mark with a banner that screamed: this is not a crisis, we are not willing to pay for it, and we've lost our fear of demanding a change of political system and economic model.

In the context of a discussion on 15-M and the Acampada Sol, they argue that recovering public space for common use is also a way to conquer the fear of "the other" and the hostility that is generated in a city fueled by an individualistic logic:

> In a city as hostile as ours, after years of destruction of the associative fabric of the neighborhoods, and the privatization of common

spaces, it's a historical fact that thousands of citizens have decided to disobey the law that prohibits them from gathering and camping in the "Commune of Sol" and have turned the plazas and streets into places of public and open discussion. Street politics are the best politics: when the citizens recover the center of the city, when we all lose our fear, [. . .] when the walls fill up with ideas, poems, and slogans. Madrid the rebellious, Madrid the beautiful, Madrid without fear.

Not surprisingly, the focus on fear has been central to a slogan used later by Podemos, "Fear has changed sides," since one of the JSF authors is none other than Podemos cofounder Íñigo Errejón. The close focus on Madrid also reflects the very localized nature of Madrid's 15-M network, a feature that represents one of its core strengths (in that it provides focus and strong connections between local actors), but also a certain limitation of vision and scope of action. Like the language and frames of the PAH and 15MpaRato, JSF has an emphasis on the commons, collective mobilization, and a reclaiming of democracy, but a stronger reflection of the squatter and right to the city movements' language, which reflects the collective's autonomous local lineage.

Unsurprisingly for a country with one of the highest youth unemployment rates in the EU (almost 50% in 2011–2015, surpassed only by Greece), JSF has a strong focus on the impact of unemployment on youth, which led to the creation of another political project that tackles this issue, Oficina Precaria.

Oficina Precaria (Precarious Office)

Oficina Precaria is a project related to but autonomous from JSF, and which shares a cross-over of some core activists. Precarious politics have a strong tradition in Spanish (and Italian) movement politics (Arribas Lozano 2012; Precarias a la Deriva 2004), and precursor groups that have been influential in Madrid include Precarias a la Deriva, or Precarious (feminine plural) Adrift, a feminist collective that theorized precarity during the GJM. The theorization of precariousness includes the idea that one is not simply in an objective state of precariousness, but one is also a precarious subject. This reflexivity pushes activists beyond a specific set of demands for labor rights to an exploration of the underlying construction of a subject who is living with no guarantees because of the flexibility

IMAGE 9.3 Members of Oficina Precaria, May Day march, Madrid 2014.

model of contemporary capitalism. The "precariat" is made up of subjects who may or may not be working and are mobile, flexible, and unstable. Precarious subjects pursue strategies to navigate their precarious existence, including attempts to create alternative means of meeting needs that were formerly met by either the state or the market. In this active sense, precariousness provides an impetus (as do all crisis situations) to create alternatives while developing a critique of the system that creates the precarious subject in the first place. As a political issue, it is linked to a wider critique of the hyper-flexibility of labor contracts in contemporary capitalism, which disproportionately affect young workers (under 35) and their resulting economic vulnerability.

The issue of precarious labor has been important in Spanish autonomous social movements since the 1980s and was central in the student movements in Madrid in the period right before the global crisis (Ferández González 2014; Zamponi and Fernández González 2017). The critique of labor from autonomous movements has always included a critique of majority unions—in Spain these are the CCOO and the UGT, which are seen as too cozy with government and social partnership schemes, too concerned only for their own members rather than workers as a class, and too reluctant to put their weight behind grassroots protest unless they can control them or benefit from them. Oficina Precaria's call to protest for the traditional May 1, 2014, workers' march reflects this:

> We are convoking a 1st of May march for those who don't identify with the large unions' call to protest or who do not want to participate in them because of how they are organized.

The critique of the unions' way of doing politics does not necessarily translate into a rejection of unions *in toto*, nor of their power to mobilize. As Carlos of JSF and Oficina Precaria put it:

> Hey, politics isn't the periodic table, it's not composed of pure elements. It's composed of tensions, contradictions, and processes, and [. . .] contradictory, tense and conflictual things happen, like, for example, that the unions are sometimes social actors of the first order that mobilize mass protests, and sometimes they are social actors of the first order that fuck over the workers! [laughs]

Verónica, another member of both JSF and Oficina Precaria, spoke of the large unions' inability to address precariousness:

> I think the role of the large unions is declining in importance: they are more removed from reality every day. . . . They insist on maintaining their power in sectors that were not affected by precariousness because they were very strong, like the industrial sectors, but those sectors too are becoming precarious, so they are holding onto the facade of something that is completely crumbling at its foundations.

The trend toward extremely flexible contracts and a marked increase in temporary work that acutely and disproportionately affects youth means that the traditional model of union membership organized within specific sectors and companies cannot effectively accommodate these precarious workers, despite major unions calling attention to the problems of precarious youth employment. Oficina Precaria combines the critique from autonomous, self-organized social movements of both the large unions and the conditions of precarious workers and youth workers into a collective that hopes to offer a relevant contemporary reading of the crisis and some alternatives to it. Like the PAH, which it explicitly references as an influence, it breaks with *asistencialismo* or welfarism based on a client or charity model, and tries to constitute precarious workers as empowered political subjects with rights and demands, as opposed to victims of the system. Verónica, one of the founders explains:

> The Precarious Office tries to break with the Offices of Social Rights that come out of autonomy (*autonomia*), because we felt that it was really too much of a client/helper relationship and we didn't want to just give advice, we wanted to engage in the political terrain.

She is referring to the ODS (Oficinas de Derechos Sociales) set up in many social centers around Spain as a form of social syndicalism, strongly rooted in autonomy, that seek to develop tools to foster processes of collective self-organization in the face of precariousness, but also work for immigrant rights and access to housing.

Verónica elaborates on the influence of the PAH on their political practice, particularly their successful method of building the movement through reciprocal solidary action:

> They really understood that they need to establish a strong connection between the people that are going to be evicted and the activists [. . .] Above all they're actually giving an answer, they are coming up with a solution [. . .] they actually offer alternatives.

Offering solutions and collectively self-organizing, as opposed to simply protesting and demanding rights, is an element of autonomous ethics that has evolved and strengthened within the 15-M network. The Oficina Precaria's ambitious plan of action never materialized into a sustained and powerful movement, but it included:

- Holding office hours in a central squatted social center in Madrid, where it provided legal advice on workers' rights.
- Working with institutions by contacting a sympathetic work inspector and providing him with anonymous formal complaints on abuse of internship agreements so he could pressure companies to hire the interns rather than face a fine.
- Facilitating and encouraging the creation of cooperatives.

- Direct actions such as the *escrache precaria* where they leafleted customers of companies with abusive labor practices. They have also done humorous actions such as the satirical "neoliberal tide" action, where they demanded bankers be freed.
- Media engagement both in mainstream and alternative media, with a savvy use of digital technologies and social media, videos, testimonials, etc.
- Campaigns that combine direct action with social media, using the same strategies and organization as JSF, such as *No más becas x trabajo* (No more work-study internships for work).
- Organizing workshops/debates.

Like the activists in JSF (many of whom are the same people), Oficina Precaria coordinated its activities through assemblies and held a yearly form of "refresh." In 2014 members reflected on how their precarious existence affected their activism, and this led them to do two things: become more flexible in their expectations of themselves and each other, and become more formally coordinated and established in their organization, by creating the role of an office coordinator who could make sure the office

IMAGE 9.4 Pablo Padilla (JSF and Podemos) speaks to the press, Madrid 2015.

was opened, that spokespeople for media appearances were coordinated, and other tasks. As with JSF, their precariousness means they are often not in a position to commit as much time and energy to politics as they would like. Following the eviction of the Patio Maravillas in 2015, they faced an even greater challenge: a lack of a physical space in which to carry out their activities, which were put largely on hold awaiting a new space.

Like JSF, the Oficina Precaria is committed to feminism as a core principle, and it adopted the 15-M practice of using the feminine plural, as explained on its website:

> All of the articles on our website are written in feminine plural, but it should be understood that we are speaking as much about men as we are about women, we are speaking of precarious workers [of both sexes]. [. . .] This small violation of grammatical norms is a feminist gesture that tries to call attention to the fact that women are still discriminated against in our society, especially in the political sphere and in the world of work. Because the fight against precariousness cannot be separated from the fight against patriarchy.

Members highlight the feminist critique that work should not be equated with employment, and that other sources of expropriation, such as care work, informal labor, and social reproduction are disproportionately female.

The Oficina Precaria combines an ethos that encompasses core principles shared by many 15-M collectives, advocating for a politics that is proactive not reactive, based on collective self-empowerment not service provision, framing political demands around dignity, labor, and social justice, and breaking from ideology-based politics to praxis-based politics by politicizing the everyday reality of precarious people. Its analysis of precariousness is connected to critiques of the crisis and austerity, housing, the right to the city, youth, feminism, and cooperative-based social syndicalism. Emigrant Spanish youth have set up other Oficinas Precarias in a few cities around the world, including Edinburgh and Berlin, which together with JSF influenced the creation of the *Mareas Granate* groups designed to highlight and politicize what their "exiled" members consider to be "forced emigration" as a result of the crisis and austerity.

Spain's indignant "Youth Without Future" faced the post-crisis scenario by demanding the right to a dignified future, highlighting the costs and consequences of austerity politics, and who bears the burden. Although groups like JSF and Oficina Precaria focus primarily on youth as political subjects whose politics connect directly with their lived experience, they adopt a holistic and interconnected perspective that joins diverse areas (education, housing, healthcare, employment, precariousness, and emigration) and identifies a matrix of responsibility and beneficiaries of the status quo (bankers, politicians, complicit media) against which they clearly direct their demands.

Groups like JSF, which influenced 15-M directly, have also produced a number of Podemos's political representatives and office holders, providing a link of continuity between 15-M and Podemos that is easy to miss unless one traces the groups' genealogies. These cases also show the transmission of influence throughout the network that connects diverse collectives, including *V de Vivienda* and the PAH. Narratives, frames, types of action, campaign slogans and key demands, and even aesthetics are shared freely across groups and adapted to each issue area. Together they weave an overarching anti-austerity and pro-democracy master narrative and build the movement.

* * *

I began Part III by arguing that seeking formal institutional or organizational infrastructures would not reveal the contours of autonomous movements. Despite the variety of specific issues and organizational forms each group takes, a shared matrix of critique of really existing democracy and austerity politics connect all these groups, from the pensioners of *preferentes*, to the technopolitical activists of 15MpaRato, to the assembly-based chapters of the PAH, to the indignant youth.

Although each group has its own identity, they all see themselves *and each other* as forming part of the broader 15-M network. It is in this shared sense of belonging, manifested through reciprocal ties, alliances and solidarity, shared critique and contestation, and shared commitment to a 15-M "way" of doing politics that we can find the contours of the 15-M movement, even in the absence of any common formal label or organizational structure.

Note

1. As they are public hunger strikers, and with their permission, I am using Jorge's and Alex's real names.

PART IV

From 15-M to Podemos

10

15-M and Podemos

EXPLAINING THE PUZZLE OF THE "ELECTORAL TURN"

Podemos has enacted a masterful strategy and without a doubt have been the most intelligent and efficient electoral actors of all of us who have entered the fray.

—X Party

ONE OF THE unintended "consequences" of 15-M that has drawn worldwide attention has been the birth of the new political party Podemos.[1] Podemos was presented officially on January 17, 2014, in a theater in the Lavapiés neighborhood of Madrid with the reading of a manifesto called "Making a Move[2]: Turning Indignation into Political Change" (*Mover Ficha: Convertir la Indignación en Cambio Político*) (see manifesto in Juan Luís Sánchez 2014).[3] The original proposal was for the creation of a political tool based on a participatory citizen *movement*, "not as party but as a participatory method in which the people will decide," which would seek "unity with all the anti-austerity forces on the left," and making explicit reference to IU, the CUP, the SAT, ANOVA, and the Citizen Tides (Castro 2014; Podemos 2014).

Just four months later, Podemos burst onto the national and world stage with its remarkable results in the 2014 European Parliamentary (EP) elections, wining over five million votes and five seats in the EP. Podemos forms a part of the story of 15-M and continues to form an important part of the Spanish "political laboratory," not only in its national incarnation as a "hybrid" party, but also in its coalitions with numerous electoral platforms (called "municipal lists" or "parties of change") that managed to govern major cities in Spain, including Madrid and Barcelona. For some the diversity of these coalition "pop-up" party lists make them truer inheritors of 15-M than Podemos, yet without Podemos these coalitions would

Democracy Reloaded. Cristina Flesher Fominaya, Oxford University Press (2020). © Oxford University Press.
DOI: 10.1093/oso/9780190099961.001.0001

IMAGE 10.1 Members of the Boadilla Podemos Circle, March for Change, Madrid 2015.

likely not have had the success they have enjoyed so far. It was Podemos that took the early leap of faith, successfully seized a political opportunity, and transformed Spain's political landscape, breaking the hold of bipartisan dominance for the first time since the Transition.

Podemos is an unintended consequence of 15-M. Its success requires careful explanation, as it poses one of the most intriguing puzzles presented by the 15-M movement: How could a movement that was so critical of representative democracy, so adamant about independence from parties and unions, so embracing of a prefigurative and participatory form of democratic practice, and so committed to decentralized logics of action, have a large number of its members embrace the Podemos electoral initiative less than three years later, while *still claiming allegiance to the spirit of the movement*? In other words, the activists who left movement assemblies to join Podemos "circles" had not undergone a conversion process whereby they had suddenly "seen the light" and recognized the futility of movement organizing when "real" political change takes placed in the institutions. On the contrary, they continued to maintain a commitment to grassroots mobilization.

IMAGE 10.2 Thousands fill the streets for Podemos March for Change, Madrid 2015.

The tensions between Institutional Left and autonomous politics is a long-standing defining feature of the European and Spanish social movement landscape, and Podemos is not the first party to try to channel and galvanize autonomous movement actors for electoral purposes. Recall the remarkable rise of the German Greens in the 1980s, and the ensuing debates between *realos* and *fundis*, or between so-called radicals and reformists within the party, as it struggled to maintain a balance between movement and party. It is tempting for those who embrace institutional politics (or classical political theories about party formation) to see Podemos as the "natural" evolution from (naïve) mass mobilization to "real" (mature) politics. I reject this argument as wishful thinking and insufficient to explain the electoral turn.

Spain's autonomous network activists have always tolerated multi-militancy (including activists who also participate in parties), so long as they left those allegiances largely outside autonomous spaces, forming temporary strategic alliances on certain campaigns or protest events. During the 1980s there was also a massive demobilization in movements when the PSOE appeared to represent many of the political demands that diverse social movements (many of them institutionally oriented in any event) were making. Never before, however, had there been a widespread transfusion of *autonomous* movement activists, explicitly committed to an autonomous nonpartisan collective identity, into a political party. So how did 15-M activists overcome their cognitive dissonance to cross the Institutional Left/autonomous divide and try to combine these two very different logics of collective action? How were they persuaded to engage in electoral politics while maintaining an autonomous 15-M collective identity? It is this that requires explanation.

I argue that party founders and early supporters needed to engage in extensive discursive work to enable 15-M activists to overcome their cognitive dissonance and realign their activist identities to embrace the electoral turn. In the process, Podemos was assisted by a number of political opportunities that the party successfully exploited. I make five key arguments that work *synergistically* to explain this puzzle. In Section I: *Podemos as a precursor to 15-M*, I argue that we should understand Podemos not only as an outcome, but also as part of the movement's origin story. In Section II: *The Democratic Turn*, I argue that, as I have shown, 15-M was *already* shifting from a pure autonomous to a more hybrid movement that engaged with democratic institutions (see also Flesher Fominaya 2014a, 2017). In Section III: *Podemos as a hybrid party*, I show how Podemos drew on five key sources of legitimacy and discursive persuasion to facilitate 15-M activists' transition from autonomous nonpartisan actors to party supporters. In Section IV: *Frustration*, I argue that in the midst of the crisis, government impermeability to movement demands led to widespread frustration with the lack of tangible results of mass mobilization, facilitating the receptivity to an institutional option and opening a political opportunity for Podemos. In Section V: *Cognitive liberation*, I argue that Podemos's surprising and stunning European Parliamentary Election win triggered a mass rally around the new party. Finally, in Section VI: *The unconvinced*, I explore the narratives of 15-M activists who did not embrace the electoral turn, but were largely sympathetic to the party. While some of these factors are relatively straightforward, others require further unpacking. I will take each of these in turn, beginning with the most provocative.

I. Podemos as a precursor to 15-M

How can Podemos be said to be a precursor to 15-M if the party was not created until three years after 15-M? The answer lies in a two-fold continuity between the pre- and post-15-M scenario with regard to Podemos's communicative strategy. The first continuity lies in the role that Podemos's founders played in preparing the discursive terrain for 15-M through developing and propagating key anti-austerity and pro-democracy narratives, and the continuity between that discourse and the communicative framing strategies they used to form the party. The second continuity lies in the initial actors who formed and supported the project, many of whom came from the GJM, JSF, and Izquierda Anticapitalista (IA), all precursor actors in 15-M, and later formed the core of Podemos.

We could trace the origins of Podemos to 2010, with the emergence of *La Tuerka*, a local political TV show designed to exploit the opportunity of an economic crisis that was beginning to undermine dominant social consensus by recognizing that "the principal scenario of political confrontation is communication" (Iglesias 2015). From here we can trace the development of a powerful communication strategy that played an important role in preparing the discursive terrain for 15-M and, later, the launching of Podemos.

But Podemos's origins go back further. Luis Giménez, one of the participants in *La Tuerka*, its spin-off *Fort Apache*, and, later, part of Podemos's communication team, traces the origins of *La Tuerka* back to 2006, when a group of students dressed in white overalls, burst into the cafeteria in the Faculty of Political Science and Sociology at Madrid's Universidad Complutense, megaphone in hand, to announce the creation of the university association *Contrapoder* (Counter Power), driven by the idea that all political action in the university had to be grounded in "easy and fun" collective disobedience (Dominguez and Giménez 2014).

The use of white overalls wasn't random. It was directly influenced by the autonomous Italian movement *Tute Bianche*, whose protests during the GJM were inspired by the Mexican Zapatistas, and whose Spanish homologue was the Global Resistance Movement (MRG), whose main spokesperson was none other than Pablo Iglesias. Iglesias's fascination with the Zapatistas and the *Tute Bianche* inspired his doctoral thesis on Italian and Spanish disobedient movements. Iglesias's interest in the power of discourse and political communication, combined with his desire to keep politics grounded in social movements and outside the realm of Institutional Left politics, led him to experiment with the creation of new forms of political identity and communication. My own point of reference is earlier than Giménez's (who comes from a later generation). It comes from 2002, when Pablo and I spent several hours discussing the limits and possibilities of political and theoretical discourse in the context of a "postmortem" of a short-lived political space we both took part in. Central to this discussion was his understanding that effective politics requires the ability to translate theoretical expertise into language everyone can not only understand, but also be comfortable using, and which will foster their participation.[4]

Alongside *Contrapoder* (which later semi-morphed into JSF), which formed part of an active Madrid university student network, was a group of professors organized in *La Promotora del pensamiento crítico* (The promoter of critical thought), which included Iglesias, Monedero, and Errejón, who were using insights from Latin American political change to explore a renewed understanding of the Spanish Transition, a project that combined academic and activist orientations and sought to traverse the university and Madrid's social movement spaces (such as the Patio Maravillas social center) (Giménez in Domínguez and Giménez 2014).

This period of student and university activism prior to 2008 was important in continuing the development of a critique of neoliberal policies and Spanish democracy from the GJM, as well as experimentation with civil disobedience by a new generation of activists, despite the period of economic expansion and "progressive" social democratic governance in which it developed. However, the "prosperous" socioeconomic context of the time also limited its ability to reach beyond a relatively small group of people. From 2007 to 2010 in particular, student contestation around issues such as the Bologna university reform was embedded in a wider critique of neoliberal economic policies, which laid the foundations for a critique of the crisis once it hit. By 2008 the first shock of the crisis was felt, and the long-cherished dream of GJM activists to "break out of the activist ghetto" joined the desire of critical academics to break out of the university walls. In this endeavour, *La Promotora* organized a series of seminars and debates with the objective of using them as political tools that would reach a wider audience. One such debate was "The Left to the Left of the PSOE." Pablo Iglesias chaired the debate, which included representatives of United Left (Izquierda Unida, or IU), Anticapitalist Left (IA, Izquierda Anticapitalista), Squatted Social Center (CSOA), Patio Maravillas, and the Galician Nationalist Bloc party (Bloque Nacionalista Galego, or BNG) (Giménez 2014). Ariel Jeréz, a long-time activist, member of *La Promotora*, and inner circle member of Podemos founders, remembers this time:

In 2008 we created *La Promotora* of critical thought, with Pablo (Iglesias), Íñigo (Errejón), Juan Carlos (Monedero), Carolina (Bescansa), Pablo Sánchez León, me, and several students. We were trying to work on shared critical themes and create a common public for them.

Two key concerns occupied the group, critically reflecting on the Transition and finding formats through which to effectively reach their intended audience. Despite inviting exciting and distinguished guests, their events had at most 30 participants.

To combat this they borrowed a format from a popular TV show (*59 Seconds*), giving guests 99 seconds to respond to debate questions. Their first debate on the Transition, human rights, and generational change brought in 700 people. They recorded the debate and put it online:

The next day Paco Pérez, from Vallecas television station, called me up and said, "Hey, who's the guy with the ponytail? Ask him if he wants to do a television program here in Vallecas," and the next week Pablo was doing *La Tuerka*. So it was four years of that process that had a lot to do with this reflection about format. As a working group we really put our energies into this idea of media activism, into the power of social networks. [. . .] It would be impossible to understand Podemos without the experience that Pablo had during this entire media communication learning process—well, you know he's always been a great communicator—but he finally began to understand a series of things that makes Pablo (as much as many people would prefer that it wasn't so) one of the most important resources that we have in Podemos.

Victor Sampedro, an activist and professor of media and communication, highlights another crucial aspect of this communicative development process: Pablo Iglesias's ability to see the political importance of the Spanish political *tertulia* format (a particular form of debate between intellectuals and pundits that is often cacophonous and not particularly sophisticated), and the possibilities offered by using it to present debates on *La Tuerka*. Unlike Jerez and Sampedro, who saw Tele K "as a boring, old-fashioned station," "stuck in neighborhood struggles and very I U influenced," Iglesias seized the opportunity and began to experiment with transforming the hegemonic *tertulia* format, elevating the caliber and calming the tone of debate:

> (Sampedro) Pablo does something very intelligent, which is to get the second-string right-wing *tertulianos*—not the big shots like Jiménéz-Losantos, no—he grabs the young people from the FAES [a right-wing think tank linked to the PP] and he starts using them as sparring partners, and trains himself more. He studies theater, does his master's in cultural studies at the Carlos III, and all the while he keeps developing his ability to transform this hegemonic political format, because he controls the production and he uses his guests to completely pummel them discursively, by working out his answers to the questions beforehand. So [he begins to gain] visibility.

The importance of a social media ecology was also crucial in reaching wider audiences, as Sampedro highlights:

> Pablo starts to create these media pills that go viral in the public digital sphere, and here is where he encountered the independent television stations in other countries that produced *Fort Apache.*

Sampedro and I discussed the politically problematic issue of producing a program financed by Iran's public television, for which Iglesias has been severely criticized (along with the relationship of members of Podemos with Venezuela's government through their work with the CEPS foundation; see below). As Sampedro tells it,

> Pablo manages to go viral using his own media, using social networks, and taking on the next younger generation of cyberactivists who were 20 and 30 years old, some of whom work on free culture in the digital sphere. [. . .] So he says Iranian TV? OK, Canal Sur of Venezuela? OK, great we'll take that money and use it for *La Promotora.* The key thing is that the production arrangement is a closed deal—in other word, you buy my program, but you have no control over the content. So this generation of political actors are free political communicative subjects in their own right (*en pleno derecho*), and they act as such, without any complexes.

Pablo Iglesias's media development wasn't the only training in political communication during this period. Íñigo Errejón and other members of Podemos spent time in Venezuela working as political communication advisors to different public institutions via the CEPS foundation.[5] One member told me that although he wasn't enamored of *Chavismo*, the experience was a powerful awakening to the possibility of translating a new social "common sense" into an institutional political force. This experience was later brought to bear on the political communication strategies of the party, developed primarily by Errejón.

By 2010 the effects of the crisis were being felt strongly, and the small team putting together the *La Tuerka* program included people from *Contrapoder*, JSF, and *La Promotora*. As with Madrid's autonomous movements, there was no formal structure or organizational connection between these different political spaces, but they were connected organically through personal ties and multi-militancy (see Hector Meleiro, in Giménez 2014, 30). Everything was done on a shoestring, and no one made any money at all initially. The early programs were done in a very underground style, covering social movement activities very closely, and drawing on the pool of human resources in Contrapoder and JSF to provide political content in an ad hoc fashion. Everyone saw the production of the program as an act of political activism, and it was a crucial media training ground for all involved. Over time, the organization became more structured, with people in charge of different working groups and higher production values. As the program improved, the audience numbers jumped dramatically. By January 2011 (four months before 15-M), millions were watching via YouTube. Around this time they appointed a salaried coordinator and producer, and registered themselves as a cultural association, CMI Productions. By the general elections of November 2011, Izquierda Unida hired Errejón and Iglesias as campaign advisers, and they used CMI Productions to create publicity spots that they themselves wrote. CMI Productions also created videos for other collectives such as JSF (pro bono) and for Bolivian public television (Giménez 2014).

Those involved were keen to reach audiences beyond their natural sympathizers, and to reclaim concepts such as "nation" and "country" that they felt had been appropriated by the Right and abdicated by the Left. This led to a debate with the leader of the Popular Party's New Generations (Nuevas Generaciones), Ángel Carromero, on October 12, 2011 (Hispanic Day), which marked a turning point in the program. Errejón and Monedero argued that the appropriation of the Spanish flag as a symbolic representation of the nation-state enabled the Right to claim representation of the majority based on nationalist sentiment to the exclusion of leftist political agendas and alternatives (Giménez 2014). "Little by little they began to open the door to other commentators, and the set of *La Tuerka* became more and more diverse, which in turn enabled it to reach a wider audience" (Gimenez 2014, 37).

Iglesias's opening monologues in *La Tuerka* (which he hastens to say were written by a team of people, but which bear his unmistakable stamp) were beautifully written, compellingly argued, took no prisoners, and delivered with a communicative power that has characterized his public speaking for many years. Iglesias, and later Monedero, took aim at those responsible for austerity policies, and at those who benefited from the crisis, passed the cost to the public, and helped themselves to public money through fraud and corruption. Whenever anything of note happened in Spanish or global politics, or on the streets of Spain, *La Tuerka* was there to provide often brilliant critical commentary that managed to express and shape the zeitgeist to perfection. When Ada Colau called a senior banking official a criminal during the parliamentary intervention that would make her known across Spain (see Chapter 8), Iglesias offered a monologue on the meaning of political radicalism. Although Errejón is often considered the most theoretically and strategically sophisticated of Podemos's founding cupula, Iglesias's monologues have the rhythm and power of a born orator, weaving cinematic references with political theory and not being afraid to go out on a limb. It was this ability to read the political moment, to critique it and mobilize energy around it, developed acutely during the hundreds of hours of work on *La Tuerka* and during his many political debates on major TV *tertulias* that explain in great part the later communicative success of Podemos's political campaigns.

Both Iglesias and Monedero managed to find enough common ground, common sense, and transgression to channel a significant part of public opinion in the context of the crisis. They were also establishing political legitimacy with those who would become 15-M activists. And the show didn't only provide commentary, it also laid out the central tenets of a political philosophy and a political strategy, preparing, without knowing it at the time, the groundwork for what would later become Podemos. The deliberate and reflexive reclaiming of discursive space from the Right would later take the form of claiming political space from both the Right and the PSOE with the creation of the party.

Iglesias's mediatic qualities were noted by the mainstream, and he began to be invited to mass media *tertulias* on both left- and right-wing shows, where audience share increased each time he appeared. Soon the "guy with the ponytail" was becoming known across Spain, as were his forceful arguments against austerity and the democratic deficit.

The eruption of 15-M in 2011 provided a new social climate that further opened the discursive framework of political contestation against the crisis, against austerity politics, and for a new form of democracy. If *La Tuerka*'s team felt personally closer to those groups that make up the DNA of 15-M (e.g., the PAH, JSF, squatted social centers), they also wanted to serve as a point of connection between the more Institutional Left actors of Spanish politics and 15-M (Giménez 2014,41; and Jeréz, above). Actors who would later become the visible face of Podemos, then, were key actors in generating the very 15-M discourse that fueled the movement. Pablo Iglesias, as the most visible face of *La Tuerka* and *Fort Apache*, and of the widely viewed television political *tertulias*, had significant activist and critical "street cred" as someone who very effectively channeled what so many people were feeling, and reflexively and strategically developed a counter-hegemonic discourse that prepared the terrain for Podemos and 15-M's wider resonance in a significant way by delegitimizing existing political elites.

There was a synergistic relationship between *La Tuerka* and 15-M, each providing legitimacy to the other, and both developing the political terrain that would then be capitalized on to create the movement-party "Podemos" in 2014. Iglesias himself recognized the crucial role of media and communication in Podemos's success, saying of the contrast between 15-M and Podemos, "What is the difference between a social expression and a political one? The machine. And what is the key to the Podemos machine? A party? No. The capacity to intervene in the media with a discourse that works. [. . .] Everybody knows that the most important battles are fought in the media" (Lago 2015).

The importance of the political communication strategy is underscored by a final point: Podemos was by no means the only, or even the most intuitively "natural," heir of 15-M. Prior to Podemos's emergence, other parties, notably Partido X (X Party) in 2013, had developed an initiative organized as a digitally enabled participatory citizen tool that very clearly cleaved itself to the principles and discourse fueling 15-M. In line with 15-M political culture, Partido X rejected media leadership and adopted anonymity; it advocated citizen control of "real democracy" and political responsibility; they embraced a nonconfrontational philosophy that worked for the common good and rejected ideological divisions (see Chapter 7). But Podemos's media strategy, which combined local TV, social media, and breaking the mass media barrier through the *tertulia* participation of Iglesias, was crucial in making the Podemos option visible to the electorate, as Partido X recognized in its analysis of the 2014 European election results (in which they won 100,115 votes). During the election campaign, Partido X had a total of 23 minutes of television coverage, while Podemos had about six hours. Partido X summed up the key to Podemos's success:

> They have prepared their terrain due to the efforts of Pablo Iglesias and the colleagues (*compañeros*) who created *La Tuerka*, with great ability and without anyone's help. (Partido X 2014)

II. The "democratic turn"

15-M's "democratic turn" represented a shift from pure autonomy to a reclaiming of democratic institutions for citizen benefit, lending a greater disposition to institutional engagement as an arena of political action. Many 15-M activists were willing to leave their comfort zones to engage directly with political and economic institutions, whether via bank occupations or negotiations with bank managers (e.g., the PAH), directly engaging with parliamentary commissions and actors (e.g., No Somos Delito), taking those responsible for fraud to court when the state failed to do so (e.g., 15MpaRato), and so on. While it is true that they do so from an explicitly nonpartisan standpoint, and actively contested any media accounts that suggest otherwise (e.g., the PAH's #Somos APAHrtidistas [We are nonpartisan] campaign), the movement was also moving toward a hybrid form of autonomy that engaged with institutions much more than before (see Flesher Fominaya 2015e, 2017; Martínez 2016).

However, this predisposition to engage with institutional politics is not enough to explain the electoral turn. This shift required many other intervening factors to enable it (see Section III below), and it still feels awkward to some 15-M activists, such as Pepe, who I ran into in the Puerta del Sol on the eve of the elections of May 25, 2015:

> It's a very strange feeling for me because I've gone from "They don't represent us!" to "They do represent us!," and it's weird because I have really mixed feelings about it.

I had just been with a group of other 15-M activists, two of whom had told me they would not be going to any campaign closing ceremonies, as political parties "were not their thing at all." Despite the refusal of some, there is no question that a critical mass of activists did lend their active support to Podemos and, later, the municipal lists.

Despite the strong nonpartisan orientation of 15-M's political culture, some activists in Acampada Sol wanted a party to develop from the movement from the beginning. Not all 15-M activists were committed to autonomy as the only political form. Some saw it as a complementary activity to other forms of political engagement, and many were already participating in preexisting political parties, or created alternative parties post 15-M, including Institutional Left IU, radical-left Izquierda Anticapitalista, ecologist party Equo, liquid democracy/Internet party Partido Pirata (Pirate Party), or the Internet party Partido X. In November 2013, prior to Podemos's formation, Madrid's Traficantes de Sueños bookstore, known for its autonomous orientation, held an event called "Assaulting the Ballot Boxes," which involved Tania Sánchez (of IU, later of Podemos) and Miguel Urbán of Izquierda Anticapitalista (later of Podemos) (Díaz-Parra et al. 2017). However, until Podemos's electoral success, no one saw these parties (new or old) as anything other than marginal oppositional options rather than viable contenders for state power or control of government. Podemos's success opened up possibilities not just for Podemos, but also for these other parties.

Some 15-M activists justified participation in the electoral turn as a guarantor of democracy within the new formations, combined with an "if you can't lick 'em, join 'em" logic, as I witnessed in a DRY! Madrid assembly. In the context of a debate about participation in the electoral initiatives and an information session on the process of the creation of Ganemos Madrid (later part of Ahora Madrid) in which Podemos was a driving force, some enthusiastic members of the assembly argued that since institutionalization was by then inevitable, it behooved members of DRY! to be actively involved to ensure democratic control and transparency throughout the process. Some DRY! Madrid members became enthusiastic supporters, others were already members of smaller parties such as Equo and Pirates Party, and others remained committed to autonomy to the exclusion of electoral politics. DRY! Madrid later configured its own list for the Ahora Madrid process, causing some casualties to the assembly in the process—an example of political fallout from the "Podemos effect." As Blanca of Ion Radio put it, Podemos did what many were asking of the 15-M movement from the beginning: to make the move to the electoral sphere.

III. Podemos as a hybrid party

At its inception, Podemos fashioned itself as a citizen's movement rather than a party, only establishing itself as a party after a participatory process led to its foundational assembly in Vistalegre I. Podemos can be understood as a *hybrid party*, a party that seeks to maintain links to, but also characteristics of, participatory democratic social movements, while still being firmly committed to winning elections.

Although often grouped together with Syriza and Italy's 5 Star Movement party, Podemos is not exactly comparable to either (but see a systematic comparison of the three in della Porta et al. 2017). In contrast to Syriza, which is essentially a preexisting Institutional Left party that managed to grow following mass mobilization in Greece in the acute crisis context, Podemos did not exist prior to 15-M. Italy's Movimento 5 Stelle, on the other hand, made very effective use of movement discourse and discontent to position itself as a movement-party (as its name clearly indicates) and also had a charismatic leader, but did not arise from, nor has it managed to achieve, widespread legitimacy or support from grassroots or autonomous activists. Podemos has a very particular relation to 15-M, which it draws on discursively and practically for crucial support, resources, and legitimacy. Initially, therefore, it needed to develop a strong connection to its movement base in order to effectively mobilize its vote (though the extent to which it will continue to need to do so is an open question).

Podemos and the municipal lists "of change" knew that they would need to work hard to enable their autonomous activist base to overcome their cognitive dissonance in making the transition from nonpartisan autonomous activists to party/electoral supporters. In this endeavor they drew on five key sources of legitimacy and discursive persuasion, emphasizing:

- the roots of the party in 15-M,
- the guarantee/incorporation of key demands and elements of 15-M, political culture in a hybrid movement/party,
- the activist credentials of party leadership,

- the blurring of the social movement/party binary, and
- the moral imperative to save democracy for the people.

The roots of the party in 15-M

From its first manifesto, which mentions 15-M twice and indignation (the root of *indignados*) five times, to its presentation to the press in January 2014, during which it also repeatedly mentioned 15-M, to this day (2019), when it continues to make reference to the movement regularly, Podemos has framed itself as a movement/party born out of the 15-M movement. Yet it is also careful not to be seen to be appropriating or capitalizing on the movement's identity directly. The party also couldn't exclusively identify with 15-M, as it needed to also speak "in the name of the people" and appeal to non-15-M voters.

Podemos was not alone in making the argument for the roots of the party in 15-M. Ada Colau, in an interview as candidate for mayor of Barcelona in December 2014, said,

> This year has been marked by the irruption of Podemos. But it is important to stress that Podemos is not just Podemos, it is the maximum expression of a democratic revolution that has been brewing for several years and that has had various phases, the PAH, 15-M, the [citizen] tides (*mareas*). We have gone from mass mobilization [. . .] to searching for effective tools to defend the lives of the people. (Ayllón 2014)

As I argued above, and as the party founders discuss in a collective history of Podemos (Guedán 2016), the political roots of Podemos go back much further than 15-M. However, 15-M was essential discursively (both in lending legitimacy to the party and preparing the political terrain for it) and materially, by supporting it with resources and an organizing base. The early "circles" (Podemos assemblies) of the pre-party political project were filled with people from 15-M assemblies, as Tomás recalls:

> As soon as my neighborhood circle was established, at the end of March 2014, I became super active in the party. During the first week everybody in my circle were super 15-M, and every 15 days we would have [a Madrid-wide assembly of all the circles] and everybody there was 15-M too. The profile and spirit of the (Podemos circle) people in Madrid—and Madrid was clearly the heart of

the whole thing—were 15-M. There were around 20 people in the smallest circles and 80 in the larger circles and little by little they became practically filled with people from the 15-M assemblies that were still active.

Tomás, who worked in the communications group, highlights how 15-M activists used their skills and resources to help create the project:

> The coordination of the circles both in terms of face-to-face assemblies and e-mail communication was super smooth, and was facilitated by the enormous experience of all of those 15-M people with that strong assembly (*asamblearia*) tradition.

Integration of key elements of 15-M political culture

As a hybrid movement party born from, inspired by, and seeking to translate and channel 15-M, Podemos integrated the core anti-austerity and pro-democracy demands of the movement, and the core elements of 15-M political culture that I have highlighted so far: (1) autonomous participatory democracy, (2) hacker ethics through digitally enabled participation, and (3) a commitment to feminism (initially to gender equality and the fight against sexist violence; later to a more explicitly feminist agenda). The extent to which Podemos is seen as having managed to integrate these elements goes a long way to explaining the legitimacy the party has been able to maintain in different sectors of the activist community, and I will return to this assessment in the next chapter. For now, I am simply sketching out the central "promises" of the movement/party project that Podemos presented.

Autonomous participatory democracy

The appeal to autonomous principles and *asambleario* processes was clear from the beginning of the project's announcement. From its inception Podemos framed itself as a participatory project that would rely on "society" to determine whether or not it would flourish. At the project presentation (January 17, 2014), it claimed that if it didn't get 50,000 signatures in 20 days, it would take a step back, taking that as an indication that "that was not what society wanted." The party/project (at that point) would be based on participation of assemblies and committees (later "circles"). Iglesias declared, "This isn't a party or an electoral list, it is about a wide process that wants to culminate in a popular candidacy for the European elections" (Juan Luís Sánchez 2014).

Hacker ethics

All of this participation would be fostered by a commitment to technopolitical democracy, where participatory digital tools would be used to create maximum participation in proposals and decision-making. Podemos's first director of organization, Miguel Urbán of Izquierda Anticapitalista (later Anticapitalistas) said at the Podemos's presentation, "The idea is to build a bottom-up process where we combine on- and offline participation . . . we will open up a collaborative wiki to build the program." This gave the "promise" that the direction of the party would come from the people involved and not from the party leadership. In addition, the party would use the Web to ask citizens for donations, so that "we don't ask for a single Euro from the banks that we want to expropriate and the politicians we want to dethrone."

Podemos soon created a buzz for innovative use of digital tools for participatory decision-making through Plaza Podemos and its use of Redditt, to propose and debate the different political, organizational, and ethical documents that would configure the structure of the party. It also used Agora Voting and Appgree at Vistalegre I (officially called *Asamblea Sí Se Puede*, or "Yes We Can Assembly"), the first constituent "citizen" assembly of the party, at which participants voted and the documents voted on would be presented. The digital voting and communication tools were presented to the press during the assembly agenda on the first day to explain how they assisted the participatory process. Party cofounder Carolina Bescansa declared that the Citizen's Assembly's participatory process made Podemos "the most deliberative party in history" (Rivero 2015, 151).

Many 15-M activists committed to technopolitics and excited by its possibilities embraced the electoral initiatives because they believed that digital technologies allowed for meaningful grassroots participation for the first time ever on a mass scale. People like Pablo Soto (a coder who developed the P2P program Blubster, used by over 30 million people, and who later ran Ahora Madrid's citizen participation office), Miguel Arana (one of the first occupiers in Sol, and who works with Soto), Edulix of Ágora Voting (who designs and implements the voting systems used by Podemos), and many others in Spain's thriving digitally enabled media and democracy movement share a belief in the power of collective intelligence and digital tools as mechanisms for participatory political transformation,

and a strong identification with 15-M. Podemos's commitment to digitally enabled democracy facilitated the transition from movement to party
identity for activists in 15-M, helping them realign their interpretive frameworks to overcome cognitive dissonance (Romanos and Sádaba 2015).

What is more, as activists who want to "hack democracy," they are *already* oriented to having digital tools used as a means to close the gap
between institutional actors and citizens in political decision-making. The
Collective Intelligence for Democracy Lab in Madrid, coordinated by Yago
Abati, for example, lays out this vision for "real democracy":

> We need new [network technologies] to help us move towards real
> democracy [. . .] to enable us to undertake distributed forms of po-
> litical action and collaborative decision-making, to achieve a new
> commons oriented democracy paradigm.

Feminism

A basic commitment to feminism, or at least gender equality, has been
an expectation on the Spanish Left for decades, and in 15-M the demand
for feminism came to be a core part of the demand for "real democracy."

The commitment to feminism in Podemos has had a striking evolution since its inception, and of the three elements of 15-M political culture
discussed here it has fared the best over time (see Chapter 11), despite
starting out as the *least* explicit and defined element. Despite having
"Zipper candidate lists" (women in alternate positions), an explicit commitment to "women's rights over their own bodies," freedom of sexual
orientation, and a fight against gender-based violence in the original foundational manifesto, there is no explicit commitment to a *feminist* agenda
in the manifesto (the word doesn't appear), and the founding cupola of
the party was overwhelmingly male. Interestingly, Podemos's voter profile is the most masculine in Spain (Claveria 2016; Metroscopia 2015). As
I discuss in the next chapter, the party's masculine profile and internal
dynamic is a continuing point of debate, but initially there was at least an
assumption of gender parity and a commitment to women's issues consistent with "progressive" Left parties.

Integrating all of these political cultural elements was essential in
facilitating the political transition from grassroots activism to the electoral
sphere, given how important praxis is to 15-M activists' political collective
identity. Podemos's ability to frame participation in ways that resonated

with movement principles and practice meant that Podemos didn't initially look or feel like established party politics, but rather an extension of the creative forms of experimentation with politics and democracy that characterized the movement. Note too that as a hybrid party linked to a particular movement, Podemos is different from so-called Internet parties[6] (e.g., the Pirate Party, Partido X), which are framed primarily around the hacker/technopolitical element of political culture. In other words, the success of Podemos rests in great part on its synchronicity with the 15-M movement, which transformed the wider political climate in which Podemos emerged.

The movement/party linked the promise of 15-M political culture to the core demands of the movement, declaring itself as anti-austerity and pro-democracy. At Podemos's presentation, Iglesias said,

> It seems like this crisis has become the best excuse for a privileged group to hold democracy ransom and to destroy social rights. [. . .] The problem isn't that we have a right-wing government. [. . .] We are leftists, that much is obvious, but what we are saying goes much further than ideological labels—we are saying that we need to defend decency, democracy, and human rights.[7]

As a hybrid *movement*/party, Podemos had to be seen as a party that sought to integrate the 15-M position of not being on the Left or the Right. But as a widespread citizen movement, it also had to be careful not to explicitly align itself with any particular leftist party. The founders initially worried that Iglesias's and Monedero's leftist past would come back to haunt them, thereby blowing their legitimacy as a "new" movement/party capable of appealing to 15-M's "nonpartisan citizen" as political subject (Rivero 2015). At the same time, in order to garner support from the base, it had to have the support or at least tolerance of the existing leftist formations, leading to a sort of dance between distancing itself from IU, the largest existing Leftist party federation, but also offering an "open hand" to all parties, including IU, which shared similar goals.

Activist "street cred"

Podemos's cupola, especially Pablo Iglesias, Íñigo Errejón, and the early Izquierda Anticapitalista and JSF faction, had considerable activist street cred (this also applied later to many of the municipalist candidates, especially Ada Colau). In answer to the question of how a nonpartisan movement could have embraced Podemos, Blanca, an alternative radio activist, mentioned Pablo Iglesias's activist persona: "We (activist journalists) just saw him as one of us. We felt very close to him."

Many of the "faces" of the party on the original list, and later on the many lists for internal and electoral candidacies, were activists with connections to reputable movement spaces (e.g., 15-M, PAH, Patio Maravillas and other neighborhood associations and squatted social centers, the GJM). Of the 62 people voted to the Citizen's Council after Vistalegre I, 28 had explicitly activist biographies, and most of the people occupying the top spots did as well.

Pablo Iglesias and other Podemos founders also put in considerable legwork, going from one collective to the other presenting the project and asking for support over a period of several months before presenting it in the theater of Lavapiés, one of the most historically activist neighborhoods of Madrid.

The moral imperative, reluctant politicians, and blurring the movement/institution binary

Podemos' (and the municipalist) leaders also developed a very effective narrative about the need for continued activism, thereby not creating a binary choice between movement and party, but rather validating street activism as a core "party" activity.

This was linked to a very believable narrative about how high the stakes were. In the midst of a crisis and palpable human suffering, the appeal to an institutional remedy was convincing, especially given the continued commitment to austerity politics from the governing parties. As Iglesias said at the presentation of Podemos,

> If ordinary people don't do politics, other people will do politics for us, and that's very dangerous.

Ada Colau, leader of Barcelona list *Guanyem*, addressed this in December 2014:

> The citizens have been ahead of the institutions in defending citizen rights: stopping evictions, defending hospitals against privatization, and that cycle is not over. Many of us, who have no particular

interest in having a political career, have had to rethink this, because the hijacking of our institutions is threatening our rights and
democracy. [. . .] It isn't true that the movements have emptied out
into Podemos or Guanyem [her party list at the time]. [. . .] Look who
is propelling Podemos forward. There is a harmony with the movements, not a disembarkation from them. We have learned from the
Transition and the subsequent demobilization.[8] [We] are very con-
scious of the need to maintain the autonomy of the movements
[. . .]. We are going to need more mobilization than ever. Whoever
wins these elections. (Ayllón 2014)

This message would be repeated even after election victories in Madrid
and Barcelona. Colau's narrative establishes the activist legitimacy of the
people behind Podemos, their origins in 15-M and activism, the harmony
between the movements and the new parties, the respect for movement's
autonomy, and the continued need for mobilization. It also positions the
leaders of these electoral initiatives as *reluctant* politicians, in unspoken
contrast to politicians in it for power and self-interest. Katrina, a member
of the Podemos Citizen's Council, explained:

Working within Podemos for me stems from two motivations.
One is to find that fastest way to solve the urgent problems we are
facing, and to pressure from the inside to make those issues non-
negotiable. [. . .] I find that in my day-to-day work I can shape the
agenda of our program. [. . .] The other has to do with this idea that
we can win [but] civil society has to keep fighting in the streets and
putting pressure on [politicians]. I live between that double identity,
I'm in Podemos but I am still an activist, I am not such an insider
that I can't be critical, but not such an outsider that I can't have influence on the party.

Threat to democracy

Another strong theme of Podemos and the municipal lists was the idea
that democracy was under severe threat from the rampant corruption
of the governing political parties and the revolving doors between busi-
ness/finance and politics, which was also a key theme of 15-M activism.
Podemos and the other municipal parties "of change" were framed as

activists who had become reluctant politicians and were making a necessary sacrifice in order to safeguard democracy for the common good. In
2014 Tania Sánchez (at the time in IU, now in Podemos) and Ada Colau
gave a joint interview in which they declared the following:

> Beyond social movements, there has been a traumatic realization
> on the part of citizens as a whole that delegating politics has led to
> the privatization of politics, a confusion between private and public
> interests, revolving doors, generalized corruption. We should never
> delegate again, democracy does not happen on its own, it isn't an
> ending point as they sold us with a certain narrative about the
> Transition, it is a starting point, a permanent gerund, and if not,
> there is no democracy. (Corcuera 2014)

The use of the phrase "privatization of politics" implies economic gain
by the political class through the privatization of public goods and services
(as well as fraud and corruption). This goes much further than simply
denouncing an out-of-touch elite that is too distant from citizen needs,
or critiquing a "professional" political class that follows rules and codes
divorced from those that govern "ordinary people." Instead, the link to corruption and personal gain continues the trope of politicians who not only
do not represent the people, but also become wealthy at their expense,
who actually benefit from the "crisis." The language is also not individualized: it doesn't focus on a few bad apples, but on a systemic crisis that
threatens the democratic system as a whole. As Colau argued in another
interview, "If we give in to structural corruption we are lost as a society"
(Gil 2014).

The moral imperative to save democracy was not just a discursive
ploy to the gallery, but was a theme that emerged in my interviews
with members of Podemos, who reflected on their sense of moral ob-
ligation to fight austerity and support democracy. Alejandro, another
former member of JSF, now a member of the communications team,
addressed this:

> None of us saw ourselves in institutional politics, it's not like that
> ever fit into our life project, and I really don't see myself in this long
> term. There are so many other things I want to do with my life, and
> this is a real drag in a lot of ways. But if there is a possibility to win,
> and to change things, then I feel like I have to do it.

Podemos and the municipal party/lists consistently delegitimize established political elites, while simultaneously relegitimizing democracy, democratic values, and civil society. Podemos's initial onslaught against corruption in the political classes centers around the term *casta*, or "caste," to describe an elite divorced from the citizens, who used public institutions to advance their own interests. In late 2016 the party introduced a new buzzword, *trama*, or "plot," and launched a "TramaBus"—a large blue bus in the shade of the Popular Party's color, covered with large iconic images of Popular Party leaders either charged, convicted, or strongly associated with corruption (and also PSOE former president Felipe González). Within days of the TramaBus initiative, a new corruption scandal in the PP broke, prompting Podemos to joke (in tweets and videos), "We swear we did not time the TramaBus to coincide with these new allegations of corruption."

The *trama* campaign culminated in the launching of a widespread process for a citizen consultation for a motion to censure the Popular Party (in April 2017), following new evidence of corruption and looting of public institutions (specifically, in this case, the public water of Madrid, the Canal de Isabel II, leading to the resignation of the PP leader in Madrid, top politician Esperanza Aguirre, and the investigation of the PP's president of the Community of Madrid, Cristina Cifuentes).[9] This paved for the way for the later motion of censure that brought down Rajoy's government in 2018 (Flesher Fominaya 2018).

The fight against corruption and for transparency is continually linked to an *alternative relegitimized* form of democracy, based on participation and citizen mobilization. As Ramón Espinar, then general secretary of Podemos Madrid, declared, "The biggest threat to democracy is for corruption to become normalized" (in Sánchez 2017). The solution to corruption, he argued, was participation by

> The people, the people, the people (*Pueblo, pueblo y pueblo*). Only citizen participation, mechanisms of transparency, and citizen vigilance of politics can reverse institutionalized corruption.

Espinar contrasts this with an alternative view to existing democracy by arguing that the proposed motion of censure can only take place—"like all fundamental issues"—after the bases have been consulted, and he clarifies that this does not mean Podemos should just consult *its* bases, but that it should lead a process open to *all citizens* in which they can decide whether or not to go forward with it. As secretary general for Madrid he had called for the full Executive Council and Citizens Council of Podemos, the secretary generals of all the municipalities, the Assembly of Madrid, and all the leaders in Podemos with competence in the area to discuss the motion of censure, but "not even all of these people are legitimated to take a decision of this magnitude." That task, he argued, is up to the citizens, "like all strategic, crucial decisions in the party" (ibid.). As we will see in the next chapter, this last claim would be contested by many, but *discursively* it shows how Podemos works to both delegitimize really existing democracy and relegitimize democracy as a principle and set of values that must be upheld, while putting Podemos forward as the party to lead and coordinate this process. Note too that throughout this discussion the critique of capitalism is implicit, but never explicit, in keeping with the discursive strategies developed in JSF, Oficina Precaria, and related projects (see Chapters 2 and 9).

IV. Frustration

By 2014 the 15-M assembly/movement was in decline, fueled by fatigue, cooptation in some assemblies, and a natural post-boom attrition (Freeman and Johnson 1999; Snow and Benford 1992; Tarrow 1993). While some blamed Podemos for "depopulating" the assemblies, the truth is that many were struggling to maintain momentum by the time Podemos and the municipal lists came along. As Sara, a 15-M activist said to me,

> The assemblies were already much smaller by then. The young people lost interest quickly when they realized that assemblies in the neighborhoods don't reproduce the euphoria and excitement of the occupations—they want that buzz, not endless hours of assemblies.[10]

As David Aristegui put it,

> Activists last as long as they last, it is impossible to maintain a cycle of intense protest indefinitely. Besides, it is profoundly elitist and exclusionary. Who can do it? Students and professional activists, and when movements become co-opted or led by students or professional activists you need to stop and say, "Let's rethink this." In this case people opted for *municipalismo*; I am not really in agreement with that, but I do see it as legitimate.

"Activism fatigue" was coupled with frustration that mass mobilizations had led to very little if any positive concrete change, due to the PP and PSOE's refusal to change their austerity policies or engage in meaningful democratic renewal. Instead, the parties seemed impervious to the waves of corruption and fraud scandals, many uncovered by 15-M activists.

Alejandro, a member of JSF who later joined the inner circle of Podemos, summarized a widely shared feeling among activists who decided to make the transition from movement to party activism:

> We've seen millions of people on the street in the Marches of Dignity (22-M, *Marchas de la Dignidad*), we have participated in three huge general strikes . . . [. . .] we've seen the PAH network and the stop evictions campaigns do an amazing job, we've seen them organize a popular legislative initiative, we've seen the creation of [. . .] neighborhood solidarity networks, this incredible range of social struggles that have gone farther than anything we could have imagined in this country. We've also seen a more insurrectional strategy—a [much higher level of confrontation] [. . .] and we've seen a level of intellectual reflexive effervescence in the universities, and none of that made any difference. The Popular Party continued its repression, deepened the austerity cuts, made the laws harsher, every day we had more people arrested [. . .]. And little by little, all of that makes you start to rethink things, and little by little, people [. . .] start to see [. . .] that we need to use the institutions [. . .] to construct an electoral tool that can help to transform that social majority, the new common sense into the political, so I think that's been a generational shift.

Tomás, a 15-M activist very active in Podemos, remembers the initial feelings in the 15-M network:

> There were people who for a long time felt that there had to be some kind of storming of the institutions, that 15-M had to do that without losing the local neighborhood activism [. . .]. But there were also people in 15-M who thought that was Satan's work, that would just reproduce what happened to the citizens' movements when the PSOE emerged in the 1980s [. . .]. But then there were those of us who thought that just doing micropolitics meant that we were never going to be able to tear down the establishment or change the status

quo, [. . .] not in your fucking life! So if you want to change that, you have to try to create mechanisms from citizens movements that cross-contaminate this project of transformation and assault on the institutions, without losing [. . .] those aspirations, that methodology, and to create spaces that can enrich that process. And we saw in Podemos not the best option, but the *only* option.

The lack of permeability of political elites and institutions to the demands of the 15-M movement has been a widely shared narrative to explain 15-M's electoral turn (see Feenstra 2015; Fernández-Savater 2015a). Clearly it was an important factor, but it did not *automatically* translate into mass support for a new party (as the relative failure of other credible 15-M-related hybrid parties shows); instead, conversion required an effective and concerted strategy, and Podemos and the municipalists delivered.

V. Cognitive liberation

Many activists were not convinced, despite all of these factors. Scale shift came after Podemos's first stunning electoral win in the European Parliamentary elections. Those activists reticent about leftist institutional politics—in part because they never managed to achieve any results—suddenly believed it was actually possible not only to run in elections, but to *win* them. The Podemos victory therefore produced a sort of collective "cognitive (and emotional) liberation" by proving that winning was actually possible. Activists involved in other parties were persuaded to renew their efforts in coalitions with Podemos at the municipal and regional level, fueling great excitement in Madrid, even in the absence of great enthusiasm for Podemos itself. As Blanca of Ion Radio put it, "People were waiting to see if it worked. Like, if it works, I'll join. That's kind of human nature though isn't it?"

Katrina, a 15-M activist who is a key member of Podemos, explains that she didn't even consider joining the party until election night:

I joined when I saw Pablo at the May 25, 2014, press conference after winning five seats in the Euro-parliament. I knew him from the *tertulias*, which I didn't like much to be honest. [. . .] But when he came out and said "We didn't create Podemos to play a testimonial role but to win the elections," I thought OK, we have shifted our focus from the loser Left who suffers defeat after defeat. [. . .]

I have seen so many people who have experienced first-hand the effects of this crisis and [. . .] finally someone who was proposing to actually beat the PP and the Right, I thought, "that is my party."

Pablo Padilla, formerly of JSF and now in Podemos, argued,

There are certain limits that can only be transcended with institutional tools, but not everything can be done from the institutions either, the role of social movements is still crucial. You can ask Podemos and the institutions to do certain things, but not all. Don't ask a hammer to know how to unscrew something. [. . .] My political self is nothing like it was four years ago; it has changed out of necessity brought on by events [. . .] and this influenced my decision to enter Podemos. (in Carvajal 2016)

Although the electoral success increased the process of cognitive liberation and swelled the numbers of supporters, Tomás's narrative shows that without a core of early believers, the project would never have gotten off the ground:

We thought that there was a possibility that we could actually achieve a storming of the institutions, so we totally went for it, with all our energy. I think that idea was shared by lots of people in 15-M who joined the Podemos project early on, but who with time have become really disillusioned with the whole process of structuration and consolidation. But I still feel that this is a historic opportunity that I can't turn my back on.

VI. The unconvinced

Of course, not all 15-M activists were convinced. Some activists saw Podemos as coopting a nonpartisan movement, betraying the idea of direct democracy, reproducing the politics of charismatic leadership, and just being a revamped version of IU (see Flesher Fominaya 2014c). As one 15-M activist tweeted following the elections, "I wonder how long it will take for some people to stop doing things for themselves and start expecting Pablo Iglesias to do it for them."

Canino of Barrio Canino Radio told me (in 2015) that while many people have not gone for the electoral/institutional option, what *has* shifted is their feeling toward those that have, since many are former or current fellow activists. If in the past the tendency would have been to seek confrontation, now they respect those who enter the electoral fray. In the same conversation, Blanca of Ion Radio felt that there might also be a wider evolution of more hardline autonomous spaces in which even libertarian groups are considering working with the institutions. Not opting to go into institutional politics is not anti-political (as some have labeled 15-M, but few, if any, in the movement would). Jon Aguirre Such, one of the more visible faces of 15-M, did not make the move into electoral politics, but he stresses that this in no way means he isn't involved in politics: "What I and many others are doing is simply politics by other means" (in Carvajal 2016).

Outspoken critics of Podemos remain unconvinced by the project as a mechanism of meaningful democratic social transformation (see Mateo Regueiro 2015). Activist philosopher Amador Fernández-Savater (2015a), takes a somewhat more benevolent view but sees Podemos as limited in its transformational potential:

> [A change of political power into the new parties is no small thing]. I will vote for whoever needs to be voted for in order for that to happen [. . .] but voting isn't "changing your life," it takes five minutes. [. . .] There is this standard analysis: suddenly the politicization of 15-M reached a glass ceiling (the closing of parties to any change), there was an impasse and a sense of discouragement, and then we entered another phase, the "assault on the institutions" to unbolt the door (Podemos, etc.). To me this analysis is a real "block" to our thinking. It doesn't allow us to advance at all.

Many activists who were initially unconvinced later joined the party, or will vote for them. Yet, as with the initial massive influx into the 15-M, the initial ingress into Podemos has also subsided, and the honeymoon phase has given way to a deeper critique. The decision of some activists to leave after joining (still far fewer than those who decided to join), or to become an internal critical faction, is in part due to the extent to which they see the party as having failed to fulfill its promises or its capacity to represent in practice the spirit of 15-M to which it appeals discursively. I turn to this in the next chapter.

Notes

1. In this book I limit my discussion of Podemos to its relation with 15-M, its activist base, and its internal critics. Readers interested in voter profiles and electoral analyses of Podemos can see Rodon and Hierro 2016; Fernández-Albertos 2015; Metroscopia 2015; Claveria 2016; Lobera 2015; Lobera and Rogero-García 2016; Flesher Fominaya 2015d).

2. As in a game of chess.

3. Translation available from Cunning Hired Knaves 2014).

4. It was an issue both of us were thinking a lot about at the time, and which I later wrote about in relation to collective identity formation in movement groups in my dissertation (2005).

5. The Centro de Estudios Politicos y Sociales (Center for Political and Social Studies), whose earnings financed the origins of the party, leading to allegations that the party was funded by Venezuela's government, since that government, as well as a number of other Latin American governments, were clients of the foundation.

6. According to Fish (2015), "Internet Parties are unique amongst political parties for their emphasis on the Internet as a policy issue, party organizing system, policy generating tool, and lastly, a political fetish."

7. The video is available from Podemos 2014 or http://www.eldiario.es/politica/ politologo-Pablo-Iglesias-candidatura-dispuesto_0_219078268.html.

8. She is referring to the demobilizing effect of the rise of the PSOE after the Transition.

9. This looting had been denounced in 2014 by the Platform against the Privatization of Water, which forms part of the 15-M-related "Blue Tide" (Marea Azul 2014).

10. When I spoke with two young members of a Podemos circle in Andalucía at the Podemos "March for Change" in 2015, they told me they were struggling to keep young people involved in Podemos, because they found the assemblies boring and didn't want to give up their Saturday mornings.

11

Podemos

A HYBRID PARTY?

The main tendencies within the party hoped for more decentralization, more power for the grassroots, and a more proportional system, but the bases have voted for more Pablo.

—NURIA ALABAO (2017a)

THE RISE OF "progressive" hybrid parties such as Italy's Movimento 5 Stelle (5 Star Movement), Syriza in Greece, and Podemos in Spain in the wake of the post-crisis mobilizations have renewed interest in these parties' ability to regenerate democracy (Chironi and Fittipaldi 2017; della Porta et al. 2017; Rodon and Hierro 2016; Tormey and Feenstra 2015; Treré and Barassi 2015; Mosca 2014). The very term *hybrid party* embraces an internal contradiction between movement and party logics of collective action. Hybrid or movement parties—initially at least—need to satisfy and maintain legitimacy with their movement base, which in the case of Podemos is 15-M. Since its inception, Podemos has struggled to satisfy the expectations of its activist base and to strike a balance between (horizontal) movement and (vertical) party, a challenge all the more difficult given the 15-M movement's commitment to participatory democracy. Criticism came at the very beginning, starting with those unconvinced by Podemos's initial self-presentation as a radically participatory citizen movement, as this reaction from a young libertarian 15-M activist, Raquel, shortly before the May 24, 2014, elections, shows:

> The other day Podemos was in the Plaza of Oporto, and people were saying "Did this come out of 15-M?" It was like people wanted to be

Democracy Reloaded. Cristina Flesher Fominaya, Oxford University Press (2020). © Oxford University Press.
DOI: 10.1093/oso/9780190099961.001.0001

convinced that it had, because they needed to believe in something. I don't believe it. Podemos didn't come out of 15-M. It started because that guy was on a TV program that a lot of people saw and since he became famous he used that. But he was in the Communist Party [. . .] and then he left. So he has these Marxist ideas but he didn't believe in the Communist Party and now he's creating a new party and they're [using 15-M but swapping assemblies for circles]. Like Leninist circles that contribute to the Vanguard, which is them. I see them as a new version of IU.

Raquel's critique was part of only one of many debates within the party and 15-M around the tension between vertical and horizontal logics of action that the rise of Podemos unleashed. These debates reflect the promises and limitations of the three core elements of 15-M political culture I have analyzed here: horizontal participation and autonomy, digitally enabled technopolitics, and feminism. They illuminate the internal contradictions of pro-democracy hybrid parties, and raise the question of whether movement parties can be a powerful force for democratic regeneration or are doomed to being oxymora.

Early internal critiques of Podemos

Tensions between 15-M activists, Izquierda Anticapitalista (IA), and the cupola were present in Podemos even before it was a party. As Tomás, who was involved early on in one of the first Madrid "circles," explained, there were three initial profiles in tension: the founding professorial "clique" of about 20 people, the more radical IA members, and the people filling the circles from 15-M:

> There was a real tension between people who were coming out of 15-M, who were really looking for horizontality, and those who were looking for a more vertical, efficient party.

Tomás told me that the university-based group had "far too much admiration for the fathers of the nation (the party founders)," and "that whole group began to fill up the organizational cupola of the party." He argued that tensions fell along two lines: on the one hand, between 15-M activists committed to horizontality and IA and the Podemos cupola, and on the other, between IA and the Podemos cupola:

A lot of people have the impression that the university cupola was looking for speed and verticality, and that IA was looking to slow down the project, but I think that is completely wrong. Sure, there were some ideological differences between them, but the conflicts were more about egos and affinity groups.

At one point there was a real possibility that Podemos Madrid was going to split from Podemos, but in the end the people from IA decided to stick with the project—people realized that a split would have scuppered the whole thing before it even got started. It was a combination of the fact that IA had provided a lot of the initial infrastructure and resources for the project but had absolutely no say in the decisions that were being made, on the one hand, and the feeling of a lot of people in the circles that they were not central to the project either. At the time the leadership of the party was really pushing for this idea of efficacy, which made some sense but was very badly handled. They could've sacrificed a little bit of efficacy in order to be able to integrate a lot of the people who had given so much to the project during those months. So even before we get to Vistalegre I, even in the run-up to the preparatory conference for the *preparation* of Vistalegre I, and even before that, in the conference to choose the candidates for the European Parliamentary list, these divisions and tensions are already there.

These early tensions in the nucleus of the developing project in Madrid later became more visible, shortly after the initial euphoria and rapid increase in membership following the European Parliamentary election success. The first widespread sense of disillusionment from 15-M activists who had placed their hopes in Podemos came with the party's first constituent assembly, known as Vistalegre I.

Vistalegre I

The period leading up to the first constituent assembly of Podemos in October 2014 was full of promise and activity. Because the political program and organizational structure of the party were yet to be defined, participants could project their own desires onto it. As long-time autonomous free software/culture activist David Aristégui pointed out in November 2014, Podemos's media presence anticipated its actual existence as a consolidated party:

Everything is hyper-mediated. The paradigmatic case is Podemos, which has hyper-representation in the media but nobody actually knows what the electoral program is because it hasn't been developed. So the Corporation's image goes before the Corporation. [. . .] In reality no one knows the party's opinion on a whole series of issues. Podemos encompasses many different things. There are animal-rights collectives, scientists, collectives from the armed forces and even police, pacifist, and environmentalist circles. At some point they're going to have to take a stand. You can't make everybody happy. [. . .] The minute they say "We believe this about the national defense, about gender violence, about laboratory research on animals," that will affect how people orient themselves toward the party. But since they haven't said anything, everyone projects their own needs onto Podemos like some sort of salvation movement.

Many were pinning their hopes on the constituent assembly, officially called the Citizen's Assembly Yes We Can! of Podemos (Asamblea Ciudadana Sí se Puede! de Podemos), but known as Vistalegre I. The event (October 18–19, 2014) followed a one-month period of participation in Plaza Podemos (Reddit), during which people could "transact" with the promoter groups to modify the proposals that would be voted on to define the political lines, organizational structure, and ethical code of the new party. Anyone who registered was eligible to participate in this process.

Although in theory proposals could come from anyone (some 350 proposals were registered), in reality two main competing sets of proposals emerged, both arising from particular factions in the party. One, *"Claro que Podemos!"* (Of course we can!"), revolved around the figure of Pablo Iglesias and the cupola (Monedero, Errejón, Bescansa, and Alegre). The other was spearheaded by two of the Euro-parliamentarians, Pablo Echenique and Teresa Rodriguez, and integrated 30 different proposals under the promoter group *Sumando Podemos* ("Adding up Podemos," or "Joining forces we can"). Initially, this proposal had the support of all four Euro-parliamentarians except for Iglesias, but ultimately MEP Tania Gonzalez lent her support to the Iglesias team. The *Sumando Podemos* proposal only addressed the organizational structure of the party, which was the most contentious issue. It reflected a multiplicity of influences in 15-M political culture and social movements in Spain, including a mix of ideas drawing on digitally enabled democratic imaginaries (i.e., liquid/

cyber democracy), as well as more geographically rooted autonomous imaginaries. These participatory visions stressed the need to maintain the social movement side of Podemos, seeing it as not only a tool to win elections, but also as a way to foster citizen participation and oversight. Suggestions included using a lottery system for representation on the Citizens Council, online multiple referendums to enable consultation on issues, greater autonomy and power for the circles and the autonomous regional party organs, multiple secretary generals (as opposed to one), and multiple spokespeople. In this pre-constituent phase, everything was up for debate and anything seemed possible.

The organizational proposal coming from the party cupola was very different. Although they incorporated some suggestions for increased participation, including lowering thresholds for revoking the secretary general (20%) and opening up internal debates within the party (10%), giving more autonomy to the regional organizations within the party (each of which would have their own secretary-general), and sharing power with the Citizen's Council (which would determine the overall political line of the party and the internal organization of key posts), the overall model proposed was a far cry from the participatory party many had hoped for. The cupola insisted that voters had to vote for all three documents of one team or the other, rather than freely deciding from all the options, which sparked great criticism. Furthermore, Iglesias declared that unless his proposals won, he would not lead the party, knowing that his leadership was one of the party's strongest electoral assets. He also declared that whoever "lost" at Vistalegre should stand aside—a clear allusion to the high likelihood that he would win and that the opposing project, backed by many members of Anticapitalistas, and notably Teresa Rodriguez, should "stand down" if defeated. This all or nothing, "with me or against me," approach was disturbing for those who felt it did not bode well for a truly participatory hybrid party.

In her speech in Vistalegre I, MEP Teresa Rodriguez responded to Iglesias's declarations: "We are the protagonists of a historic process. Our document is the result of 35 different teams and their work. Elections are not won by one secretary general, nor by three, nor by 100, but by the people. Power is won by the people. Whatever comes out of this process, we are not going to stand aside, we're going to take a step forward." In her speech, Carolina Bescansa, party cofounder and member of the Iglesias team, also claimed democratic legitimacy for "her side":

We're proposing the most democratic, capable, deliberative, and transparent organization in the history of our country. . . . Podemos needs intelligence, astuteness, and hard work to coordinate the efforts of the thousands of people who are Podemos today and the thousands and thousands that will be Podemos in the coming months.

While in principle "anyone" could propose and participate, in reality few people were going to read through 350 proposals, much less vote for any that were not coming from the party leadership. In a hyper-mediatized environment in which anyone could participate, whether they actually were active in Podemos or not, the general public (whose only point of contact or reference with the party was likely to be what they saw of Iglesias or other cupola members on television) were going to be able to carry the day over active grassroots participants in preparatory circles and movement spaces leading up to the constituent assembly. In this way, the cupola maintained its control through adopting a participatory mechanism "open to all." Much was made (by Podemos and by international media) of the digital tools offered for voting, debating, and communicating with party members, before, during, and after the assembly. The media and activists enthused by digitally enabled democratic imaginaries hyped the use of tools such as Appgree, Loomio, Agora Voting, and Plaza Podemos (Reddit). Speaking shortly after Vistalegre I, David Aristégui reflected on the shortcomings of the process from a participatory point of view:

The minute you take a step back and look at Podemos you can see that a small group of people have decided everything. A small group of people prepared the Citizen's Assembly. A small group of people forced everyone to vote for their proposals in a package. They have chosen the ethical, organizational, and political principles of the party. They are going to decide on the candidate lists [. . . and] will define everything in the general assemblies. But everyone is super happy because they can vote on their cell phone and they don't actually have to go to these face-to-face assemblies. [. . .] In fact it's really fantastic because [. . .] they actually have an iron grip of Leninist control that I don't think even the Communist Party of Spain has, but they've managed to dress it up in this amazingly strong narrative of internal democracy. [They can claim democratic legitimacy pointing to the number of votes they got], but how is anyone going to compete with the promoter group of Pablo Iglesias? On the last day of the assembly when they were presenting their package of organizational, ethical, and political documents to the vote, Pablo Iglesias was on primetime television with Jordi Evole [a famous TV presenter]. I mean who can compete with that? It's impossible. So there are a lot of really brutal contradictions there.

His comments highlight the ways "digitally enabled" participatory mechanisms can mask the reproduction of vertical power structures and a shallow form of participation.[1] In the event, Iglesias's team's proposals won by a landslide, even though the opposing proposals were supported by many more working groups active within the base of the party. The results opened up a first wave of disillusionment and a "reality check" of what it meant to compete in an open and hyper-mediated forum, where, ironically, those calling for greater power and participation for the base were outvoted by a public that preferred to vote for the party leadership without bothering too much about the details. Those heavily invested in a participatory model were left in a "minority" position and simply couldn't compete with Iglesias's media power.

In its initial "sales pitch," Podemos made much of the "circles," which were supposed to provide the mechanism for grassroots, bottom-up participation in the party, but Vistalegre I left the circles without even a consultative role, much less any power. For David Aristégui, a member of a Podemos circle, the benefit of the circles is that they provide interesting arenas for debate. Such debate, however, had little or no influence on the party executive (referred to indiscriminately as the promoter group, the cupola, the nucleus, or hard core). Aristégui provides me with a dizzying typology of the plurality of the circles, by theme, region, and organizational and communicative form, including "the joke circles that are super popular like the Death Star/Star Wars Circle."

Aristégui pointed out that even something seemingly as "participatory" as having many circles in fact strengthens rather than weakens the cupola, because it lends cosmetic legitimacy without affecting their power, because the circles are not consultative organs:

> They are not organs at all, they are just participatory spaces, but not real participatory spaces. [. . .] Since everything's going to be voted case-by-case and anyone can vote without being in a circle, there

will always be an advantage for the promoter group—so as far as they are concerned, the more votes the better [. . .] and no power at all for the circles. [. . .] I doubt that they've read a single proposal, a single resolution or suggestion that has come out of the circles. [. . .] It's also true, however, that so much material is produced and there are so many circles, that if they actually read all of it, it would be impossible for them to actually incorporate all the different demands. [. . .] So they've managed to transmit this image of a party that is absolutely democratic, and the media has been really generous with them and held them up as a sort of democratic success story.

Tomás also expressed regret at the devolution of the circles away from the 15-M spirit that initially characterized them:

The circles have become support groups for campaigning or for providing infrastructure or resources to the Podemos project, and I don't think that they should become that. It's not bad that they do that, but they need to maintain their independence and their freedom—that proximity with the citizens based movements like the neighborhood assemblies and other projects. . . . In my neighborhood that's been lost. [The original 15-M people have left].

The critique of Podemos as a party controlled by the cupola was widely shared among 15-M activists in and out of the party, even those, like Aristégui, broadly sympathetic to it. An even more emphatic critique of Podemos was expressed in a book by activist-intellectuals called *Hasta luego, Pablo* (See You Later, Pablo) (Regueiro 2015). One contributor, Rafael Cid, wrote about Vistalegre I:

After the definitive verdict emitted by electronic ballot last November as the crowning moment of its organizational process: Podemos is the party of Pablo Iglesias. With the exception of Santiago Carrillo (leader of the Spanish Communist Party), never in the history of Spanish democracy has any political leader held such enormous power. And in the case of the organization of Pablo Iglesias, great admirer of Carrillo, they have the Orwellian advantage of being able to present themselves as the party of the people. [. . .] Everything in his executive organizational structure has been articulated in a presidentialist format, all enveloped in a huge wave of popular and media enthusiasm. Because, against all political prudence, each monopolizing decree ordained by Pablo Iglesias has been met with unconditional surrender by the bases. He eliminated the possibility of a collegial leadership of the party using the rancid short-term discourse of efficiency; he imposed his programmatic agenda with threats of resigning if they weren't accepted; he stigmatized all possible competitors by encouraging the minorities within the party to step aside for the good of the cause, and he culminated his triumphal journey by achieving what has never before been seen in democracy: that those below willingly and proudly give up almost all their power to those above. (Regueiro 2015, 19–20)

Cid later cites an article published in *Infolibre* by Luis Alegre, a member of the Iglesias promoter group, in which Alegre declared,

"Podemos isn't a meeting of housewives, the long-term unemployed, or idealistic youth. It's not a spontaneous movement around a shared cause, like the evicted, public health workers, or taxi drivers. Podemos is the product of a laboratory, designed by specialists in framing, in storytelling, in persuasion, in political communication." (Alegre, quoted in Regueiro 2015, 27)

Little wonder that this type of discourse celebrating the party as an intellectual elite-driven master plan (and juxtaposing it with derogatory allusions to 15-M activism and housewives!) would meet with a profound rejection by many 15-M activists, both inside and outside the party. 15-M activist Reyna sums up this feeling:

For me all legitimacy was lost with Vistalegre I. Pablo's blackmail was the final straw—if you don't want to let people decide freely, then you are actually not in favor of participatory democracy, are you? On the other hand, you've got Errejón moving everything to the center. It is one thing to change discourse to attract more people, but you can't jettison the party program as well! The idea is to *keep* the program and change the *discourse*. So, that was it for me. Game over.

Opening the party or just another party? Critical voices grow louder

By early 2015, the early criticisms voiced during Vistalegre I were getting louder, both from 15-M activists and from a critical sector within the party associated with then secretary general of Podemos in Aragon, Pablo Echenique, and members of Anticapitalistas (IA), coming to a head in June. 15-M Granada's tweet summed up the feeling that Podemos was becoming too instrumental and straying from its original purpose:

> [They've gone from] turning Podemos into a political tool for citizens to converting the citizens into a political tool for Podemos. (June 11, 2015)

Recognizing the loss of grassroots support, Echenique and several hundred other members of the critical sector signed a manifesto titled "We Open Podemos: For a Constituent Candidacy" (*Abrimos Podemos: Por Una Candidatura Constituyente*), which criticized Podemos for running the risk of turning into "just another party." This new wave of debate followed an earlier one centered around whether or not Podemos should present itself for local and municipal elections as "Podemos," and if so, how. As the general elections loomed, lines were drawn between those who clamored for an open process that would integrate multiple small lists, parties, and candidates, a process known as "confluence," and those who felt strongly that Podemos needed to maintain its own identity as a political party. This debate consumed a great amount of energy within the party and its grassroots base.

Each side of the debate tried to anchor their rationale in the lessons they drew from the results of the 2015 autonomous and municipal elections. Those supporting Echenique's sector believed that the remarkable electoral results in Barcelona and Madrid that brought the municipal lists to power (Barcelona en Comú and Ahora Madrid) meant that Podemos must also present itself for the general elections in a joint list with IU and/or other small parties or projects. The *Abrimos Podemos* document states: "The question [is] whether Podemos aspires to become just another party that [upholds] a regime in crisis or whether it will take advantage of this historic opportunity to contribute to a true transformation of democracy." In order to live up to the challenge, Podemos had to be "in social media and on TV, but also on the streets." With regard to organizational structure, the critical sector called for the circles to "regain their role as spaces of debate and face-to-face political decision-making." Unlike with Vistalegre I, this time critique extended to political priorities, not just procedures, including a return to the party's defense of the universal basic income and a firm commitment to a citizen audit of the debt in order to "break with the corrupt oligarchic regime" (two core promises in the European Parliamentary elections). They argued that Podemos needed to "avoid reproducing the bad practices of political parties under the pretext of urgency, exceptional circumstances, and supposed meritocracy."

The *Abrimos Podemos* document reflects primary demands from the grassroots base and core elements of 15-M political culture: a strong commitment to pro-democracy and anti-austerity politics, strengthening the role of the circles as decision-making spaces, and a commitment to openness and plurality by integrating as many different political currents under the umbrella of Podemos as possible. The opposition between the "face to face" and the virtual (two coexisting imaginaries in 15-M) mirrors another distinction between the internal and external face of the party, with "face-to-face" interaction being characterized as neglected as the cupola seeks ever more media impact via TV and social media. Within this narrative, the plurality and openness of the municipal list processes were seen as a clear indication that this approach was not only truer to the principle that inspired the party (and of course the 15-M movement), but also would result in stronger election results.

Those on the other side of the debate had a very different reading of the election results and of their implications for the general election strategy, especially with regard to any proposed alliance with IU. Podemos had from the beginning positioned itself as a genuinely new party that was not beholden to orthodoxies from the past, nor interested in sterile debates between the Left and the Right, but which sought common ground that would serve citizen interests across the nation (*la patria*). Joining in an open alliance with IU would seriously undermine that claim, as IU represents the "old Left" in Spain, and was strongly associated with diverse leftist currents that have yielded poor electoral results for many years. Politics scholars (within and beyond the party) also understood that what works in the cities of Spain is not what produces electoral results in the countryside—an important constituency in a general election. Furthermore, they understood that it was not a simple question of adding together the votes that IU would win plus the votes Podemos would win, since a joint list would dissuade some voters from casting their vote for Podemos, just as it would encourage others.

IU, for its part, made some noises about no party imposing its hegemony or superiority, despite Podemos clearly occupying a leadership position in terms of potential electoral results. The critical sector of Podemos took an intermediate position to IU, declaring that Podemos had to recognize that "it wasn't the only instrument of change in the country," but at the same time that "nothing would be possible without Podemos" (recognizing the crucial role played by Podemos in all of the major municipal initiatives "for change"). Errejón and Iglesias at this time were seen as the united leadership of the party (the cupola) who resisted any such call for change.

For grassroots activists on the side of the debate that *opposed* "confluence," specifically with regard to IU, an alliance with IU would signal becoming "just another party," since despite its support for progressive issues, IU has also been notorious for trying to instrumentalize grassroots movements and co-opt social movement spaces. For anarchists and autonomous activists who were also critical of the Second Republic (and of IU), support for Podemos would be diminished greatly by the alliance. The "Black Card" scandal in 2014, in which some IU Madrid members were involved (see Chapter 7), had further contaminated IU as a political brand that could hope to represent or be associated with a new noncorrupt political party, one of the cornerstones of Podemos "anti-*casta*" political identity. For those committed to the idea of moving beyond Left and Right understandings of politics, joining with IU would also represent a major step backward. IU (and the associated Republican flag) represents a re-opening of the strong cleavage between Left and Right that still dominates so much of Spain's political culture, a cleavage many (but not all) of the younger generation would like to dispense with once and for all.

In a remarkably candid interview in June 2015 (Picazo and Deláz 2015), Pablo Iglesias revealed his own strong desire to leave IU behind and chart a new course for Podemos, unencumbered by the symbols and political tics of the past. This desire was also underscored by his interpretation of the municipal wins in Barcelona and Madrid and their lessons for Podemos with regard to the general elections:

> Barcelona en Comú didn't win because the EUiA, ICV, and other political parties [were integrated into the list]. They won because Ada Colau was leading the project and because they managed to signal it was something new. It has a lot to do with how Podemos won

the European elections. That is the key to the success of Barcelona en Comú and Ahora Madrid. It doesn't have to do with the parties that were integrated into those lists. Ahora Madrid did not include IU, who ran on a separate candidacy [. . .]. We respect other parties' identities and we want them to respect ours.

Iglesias stressed that an election win could not rely solely on support from leftist voters:

It's not enough for the Left to like our program. [. . .] What is needed is a new social majority that identifies with your discourse, with your proposals, and within that social majority there are going to be a lot of sectors who are going to say: "Being on the left doesn't form part of my identity."

Iglesias then gave full rein to his frustration with those insisting on an alliance with IU:

[To the old Left I say] you're ashamed of your country and your people. You think people are idiots who watch trash television and that you are very cultured. You love to wallow in a sort of culture of defeat. The typical melancholic, bored, bitter, leftist lucidity of pessimism: "Nothing can be changed, people here are idiots, they're going to vote for Ciudadanos, but I prefer to hang on to my 5% (of the vote), my red flag, and my whatever." I can respect that totally, but leave me out of it. [. . .] Stick to your existential pessimism, cook yourself in your sauce full of red stars, but don't get near us, because you are precisely the people who are responsible for the fact that nothing in this country has changed.

In the same interview, Iglesias made absolutely clear that there was "zero possibility" of a pact with IU for the 2015 general elections.

While many people sympathized with his position, others who shared the "Left fetishism" were adamant about the need for "confluence," and they made their voices heard. Confluence became a buzz word repeated ad nauseum, with those using it always mentioning the municipal election results as "proof positive" that a joint candidacy was the answer (despite IU not forming part of the Ahora Madrid candidacy at all!). The cynic in me read those demands as a desire for IU to not be left out of what looked like the first real electoral possibility of victory in decades, even if it meant scuppering the chances of that victory, and I strongly shared Iglesias's interpretation of the election results.

Although Iglesias later bowed to pressure (or changed his mind), and Podemos ended up running a joint candidacy with IU in the second round of the general elections in 2016, I maintained then and still feel that this was a very costly mistake. Podemos's early success lay in mobilizing non-voters disenchanted with politics as usual. Despite having a young, intelligent, and charismatic leader (Alberto Garzón), for most Spanish voters, IU represented the old Left, and politics as usual, not the future. At the same time, those *not* necessarily pressing for an IU joint list, but who were instead encouraging an opening of the party to a more pluralistic bottom-up process that respected and recuperated their grassroots support, were making a legitimate and widespread critique and demand that reflected the continuing influence of autonomous political culture and its manifestation in 15-M, as well as the vertical and top-down nature of Podemos leadership and decision-making. This is an important and ongoing internal tension within the party (irrespective of the discussion about IU), which has been exacerbated by other splits and tensions over time.

The disparity between the power of the executive and the rest of the party was thrown into sharp relief in the process of the party primaries (creating the electoral lists) for the general elections in July 2015. Over 900 officeholders in the party and the leadership of five regional divisions of the party publicly rejected the regulation approved by the national executive, alleging that it lacked guarantees for pluralism or participation (*Infolibre* 2015a, 2015b). The criticism centered around two main features: the use of closed lists, which obliges people to vote for an entire team as opposed to being able to select the individual candidates they most prefer (*listas plancha*), and the use of a single national constituency rather than regional lists within each autonomous community. The closed lists meant that Iglesias's team was likely to win, and therefore control the vast majority of the party. The single national constituency meant that the party executive could position their own people in the autonomous territories even if they didn't have local support in those territories (another form of controlling the party from the top) (Díaz-Parra et al. 2017; *InfoLibre* 2015a, 2015b).

In November 2015 there was another outcry from critical sectors of the party, when Internal Regulation Article 7.2 was invoked to allow the party executive to recruit prominent people to occupy top spots on the autonomous community lists, overriding the primary election results. In the aftermath of the outcry, some of these political "celebrities" resigned their spots on these lists (El Plural 2015). Meanwhile, party insiders told me the primary processes had been exhausting, consuming enormous amount of the party's political energy, and leaving little time for much else. Jockeying for position on the lists also had damaging consequences for relations within different circles and regional sectors of the party. Participation in the primary and internal voting of the party had declined steadily since Vistalegre I, with decreasing percentages of the 380,000 registered members voting each time (see Table 11.1).

In 2016 new tensions appeared and public spats damaged the party's credibility, notably a hyper-mediatized rift between Errejón and Iglesias, up until that point seen as a dynamic duo of close friends. The strong focus on the leadership dispute between the two men already represented a deeper problem from the perspective of many grassroots 15-M activist supporters, who already questioned the vertical and "alpha male" leadership of the party, as well as its drift toward becoming "just another party." The "electoral war machine" rhetoric of Iglesias and Errejón during the 2015 campaign alienated 15-M former supporters, who began to feel Podemos's leadership had lost the plot in their quest for electoral victory. Phrases such as "the heavens aren't stormed by consensus but by assault," and overly strategic and artificial-sounding repetition of key phrases (e.g., la casta) in every sound bite, distanced the leadership from the base. It seemed, too, as if Podemos leaders had begun to spend most of their time talking about themselves and little time talking about the people, austerity, or the crisis. More importantly, "confluence" was not helping, because the many innovations and achievements the new municipal governments were making could not be effectively capitalized on, since Podemos's name did not feature municipally, despite forming the core of the projects in cities like Madrid. Suddenly it seemed that Iglesias and Errejón were

Table 11.1 Declining Participation in Internal Votes (Podemos)

October 2014	Vistalegre I	54.4%
November 2014	Secretary General and Citizen's Assembly	42.6%
December 2014	Municipal Primaries	34.6%
April 2015	Autonomous Primaries	20,1%
July 2015	General Election Primaries	15,8%

Source: Carvajal 2015

losing touch with the people that had garnered them so much support in the first place.

In my political reading of this period, Iglesias's own words come back to me: that Barcelona en Comú won because of Ada Colau, and that, likewise, Ahora Madrid's campaign was won by mobilizing around the figure of Manuela Carmena, whom most people had never heard of three weeks before she won the election. While cults of personality are not a trait of Spanish politics any autonomous activist would consider a good thing, both women practice a very different form of political expression from the masculinized Spanish political norm: they exude warmth and emotion, and they do not perform a politics of confrontation despite being forceful, clear, and passionate about their positions. There are no pumping fists, they repeatedly speak about caring and nurturing, and Colau has been moved to tears in more than one speech discussing the impacts of austerity, the human drama related to the crisis, or other important social issues. As one member of the Ahora Madrid City Council team told me,

> On election night (after the autonomous and municipal elections), Pablo (Iglesias) came onstage, and he spoke, and he got the applause in all the right places. And then Manuela (Carmena, mayor of Madrid) came out, with her little handbag clutched under her arm, and she spoke, and she just moved people emotionally. He appealed to their heads, but she won their heads *and* their hearts.

The irony is that Iglesias can and has moved people deeply with his words when he speaks from the heart, and both he and Errejón's self-presentation differs from that of established Spanish politicians. How one evaluates them depends in large part on the point of reference: established party politics as usual, or progressive and innovative forms of political communication. In an extremely hostile and challenging media and electoral environment, in which the PP and PSOE's electoral campaigns (supported and propagated by various mass media outlets and pundits) seemed to rest entirely on an anti-Podemos platform, they were following their election "war machine" playbook to the letter. But the master strategy Iglesias and Errejón had developed to win the elections just wasn't coming across in a genuinely moving way. It seemed now it was they who were misreading the moment, and perhaps taking a leaf out of Colau and Carmena's book, with their commitment to "feminizing politics," might have helped. Indeed, it may have worked to close the gap between male and women voters (Claveria 2016). Certainly, many within Podemos were demanding a new form of politics, and this time they were not only demanding a more open and participatory party, but also a more feminist one. Up to then, the tensions between autonomous and Institutional Left politics (see Flesher Fominaya 2007a) had played out primarily around autonomous (e.g., demands for greater participation) and technopolitical frameworks (e.g., demands for liquid democracy) of 15-M political culture. Now the third key component, feminism, and the de-patriarchization of politics, was coming to the fore.

Feminizing the party and the 2016 battle for Madrid

On April 10, 2017, in the inaugural speech of her new party, "Un País en Común" (A country in common), Ada Colau (mayor of Barcelona) articulated the party's feminist agenda in words that illuminated a wider trend in the sectors of Podemos and other new/progressive parties that explicitly advocate for a feminization (by which they mean de-patriarchization) of politics. Colau's speech didn't place feminism as an additional component of the party's politics (i.e., add women and stir), but rather as an essential defining feature of the party's ideology. Colau is a political figure of enormous resonance among activists in Spain and an important political reference across the Left, including Podemos. At the end of her speech, Colau asked, "What does it mean to say we are in common [Comúns]?" After giving a number of reasons, she said.

> [W]e are in common because we are profoundly feminist. We are feminists not only because this is a space that women can make theirs without asking for permission, not only because we believe it is a priority for our members to fight [. . .] sexist and patriarchal violence [and for equality]. I think the most important reason we are in common and we are feminists is not only because we want to win, [. . .] [but] because we have come to change the meaning of the word(s) "to win." We want winning to mean something radically different from what it has meant in the past. We want winning to mean doing politics for the people, with the people, and making people the only priority of public policy, because we want to shout that care, empathy, and cooperation must be the norm and not the exception, and that [. . .] nothing [is] as important as the welfare

of our children, our disabled people, our grandparents, because nothing, nothing, is as important as human life.

Colau described the internal dynamics of the party, where "women can make the space their own without asking for permission," and its feminist policy orientation. Her repeated reference to the commons also reflected both autonomous and technopolitical imaginaries. The *feminist-ization* of politics was a core task of feminists in 15-M (and previous feminist generations), and was also an issue for feminists within Podemos since its inception. The term *feminizar* can be translated as feminize, but a more accurate if awkward term would be feminist-ize, as the point is not to make the party more female, but more feminist, independent of gender. While I will use the term *feminize*, I am referring to a process of de-patriarchization, which includes integrating and promoting women, but reads politics as a whole through a feminist lens.

In Podemos in 2015, making the "space their own without asking for permission" was not easy for some women in the party. One member of the Citizen's Council, Katrina, reflected on this:

> More than a masculine profile, I would say the party suffers from very masculinized internal dynamics. One example is the way that the supposed need for speed is a way to not take care about who gets left out when you work crazy hours, don't close the office, work all weekend . . . mothers with kids have to be super-human to keep up with that in the party. Of course, there are certain times when you need to do that, but it is used to leave people out, and [. . .] it is also a problem because it creates this way of life that is a bubble divorced from the real world. [. . .] It's also a way to be able to take decisions without anyone objecting, because they can't be there all the time, and that's what worries me most.

In addition to the exclusionary pace and lack of attention to work/family balance, Katrina points to forms of everyday sexism during meetings:

> Women speak much less, much, much less . . . to give you another very specific example, if Pablo or Íñigo speak, everyone is quiet, but if Carolina Bescansa speaks, people start chitchatting amongst themselves, and it's like, "What the fuck are you doing?"

Katrina connects these dynamics to the effort it takes women to continue in these spaces:

> [It] is really, really hard. I have never faced the level of sexism I have in politics, I had never seen the extent to which there is this cut off point, and you get left out, but the men don't. And it isn't like we are these little lambs who have no analysis and are not aware of what is being done to us. When we have to go as spokespeople on TV shows or whatever it is terrifying.

Katrina is referring to the everyday micro-sexism in the party, in inter-actions with media professionals, or when carrying out public party duties, where women are given less visibility and respect.

The lack of attention to feminism in the party was critiqued by many within Podemos, a tension that culminated in 2016 when an internal power struggle within Podemos Madrid centered in part around this issue. Madrid politics tend to play a central role for national parties in Spain because it is usually where the heavy hitters within the party are based (as well as the focus of media attention), and Podemos (despite hav-ing some very strong leaders in autonomous communities) is no excep-tion. The Madrid primaries in 2016 had two phases (as in Vistalegre I), the first for documents (proposals on organization and political strategy), the second for secretary general and members of the Citizen's Council in Madrid. One team, led by Rita Maestre, Ahora Madrid's spokesperson and city council member, *Adelante Podemos con la Gente* (We can go forward with the people), presented eleven documents on organization, equality, and political content and strategies.

In an interview, Tania Sánchez, a member of parliament for Podemos, (former IU Madrid MP, and cofounder of an alternative party[2]), explained the priorities of the *Adelante Podemos* team in terms that echo Colau's words above, and also integrate arguments from the previous debates about participation and connection to social movements:

> Our team has put together a whole series of proposals with innova-tive mechanisms that have the objective of decentralizing and fem-inizing politics so that we can change the way that politics is done in Podemos. Podemos is the party that has the strongest difference between the male and female vote, which undoubtedly has to do with the fact that we exude testosterone. So we need to overcome

this and exude sensibility and cooperative ways of working, like people like Manuela (Carmena) or Ada (Colau) do. They are absolutely uncompromising in adopting political positions that defend the interest of the majority, but completely innovative in their forms of doing politics, because we don't need more machismo, we need less. [. . .] Podemos has to be capable of continuing [to construct] new imaginaries.

The dominant narrative in the Madrid primaries across candidacies was a reconnection with "the streets," following mass resignations from party organs in protest against the top-down nature of the leadership, causing important divisions in the party. Tania Sánchez situates the proposals of the *Adelante Podemos* team within this framework:

In order to make this transition from electoral machine to a normal organization, Podemos needs to ensure that all of its organs represent the full plurality of the party. [First], there has to be proportionality in the lists. It doesn't make any sense that if somebody has [. . .] 49% of the votes suddenly they control 80% of a given party organ. That's madness and it makes us lose plurality and really good people. And the second thing [. . .] is that we should be capable of not perpetuating this organizational culture in which one person wins and the other person loses, and in which there is a constant battle.

Both teams appealed to 15-M and the need for increased participation with the grassroots and the citizens. Sánchez, however, contrasted the two teams' visions of Podemos:

One understands it as an organization of militants that is situated as a vanguard that drags society along behind it, and the other understands it as a political organization for the 21st century in which its connection with the daily life of society [. . .] enables it to be a tool to articulate individual needs. We defend the latter model. [. . .] Podemos needs to be a tool that empowers civil society, [. . .] I think that's what 15-M did and I think that's the best legacy that we could pay homage to.

The *Adelante Podemos* team's conception of "winning" and its link to the desire to *feminize* politics and connect with the people reflects similar discourses in Ada Colau's speeches and also those of Manuela Carmena in Madrid. The emphasis on material needs also reflects the particular feminist prism through which the drive to feminize politics in Spain is articulated. In their press statement following their victory in the document votes, *Adelante Podemos* declared, "People have decisively voted for a political organizational and equalitarian project to beat the Popular Party."

The opposing team (considered to be the Iglesias faction, which now reintegrated important members of IA) also positioned itself as "the only team capable of leading a plural Podemos," appealing to "the circles," "participation," and "a new form of doing politics," but without articulating an explicitly feminist discourse (despite having veteran feminist Beatriz Gimeno on the team), nor really questioning the internal mechanisms of the party other than to point out organizational deficiencies in the statutes voted for in Vistalegre I. Espinar argued vaguely (in line with IA's critiques) for a different role for the circles, but given that Iglesias and the cupola had denied them any real power, this discourse rang hollow. Although there was an appeal to reconnecting with the daily lives of people ("as in 15-M"), the overall language was much more strategic and oriented toward winning the elections (see, e.g., the interview with Espinar in Gutiérrez 2016).

Unfortunately, the push for more reflexivity about feminism and organizational political culture was largely lost in the media framing of the primaries as a battle between Iglesias and Errejón, two alpha males fighting for leadership of the pack. In a classic double standard applied to women in politics, both Maestre's and Sánchez's past romantic relationships with Errejón and Iglesias (respectively) were reported on in the media, (in contrast, Espinar's, Errejón's, and Iglesias's romantic entanglements were irrelevant). Party insiders and critical journalists also framed the contest as a confrontation between Iglesias and Errejón, not only reproducing the masculinized trope of politics as a confrontation between leaders, but missing the more interesting and significant elements of the debate. The language of feminization and "winning" in Colau's and Sánchez' words reflects a reframing of politics that continues to fuel debate within Podemos and other progressive parties in Spain, and is an important legacy of 15-M feminist pedagogy and other feminist activist spaces in Spain.

Whatever impact the "Podemos effect" had on 15-M assemblies, it has also opened up new spaces of debate, such as the four-day Podemos University Conference organized by the Podemos think tank Institute 25M Democracy. This event was explicitly framed as an attempt press pause after the "war machine" period, to "stop and think about the new political, social, and cultural context that opens up before us." Ten of the 77 sessions addressed feminism and gender, seeking not only to address gender inequality, but also to transform the party's political culture, discourse, and understanding of politics (e.g., empowerment, participation, values) in a feminist direction.[3] Debate was profound and provocative.

With regard to gender, the vote for secretary general revealed an on-going and problematic trend within the party: although voters preferred the *content* of 10 out of 11 of the documents presented by Rita Maestre and her team, they still voted for Ramón Espinar as secretary general. Although women candidates have done very well in Podemos's internal elections, two general features worthy of reflection have characterized the votes: First, the zipper lists (alternating male and female candidates occupying the seat, regardless of the percentage of the vote) have actually benefitted men in some cases (including Espinar), raising them up (in some cases over 10 spots) into seats over women who received more votes. In other words, in the first Madrid internal elections in 2015, women would have outnumbered men had it not been for zipper-list allocation of seats. Ironically therefore, they were *disadvantaged* by the mechanism put in place to guarantee gender parity. Second, support for women candidates has one important exception: the top spot. Here, the glass ceiling becomes visible, with voters still seeing men as more qualified to lead than women. In the first internal elections of the party, this resulted in 13 men and 3 women autonomous community secretary generals and 13 men and 2 women at the municipal level (for cities with more than 2,000 registered militants). In 2017 the ratio was slightly better, with 4 female secretary generals and 11 men. Since obviously gender parity cannot be solved by zipper lists for uni-personal elections (such as electing the secretary general), simply having a participatory process is not enough to guarantee gender parity in party leadership (Flesher Fominaya 2015c). Ariel Jeréz admitted to me (in 2015) that "the lesson had been learned" and that discussions were ongoing as to how to improve. By November 2015, the zipper list system was modified to not be used "when it could disadvantage women." But Madrid's vote to elect Iglesias's (male) candidate Espinar, by a healthy margin, despite voters preferring 10 of 11 documents presented by his female opponent Maestre, still leaves the glass ceiling and the relation between gender and participation a troubling and unresolved question.

The internal pressure from active feminists in the party, as well as strongly influential feminist political leaders related to Podemos through alliances such as Ada Colau and Mónica Oltra (of *Compromis* in Valencia), has transformed the party's feminist orientation significantly. A comparison of the documents from the first manifesto with the documents drafted for Vistalegre I and Vistalegre II is striking. In the first manifesto, the word feminist/m is not used at all. In Vistalegre I, there was little attention to feminism, gender equality, or LGBTQ issues in the majority of the proposals. Although one feminist proposal was made, it received only 7.01% of the vote (Calvo and López 2015).

By Vistalegre II, thanks to the active work of feminists in the party, there had been a radical transformation. A separate extensive document devoted exclusively to feminism and gender equality was presented by each of the main competing factions, one of which even included a guide on managing everyday sexism and heteronormativity. The language had also changed to reflect the feminine plural widely used by 15-M activists in most instances. Pablo Iglesias's team was called "Podemos for all [fem. pl.]" (*Podemos para Todas*), and presented a separate "Document on Equality" titled "Feminism for all [fem.] and all [masc.]," which, once you clicked past the cover page took you to a document titled "Feminism in Movement for All [fem. pl.]," a 36-page document shared with the team led by Anticapitalistas members Miguel Urbán and Teresa Rodríguez. In Iglesias's team's organizational document "Govern by Obeying," he states under general principles (p. 14), "We need a Podemos that is united, transversal, feminist, pluri-national, decentralized, in movement, and prepared to govern." His political document, "Plan 2020," includes a subsection under "organizational tasks" called "De-patriarchizing Podemos," in which he declares this as an organizational priority. For their part, the team led by Íñigo Errejón, "Recovering Excitement/Hope"[4] (*Recuperar la Ilusión*), which included the Madrid faction led by Rita Maestre, presented their "Document on Equality" called "Feminism in Movement for All [fem. pl.]: With us [fem.pl.], yes, we can, popular feminism to win a country" (*Feminismo en movimiento para todas: Con nosotras, sí se puede, feminismo popular para ganar un país*).[5]

Vistalegre II

In the lead-up to Podemos's second Constituent Citizen's Assembly, Vistalegre II, media attention to the rift between Iglesias and Errejón had intensified at the cost of coverage of Podemos's virtues or achievements. Far from looking like a citizen assembly or consultation with the base (which was purportedly the purpose of the refounding of the party post-elections), Vistalegre II became instead a public referendum on Iglesias's continued leadership. If the feminist issue had gained relevance, the deep critiques of party verticality were not softened by Vistalegre II. Quite the opposite. Not only was the debate centered between two cupola members who to most people represented two variations of top-down internal organization (leaving a truly participatory option out altogether), the rift between them reflected a political culture of "war," a far cry from the culture of consensus, dialogue, and plurality that many party activists were calling for.

The way decisions are taken in a party are crucial in determining the distribution of internal power, and hence its degree of internal democracy. Echenique, who had argued in Vistalegre I for greater proportionality, this time pushed for the Desborda system, which favored majorities (i.e., Iglesias and his list, which Echenique now formed part of). The only improvement over Vistalegre I was that the lists were now open, if weighted to the most voted. Although Iglesias's proposal for the internal voting system won by 41% of the 100,000 votes, almost 60% of those who voted opted for a more proportional form of representation that would enable the inclusion of minorities in the party's governing bodies. Errejón, who until Vistalegre II had not been a proponent of greater internal democracy in the party, now appealed to the base to allow for the integration of minority positions. He argued that the verticality of the party voted for in Vistalegre I was justified due to "exceptional circumstances," but that now it was time to open the party up. His team's proposal received only 2,000 fewer votes than Iglesias's. The critical *Anticapitalista* sector got just over 10%. As critical journalist Alabao (2016) concludes, "To be sure, Podemos at this point is certainly far from that tide of hope that it [could channel] all of 15-M's energy into a movement-party. . . . If [Podemos] wants to be a tool for institutional change and not just another wheel in the established machinery, it needs to leave behind the plebiscitary model and the vertical political culture that currently characterizes it."

Particularly galling for critics was the fact that the "assembly" in fact presented a fait accompli, since voting ended half an hour after the presentation of the final document, meaning any "debate" would have little effect on the outcome, rendering the "congress" a sort of performance spectacle rather than a forum for the debate of proposals. Iglesias once again threatened that unless all his documents were voted for, and unless his list won the majority vote, he would resign. There seemed to be little effort to engage in the transactions that characterized Vistalegre I's negotiations, and competing documents had entire sections that were practically identical to each other, evidencing the war of factions over the war of ideas.

Iglesias's team won all of the documents (ethical, political, organizational, and equality) and was the most voted list, leaving him with control of the Coordinating Council and Citizen's Council. The Desborda system gave Iglesias 60% control of the Citizen's Council, with 50% of the vote, giving him an absolute majority, with 37 councilors on the Citizen's Assembly versus 23 from Errejón's team and 2 from the Anticapitalista-Podemos en Movimiento list. Once again there was a "glass ceiling" in terms of the vote's gender breakdown: of the top 10 most voted for candidates, only 2 were women,[6] and although both were very worthy candidates in their own right, with high profile roles in the party, both had sentimental relationships with either Errejón or Iglesias, which, whether it influenced the vote or not, reinforces the alpha-male trope. All in all, from the perspective of those hoping to increase proportionality and pluralism in the party, the outcome of Vistalegre II was a crushing disappointment.

The division between Errejón and Iglesias was both organizational and political. Errejón, in advocating for a more proportional mechanism of distribution of power within the party, appealed more to party activists hoping to maintain a greater connection to social movements and some of the spirit of 15-M (although many would argue that neither Errejón nor Iglesias were genuinely interested in doing that). In theory, this position should put him more in line with the Anticapitalistas' (IA) critical sector. However, Errejón's political line is more centrist than Iglesias's, which alienates him from the harder left-wing positions of Anticapitalistas and other activists who identify strongly with the Left. For his part, Iglesias's political line is more clearly leftist but so is his vision for the more vertical internal organization of the party, seen as illegitimate by autonomous activists. The critical sector of Anticapitalistas is caught between support for Iglesias's political line but rejection of his reproduction of Institutional Left/vertical organizational structures and centralized control of the party.

While Iglesias has been successful in maintaining top-down control of the party, this has come at a high cost, because the lack of legitimacy from the perspective of autonomous and 15-M activists has led to waves of resignation during the short life of the party. The desire to control the party from the center led to the imposition of often inexperienced leaders in the regional organs of the party, who had little connection with local party politics, and who saw their authority as stemming from their proximity to the party executive, as opposed to stemming from legitimacy gained by working closely with people on the ground.

The culture of war criticized by many has by no means been limited to the rift between Errejón and Iglesias. Competition for positions on electoral lists within the many circles and within the internal organs of the party have further debilitated it, leading one party insider to comment that "the bloodletting in the circles over the configuration of the electoral lists has left scars that will take a long time to heal." Competition for the top spot in each region also divided circles and party organs into factions.

The politics of confrontation symbolized by Vistalegre II led to widespread debate in critical sectors over the culture of war within the party that was linked to a feminist critique of masculinized political culture. Alabao (2017b) wrote of the challenge of democracy in Podemos, that it wasn't just a question of introducing mechanisms that could effectively deal with dissent, but of dispensing with the culture of competition and war, and creating a more feminist organization "which does not mean putting women in positions of power—although that's important—but women who question power itself and the way that it's exercised as a means to creating a more egalitarian structure." Women were by no means the only feminists critiquing the party, as many feminist men shared this analysis. One party member said of the competition between Iglesias and Errejón, "What really gets me is the stupidity. Does anybody really think there's going to be a winner here?" A 15-M activist and critic commented on Facebook (in February 2017), stating,

> These types of warrior discourses are the most [. . .] seductive because they have an element of virility. [. . .] But look where all this Schmittian thinking has gotten Podemos: neither to reform nor to revolution, only to an internalization of the logic of war. And after all this, the most they can hope for is for the party to survive. If we don't manage to think about politics in another way that doesn't overcome this macho warrior fantasy, we are lost. [. . .] Anyone who

thinks that [the renewal of] "the political" can consist of destroying relationships [. . .] has understood absolutely nothing.

The real cost of the organizational model proposed by Iglesias and voted for by his loyal voting base (and the Vistalegre stadium was *full* of his loyal fans) is that it marginalizes, silences, and therefore alienates so many of the most committed activists within the party, and negates the possibility for these rich debates to flourish within the heart of the party. In the lead-up to Vistalegre II, the great debate was whether or not it would be possible to open up the party and rectify the problems caused by the internal mechanisms decided on in Vistalegre I. After Vistalegre II, the party was left with a more presidentialist model than ever. As Alabao (2017a) writes with regard to Vistalegre II,

> They have voted to allow the secretary general to ask them by Internet—as they have up to now—whenever he encounters problems in the executive leadership of the party: allowing him to design the timing and the form the question takes. They voted to allow the state assembly to revoke decisions taken in the autonomous communities, and even to provoke citizen assemblies in any part of Spain to replace local party leadership—as has already happened in Galicia. They voted for the Desborda system—with all the problems it entails—to be the voting system used to elect all party organs and officials.

The situation that has arisen in Podemos throws into relief the core issues that need to be grappled with in digitally enabled participatory scenarios that are still based on a plebiscitary model. These take the quantity of participation as an indicator of democratic participation, rather than the quality of participation, especially in a hyper-mediatized scenario where party leaders, especially ones with a strong media presence like Iglesias, will be favored. Of course, in one superficial sense this reproduces classic political debates between participation and voting of the "ignorant masses" versus "enlightened leadership" (see Chapter 1). In light of this discussion about the relation between 15-M and Podemos, however, it takes us back to the core demand for greater and "real" democracy in 15-M, where democratic decision-making was seen as involving genuine discussion and a desire to reconcile opposing views, to seek consensus and plurality, and not to reduce participation in politics to voting every four years.

The autonomous action principle of *quien lo propone se lo come* (literally "who makes the proposal, eats the proposal") refers to the idea that people involved in taking a decision should also be deeply implicated in carrying it out, and unless people are willing to work to put their proposal into action, they should refrain from proposing or deciding. People who only come to assembly to push their agenda (or that of their leader or party), but do not "stick around" to do any real work, are seen as less legitimate and less entitled to take decisions than those involved in the day-to-day work that keeps the assembly alive, as well as less aware of the real issues surrounding any decision, given their distance from the everyday reality of the political work. From this perspective, in the Podemos scenario, the internal voters (some 480,000 registered in 2017) whom Iglesias's plebiscitary and presidential model can appeal to for decisions are like those illegitimate assembly interlopers—their level of commitment is questionable (in part because it is impossible to measure the extent to which they are involved)—when compared to those who work inside the party. As decided in Vistalegre I, the Podemos voter, as Alabao (2017a) points out (echoing Aristégui's analysis above), is not even asked to become a member of the party in order to vote:

> The technocratic justification for this was to create a party that didn't resemble any other. But what was really behind it was a model that didn't have to distribute power to the bottom, to the actual organization or to the circles; instead, it only had to ask the opinion of tele-spectators who could participate from home via an easy click. Nothing else is asked of them.

The party primaries of April 2018 witnessed a further round of internal critiques from some factions, such as *Podemos en Movimiento*, who boycotted the process, arguing Podemos was squandering valuable political capital at a time when the Popular Party was vulnerable. It is ironic that the party built on a movement whose fundamental critique of really existing democracy was that democracy didn't only consist of voting every four years should end up constituting itself as a party where, for most people, participation consists of voting every four years on issues decided by the leadership of the party. A party where the internal voting mechanisms are weighted toward the majorities and have enabled the minority control of the party from above and from the center, a system that has marginalized or expelled dissenting voices, fostered a culture of war and factionalism and all-or-nothing politics. Podemos's leadership's legitimate fear that the party would be co-opted by traditional leftist actors paradoxically influenced their own tendency towards verticalism in order to maintain control of the organization. At the same time, they legitimately feared a loss of control through purely participatory mechanisms from the more radically horizontal elements in the party, such as choosing representatives by lottery, or control of the party from below through the circles.

Podemos: A Hybrid Party?

Whether or not something of the initial vision and promise of a hybrid party that truly connects to its social movement base and seeks to create a new political form that overcomes the dividing line between movement and electoral collective action logics can be salvaged is an open question. For some, the party has passed the point of no return. In the words of one well-known and influential 15-M activist, "Podemos has utterly ceased to interest me politically. It has simply ceased to be credible." Another, a political scientist, declared the party "[t]he least internally democratic party in Spain."

Podemos occupies an ambiguous space between two logics. One is an autonomous logic that seeks to constitute popular power outside and beyond the state, and beyond any specific identity, a radical egalitarianism based on the idea that anyone and therefore no "one" (group, interest, identity) can represent the people. This is the logic of the 15-M *ágoras* in the plazas, which work through particular spaces of action, but also against specific anti-austerity politics like the anti-eviction actions of the PAH, that connect to the daily struggles of lived experience, attempting to transcend Left-Right cleavages. The other logic (manifested also by Melenchón in France and Corbyn in the UK) is based on leftist interpretations of Laclauian populism that appeal to the shared history, nation (*patria*), and identity of "the people" and seek to reclaim these from the Right. The loss of Errejón to Más Madrid, following bitter and publicized internal disputes, dealt a deep blow to the party's reputation, its vote at the Community of Madrid level, and its supporting base. How big an impact this will have at the general elections remains to be seen.

Sympathetic or critical observers and participants in the party agree on one thing: Podemos would not exist without 15-M. However, as I argued in Chapter 10, in a certain sense Podemos (or the political projects of those behind it) plays a part in the origin story of 15-M. And if Podemos would not have been possible without 15-M, 15-M would not necessarily have produced Podemos. That achievement belongs entirely to those visionaries who fueled the original initiative and persuaded so many others to follow and support the project, overcoming their "cognitive dissonance" to facilitate the transition from movement to party.

Despite deep differences between the visions and practices of democracy in the movement and the party, all share a desire to break with the Culture of the Transition, to break with the practices of really existing democracy, and to push for a strong anti-austerity agenda and the renewal of Spanish democracy. Podemos has also supported numerous strikes, increased attention to the problems of precarious workers and the gendered costs of austerity, spoken out against repression and the Gag Law, stood up against sexist violence, and actively supported and participated in countless 15-M-related political actions and issues. In this sense it *can* be said to represent the movement.

Critiquing and exploring the challenges of hybrid parties as they seek to reconcile horizontal and vertical forms through the case of Podemos in no way diminishes the party's remarkable achievements. Podemos has broken with the bipartisan alternation of power established in the pacts of the Transition. It has managed to breach the seemingly impenetrable walls of an electoral system designed to keep power distributed between two main parties,[7] opening up political space not just for Podemos, but also for the resurgence of the right-wing party Ciudadanos, which has appropriated some of its central discursive elements and demands for democratic renewal (again unthinkable without 15-M). It has transformed the political landscape by proving that elections could be won on the basis of grassroots movement support and independently of private financial backing. It has delegitimized established politics but relegitimized party politics by calling for a reclaiming of public institutions for citizens, with politicians that are independent of vested interests. The salary caps and obligatory donations to grassroots movements (of the elected official's choice) break with the separation of political elites from the lived reality of "average citizens."

Although other post-15-M parties and collectives were discussing electoral initiatives (e.g., Partido X, municipal list initiatives), Podemos managed to get there first, successfully achieving the cognitive liberation of the electoral "Sí se puede," acting as a huge motivator to push those other initiatives forward and to galvanize energy and support, and later acting as a key partner in the municipal lists that have had an even greater direct influence on Spanish politics through the control of some of Spain's major cities. Iglesias and other Podemos officials have managed to speak for a sector of disadvantaged people in Spain who have not felt identified with the classical Left parties, and Podemos has precipitated internal crises of the seemingly immovable PSOE. It and 15-M-related activism laid the groundwork for the PSOE's successful motion of censure in 2018 that finally removed the PP from government (following a series of corruption scandals that Podemos worked hard to keep on the political agenda) (Flesher Fominaya 2018).

The loss of Errejón to Más Madrid, following bitter and publicized internal disputes, dealt a deep blow to the party's reputation, its vote at the Community of Madrid level, and its supporting base. In the general elections of November 2019, the Unidas Podemos ticket (in colation with IU, Equo and En Común Podem) lost 8 seats with respect to their April 2019 results, ending up with 34 (a far distance from the 71 seats they won in 2016). For his part, Errejón made the leap to national politics, presenting a new party Más país and gained 3 seats, far from his supporter's expectations.

Yet despite the relatively poor results, in January 2020 Podemos was poised to enter government in coalition with the PSOE pending a successful investiture. The demographic profile of voters (a very high average age for PP, and a much younger profile for Podemos)[8] indicate that, barring any further reversals in its fortunes, Podemos represents an important part of the future vote and can therefore potentially play an important role in government. And it has done all of this in a remarkably short period of time, without external funding, relying on crowdfunding, and managing to run the party on a fraction of the budget of the established parties, with transparency and accountability.

If it breaks with 15-M in some of its forms and spirit, Podemos represents continuity in its political demands: it has challenged austerity politics and their justification, continuing the critique of 15-M that politics needs to place the interests of citizens above those of elites, and it has relentlessly denounced corruption, demanded transparency, and delegitimized "la casta" and exposed "la trama." At the same time, it has relegitimized electoral politics for a significant number of people who had been alienated and self-disenfranchised from representative politics—even many 15-M activists, who moved from shouting "They don't represent us!" to "They do represent us!"

While the trajectory of Podemos may suggest electoral and movement logics are so fundamentally opposed as to render progressive hybrid parties oxymora, I remain optimistic that the core political cultural frameworks of 15-M and similar movements can still bear fruit on transforming new party logics. The ongoing debates around feminizing politics, the critical push for greater internal democracy, and the continuing experimentation of digitally enabled democratic visionaries in movement/party political laboratories all give reason for hope.

Notes

1. For a provocative discussion of this in Italy's 5 Star Movement party, see Treré and Barassi 2015.

2. *Convocatoria por Madrid*, cofounded with Equo and others, a short-lived initiative that was soon integrated into Podemos, although the Green party Equo retains its party identity.

3. All of the sessions can be viewed at https://instituto25m.info/universidad-de-podemos-2016/.

4. *Ilusión* is not directly translatable but refers to a combination of hope and excitement, as in looking forward to something good happening.

5. In July 2018 Colau and Carmena took their feminizing politics message to the United Nations. In a session on Cities for Adequate Housing, Colau stated, "It is in the cities where we are feminizing politics out of sheer need—we are the government of everyday needs, we understand there is nothing more important than human life, and we cooperate to find common solutions, and that is what we call feminizing politics. We invite all states to join in this revolution and to feminize politics."

6. The results of the vote (unmodified for gender parity) can be found here: https://vistalegre2.podemos.info/wp-content/uploads/2017/02/155015.results.pdf.

7. But, in fact, according to some analysts, this electoral shift began with 15-M in 2011, see Partido X 2014. For analysis of the evolution of the vote, 15-M and Podemos, see Revilla et al. 2015.

8. See Metroscopia 2015.

PART V

Conclusions

12

15-M Political Culture, Collective Identity, and the Logic of Autonomous Networks in the Digital Age

THROUGHOUT THIS BOOK I have shown how 15-M's political culture and collective identity followed an autonomous networking logic to build the movement and mobilize against austerity and for democracy. Following this logic, the movement built social capital, based on reciprocal solidarity and alliances, and developed shared master frames about the crisis and austerity, moving beyond prefigurative democratic practices within the movement to contest hegemonic discourses about democracy and the crisis, and to offer alternatives visions of democracy that contributed substantive content to a "real" democratic imaginary.

Autonomous organizing logics defy the "recipes for success" in canonical social movement literature. Resource mobilization theory, for example, emphasizes the role of strong formal organizations and the ability to attract and maximize external resources (Zald and McCarthy 2017). Political process theory stresses the importance of favorable political opportunities, in the absence of which movements would not succeed, no matter how well organized and financed (Edwards 2014; McAdam 1982). Gamson's (1990 [1975]) classic work *The Strategy of Social Protest* established that the three factors most likely to contribute to movement success are centralized power, bureaucratic organization, and ideological convergence (the absence of factionalism). Others have emphasized the importance of strong professionalized leadership and organization

Democracy Reloaded. Cristina Flesher Fominaya, Oxford University Press (2020). © Oxford University Press.
DOI: 10.1093/oso/9780190099961.001.0001

(Morris and Staggenborg 2004; Staggenborg 1988). Despite numerous critiques and alternative formulations (Gerlach and Hine 1970; Gerlach 2001; Goldstone 1980; Goodwin and Jasper 1999; Jasper 2010a; Piven and Cloward 1979, 1991), the idea that vertically organized, formally structured, well-resourced, and institutionally integrated movements will be most likely to succeed is widespread and persistent.

The tendency to focus on formally organized movement organizations, coupled with a state centric bias in analyzing movement effects (Giugni 1998; Giugni et al. 1999), has contributed to the marginalization and invisibility of autonomous movements in the literature. This has been exacerbated by two other tendencies: to consider mobilization (e.g., protests) to be the primary or most significant aspect of social movement activities (Melucci 1989, 2003), and the auto-invisibility of autonomous movements, whose refusal to mobilize under flags, banners, and other identity markers makes recognizing their role in mobilization difficult in the absence of inside information.

Uncovering the role of autonomous social movements in mobilization, and its impact, therefore, requires an approach that enables access to their subterranean spaces of experimentation, an approach that also enables the researcher to triangulate activist narratives and self-representations with other ethnographic data. Understanding the internal dynamics of autonomous movements not only enables an exploration of prefigurative praxis within movements (Blee 2012; Juris 2008; Maeckelbergh 2009; Polletta 2012), but when combined with a genealogical approach and secondary sources, it does much more: it enables us to understand the dynamics of movement emergence and consolidation (Freeman 1999; Melucci 1989), as well as the relationship between movement political culture, collective identity, and praxis *within* the movement and its impact on the wider political field.

The challenge of building large movements across heterogeneous groups of actors has led scholars to consider the contexts or circumstances within which diverse actors are likely to work together, focusing in particular on political opportunity structures (Eisinger 1974; McAdam 1982; Meyer 2003; Tarrow 2011; Tilly 1978). In considering internal movement-building processes, scholars have focused on the role of resources, effective recruitment, influencing authorities, and achieving new gains for group members (Gamson 1990; McCarthy and Zald 1977; Meyer 2003; Piven and Cloward 1979), within a framework that sees movements as a series of alliances between discrete social movement organizations

(SMOs), (Diani 2015; Diani and McAdam 2003; Zald and McCarthy 2017). In this book, I have argued that movement political culture, collective identity, and praxis are crucial elements of movement building in prefigurative autonomous movements.

My analysis of the 15-M movement shows that in times of crisis, autonomous networks can enable rapid mobilization, but also, more importantly, in the wake of mass mobilization, autonomous networking logics can build and sustain heterogeneous *movements* across multiple issues, identities, and ideologies, even in the absence of abundant movement resources, formal organizational structures, professional and formal leadership, and favorable institutional political opportunities. Although economic grievances facilitated public receptivity to the movement's claims, it faced other significant challenges, including a state that refused to change austerity policies in response to movement demands (thereby increasing the difficulty of maintaining a belief in the possibility of winning), and criminalized protest, dissent, and poverty (thereby increasing the costs and fear associated with mobilizing).

Autonomous networking logics have long faced challenges in their execution, including informal hierarchies, de-facto leaderships, personalized conflicts, burnout through assembly fatigue, and the paradoxical conversion of autonomous principles into counterproductive orthodoxies through a lack of critical reflexivity in their adoption (Flesher Eguiarte 2005; Freeman 2013). A commitment to horizontality is always navigated in tension with more vertical logics of action (Flesher Fominaya 2007a). Autonomous groups face the constant threat of self-destruction if they fail to strike a balance between efficacy and process in a way that satisfies participants, and conflicts over strategy and priorities are rife (Flesher Fominaya 2007b, 2010). In 15-M the salience of feminist and technopolitical ethics acted as synergistic correctives to some of autonomy's potential shortcomings, as well as providing values and substance to the movement's democratic imaginaries.

Movement culture provides actors with a common set of references, a bundle of practices and orientations to group interaction that set boundaries for legitimate behavior (which are contested and dynamic, but also relatively stable and coherent) (Bourdieu 1977; Crossley 2003; Flesher Fominaya 2016a; Jasper 2010b). Movement political culture is closely connected to movement collective identity, because autonomous actors recognize and accept each other as belonging to the same movement largely on the basis of shared cultural praxis (a whole way of struggle loosely defined around core principles), and this works to sustain the movement and build cohesion over time. The specific ideational frameworks that underlie the movement's political culture also have crucial implications for the way the network evolves and the kind of politics it pursues. 15-M political culture does not form a neat and coherent alternative model of democracy, but rather what are known as *ideas fuerza*, or core ideational frameworks, that motivate action, or praxis. I have argued throughout that the movement political culture is fueled by three core ideational frameworks, which I have synthesized as autonomy, feminism, and technopolitics (see Table 4.1). These different core frameworks are rooted in specific political movement traditions and imaginaries that come into tension with each other but can also combine synergistically. Three Acampada Sol slogans after the camp was "packed up" sum these up: Autonomy: "We'll see you in the neighborhoods;" Feminism: "We are moving to your consciousness;" and Hacker Ethics: "We'll see each other in cyberspace."

Here I explore the strengths and limitations of 15-M's autonomous collective identity, the synergies and tensions between its core ideational frameworks, and the continuing power of collective action networks in the digital age.

15-M collective identity: Strengths and limitations

The collective identity of the 15-M movement rests largely on embracing a commitment to the three core frameworks discussed above, to a greater or lesser extent. Crucially, it is the inclusivity and elasticity of the autonomous collective identity that not only defines membership but actively works to *expand* it. That is, you need to be committed to inclusivity and diversity to belong, and this requirement in itself, in theory, works to expand the scope and frame of belonging in the movement. This idea comes from the autonomous tradition and is what I have termed elsewhere (Flesher Fominaya 2015a) as "the paradox of anti-identitarian collective identity." In Acampada Sol, from the very first moment, any symbols or flags that could be divisive were removed or left out. But autonomy needs to be constantly reflexive and critical, and it ceases to work if it becomes complacent and gels into orthodoxy or prescription (Flesher Eguiarte 2005). The ripping down of the feminist banner that read "The revolution will be feminist or it won't be a revolution" was a perfect example of this, as was the "consensus orthodoxy" that confused consensus with unanimous agreement. As I have argued elsewhere (Flesher Fominaya 2015b), breaking out of the activist ghetto and reaching "the people" was a long-term ambition of autonomous activists in Spain, one tied deeply into the anti-identitarian framing of autonomy's political subject. The "politics of anyone" (Lawrence 2013) in 15-M did initially work to overcome traditional political cleavages between the Left and the Right, but the nomenclature of "citizen" and the appeal to "we the people" also rooted "anybody" very firmly in the Spanish terrain, lessening its universalist and internationalist imaginary, a source of critique for some participants.

This ambiguity reflects the tensions between autonomous collective identity and the Laclauian populist constructions of "the people" strategically embraced by JSF and Podemos. Where, for example, does an undocumented migrant stand in relation to the label "citizen"? Who among "ordinary citizens" can spend endless hours in the plazas and assemblies? It is no coincidence that two core socio-demographic movement groups are youth (who have less family and work commitments due to unemployment) and old-age pensioners such as the *iaioflautas/Yayoflautas* who are at the end of their working lives. In addition, the "we the people" formula (later expressed in Occupy Wall Street as "we are the 99%") also runs the risk of glossing the myriad forms of exclusion and marginalization that traverse the 99%, including racism, classism, sexism, and heteronormativity (Calvo and Álvarez López 2015; Flesher Fominaya 2015c; Fernández-Savater and Rancière 2014). The "politics of anybody" (Moreno Caballud and Grabner-Coronel 2015) therefore requires active and concerted pedagogical practice in order to genuinely include—and erase hierarchies between—participants, as the feminists in the squares discovered almost immediately. It was through their concerted political action, and not simply through the "inclusivity" formula, that feminism became a core ideational framework within the movement (and not everyone would agree with me that it succeeded). Although participants subscribe to an anti-racist ideology, and many work actively on migrant, refugee, and anti-racist work, there has not been an active integration of people of color and non-Spaniards into the movement as a whole (although this varies by group and area of activity). The mastery of linguistic codes and movement cultural practices creates internal cohesion, but also barriers to the integration of those who don't or can't easily master them. Again, active reflexivity and pedagogical work is necessary to overcome these barriers. Recognizing too that intense activism is itself inherently exclusionary helps explain the appeal of digitally enabled democratic imaginaries, as they are perceived to enable participation outside fixed places and times (e.g., three-hour assemblies in urban squats) in a never-ending assembly that takes place in the "neighborhood patio called the Internet."

When rooted in a consolidated movement culture, autonomous collective identities can serve to build strong movement networks in the absence of formal organizational structures and strong ideologies, and across heterogeneous issues and identities, providing part of the glue that enables reciprocal alliances to form and movement social capital to develop (Diani 1997; Diani 2015).

Core ideational frameworks of 15-M political culture: Synergies and tensions

The autonomous tradition is very locally rooted in *urban* movements. It is no coincidence that key members of the municipal movements (including the mayor of Barcelona) come from squatting movement traditions that have thought deeply about the urban landscape and its problems for many years, as well as developing a reimagining of urban life based on a commitment to inclusivity and the material and social needs of citizens. Here the influence of feminism has been a crucial source of inspiration, and Ahora Madrid and Barcelona en Comú's mayors have an explicit commitment to not only "de-patriarchizing" but also "feminist-izing" (*feminizar*, or "feminizing" in their terminology) politics and the city. This vision goes far beyond combatting gender inequality and sexist violence to reimagining a caring city that prioritizes the needs of its most vulnerable and places the good of the commons above particular interests. Feminist imaginaries in 15-M have filled the floating signifier "democracy" with specific substantive content, which cross-contaminates with autonomy, environmentalism, anti-militarist, squatting, queer, and other movement traditions.

The long-standing cross-contamination of autonomous feminist and anti-militarist movement cultures in Madrid also provided the commitment to nonviolence that characterized most of the 15-M movement from the beginning. This too was actively juxtaposed to the violence of austerity and capitalism and its inherently divisive and competitive ethos:

Rooted in the base of the movement [. . .] is [. . .] a culture of peace and democracy in response to the violence of funding cuts and the precariousness of the state of living, [instead of the fear and hatred fuelling the rise of] xenophobic parties [in other countries]. (Nanclares and Horrillo 2017)

Feminismos Sol understands its activism as offering "[p]roposals that place people at their center, taking into account their diversity, needs, and desires, and questioning the order of things established by the markets" (Caravantes et al. 2016).

The locally rooted nature of autonomous politics in Spain comes into tension with technopolitics in three ways that 15-M activists had to navigate. First, the face-to-face assembly model is rooted in place, specifically the neighborhood, a key "trope" in the imaginary that is a quasi-fetish in *asambleario* politics, whereas hacker ethics are rooted in the placelessness of cyberspace, which offers the possibilities of defying space-time boundaries. 15-M brought the two into greater communication. One day I ran into Julián, a member of the 15-M HackLab. He told me excitedly that the HackLab had had a really great assembly and they had taken a big decision. I asked him what it was, fully expecting him to tell me something about digital tools or cyber-politics. He said, "We realized that what we really need to do is get out in the neighborhood and talk to our neighbors, especially the older ones who are really missing out on this whole digital thing. We need to understand where they are coming from and help them get connected!" In pure Madrid autonomous style, their democracy "hack" started with talking to the neighbors!

The second tension arises between the slow, participatory, active listening aspect of *asamblearismo* and the speed and agility of technopolitics. The 15-M reappropriated Zapatista slogan "We are going slow because we are going far" is great for imagining new worlds, but sometimes changing things requires speed. Digital tools enable rapid communication, and the interpenetration of the assemblies with these tools means face-to-face assemblies can be connected with people who aren't physically present but are online, so decisions can be taken more quickly, collaborative documents can be written in situ, campaigns can be designed and consulted on collectively during meetings, and the whole assembly can be live-streamed if desired.

Finally, *asamblearismo*'s "sovereignty of the assembly fetishism" with its attendant occasional "consensus obsession" comes into tension with the unmediated autonomy of action of techno-politics. Manuel of Xnet and 15MpaRato doesn't see the need for consensus and approval to take action, and explicitly contrast their forms of technopolitical networking with assembly-based horizontalism:

All we need to do is say, "Listen, we're going to do this, do you want to help us out?" And that's how it works, and it works well, and you don't have to ask for anyone's approval and nobody needs to represent you. I think that in the 21st century we should have arrived at a point where society is sufficiently mature and empowered to be able to do this.

The shifting of decision-making completely online and outside the assembly can and has led to serious tensions and problems (Flesher Fominaya 2016b). In this way the *asamblearia* tradition acts as a corrective to the potential unaccountability of technopolitics, but the autonomous hacker ethic embodied by groups like 15MpaRato also enables a rapid response to changing conditions. Key to the balance between approaches is the *legitimacy* of the actors, who will be forgiven for taking action without consultation as long as they are seen to be acting for the common good and in line with the general principles and commitments of the movement or group as a whole. The hacker ethic commitment to transparency and "open source code" (letting others see how you have done what you have done, and allowing them to evaluate it, replicate it, and, hopefully, improve it) facilitates this legitimacy.

Hacker ethics and digital democratic imaginaries have strong synergies with autonomous politics, especially when autonomous movements seek to re-engage with the state and its institutions directly, as in 15-M. Digital tools facilitate communication but also enable political objectives by providing solutions to some of the problems inherent to really existing democracy. These include oversight of corruption and fraud through whistleblowing and collective intelligence mediated online, and the digitally enabled implementation of innovations and improvements (transparency of institutions through online information sharing maximum decision-making and consultation of citizens enabled by online tools, including voting on budgets; etc.) (see also Romanos and Sádaba 2015). The rise of monitory democracy as a key element of the politics of movements like 15-M and hybrid parties like Podemos is greatly facilitated by digital tools and the internet (Feenstra et al. 2017).

The cross-contamination of organizing traditions fueled a process of "cognitive liberation" enabling long-standing political desires to be materialized in new forms. Canino, a community radio activist, told the story of how he and other radio community activists had long been frustrated by the organizing model of their local community radio stations, which were governed by boards of directors. When they encountered 15-M's Ágora Sol Radio they realized that the horizontal *asambleario* organizing model could be a challenging but radical way to produce community radio. They decided to become not just a community radio but a *guerrilla radio* based on a technopolitical, and not just an *asambleario*, imaginary:

> We wanted to disseminate the organizing model we use in Ágora Sol Radio, what in free software terms we would call liberating the source code, so, not just produce radio from the squares, but explain to others how to do it so they could [. . .] replicate it, improve it, and put it at the service of the commons. We wanted to apply the concept of sustainability to a process of horizontal, self-organized (autonomous), associative, and collaborative communication, through welcoming people to learn with us, but also going out and doing workshops and encouraging ourselves and others to do much more of this work of showing others how it is done.

This cross-contamination of autonomy and technopolitics (and indeed feminism and autonomy) predates 15-M but was given an accelerated intensity through the process of occupation and the subsequent explosion of movement activity. With respect to the development of a new democratic imaginary, there are key points of synergy between autonomy, feminism and technopolitical frameworks, which are manifested in the Spanish political laboratory in myriad ways.

All take *the subversion of identity* as a key problematic, all see reconciling *inclusivity and diversity* as a central challenge, all understand knowledge sharing as a means of redressing power imbalances, and all challenge the idea of "experts" and "leaders" as separate classes of people who can use this to legitimize the exercise of power. The challenge to experts is very different from anti-intellectualism. It is not against expertise or professional knowledge per se, but rather against certain groups of people claiming it as their exclusive domain. All three core frameworks seek to fundamentally transform social relations. Together they pose a profound challenge to dominant narratives about the way contemporary society should be organized, socially, economically, and politically, and offer instead a vision of collective self-empowerment through active and participatory citizenship. In Spain, they also work to shape and sustain specific networks that engage in collective action.

Autonomous networks in the digital age

In the wake of global protests following the financial crisis, the role of digital media has been put forward as an explanatory factor to explain the emergence and strength of mobilization, including 15-M, and to argue for the power of social media to mobilize weak ties in the absence of organizing structures in the emergence of the protest and subsequent encampment (Bennett and Segerberg 2012, 2013; López, et al. 2014; Anduiza et al. 2014, Gerbaudo 2012). Bennett and Segerberg's conception of the logic of connective action has become very popular in social movement literature as revealing a fundamentally new and determining factor in mass mobilization and movement organizing. They link their argument about the role of ICTs in contemporary mobilizations (including 15-M) to a theory about the centrality of personalized expression and individualism in contemporary society. Others have also argued for a link between internal architecture of social media platforms, such as Facebook and Twitter, and the extent to which they are characterized by a "logic of self-centered participation" (Fenton and Barassi 2011, 183) "that privileges the individual over the collective, the formation of temporary online crowds rather than social movements" (Kavada 2018, see also Tufekci 2014). In this way social media architecture is connected to a purported self-seeking entrepreneurial individual shaped by the very neoliberal logics embedded in social media (Brown 2015; Kavada 2018).

These arguments rest on a distinction between peripheral crowds (of individual personalized entrepreneurs exchanging interpersonal action frames online), who follow an aggregational logic, and networked nodes of activists on the ground, who somehow escape the individualized logics of social media platforms. The problem with these arguments does not lie in the recognition of looser organizational structures facilitated by digital tools, but in seeking the emergence of mass mobilization in the preexisting individual attributes (including beliefs and ideas) of participants who then need to align their collective action frames with those of a movement and its ideology—a long tradition in social movement studies (see Munson 2008). The problem with this argument is that the shared beliefs, ideas, and collective action frames (and collective identities) that fuel movements develop primarily through participation in social movement activities, not in isolation from them and prior to them. In order to understand what is happening online, we actually need to understand what activists are doing on the ground when they engage with digital tools.

We need to consider such use within the broad media and movement ecology within which activists operate (Flesher Fominaya and Gillan 2017; Mercea et al. 2016; Treré and Mattoni 2016; Kavada 2018). This means observing how they actually engage with these tools, the strategies they develop, and how they evaluate their effectiveness and importance. But it also requires paying attention to how ideational frameworks and movement political culture shape communicative and organizational practices. Doing so reveals their profoundly collective nature.

Gerbaudo (2012) adopts this approach to an extent in his book on social media and social movements, including 15-M. His argument has many merits, such as debunking the seemingly spontaneous nature of mobilization and contributing to the understanding of collective identity formation online. Although he presents his argument as against techno-determinism, he privileges and attributes a power to social media that is overstated, and claims a greater rupture with previous collective action logics than is merited. Like Bennett and Segerberg (2012), Gerbaudo understands the rise of individualism as a determining feature of contemporary society, and interestingly focuses on individual communicators in the movement, whom he sees as the invisible de-facto leaders in the shadows that enable the façade of networked horizontalism to prosper.

Gerbaudo (2012) posits a distinction between reluctant anti-leaders (13) and followers (19), in which communication activists are orchestrating or choreographing mobilization between dispersed individuals. Social media allows individuals to assemble, to fuse a collective identity (e.g., 29, 35–36, 77), and to channel emotions into collective indignation. His line of argument falls prey to the conflation of mobilization (protest event) with social movement (collective actor), and a privileging of mobilization as the key aim of activist communication strategies. He argues (13) that social media has led to the rise of soft forms of leadership that "exploit the interactive and participatory character of the new communication technologies," a problem he argues is only now beginning to be openly addressed (101). Yet the problems of informal leadership (generally) and power imbalances resulting from individuals' control of communication technologies in horizontal movements (specifically) have long been reflexively and critically documented (Flesher Fominaya 2016b; Juris et al. 2013; Pickerill 2004) by scholars and activists of autonomous movements, prior to the emergence of social media.

In a variant of the "connective action" argument, Gerbaudo (2012,138) argues that "within contemporary social movements, with their stress on informality and the adoption of 'friendship' as the frame for interpersonal interaction, communication and organization become by and large impossible to separate from one another—so deeply embedded, so tightly woven together that they become indistinguishable." My research shows, however, that digital ethnography and qualitative research enable one to clearly separate organizational and communicative practices, and to see how movement communication practices are *embedded in* organizational practices. This requires disentangling widespread communication online during visible protest from the communication practices and strategies within social movement groups that precede, traverse, and follow specific protest events.

My research on Acampada Sol, JSF, DRY!, the PAH, and 15MpaRato shows that those communication strategies were carefully and collectively developed behind the scenes, through an active and reflexive network-building strategy, down to the specific content of tweets and the timing of the social media campaigns. In many groups, the content of specific tweets for Twitter campaigns was developed in and out of assembly Titan Pads (collaborative documents), to which other groups, organizations, and collectives in the network were often invited. The tweets were then collected in a paste-bin to which other groups were given access and instructions on when (day and time) they should begin tweeting them. Communication strategies were developed following specific protocols to ensure consistency with the assemblies' values and agreements, as is the case with DRY! Madrid's secret Facebook page, where the Facebook posts they later publish publicly are debated, modified, and require the support of at least three members of the assembly before they can be posted. These campaigns were sometimes, as in the case of JSF, worked out in great detail up to a year in advance. Press releases and scripts and guidelines for spokespeople were also worked out beforehand. They were the result of collective debate that took into consideration the preferences and work of other actors in the network. While not everything has to go through consensus or formal assembly, the desires of the collective are taken into consideration and only broken in exceptional circumstances, and often at high cost to group cohesion and individual reputation. All of these examples show that it is indeed possible to disentangle organization and communication by engaging in an ethnography of digital practices, and that clearly these practices do not reflect the individualized exchange of collective action frames as Bennett and Segerberg argue.

Despite Gerbaudo's *own data* highlighting many of these characteristics for Madrid's 15-M, and the evidence he provides on the importance of concerted action by activists engaging in communicative strategies, he nevertheless concludes that, "What we are witnessing here is thus not only an equivalence between organization and communication, but arguably also a reversal of their mutual relationship. . . . It is communication that organizes, rather than organization that communicates. As a corollary, communicators also *automatically* become organizers, given the influence they can have through their communications on the unfolding of collective action" (2012, 139; emphasis mine). There are number of problems with this bold statement, which fails to take into account several considerations about social movement actors' use of media.

First, activist use of social media serves to do much more than mobilize to protest on the ground, and is often geared to contesting hegemonic narratives. Second, even the most strategically developed communication plans by influential actors often *fail* in their attempts to spur or shape mobilization, which highlights the lack of necessary correspondence between on- and offline mobilization, and the difficulties of influencing what happens online, let alone offline. Third, during periods of peak mobilization, instigating actors (the communication activists) quickly lose control of the communicative sphere. Recall the descriptions of absolute chaos in the communication cadre of Acampada Sol (Chapter 4), where any illusions of total control over message and strategy were quickly dispensed with, and where there were multiple sources of information (spokespeople, accounts, websites, etc.). Fourth, influential social movement "communicators" (even power tweeters like Fanetín) are not acting in isolation but are embedded in the social movement community. Fanetín, for example, actively participates in a number of collectives and organizations and contributes to the collective development of their action campaigns. A spokesperson, tweeter, or Facebook content producer who goes off-script, or unilaterally decides to hijack a movement communication systems or platforms (e.g., Acampada Sol, tomalaplaza, or DRY!), will be met with strong sanctions from the community (as numerous such attempts have shown over the years). Finally, privileging communication over other movement practices precisely ignores the way communication strategies and practices are *embedded in specific organizational logics* and supported by the many other resources in the network (as Aristégui pointed out so forcefully in Chapter 4). Far from representing a break with previous networked social movements then, as Gerbaudo (2012, 30) and others argue,

15-M is in fact a testament to the continuing importance of networks in social movement configuration in the digital age.

By attributing wider social processes such as the rise of individualism to movements, scholars adopting these arguments are neglecting the importance that collectively developed counter-hegemonic ideational frameworks have in fueling movement organization. Autonomous movements are not immune from neoliberal logics, of course, but are actively, reflexively, and prefiguratively working to contest them. In contrast to some libertarian ideologies, in Spain (and elsewhere in Europe, Latin America, and North America) the commitment to autonomous principles is not based on a conception of the atomized liberal individual, but on a collective actor (Flesher Fominaya 2007a). The decentralized, nonhierarchical, anti-identitarian, and anti-ideological logic of autonomy predates the mass adoption of digital tools, despite having deep synergies with their architectures, and despite the way these digital tools have influenced the autonomous imaginary (and been influenced by them). Collective logics do not represent "old" ways of organizing that are giving way to "new" connective action logics (Bennett and Segerberg 2012). Collective and connective logics are not antithetical, but mutually enhancing, and mutually constitutive.

Digital tools are ubiquitous to contemporary mobilizing and are as likely to be used by the Taliban as by progressive pro-democracy movements. What I hope to have shown here is that as important as digital tools are, even more influential for 15-M has been the integration of a technopolitical hacker *ethic* that enters into synergy with other movement traditions to fuel collective action located in specific networks (see also Romanos and Sadába 2015). This ethic is not rooted in individualism but in harnessing the power of the collective, which makes it strongly synergistic with autonomous collective action logics, not antithetical to them. The movement has from the beginning integrated on- and offline forms of action, sometimes initiating online (as with Estado de Malestar, DRY!) before going offline, other times working in the other direction (PAH, NSD, JSF, 15MpaRato), and other times never going online as a group (the *preferentes* pensioners). From the planning of the first 15-M protest, the movement has been built step by step by concerted collective action on the ground, by DRY! Madrid members going from one assembly and group to another, through the intense collective exchanges in the squares and the circulation of activists flowing through the networked squats and physical spaces of Madrid, Barcelona, and other cities and towns. Through these exchanges these activists built up shared master frames and narratives about the crisis and austerity and their own resistance to it. They established solidarity through acts of generosity and courage, physically blocking evictions, plastering the walls of banks and government buildings with stickers, occupying them with their bodies, sitting or dancing in protest, deafening elite narratives with whistles and banging on pots and pans, and filling the streets with *batucadas* and the strains of the "Solfónica," who set critical political lyrics to classic Spanish songs. They expressed their indignation but also their hope and commitment to life and joy through creative and humorous direct actions and street performances. They actively worked together to build and sustain the network through sharing resources and information, drawing on their collective intelligence, expertise, and creativity.

Crucially, ethnographic exploration of 15-M digital engagements reveal that their use is *collectively* self-reflexive and *collectively* designed and enacted, following a deep commitment to a logic of collective (not individual aggregational) connective action. It is these ideational frameworks that are completely overlooked in theoretical narratives linking social media use, hypothetical individualistic entrepreneurial citizens, and contemporary mobilizations. In 15-M, the collective actor is central precisely because the movement seeks to rupture the individualistic logic that capitalism and the post-political relentlessly attempts to constitute.

While new tools indisputably change mobilizing and organizing practices, what I contest is that the logics of mobilization have fundamentally changed (see also Fernández-Planells et al. 2013), at least not in the case of 15-M. While not discounting the importance of the effects of particular social media affordances on communication (Juris 2012, Antolín 2014, Gerbaudo 2012), what I have challenged here is the reading back from online interaction patterns to explain movement political participation, organization, and communication, ignoring the ideational frameworks that shape their use. I have argued instead that a hacker or technopolitical ethic—that is, a digital *imaginary*—has been crucial. This ethic does not work in isolation from other important frameworks, such as a commitment to autonomy and feminism, that also shape the use of digital tools and media. Digital ethnography enables us to trace the way movement communication practices are embedded in organizations, which are themselves connected to other groups in the wider network, all of whom coordinate and collaborate to instigate what then becomes visible online. These collaborative and coordinated digital practices also shape *internal* organization, which structures offline mobilization and many other move-ment practices. In the digital age, autonomous prefigurative movements like 15-M bring together connective and collective logics of action not just to protest, a fact often overlooked by those who study social media and movements. They also use them to directly take on institutional targets (such as the bankers targeted by 15MpaRato), to engage in processes of democratic experimentation and movement building, to reclaim and transmit movement knowledge from the past, and to harness collective intelligence to create new knowledge, expertise, and imaginaries.

The continued relevance of the movement "network" in the digital age

Autonomous logic is a networked logic, and technopolitical imaginar-ies have facilitated and countered some of its inertias while also posing new challenges in the quest to effectively integrate new tools. The net-work is not just important as a metaphor, but also as a reality. It depends first of all on the availability of *physical* spaces, and when key social cen-ters, for example, are evicted, there is a detrimental effect on activism. It also depends on virtual spaces that are actively created, nurtured, and sustained. The network is *relational* and establishes the possibilities and boundaries of action. Within different assemblies there is often a concern for what others in the network will feel about a particular action or deci-sion, especially if there is a feeling that the other group or actor has more legitimacy or ownership around that issue. This can slow down action and be a source of frustration, but it can also keep relations between groups in the network flowing.

Projects and initiatives in the network move forward on the basis of flexible collaboration between a core group of committed people, often located physically in the same place (even 15MpaRato has a core that mostly live in Barcelona, share a locale, and even joke about living to-gether) and a wider network of people who offer resources, expertise, or warm bodies on the streets. Collectives don't need a lot of people to drive forward a project, but they do need to be able to establish the legitimacy, trust, and dynamism to make others want to listen to them, support them, and turn up on the streets if necessary.

At the same time, no individual group is of much use in isolation from the rest of the network, because it is the combined resources, support, and solidarity between different actors that gives them impact and "critical mass." Key actors also serve as brokers who actively work to smooth relations between different groups and build the network by bringing different groups and actors into dialogue. Digital tools, and specifically the Internet, exponentially multiply the impact of these efforts but don't replace them. Strong networks are dense, cooperative, decentralized around several nodes, characterized by frequent dialogue between members, and connected by shared narratives around common issues and goals. In times of mobilization, this autonomous network logic facilitates the integration and "aggregation of individuals" into an "overflow" (*desborde*) if they are sufficiently moved and energized by the campaign.

The possibility for autonomous networks to be mobilized, seemingly "spontaneously" in times of crisis and opportunity, is captured by this quote from the appropriately anonymous collective voice of the MLGM (2017):

> We are living through an economic and ideological earthquake, where cultural consensus breaks down from exhaustion and new political paths emerge that only recently seemed impossible. A volatile, high-risk scenario, where threats and opportunities reveal themselves in all their starkness.
>
> Our creativity, our joy, and our combative impudence are always latent, lying in wait for the next opportunity to awake. When will they rise again?

15-M established a strong political culture and collective identity, whose specific content and not just form matter in explaining the sustainability and development of the movement and related initiatives. At the same time, neither the political culture nor collective identity are fixed, but rather, in keeping with autonomy and hacker ethics, are open and elastic, lending them a dynamism that can be actively enabled in the face of changing interpretations of context and opportunities, and can circulate across and between sites. This then is the power of autonomy in the digital age.

13

Democracy Reloaded

POLITICS IN TIMES OF CRISIS

SPAIN'S 15-M MOVEMENT demanding "real democracy now" is one of the most vibrant, sustained, and influential movements of recent decades. It forms part of a wave of post–2007-2008 financial crisis protests in which participants demanded an end to austerity or greater socioeconomic justice, but also greater or "real" democracy. From Occupy Wall Street to Hong Kong's Umbrella movement, these mobilizations and movements have placed the crisis of democracy at the center of public, political, and scholarly debate, and in Europe these debates have become central to academic inquiry and reflection.

Theorists of democracy and social movements have been divided in their view of what these movements represent in terms of their "emancipatory potential" or capacity to save or at least resist the further deterioration of democracy. Scholars such as Antonio Negri (1980), Jacques Rancière (2014), Michael Hardt (see Hardt and Negri 2004), Manuel Castells (2015), Donatella della Porta (2013), Simon Tormey (2015a, 2015b), and Amador Fernández-Savater (2012a) view autonomous networked movements favorably and recognize their role in contesting the status quo and regenerating democracy, while others either argue for the additional need for the construction of renewed political hegemony of the people for example Íñigo Errejón and Chantal Mouffe (2016) or see these movements as disorganized, inchoate, and incomplete, suffering from the fatal weakness of insufficient programmatic logics, and presumably the lack of an intellectual vanguard for example, Alain Badiou (2012).

The difference lies in part in core ideas about the relationship between theories and change and between social movements and emancipatory

Democracy Reloaded. Cristina Flesher Fominaya, Oxford University Press (2020). © Oxford University Press.
DOI: 10.1093/oso/9780190099961.001.0001

politics. In one view, emancipatory social movements are scenarios of contestation and conflict, in which grassroots actors attempt to build sufficient strength to not only resist the status quo, but also produce new knowledge and imaginaries. For those with a more teleological view of social change, social movements form part of a historical progression toward an already agreed-upon end (emancipation): they are a previous stage in the progression toward a "real" politics rooted in durable organizations.

There is no theory or programmatic logic capable of leading to emancipation, and even if by some miracle a social movement possessed it, the complexity of social forces would alter its manifestation and outcome. But that doesn't mean progressive transformation is not possible. Instead of seeking an intellectual vanguard with the "right" tools or strategy to reach a predetermined end, it is more illuminating to explore the cultural logics and ideational frameworks that enable a process of democratic experimentation, contestation, and regeneration to flourish, and to tease out their limitations and challenges, not as a prescriptive recipe for success, but as a contribution to critical reflexive knowledge on political engagement that seeks a democratic society based on equality and the common good—concepts that themselves must be continually redefined through contestation and reflection.

The 15-M movement emerged in the midst of profound twin crises, a financial crisis with its ensuing austerity policies, and a crisis of legitimacy of really existing democracy. The second crisis wasn't an inevitable outcome of the first, as can be seen by the variance in its expression across national contexts in which the crisis was strongly felt. Instead, pro-democracy and anti-austerity movements both reflected and contributed to the legitimation crisis through relentless contestation of hegemonic narratives that framed the crisis and its consequences as inevitable outcomes of abstract economic processes beyond political (or human) control. The 15-M movement did so initially in the guise of a movement rooted deeply in autonomy, which saw itself as manifesting and demanding real democracy independently from the state or other formal representative institutions, such as unions or parties. Although this stance has been a hallmark of autonomous movements in Spain and Europe for several decades, the 15-M movement marked a significant rupture with previous waves of mobilization in its "democratic turn." The Global Justice Movement certainly concerned itself with the search for alternative conceptions of democracy (della Porta 2013, 72–79; Flesher Eguiarte 2005; Flesher Fominaya 2010b;

Maeckelbergh 2009, 2012), but mostly as a prefigurative set of movement practices (i.e., of consensus, deliberation, and decision-making).

In 15-M, instead of seeing democracy as something that could only authentically be practiced *within* movements and critiqued *outside* them, activists began to combine a prefigurative experimentation with democratic praxis within the movement with a demand for reform within the institutions of really existing deficient democracy. In a shift from previous autonomous movements that tended to look inward and away from the state (Holloway 2014), in the face of a crisis of political representation, 15-M activists did not ask for less politics, but *more* politics, unleashing a debate about the nature and meaning of Spanish democracy. They appealed to the rights enshrined in the constitution, and to national sovereignty, demanding a government that responded to citizen needs (Benski et al. 2013; Flesher Fominaya 2014a, 2015e; Gerbaudo 2017; Roos and Oikonomakis 2014). This is what Spanish activists meant by the slogan "We are not anti-system, the system is anti-us." And this is why the term *anti-politics*, sometimes applied to these mobilizations, is spectacularly misleading.

In the Global Justice Movement, a shared commitment to practice based on autonomous cultural logics and values (i.e., diversity, horizontality, inclusivity, direct action) enabled alliances across issues and groups (e.g., feminism, environment, indigenous rights, global justice) around specific campaigns and mobilizations for "horizontalists," but these diverse groups were not connected through a shared understanding of a central problematic. In contrast, in the period following the global financial crash, when it was precisely the deficiencies in really existing democracy that were seen by activists involved in these movements to have *led* to the crisis and to austerity politics, democracy, with its deficiencies and imaginaries, became *the* problematic around which all other issues were viewed. In contrast to the Global Justice Movement, and in contrast to anti-austerity mobilizations in other contexts such as Ireland, activists in 15-M developed shared master frames about the crisis, austerity, and democracy that enabled them to not only develop a strong collective identity, but also to effectively contest hegemonic narratives used to justify austerity politics. In this way democracy also became one core factor in enabling cross-sectoral alliances, in both *form* (the movement practices that prefiguratively embodied a "15-M" way of manifesting democratic principles) and in *content* (the diagnoses of deficient democracy and the new imaginaries proposed to replace or correct these deficiencies). I have argued that these two elements—prefigurative democratic forms and democratic imaginaries formed of core values that give *substantive* meaning to the empty signifier "democracy"—cannot be separated from each other, and that both were necessary to sustain this remarkable movement over time, just as both are necessary now to "save democracy." At the same time, activists integrated their concern with prefigurative democratic practice within movements with active engagement in the public sphere and with democratic governing institutions to reload democracy, shifting toward a form of hybrid autonomy (see also Martínez 2016).

By tracing 15-M from its origins to its consequences, I have illuminated three core questions that motivate social movement scholarship regarding movement emergence, consolidation, and outcome. A genealogical approach to the 15-M movement enables us to address explanations for the rapid emergence of mass movements across the world demanding greater democracy and greater socioeconomic justice. I have argued that the global financial crisis opened up a necessary but insufficient opportunity structure for the emergence of strong and sustained anti-austerity mobilization. We cannot understand the emergence and strength of the 15-M mobilizations by recurring to economic grievances or spontaneity arguments, but must instead adopt a genealogical approach that enables us to understand the mechanisms through which the original mobilizations emerged and developed.

In the digital age, spontaneity arguments are often coupled with narratives that posit a determining role in mobilization processes for ICTs and digital media through the power of weak ties (Bennett and Segerberg 2012; López et al. 2014; Anduiza et al. 2014, Gerbaudo 2012). The case of 15-M suggests strongly that while digital media greatly facilitate processes of rapid mass mobilization, they are not a sufficient or determining factor in movement emergence, and their role has been overstated. In the absence of preexisting networks with a culture of network building collective action, even mass occupations will not be likely to lead to the emergence of sustained mobilization over time or to new or stronger movements, independently of how strategically and effectively actors deploy digital media. In 15-M, digital media tools were effectively integrated into offline preexisting networks and newly created groups, but that face-to-face *asambleario* (assembly based) organizing practices were still crucial, and that without these "strong ties" the 15-M movement would not have emerged and sustained itself as it did. It is precisely this organizational infrastructure that enabled the movement's survival beyond the squares, in contrast to some other "occupy" movements, whose use of social media paradoxically facilitated a rapid upscaling of mobilization but were unable to sustain movement momentum beyond the occupations (see Tufekci 2017). Digital media, therefore, while a crucial tool with significant benefits for and impacts on movements, cannot substitute connective action logics for collective logics of movement organizing, communication, and network building: there is no technological shortcut to building strong and sustained movements through strong as well as weak ties (see also Tufekci 2014, 2017).

Attention to movement praxis or cultural logics does not only illuminate the central puzzle of what it means for citizens living in liberal democracies to demand "Real Democracy Now!" It also provides one answer to the question of why some post-crisis European pro-democracy movements are more resilient and effective than others. I have argued that the key to understanding what fueled and sustained this powerful movement lies in the shared political culture and collective identity that emerged following the occupation of the squares, which not only sustained the movement through reciprocal ties of solidarity and support across a diverse set of actors, but also generated a shared set of critiques and master frames across a diverse and heterogeneous set of actors and issues (e.g., housing, education, pensions, privatization of public services, corruption) that enabled the movement to effectively contest hegemonic narratives and shift the public debate and political agenda, not just about the crisis and austerity, but about democracy itself. In so doing, movement actors fostered the emergence of democratic imaginaries based on substantive as well as procedural reforms, and transformed the broader political landscape, in intentional and unintentional ways, shifting from a democratic to an electoral turn with the rise of movement-parties seemingly antithetical to their original claims and goals.

In making this argument, I am not positing a frictionless, unified, 15-M framework. On the contrary, broadly shared understandings of 15-M emerge through processes of conflict and contestation that are central to the democratic process itself. Central tensions, such as between more horizontal (movement) and vertical (institutional/representational) logics of collective action are never fully resolved, but rather are continuously subject to critique and reflexivity.

By exploring the role of ideational frameworks, collective identity, and political culture in sustaining and fueling 15-M, I am building on work on prefigurative movements that seek to embody democratic praxis and their subcultures (Blee 2012; Feenstra et al. 2017; Maecklebergh 2009;

Polletta 2012; Flesher Fominaya 2007a, 2010b), as well as work on the role political cultures and collective identity play in movement-building processes (Castells 2010; Flesher Fominaya 2010b; Freeman and Johnson 1999; Gamson 1995; Hetherington 1998; Jasper 2008; McKay 1998; Melucci 1996, 2003; Polletta 1998a). At the same time, however, I have gone a step further to highlight the crucial role that *internal* prefigurative praxis played in shaping the movement's impact on the wider political field, impacts most commonly understood in terms of factors *external* to movements, particularly political opportunities (Eisinger 1974; McAdam 1982; Meyer 2003; Tarrow 2011; Tilly 1978). I have also shown how the ideational frameworks that underlie 15-M political culture profoundly informed the way (re)new(ed) democratic imaginaries are transmitted to the public via symbolic and discursive work that shifted the public narrative about democracy, on the one hand, and provoked an institutional crisis that affected political parties and governing practices, on the other (Antentas 2016; Iglesias 2015; Revilla et al. 2015). In this way I have shown how social movements' internal cultures, practices, imaginaries, and collective identities can transform the wider political landscape symbolically and materially.

Autonomous social movements and democracy

As democracy faces a crossroads in Europe and around the world, progressive movements for democracy provide one key source of critique, reflexivity, and potential renewal. Throughout this book, I have sought to illuminate the possibilities of autonomous social movements to contribute to a process of democratic regeneration, integrating grounded empirical work with more philosophical discussions about the relationship between autonomy and democracy (e.g., Castoriadis 1997; Fernández-Savater 2012a; Hardt and Negri 2004; Negri 1980; Rancière 2011, 2014). At the same time, I have sought to bring autonomous movements from the margins to the center of social movement scholarship. Autonomous movements tend to fall outside the purview of classical social movement paradigms and scholarship due to their absence of formalized organizational structures; their rejection of clear identities; their refusal of acronyms, flags, and banners; and their commitment to "biodegradable" networks that shift and change in line with desire, effort, and opportunity. All of these factors, coupled with their anti-systemic or critical nature, have contributed to their marginality in social movement scholarship, a trend only recently changing. We cannot situate "15-M" or any movement built on autonomous networking logics in a particular set of formally organized or institutional actors (Flesher Eguiarte 2005; Juris 2008). Instead, we can more fruitfully understand 15-M as a shared prism through which all actors who take it as a point of reference understand "a whole way of struggle," and whose coherence can be found in the shared political culture and collective identity that marks it as a collective political subject that is embodied in a dynamic way. This partially embodied, partially imagined collective actor—simply called 15-M—is still continually referenced in Spain, whether in relation to positive outcomes (such as the ousting of corrupt politicians) or negative ones (such as the increasing restrictions on democratic freedoms). But 15-M offers insights for debates about contemporary democracy beyond Spain, as well as insights into how contemporary social movements should be evaluated.

Rethinking movement outcomes

There is a strong tendency in social movement scholarship to view a movement's significance as resting primarily in its ability to effect some change in the nation-state (or supranational institution), either through affecting some change in policy or law, gaining access to power holders and state institutions, or managing to shift or set the agendas of political elites, all understood as effectively posing a challenge to power holders. This state-centrism affects the very definition and understanding of social movements and their success or failures. Charles Tilly (1999, 256), for example, goes so far as to argue that social movement scholars fall prey to two key errors: "The first idea is that social movements are solidaristic coherent groups, rather than clusters of performances. The second is that social movements have continuous, self-contained life histories in somewhat the same sense that individuals and organizations have life histories. Both ideas are false, or at least very misleading."

What Tilly is trying to highlight is that movements interact with opponents, and through this interaction demonstrate the worthiness, unity, numbers, and commitment (WUNC) that analytically defines them (as bounded, contingent, interactive performances by multiple unchanging actors) and also enables analysts to measure their impact and success. Tilly (1999, 258) suggests that anybody who disagrees with his definition simply wants to talk about what interests *them*. What I hope to have shown in this book is that viewing 15-M as a series of discrete performances demonstrating worthiness, unity, numbers, and commitment would reveal little about what enabled it to emerge, grow, and sustain itself over time against tremendous challenges. These challenges include a state impervious to movement demands, which not only refused to alter austerity policies (thereby increasing the movement's difficulty in maintaining a belief in the possibility of winning), but actively sought to criminalize protest, dissent, and poverty. In this way government policy sought to marginalize and delegitimize those suffering the effects of the crisis and those who spoke out on their behalf (thereby increasing the risks, costs, and fear associated with mobilizing).

I have also shown that social movement communities *do* have cohesion, are relational, are rooted in particular shared histories, and are held together by collective identity and political cultures, despite being porous, dynamic, and traversed by conflicts and contradictions. So Tilly is right to stress the conflictual and political nature of social movements, but wrong to limit our view to such a narrow understanding of the political. If we measured 15-M success in terms of its ability to change the political agenda or policies of established national political elites, we would conclude that the movement had failed. If we measure an increase of the mechanisms that characterize "monitory democracy" (e.g., greater transparency, less corruption etc.[1]), we can see some shifts in this direction at the municipal level (in Madrid, Barcelona, and other cities with "municipal movement governments"), but only indirectly via new movement parties that have entered institutional politics and not as a direct result of mobilization. There have been limited successes in stopping privatization of public services (e.g., the forestalling of attempts to privatize hospitals in Madrid). 15-M led to the emergence of the "Citizen Tides" (which combine union activism with 15-M demands and organizing forms) mobilizing around core austerity targets, such as education and healthcare. We have seen a historic success in the motion of censure that brought down the Popular Party government in 2018, which Podemos and other observers have attributed to the 15-M movement, despite the final performance unfolding within the chambers of parliament (Flesher Fominaya 2018). The movement has had a much greater impact on public opinion, galvanizing an astonishing level of public support (Sampedro and Lobera 2014), and, crucially, increasing people's expectations for democracy and opening up a national conversation about what democracy *should be*.

Undoubtedly, the impact of the 15-M/housing movement on transforming public awareness of the housing crisis and the role of existing law and government policy in condemning millions of Spaniards to social exclusion has been remarkable. The mayor of Barcelona has managed to free the city from energy giant Endesa and has municipalized energy (Cols, 2018). Manuela Carmena, the former mayor of Madrid, municipalized public services and closed her mandate with a 54% debt reduction and a budgetary surplus of 1,072 million euros (*Público* 2019). Both have implemented participatory budget and decision-making schemes in line with their commitments to open government that have grown directly from the work of 15-M activists in municipal government (Ayuntamiento de Madrid 2018), winning international recognition from the UN (Constantini 2018).

The movement has been much less successful, however, in mobilizing around labor and unemployment. Labor unrest has been rife in Spain since 2011, but the major unions, perhaps because of their own institutional inflexibility, have been unable to fully integrate their strike actions into a wider and sustained mobilization (Antentas 2016). The 15-M movement has managed to relentlessly and effectively contest hegemonic narratives about the crisis and austerity, and has laid the blame for them on bankers and politicians, but it hasn't systematically radically challenged the underlying system as a whole—a limitation that renders it insufficiently transformative for some activists. As Carlos Taibo put it, "We need to find a way out of capitalism, not out of the crisis" (in Bastida 2013, n.p.). Given the extent to which neoliberal capitalism permeates every aspect of our lives and society, what the movement *has* achieved is nevertheless remarkable.

Transforming politics

15-M developed its own movement political culture, but it also, through its intense mobilization, transformed Spain's political landscape and shook up, if not transformed, national political culture. In the face of mass mobilization, political elites have fought back, not only to justify an economic model in which austerity cuts are seen as an unfortunate necessity, but also to defend a representative model of democracy that invests them with the legitimacy to make such choices on behalf of citizens. The Popular Party has steadfastly refused to acknowledge its responsibility for the massive cases of fraud and corruption that have been exposed in recent years, despite the direct implication of party leadership. It argues too that Spain is recovering well from the crisis (despite the Bank of Spain acknowledging that it is unlikely to recover the 60,600 million euros it spent to bail out the banks) (*Público* 2017).

Meanwhile, after a period in which the PSOE had been imploding due to its loss of votes and legitimacy in supporting the PP, its fortunes have again risen after the successful motion of censure brought forth by Pedro Sánchez in the wake of further corruption scandals (Flesher Fominaya 2018). After an internal coup ousting Secretary General Pedro Sánchez in 2016, he managed to regain command (if not control) of the party in 2017. Such has been the influence of 15-M (and the threat posed by Podemos) that in 2017 Sánchez declared that he would "represent the 15-M movement" (EFE, 2017), leading 15-M activists to declare on social media, "You have understood nothing!" and "We still remember when the PSOE ordered our eviction from the plazas!" The bipartisan model, however, is clearly in crisis, and for now any government will struggle to build sufficient support to legislate effectively.

Marisa Revilla Blanco (Revilla et al. 2015) argues that the cycle of mobilization characterized by 15-M issued forth an ideological reconfiguration that has transformed the electoral landscape in Spain. Antentas (2016, 2) goes even further, arguing that 15-M is the expression of a regime crisis in which the "assessment of the political system and its institutions is at its lowest since the Transition."

Beyond transforming the political opportunities for the emergence of new parties, 15-M forced established parties to integrate at least cosmetic changes, as Silvia Nanclares and Patricia Horrillo (in Fernández-Savater and Flesher Fominaya 2017) argue:

> There are lessons that remain from those days in the plazas that appear now in the discourse of political parties: a commitment to transparency or the search for citizen participation in more open processes. These are achievements, although many use these ideas simply as marketing. [. . .] This hack will not be immediate, but it sets forth a process of change that has no point of return.

15-M and Podemos also opened up political space for Ciudadanos, a right-wing party that predates 15-M, but whose fortunes were radically improved in the wake of Podemos, as it presented itself as a right-wing alternative that would also fight corruption.

Given how unresponsive the state has been to movement demands, it is remarkable how sustained the movements against austerity in Spain have been. This ability to sustain itself despite "political failures" points to the need to widen our gaze beyond "politics" narrowly defined when assessing the outcomes of social movements.

Transforming the political

If it is true that neoliberalism is undoing the demos (Brown 2015), then movements like 15-M are trying to counter that "stealth revolution" with a counter-revolution for democracy. While part of that involves transforming politics, which takes the form of visible performances or challenges to power holders that can be measured in policy outcomes, the most radically transformative capacity of social movements lies in their ability to transform *the political*. 15-M endeavored to transform the political in several key ways. The first attempted transformation was that of the ordinary citizen into an active political subject with a belief in their own capacity to transform society (what Touraine [1988] would call *historicity*), actively blurring the boundary between "activist" and "ordinary citizen." This belief combats the greatest obstacles to social change, which are fear (of failure, wasted energy, repression, reprisals), resignation, and apathy due to the belief that nothing can be done. "Without fear" was a key slogan of JSF and it and other 15-M-related groups understood fear as a key enemy to be overcome. Experiences in squares like Acampada Sol transmitted an emotional high fueled in part by the belief that change *was* possible (e.g., "I really thought we were in the midst of a revolution!"). Mobilizing that belief is one of social movements' key and most difficult tasks.

"People power" is probably the most radical idea of 15-M, and the hardest to get people to understand, embrace, and believe, as the activists in 15MpaRato pointed out. While 15MpaRato's concrete political goal was to uncover political and financial fraud and bring those responsible to justice, their most heartfelt desire in transforming the political was to convey the idea that "the citizens did it," that it was possible for indignant citizens to take collective direct action on behalf of the public interest. Mass media would take their victories and reinsert them into a narrative of action taken by political representatives and intermediaries, attributing to political leaders achievements made by lawyers, journalists, and hacktivists. "Sí se puede" is not just a slogan to get a party elected, it's an idea that is necessary to break through the post-political consensus that relegates politics to the realm of politicians and the belief that challenges are won and rights are gained because of elite concessions. As Silvia Nanclares and Patricia Horrillo (in Fernández-Savater and Flesher Fominaya 2017) put it,

> Understanding that democracy can only be articulated through ballot boxes and representation is mutilating the idea of constructing a society through collective means.

Transforming not just politics but the political means moving beyond demanding specific laws, better policies, or more responsive institutions (as important and necessary as these are) to raising the bigger questions about what constitutes the good society, and what kinds of mechanisms underlie the myriad inequalities that characterize contemporary society. 15-M created spaces that enabled the development of new imaginaries around these questions. This happened not through abstract discussions about democracy, but by connecting democratic imaginaries to an analysis of the nature and consequences of the crisis and austerity. Autonomous and hacker imaginaries are seen as ways to "hack" the deficient democracy that is understood as *responsible* for austerity policies. Feminism is a prism through which to understand, critique, and pose an alternative to austerity. In the context of (patriarchal) austerity capitalism, for example, "caring is revolutionary" was one of the feminist slogans of Acampada Sol. The logic of austerity capitalism, with its emphasis on individual gain and responsibility, erodes solidarity, as individuals blame themselves (and each other) for their inability to pay their mortgages, and compete with others over jobs and scarce resources. In this context, care and solidarity (and *not* charity) become a radical alternative and a constitutive political act (see also García Agustín 2015). Movements like the PAH understood this, which is why the first thing they tell newcomers is that (a) what happened is not their fault, but is a systemic problem; (b) they are not alone; and (c) the community will only survive if those who benefit from it also actively contribute to it. They offer collective self-empowerment and the creation of a commons in the face of what many initially see as their individual problem or crisis. The first shared master frame of these new imaginaries was that the nature of the crisis is *political* and not the result of abstract, unknowable, and mysterious economic forces outside of anyone's control. In the case of the PAH, for example, unpacking the "mysteries" of the deliberately obfuscating language of mortgage contracts and turning each member of the PAH into a mortgage "expert" manifested this democratic imaginary in a concrete way directly connected to the material effects of the crisis.

Spain's political laboratory cooked up new imaginaries in heterotopic and counter-hegemonic spaces. Here they generated discourses and created an alternative symbolic universe that frames political conflict and critique. These spaces were *heterotopic* in the sense that they brought together different elements not usually found together to disrupt the "order of things" that produces the normalized and disciplined subject, occupying public space in ways that redefined the possibilities of their use (e.g., plazas as political spaces and not spaces of consumption), and reclaiming "private" spaces (e.g., squats) for public use. They were *counter-hegemonic* in that they contested the "common sense" that props up the consensus around the status quo, that defines the relation between "governed and governing." They did this through the creation of alliances of diverse groups working together, juxtaposing a heterogeneous indignant people to an uncaring and unresponsive political and financial elite, who together with the juridical-constitutional apparatus form a "regime" (Errejón 2011, 139) that does not represent them. A huge banner unfurled in the Puerta del Sol the day before the 2011 municipal elections read "Down with the regime, long live the people's struggle, without fear," and "They do not represent us!" was the rallying cry.

The active building of alliances across different groups contributed to another important but often overlooked outcome of social movements: the increase in social capital (Diani 1997), or the strengthening of the network itself and its capacity to extend its limits and "overflow" them. The openness of the collective identity and political culture led to the creation of multiple hybrid spaces and organizations in which critical alternative media became mass media (e.g., *eldiario.es*, the critical media consortium El Salto), and movements became parties.

Of all the outcomes of the 15-M movement, the most potentially transformative (and to me the most unexpected) has been the resurgence of feminism in redefining the political. From small repeated acts of mundane disruption, such as the widespread use of the feminine plural, to a deep rethinking of what feminist politics could mean and look like, feminist women and men have managed to shift feminism from being a "women's" issue to becoming a prism through which to interrogate *all* of society and politics in the quest for a "Real Democracy Now!" that benefits everyone. A logic in which all fit leaves itself open to future possibilities as identities transform and shift.

Transforming the political and not just politics involves jamming the cultural, transforming consciousness, heightening emotions, inhabiting subcultural and subterranean laboratories of experimentation, attempting to create a political subject capable of transcending particular identities, engaging in the politics of the mundane and not just the discursive, and, yes, also performing visible acts of contestation in the public sphere, where the fruits of these many meaning-making labors may be expressed, preferably with creativity and joy as well as critique and contestation.

I have argued throughout that, as Castoriadis (1997), or Rancière (2011, 2014) remind us, we must dispense once and for all with viewing democracy as a set of procedures that can be applied to any ideology or values. Separating democratic forms from democratic content, focusing on digital tools or forms of media, and ignoring or marginalizing the ideational frameworks that fuels their use allows the conflation of progressive movements that are mobilizing for democratic regeneration with those who are mobilizing for an increasingly authoritarian state and the continued holding hostage of democracies for elites. In enables the conflation of right- and left-wing "populism" (terms that in any event need to be defined and unpacked), facilitating the dismissal of mass mobilizations for change as merely "the same kind of thing that led to Trump's election" (a comment I have heard numerous times in the presentation of my research). I hope by now that any reader of this book will be well aware that movements such as 15-M are the anti-thesis of movements that seek to exclude, restrict, and dominate, and which adopt hierarchies of human worth as the basis for their policies.

Attention to ideational frameworks that motivate political collective action enables us to distinguish between politics with radically different effects. The adoption of particular tools, strategies, and tactics can, and are, of course shared across ideological orientations, but this does not mean that they serve the same purpose or respond to the same motives. Participatory mechanisms can lead to the rise of Hitler and Trump, as much as they can give rise to Gandhi. Participation and greater citizen input on its own, in the absence of a democratic paideia, in the absence of a clear commitment to progressive substantive democratic values that are negotiated and renegotiated through conflict or consensus, will not lead to a regeneration of democracy. Conceptions of the common good are never fixed or predetermined, but must be subjected to critical reflection as circumstances and societies change.

It is a commonplace to argue that the Left is concerned with class and the Right with nation. If pro-democracy and anti-austerity movements have shown us anything, it is that the stakes of the new conflicts are waged around different polestars. Left-wing populist parties like Podemos are actively reclaiming the nation, and right-wing populism uses the myth of national greatness to appeal to disenfranchised working-class people. In times of crisis, where the legitimacy of really existing democracy and the economic order breaks down, the conflict is reoriented between life and capital. Between those who advocate a privileging of human, animal, and environmental well-being over the interests of individual and corporate profit, and those who don't. Perhaps the most difficult challenge of politics in times of crisis is to make these poles of conflict clearly visible despite the oversaturated, highly malleable, and rapidly changing nature of communicative space. Perhaps the relevant political questions today are no longer about Left or Right, Marxism, socialism, liberalism, or anarchism, but are much more urgent and fundamental: Do we choose democracy or authoritarianism? If democracy, for what ends and for whose benefit? Do we choose the common good over individual benefit? Do we choose life over capital?

Note

1. For a discussion of monitory democracy in Spain, see Feenstra and Keane 2014.

References

Accornero, Guya, and Pedro Ramos Pinto. 2015. "'Mild Mannered'? Protest and Mobilisation in Portugal under Austerity, 2010–2013." *West European Politics* 38 (3): 491–515.

Adell, Ramón. 2011. "La movilización de los Indignados de 15-M." *Sociedad y Utopía* 38: 141–70.

Aguilar Fernández, Paloma. 2002. *Memory and Amnesia: The Role of the Spanish Civil War in the Transition to Democracy*. New York: Berghahn Books.

Alabao, Nuria. 2016. "¿Qué Tiene Que Ver La Democracia Interna de Podemos Con El Cambio En España?" *Ctxt.Es*, December 21, https://ctxt.es/es/20161221/Politica/10199/Podemos-Vistalegre-Iglesias-Errejon-anticapitalistas-proporcionalidad.htm.

Alabao, Nuria. 2017a. "Historia de Dos Vistalegres." *Ctxt.Es*, February 11, https://ctxt.es/es/20170208/Politica/11066/vistalegre-2-podemos-iglesias-errejon.htm.

Alabao, Nuria. 2017b. "¿Por Qué Hay Una Cultura Política de Guerra En Podemos?" *Ctxt.Es*, February 5, https://ctxt.es/es/20170201/Firmas/10954/podemos-vistalegre-iglesias-errejon-guerra.htm.

Almond, Gabriel, and Sidney Verba. 1963. *The Civic Culture: Political Attitudes and Democracy in Five Nations*. Princeton, NJ: Princeton University Press.

Anduiza, Eva, Camilo Cristancho, and José M. Sabucedo. 2014. "Mobilization through Online Social Networks: The Political Protest of the Indignados in Spain." *Information, Communication & Society* 17 (6): 750–64.

Antentas, Josep María. 2016. "Podemos and the Spanish Political Crisis." *Labor History*, 58 (1): 106–31.

Antolín, Verónica. 2014. *En Los Orígenes Del Movimiento Indignado En España. Estado Del Malestar: De Facebook a Sol, Un Estudio de Caso*. Tres Años de Indignación: La Emergencia de Nuevos Sujetos Políticos. CanalUNED. http://contenidosdigitales.uned.es/fez/view/intecca:VideoCMAV-5a6f37ccb1111fe1388b45a1.

Armingeon, Klaus, and Kai Guthmann. 2014. "Democracy in Crisis? The Declining Support for National Democracy in European Countries, 2007–2011." *European Journal of Political Research* 53 (3): 423–42.

Arribas Lozano, Alberto. 2012. "Sobre La Precariedad y Sus Fugas: La Experiencia de Las Oficinas de Derechos Sociales (ODSs)." *Interface* 4 (2): 197–229.

Aguilar Fernández, Susana, and Alberto Fernández Gibaja. 2010. "El Movimiento Por La Vivienda Digna En España o El Porqué Del Fracaso de Una Protesta Con Amplia Base Social." *Revista Internacional de Sociología* 68 (3): 679–704. https://doi.org/10.3989/ris.2008.12.01.

Ayllón, Daniel. 2014. "Ada Colau: Gane Quien Gane Necesitaremos Más Movilización Que Nunca." *La Marea*, December 22, http://www.lamarea.com/2014/12/22/ada-colau-gane-quien-gane-vamos-necesitar-mas-movilizacion-que-nunca/.

Ayuntamiento de Madrid. 2018. "Cinco Nuevos Compromisos Para Avanzar En Gobierno Abierto." Nota de Prensa. *Diario Del Ayuntamiento de Madrid*, October 7, https://diario.madrid.es/blog/notas-de-prensa/cinco-nuevos-compromisos-para-avanzar-en-gobierno-abierto/.

Badcock, James. 2015. "Former IMF Boss Rodrigo Rato Arrested in Madrid." *The Telegraph*, April 16, http://www.telegraph.co.uk/news/worldnews/europe/spain/11543551/Former-IMF-boss-Rodrigo-Rato-arrested-in-Madrid.html.

Badiou, Alain. 2005. *Being and Event*. London: Continuum.

Badiou, Alain. 2012. *The Rebirth of History*. London: Verso.

Baiocchi, Gianpaolo, and Ernesto Ganuza. 2012. "No Parties, No Banners: The Spanish Experiment with Direct Democracy." *Boston Review*, February 14, http://bostonreview.net/world/no-parties-no-banners-gianpaolo-baiocchi-ernesto-ganuza.

Bastida, Alberto. 2013. "Carlos Taibo: Tenemos Que Buscar Una Salida Del Capitalismo, No de La Crisis." *Jot Down Cultural Magazine*, http://www.jotdown.es/2013/02/carlos-taibo-tenemos-que-buscar-una-salida-del-capitalismo-no-de-la-crisis/.

Baumgarten, Britta. 2017. "The Children of the Carnation Revolution? Connections Between Portugal's Anti-Austerity Movements and the Revolutionary Period 1974/1975." *Social Movement Studies* 16 (1): 51–63.

Bennett, W. Lance, and Alexandra Segerberg. 2012. "The Logic of Connective Action." *Information, Communication & Society* 15 (5): 739–68.

Bennett, W. Lance, and Alexandra Segerberg. 2013. *The Logic of Connective Action: Digital Media and the Personalization of Contentious Politics*. Cambridge University Press.

Benski, Tova, Lauren Langman, Ignacia Perugorria, and Benjamin Tejerina. 2013. "From the Streets and Squares to Social Movement Studies: What Have We Learned?" *Current Sociology* 61 (1): 541–61.

Blee, Kathleen M. 2012. *Democracy in the Making: How Activist Groups Form*. Oxford: Oxford University Press.

Bosi, Lorenzo, and Katrin Uba. 2009. "The Outcomes of Social Movements." *Mobilization: An International Quarterly* 14 (4): 409–15.

Botella Ordinas, Eva. 2011. "La democracia directa de la Puerta del Sol." La vie des idées.fr, May 24, https://booksandideas.net/La-democracia-directa-de-la-Puerta. html.

Bourdieu, Pierre. 1977. *Outline of a Theory of Practice.* Cambridge: Cambridge University Press.

Brown, Wendy. 2015. *Undoing the Demos: Neoliberalism's Stealth Revolution.* Boston: MIT Press.

Calleja, Tono. 2013. "La CNMV Investiga Al 90% de Los Bancos y Cajas Que Vendieron Preferentes." *InfoLibre*, http://www.infolibre.es/noticias/politica/2013/04/17/la_cnmv_investiga_los_bancos_que_emitieron_preferentes_2615_1012.html.

Calvo, Kerman. 2013. "Fighting for a Voice: The Spanish 15-M/Indignados Movement." In *Understanding European Movements: New Social Movements, Global Justice Struggles, Anti-Austerity Protest*, edited by Cristina Flesher Fominaya and Laurence Cox, 236–53. London: Routledge.

Calvo, Kerman, and Iago Álvarez López. 2015. "¿Nueva Política Pero Viejos Perdedores? 15-M, Podemos y Las Mujeres." *eldiario.es*, March 1, http://www.eldiario.es/agendapublica/nueva-politica/Nueva-politica-perdedores-Podemos-mujeres_0_361864204.html.

Carvajal, Alvaro. 2015. "La Participación Toca Fondo En Las Polémicas Primarias de Podemos." *El Mundo*, July 23, http://www.elmundo.es/espana/2015/07/23/55affbf1e2704e98178b458d.html.

Carvajal, Álvaro. 2016. "15-M: De Indignados a Diputados." *El Mundo*, May 9, http://www.elmundo.es/espana/2015/05/15/5554fd3fe2704e4c648b45ac.html.

Caravantes, Ruth, Haizea Álvarez, Loreto Ares. 2016. "Feminismos Sol: Cinco Años En Movimiento | Periódico Diagonal." *Diagonal*, https://www.diagonalperiodico.net/la-plaza/30189-feminismos-sol-cinco-anos-movimiento.html.

Castells, Manuel. 2010. *The Information Age: Economy, Society, and Culture.* Vol. 2, *The Power of Identity.* Boston: Wiley-Blackwell.

Castells, Manuel. 2015. *Networks of Outrage and Hope: Social Movements in the Internet Age.* Cambridge: Polity.

Castoriadis, Cornelius. 1997. "Democracy as Procedure and Democracy as Regime." *Constellations* 4 (1): 1–18.

Castro, Irene. 2014. "Pablo Iglesias Lanza La Candidatura 'Podemos' y Apela a Que Izquierda Unida Reaccione." *El Diario*, January 17, https://www.eldiario.es/politica/politologo-Pablo-Iglesias-candidatura-dispuesto_0_219078268.html.

Chabanet, Didier, and Arnaud Lacheret. 2016. "The Occupy Movement in France: Why Protests Have Not Taken Off." In *Street Politics in the Age of Austerity*, edited by Marcos Ancelovici, Pascale Dufour, and Heloise Nez, 279–94. Amsterdam: Amsterdam University Press.

Chabanet, Didier, and Frédéric Royall. 2015. "The 2011 Indignés/Occupy Movements in France and Ireland: An Analysis of the Causes of Weak Mobilisations." *Modern & Contemporary France* 23 (3) 327–49.

Chironi, Daniela, and Rafaela Fittipaldi. 2017. "Social Movements and New Forms of Political Organization: Podemos as a Hybrid Party." *Partecipazione e conflitto* 10 (1): 275–305.

Christensen, Henrik Serup. 2016. "All the Same? Examining the Link between Three Kinds of Political Dissatisfaction and Protest." *Comparative European Politics* 14 (6): 781–801. https://doi.org/10.1057/cep.2014.52.

Císař, Ondrej, and Jiri Navrátil. 2017. "Polanyi, Political-Economic Opportunity Structure and Protest: Capitalism and Contention in the Post-Communist Czech Republic." *Social Movement Studies* 16 (1): 82–100.

Claveria, Silvia. 2016. "¿Por Qué Las Mujeres Votan Menos a Podemos?" *Politikon*, July 8, https://politikon.es/2016/07/08/por-que-las-mujeres-votan-menos-a-podemos/#.

Colau, Ada, and Adriá Alemany. 2012. *Vidas Hipotecadas: De La Burbuja Inmobiliaria Al Derecho a La Vivienda*. Barcelona: Cuadrilátero de libros.

Colau, Ada, and Adriá Alemany. 2013. *¡Sí Se Puede!: Crónica de Una Pequeña Gran Victoria*. Barcelona: Destino.

Coleman, E. Gabriella. 2013. *Coding Freedom: The Ethics and Aesthetics of Hacking*. Princeton: Princeton University Press.

Cols, Carles. 2018. "Barcelona Prescinde de Endesa y Se Conecta a Su Propia Eléctrica." *El Periódico*, January 7, https://www.elperiodico.com/es/barcelona/20180630/electrica-publica-barcelona-energia-releva-endesa-6917694.

Comando Video. 2014. *SÍ SE PUEDE. Seven Days at PAH Barcelona*. https://vimeo.com/323297000.

Consejo General del Poder Judicial. 2012. "Memoria Annual," http://www.poderjudicial.es/cgpj/es/Poder_Judicial/Consejo_General_del_Poder_Judicial/Actividad_del_CGPJ/Memorias/Memoria_Anual/Memoria_anual_2012.

Constantini, Luca. 2018. "La ONU Premia Al Ayuntamiento de Madrid Por Su Portal de Participación." *El País*, June 7, https://elpais.com/ccaa/2018/06/07/madrid/1528383491_645024.html.

Corcuera, Laura. 2014. "Delegar La Política Nos Ha Llevado Al Desastre Generalizado." *Diagonal*, December 2, https://www.diagonalperiodico.net/global/24924-delegar-la-politica-nos-ha-llevado-al-desastre-generalizado.html.

Cox, Laurence, and Cristina Flesher Fominaya. 2009. "Movement Knowledge: What Do We Know, How Do We Create Knowledge and What Do We Do with It?" *Interface Journal* 1 (1): 1–20.

Crossley, Nick. 2003. "From Reproduction to Transformation: Social Movement Fields and the Radical Habitus." *Theory, Culture & Society* 20 (6): 43–68.

Crouch, Colin. 2004. *Post-Democracy*. Cambridge: Polity.

Crouch, Colin. 2011. *The Strange Non-Death of Neoliberalism*. Cambridge: Polity Press.

Cunning Hired Knaves. 2014. "Podemos—Translated Manifesto." https://hired-knaves.wordpress.com/2014/01/20/podemos-translated-manifesto/.

Dahl, Robert A. 2015. *On Democracy*. New Haven: Yale University Press.

Dekker, Paul, and Ramón A. Feenstra. 2015. "Activism and Civil Society: Broadening Political Participation." *Recerca: Revista de Pensament y Anàlisi* 17: 7–14.

della Porta, Donatella. 2005. "Deliberation in Movement: Why and How to Study Deliberative Democracy and Social Movements." *Acta Politica* 40 (3): 336–50.

della Porta, Donatella. 2012a. "Critical Trust: Social Movements and Democracy in Times of Crisis." *Cambio: Rivista Sulle Trasformazioni Sociali* 2: 33–43.

della Porta, Donatella. 2012b. "Mobilizing against the Crisis, Mobilizing for 'Another Democracy': Comparing Two Global Waves of Protest." *Interface* 4 (1): 274–77.

della Porta, Donatella. 2013. *Can Democracy Be Saved? Participation, Deliberation and Social Movements*. Cambridge: Polity.

della Porta, Donatella, Massilimiano Andretta, Tiago Fernandes, Eduardo Romanos, and Markos Vogiatzoglou. 2018. *Legacies and Memories in Movements*. New York: Oxford University Press.

della Porta, Donatella, Joseba Fernández, Hara Kouki, and Lorenzo Mosca. 2017. *Movement Parties against Austerity*. Cambridge: Polity.

Diani, Mario. 1992. "The Concept of Social Movement." *The Sociological Review* 40 (1): 1–25. https://doi.org/10.1111/j.1467-954X.1992.tb02943.x.

Diani, Mario. 1997. "Social Movements and Social Capital: A Network Perspective on Movement Outcomes." *Mobilization: An International Quarterly* 2 (2): 129–47.

Diani, Mario. 2015. *The Cement of Civil Society*. Cambridge: Cambridge University Press.

Diani, Mario, and Doug McAdam. 2003. *Social Movements and Networks: Relational Approaches to Collective Action*. Oxford: Oxford University Press.

Díaz-Parra, Ignacio, Jaime Jover Báez, and Beltran Roca Martínez. 2017. "Del 15M Al Giro Electoralista." *Cuadernos Geográficos* 56 (1): 344–64.

Domínguez, Ana, and Giménez, Luis. 2014. *Claro que Podemos*. Madrid: Los Libros del Lince.

DRY!. 2011. "Material Oficial. ¡Democracia Real YA!" http://www.democraciarealya.es/promocion/material-oficial/.

Easton, David. 1953. *The Political System*. New York: Kopf.

Edwards, Gemma. 2014. *Social Movements and Protest*. Cambridge: Cambridge University Press.

EFE. 2017. "Sánchez Asegura Que El PSOE Representará al Movimiento Del 15M." *La Vanguardia*, June 18, https://www.lavanguardia.com/politica/20170618/423486493778/sanchez-asegura-que-el-psoe-representara-al-movimiento-del-15m.html.

Eisinger, Peter. 1974. "Conditions of Protest Behavior in American Cities." *American Political Science Review* 67 (1): 11–28.

El País. 2012. "El Engaño Masivo de Las Preferentes." *El País*, September 13, http://economia.elpais.com/economia/2012/09/13/actualidad/1347534473_888418.html.

El País. 2014. "Caixa Catalunya Dio Orden de Vender Las Preferentes Como Un Producto Seguro." *El País*, July 23, http://economia.elpais.com/economia/2014/07/23/actualidad/1406101555_485412.html.

El País. 2015. "La Rey Juan Carlos Retira El 'Honoris Causa' a Rodrigo Rato." *El País*, December 22, http://ccaa.elpais.com/ccaa/2015/12/22/madrid/1450805086_609921.html.

El Plural (EFE). 2015. "¿Cumple Podemos Su Promesa de Primarias?" *El Plural*, November 17, http://www.elplural.com/2015/11/17/cumple-podemos-su-promesa-de-primarias.

Eldiario.es. 2012. "Rajoy: 'Hemos Comprado a Crédito Viajes Al Caribe.'" *Eldiario.Es*, http://www.eldiario.es/lacrispacion/Rajoy-comprado-credito-viajes-Caribe_6_75652449.html.

Errejón, Iñigo. 2011. "El 15-M Como Discurso Contrahegemónico." *Encrucijadas: Revista Crítica de Ciencias Sociales* 2: 120–45.

Errejón, Íñigo. 2015. "We the People El 15-M: ¿Un Populismo Indignado?" *ACME: An International Journal for Critical Geographies* 14 (1): 124–56.

Errejón, Íñigo, and Chantal Mouffe. 2016. *Podemos: In the Name of the People*. London: Lawrence and Wishart.

Eschle, Catherine. 2016. "Faslane Peace Camp and the Political Economy of the Everyday." *Globalizations* 13 (6): 912–14.

Eschle, Catherine. 2018. "Troubling Stories of the End of Occupy: Feminist Narratives of Betrayal at Occupy Glasgow." *Social Movement Studies* 18 (1): 1–17.

Europa Press. 2016. "La Causa Contra Rato Afecta a Medio Centenar de Empresas y Datos Informáticos Que Llenarían 728 Camiones Según ONIF." *Lainformación.Com*, February 19, http://www.lainformacion.com/policia-y-justicia/fraude/la-causa-contra-rato-afecta-a-medio-centenar-de-empresas-y-datos-informaticos-que-llenarian-728-camiones-segun-onif_wWq6uDzujr5L69D25e9py6/.

Europa Press. 2018. "Archivado El Caso Preferentes." Europa Press, May 20, http://www.europapress.es/otr-press/firmas/carmentomas/noticia-carmen-tomas-archivado-caso-preferentes-20180520080050.html.

European Council. 1993. "Council Directive 93/13/EEC of 5 April 1993 on Unfair Terms in Consumer Contracts." *Official Journal of the European Communities*, April 21, http://eur-lex.europa.eu/LexUriServ/LexUriServ.do?uri=CELEX:31993L0013:en:HTML.

Eyerman, Ron, and Andrew Jamison. 1991. *Social Movements: A Cognitive Approach*. Philadelphia: Penn State University Press.

Ezquerra, Sandra. 2012. "Discursos y Prácticas Feministas En El Movimiento 15-M: Avances y Asignaturas Pendientes." *Fundación Betiko*, January, http://

fundacionbetiko.org/wp-content/uploads/2012/11/discursos-y-praciticas-feministas-en-el-15m.pdf.

Feenstra, Ramón A. 2015. "Activist and Citizen Political Repertoire in Spain: A Reflection Based on Civil Society Theory and Different Logics of Political Participation." *Journal of Civil Society* 11 (3): 242–58.

Feenstra, Ramón, and John Keane. 2014. "Politics in Spain: A Case of Monitory Democracy." *VOLUNTAS: International Journal of Voluntary and Nonprofit Organizations* 25 (5): 1262–80.

Feenstra, Ramón, Simon Tormey, Andreu Casero-Ripollés, and John Keane. 2017. *Refiguring Democracy: The Spanish Political Laboratory.* London: Taylor and Francis.

Fenton, Natalie, and Veronica Barassi. 2011. "Alternative Media and Social Networking Sites: The Politics of Individuation and Political Participation." *Communication Review* 14 (3): 179–96.

Fernández-Albertos, José. 2015. "La Diferencia Entre El Voto a Podemos y Ahora Madrid." *eldiario.es*, June 17, http://www.eldiario.es/piedrasdepapel/diferencia-voto-Podemos-Ahora-Madrid_6_399720026.html.

Fernández González, Joseba. 2014. "El Movimiento Estudiantil Desde Las Teorías de La Acción Colectiva: El Caso Del Movimiento Anti-Bolonia En El Estado Español." PhD Thesis, Universidad del País Vasco, Unpublished.

Fernández-Planells, Ariadna. 2015. "Keeping Up with the News. Youth Culture, Social Activism & Digital Communication." PhD Thesis, Universidad Pompeu Fabra, https://www.tdx.cat/handle/10803/371740#page=1.

Fernández-Planells, Ariadna, Mònica Figueras-Maz, and Carles Feixa Pàmpols. 2014. "Communication among Young People in the #spanishrevolution: Uses of Online–Offline Tools to Obtain Information about the #acampadabcn." *New Media & Society* 16 (8): 1287–308.

Fernández-Planells, Ariadna, Carles Feixa Pampols, and Mònica Figueroas-Maz. 2013. "15-M En España: Diferencias y Similitudes En Las Prácticas Comunicativas Con Los Movimientos Previos." *Última Década* 21 (39): 115–38.

Fernández-Savater, Amador. 2012a. "El Nacimiento de Un Nuevo Poder Social." *Hispanic Review* 80 (4): 667–81.

Fernández-Savater, Amador. 2012b. "Emborronar La CT." In *CT o La Cultura de La Transición : Crítica a 35 Años de Cultura Española*, edited by Guillem Martinez. Barcelona: Debolsillo.

Fernández-Savater, Amador. 2014. "Potencias y Problemas de Una Política Del 99%: Entrevista Con Jacques Rancière." *eldiario.es*, January, 24, http://www.eldiario.es/interferencias/Ranciere-politica_del_99_6_221587865.html.

Fernández-Savater, Amador. 2015a. "Amador Fernández-Savater, En El Cuarto Aniversario Del 15M: Debes Cambiar Tu Vida" *eldiario.es*, May 21, http://www.eldiario.es/politica/nuevos-partidos-existen-gracias-creado_0_390211997.html.

Fernández-Savater, Amador. 2015b. *Fuera de Lugar.* Madrid: Antonio Machado.

Fernández-Savater, Amador. 2016. "La Asamblea y El Campamento." Unpublished. https://emakbakea.files.wordpress.com/2016/08/fsavater-la-asamblea-y-el-campamento.pdf.

Fernández-Savater, Amador, and Cristina Flesher Fominaya. 2017. "Life after the Squares: Reflections on the Consequences of the Occupy Movements." *Social Movement Studies* 16 (1): 119–51.

Fish, Adam. 2015. "Internet Parties: The Internet as Party, Policy, Platform, and Persuasive Symbol." Working Paper, MIT Press. http://eprints.lancs.ac.uk/73056/.

Fishman, Robert M. 2019. *Democratic Practice*. New York: Oxford University Press.

Flesher Eguiarte, Cristina. 2005. "The Logic of Autonomy: Principles, Praxis, and Challenges of Autonomous Anti-Capitalist Movement." PhD Thesis, University of California.

Flesher Fominaya, Cristina. 2007a. "Autonomous Movements and the Institutional Left: Two Approaches in Tension in Madrid's Anti-Globalization Network." *South European Society & Politics* 12 (3): 335–58.

Flesher Fominaya, Cristina. 2007b. "The Role of Humour in the Process of Collective Identity Formation in Autonomous Social Movement Groups in Contemporary Madrid." *International Review of Social History* 52 (S15): 243–258.

Flesher Fominaya, Cristina. 2010a. "Collective Identity in Social Movements: Central Concepts and Debates." *Sociology Compass* 4 (6): 393–404.

Flesher Fominaya, Cristina. 2010b. "Creating Cohesion from Diversity: The Challenge of Collective Identity Formation in the Global Justice Movement." *Sociological Inquiry* 80 (3): 377–404.

Flesher Fominaya, Cristina. 2013. "Movement Culture Continuity: The British Anti-Roads Movement as Precursor to the Global Justice Movement." In *Understanding European Movements: New Social Movements, Global Justice Struggles, Anti-Austerity Protests*, edited by Cristina Flesher Fominaya and Laurence Cox, 109–24. London: Routledge.

Flesher Fominaya, Cristina. 2014a. *Social Movements and Globalization: How Protests, Occupations and Uprisings Are Changing the World*. London: Palgrave Macmillan.

Flesher Fominaya, Cristina. 2014b. "Spain is Different: Podemos and 15-M." *Open Democracy*, May 29, https://www.opendemocracy.net/en/can-europe-make-it/spain-is-different-podemos-and-15m/.

Flesher Fominaya, Cristina. 2014c. "Spain's Marches of Dignity, 22M, 2014: Not Anti-Politics." *Open Democracy*, March 25, https://www.opendemocracy.net/en/can-europe-make-it/spains-marches-of-dignity-22m-2014-not-antipolitics/.

Flesher Fominaya, Cristina. 2015a. "Autonomous Social Movements and the Paradox of Anti-Identitarian Collective Identity." In *The Identity Dilemma: Social Movements and Collective Identity*, edited by Aidan McGarry and James M. Jasper, 65–84. Philadelphia: Temple University Press.

Flesher Fominaya, Cristina. 2015b. "Debunking Spontaneity: Spain's 15-M/ Indignados as Autonomous Movement." *Social Movement Studies* 14 (2): 142–63.

Flesher Fominaya, Cristina. 2015c. "El Sentido Común, Lo 'Político,' El Feminismo y El 15M." *Encrucijadas: Revista Crítica de Ciencias Sociales* 9, http://www.encrucijadas.org/index.php/ojs/article/view/160.

Flesher Fominaya, Cristina. 2015d. "Explainer: The Spanish General Election." *The Conversation*, December, http://theconversation.com/explainer-the-spanish-general-election-52545.

Flesher Fominaya, Cristina. 2015e. "Redefining the Crisis/Redefining Democracy: Mobilising for the Right to Housing in Spain's PAH Movement." *South European Society and Politics* 20 (4): 465–85.

Flesher Fominaya, Cristina. 2016a. "Cultural Barriers to Activist Networking: Habitus (In)Action in Three European Transnational Encounters." *Antipode* 48 (1): 151–71.

Flesher Fominaya, Cristina. 2016b. "Unintended Consequences: The Negative Impact of E-Mail Use on Participation and Collective Identity in Two 'Horizontal' Social Movement Groups." *European Political Science Review* 8 (1): 95–122.

Flesher Fominaya, Cristina. 2017. "European Anti-Austerity and Pro-Democracy Protests in the Wake of the Global Financial Crisis." *Social Movement Studies* 16 (1): 1–20.

Flesher Fominaya, Cristina. 2018. "Spain's Historic Motion of No-Confidence: How Can We Understand the Ousting of Seemingly Indestructible Mariano Rajoy, in Just 72 Hours?" *Open Democracy*, June 1, https://www.opendemocracy.net/can-europe-make-it/cristina-flesher-fominaya/spain-s-historic-motion-of-no-confidence-how-can-we-und.

Flesher Fominaya, Cristina. 2019. "Collective Identity in Social Movements: Assessing the Limits of a Theoretical Framework." In *The Blackwell Companion to Social Movements*, edited by David Snow et al., 429–45. Oxford: Wiley.

Flesher Fominaya, Cristina, and Kevin Gillan. 2017. "Navigating the Technology-Media-Movements Complex." *Social Movement Studies* 16 (4): 383–402.

Foa, Roberto Stefan, Yascha Mounk, Russell J Dalton, and Christian Welzel. 2016. "The Democratic Disconnect." *Journal of Democracy* 27 (3): 5–17.

Foucault, Michel, and Jay Miskowiec. 1986. "Of Other Spaces." *Diacritics* 16 (1) 22–27.

Fraser, Nancy. 1997. *Justice Interruptus*. London: Routledge.

Freeman, Jo. 1999. "On the Origins of Social Movements." In *Waves of Protest: Social Movements Since the Sixties*, edited by Jo Freeman and Victoria Johnson, 7–24. Lanham, MA: Rowman & Littlefield.

Freeman, Jo. 2013. "The Tyranny of Structurelessness." *WSQ: Women's Studies Quarterly* 41 (3): 231–46.

Freeman, Jo., and Victoria L. Johnson. 1999. *Waves of Protest: Social Movements since the Sixties*. Lanham, MD: Rowman and Littlefield.

Fuster Morell, Mayo. 2012. "The Free Culture and 15M Movements in Spain: Composition, Social Networks and Synergies." *Social Movement Studies* 11 (3–4): 386–92.

Gámez Fuentes, María José. 2015. "Feminisms and the 15M Movement in Spain: Between Frames of Recognition and Contexts of Action." *Social Movement Studies* 14 (3): 359–65.

Gamson, Joshua. 1995. "Must Identity Movements Self-Destruct? A Queer Dilemma." *Social Problems* 42 (3): 390–407.

Gamson, William A. 1990. *The Strategy of Social Protest*. 2nd ed. Belmont: Wadsworth.

Gamson, William, Bruce Fireman, and Stephen Rytina. 1982. *Encounters with Unjust Authority*. Homewood, IL: Dorsey Press.

García Agustín, Óscar. 2015. *Sociology of Discourse: From Institutions to Social Change*. Amsterdam: John Benjamins.

Gerbaudo, Paolo. 2012. *Tweets and The Street*. London: Pluto.

Gerbaudo, Paolo. 2017. "The Indignant Citizen: Anti-Austerity Movements in Southern Europe and the Anti-Oligarchic Reclaiming of Citizenship." *Social Movement Studies* 16 (1): 36–50.

Gerlach, Luther. 2001. "The Structure of Social Movements: Environmental Activism and its Opponents." In *Networks and Netwars: The Future of Terror, Crime and Militancy*, edited by John Arquilla and David Ronfeldt, 289–310. Santa Monica: Rand.

Gerlach, Luther P., and Virginia H. Hine. 1970. *People, Power, Change: Movements of Social Transformation*. Indianapolis: Bobbs-Merrill.

Gil, Álex. 2014. "Ada Colau: Si Nos Rendimos a La Corrupción Estructural, Estamos Perdidos Como Sociedad." *Público*, February 24, http://www.publico.es/actualidad/ada-colau-rendimos-corrupcion-estructural.html.

Gitlin, Todd. 2003 [1980]. *The Whole World Is Watching : Mass Media in the Making and Unmaking of the New Left*, 2003rd ed. Oakland: University of California Press.

Giugni, Marco. 1998. "Was It Worth the Effort? The Outcomes and Consequences of Social Movements." *Annual Review of Sociology* 24: 371–393.

Giugni, Marco, Doug McAdam, and Charles Tilly. 1999. *How Social Movements Matter*. Minneapolis: University of Minnesota Press.

Goldstone, Jack A. 1980. "The Weakness of Organization: A New Look at Gamson's *The Strategy of Social Protest*." *American Journal of Sociology* 85 (5): 1017–42.

Goodwin, Jeff, and James M Jasper. 1999. "Caught in a Winding, Snarling Vine: The Structural Bias of Political Process Theory." *Sociological Forum* 14 (1): 27–54.

Goodwin, Jeff, James M. Jasper, and Francesca Polletta. 2001. *Passionate Politics*. Chicago: University of Chicago Press.

Gramsci, Antonio. 1971. *Selections from the Prison Notebooks of Antonio Gramsci*. London: Lawrence & Wishart.

Grueso, Stéphane. 2011. 15M.Cc—Conversación Con Miguel Arana. https://www.youtube.com/watch?v=AocCJIR46co.

Grueso, Stéphane. 2012. "Excelente. Revulsivo. Importante." https://www.youtube.com/watch?v=cBouuM-64Ik.

Guedán, Manuel (ed.). 2016. *Podemos: Una Historia Colectiva*. Madrid: AKal.

Gutiérrez, Carmen M. 2016. "Ramón Espinar: Los Círculos de Podemos No Están Solo Para Pegar Carteles." *Madridiario*, November 2, https://www.madridiario.es/noticia/438440/politica/ramon-espinar:-los-circulos-de-podemos-no-estan-solo-para-pegar-carteles.html.

Habermas, Jurgen. 1975. *Legitimation Crisis*. Boston: Beacon Press.

Habermas, Jürgen. 1981. *The Theory of Communicative Action*. Cambridge: Polity Press.

Hammond, John. 2015. "The Anarchism of Occupy Wall Street." *Science and Society* 79 (2): 288–313.

Hardt, Michael, and Antonio Negri. 2004. *Multitude: War and Democracy in the Age of Empire*. London: Penguin Press.

Haro Barba, Carmen, and Víctor Sampedro Blanco. 2011. "Activismo Político en Red: Del Movimiento por la Vivienda Digna al 15M." *Teknokultura* 8 (2): 167–185. https://revistas.ucm.es/index.php/TEKN/article/view/48025/44901.

Held, David. 1995. *Democracy and the Global Order*. Cambridge: Cambridge University Press.

Hensmans, Manuel. 2003. "Social Movement Organizations: A Metaphor for Strategic Actors in Institutional Fields." *Organization Studies* 24 (3) 355–81.

Hetherington, Kevin. 1998. *Expressions of Identity: Space, Performance, Politics*. London: SAGE.

Holloway, John. 2014. *Change the World without Taking Power: The Meaning of Revolution Today*. London: Pluto Press.

Iglesias, Pablo. 2015. *Politics in a Time of Crisis: Podemos and the Future of Democracy in Europe*. London: Verso.

Infolibre. 2015a. "Las Primarias de Podemos Finalizan Con Un 15, 69% de Participación." *InfoLibre*, July 23, http://www.infolibre.es/noticias/politica/2015/07/23/poco_mas_del_los_inscritos_podemos_votado_las_primarias_para_elegir_candidatos_35822_1012.html.

Infolibre. 2015b. "Pablo Iglesias Presenta a Su Equipo Para Ganar Las Generales: 'Nacimos Para Esto.'" *InfoLibre*, July 16, http://www.infolibre.es/noticias/politica/2015/07/16/pablo_iglesias_presenta_equipo_para_ganar_las_generales_quot_nacimos_para_esto_quot_35519_1012.html.

Jasper, James. 2008. *The Art of Moral Protest: Culture, Biography, and Creativity in Social Movements*. Chicago: University of Chicago Press.

Jasper, James. 2010a. "Cultural Approaches in the Sociology of Social Movements." In *Handbook of Social Movements across Disciplines*, edited by Bert Klandermans and Conny Roggeband, 59–109. New York: Springer.

Jasper, James. 2010b. "Social Movement Theory Today: Toward a Theory of Action?" *Sociology Compass* 4 (11): 965–76.

Jenkins, J. Craig, and Craig Eckert. 1986. "Channeling Black Insurgency: Elite Patronage and Professional Social Movement Organizations in the Development of the Black Movement." *American Sociological Review* 51 (6): 812–29.

Juris, Jeffrey S. 2008. *Networking Futures*. Durham, NC: Duke University Press.

Juris, Jeffrey S. 2012. "Reflections on #Occupy Everywhere: Social Media, Public Space, and Emerging Logics of Aggregation." *American Ethnologist* 39 (2): 259–79.

Juris, Jeffrey S., Giuseppe Caruso, Stéphane Couture, and Lorenzo Mosca. 2013. "The Cultural Politics of Free Software and Technology within the Social Forum Process." In *Insurgent Encounters: Transnational Activism, Ethnography, and the Political*, edited by Jeffrey S. Juris and Alex Khasnabish, 342–65. Durham, NC: Duke University Press.

Juventud Sin Futuro (JSF). 2011a. *Juventud Sin Futuro*. Barcelona: Icaria.

Juventud Sin Futuro (JSF). 2011b. "Manifiesto. Juventud SIN Futuro." https://www.diariodeunjugon.com/manifiesto-juventud-sin-futuro/.

Kaldor, Mary, and Sabine Selchow. 2013. "The 'Bubbling Up' of Subterranean Politics in Europe." *Journal of Civil Society* 9 (1): 78–99.

Kanellopoulos, Kostas., Konstantinos Kostopoulos, Dimitris Papanikolopoulos, and Vasileios Rongas. 2017. "Competing Modes of Coordination in the Greek Anti-Austerity Campaign, 2010–2012." *Social Movement Studies* 16 (1): 101–18.

Katsiaficas, George. 1989. "The Eros Effect." Paper presented at the American Sociological Association Annual Meeting, San Francisco.

Katsiaficas, George. 2006. *The Subversion of Politics: European Autonomous Social Movements and the Decolonization of Everyday Life*. Oakland: AK Press.

Katzenstein, Mary. 1998. "Stepsisters: Feminist Movement Activism in Different Institutional Spaces." In *The Social Movement Society*, edited by David Meyer and Sidney Tarrow, 195–216. London: Rowman & Littlefield.

Kavada, Anastasia. 2018. "Connective or Collective? The Intersection between Online Crowds and Social Movements in Contemporary Activism." In *The Routledge Companion to Media and Activism*, edited by Graham Miekle, 108–16. London: Routledge.

Keane, John. 2011. "Monitory Democracy?" In *The Future of Representative Democracy*, edited by Sonia Alonso, John Keane and Wolfgang Merkel, 212–35. Cambridge: Cambridge University Press.

Klandermans, Bert. 1997. *The Social Psychology of Protest*. Oxford: Blackwell.

Koopmans, Ruud. 2004. "Protest in Time and Space: The Evolution of Waves of Contention." In *The Blackwell Companion to Social Movements*, edited by David A. Snow, Sarah Anne Soule, and Hanspeter Kriesi, 19–46. London: Blackwell.

Kriesberg, Louis, and Bruce Dayton. 2012. *Constructive Conflicts: From Escalation to Resolution*. Lanham, MD: Rowman & Littlefield.

Lago, Jorge. 2015. "Entrevista a Pablo Iglesias." *La Circular*, http://lacircular.info/entrevista-pablo-iglesias/.

Langman, Lauren. 2013. "Occupy: A New New Social Movement." *Current Sociology* 61 (4): 510–24.

Laraña, Enrique, Joseph Gusfied, and Hank Johnston. 2009. *New Social Movements: From Ideology to Identity*. Philadelphia: Temple University Press.

Lasswell, Harold D. 1936. *Politics: Who Gets What, When, How*. New York: McGraw-Hill.

Lawrence, Jeffrey. 2013. "The International Roots of the 99% and the 'Politics of Anyone.'" *IC—Revista Científica de Información y Comunicación* 10: 53–72.

LeFebvre, Rebecca Kay, and Crystal Armstrong. 2018. "Grievance-Based Social Movement Mobilization in the #Ferguson Twitter Storm." *New Media & Society* 20 (1): 8–28.

Linegraphics. 2011. "Movimiento 15M—Acampada de La Puerta Del Sol—Madrid 2011." *Linegraphics*.

Lobera, Josep. 2015. "De Movimientos a Partidos: La Cristalización Electoral de La Protesta/From Movements to Political Parties: The Electoral Crystallization of Protest." *RES* 24: 97–105. http://www.fes-sociologia.com/files/res/24/06.pdf.

Lobera, Josep, and Jesús Rogero-García. 2016. "De Las Plazas a Las Urnas. La Medición de La Cristalización Electoral Del 15-M En Podemos." *Pensamiento Crítico*, http://www.pensamientocritico.org/joslob0716.pdf.

Lofland, John. 1995. "Charting Degrees of Movement Culture: Tasks of the Cultural Cartographer." In *Social Movements and Culture*, edited by Hank Johnston, 188–216. Minneapolis: University of Minnesota Press.

Lorenzo Vila, Ana Rosa, and Miguel Martínez López. 2001. *Asambleas y reuniones: Metodologías de autoorganización*. Madrid: Editorial Traficantes de Sueños.

Luna, Victoria. 2013. "Rajoy Plantea Aún Más Ajustes Tras Un Año y Medio Plagado de Recortes Sociales." *20minutos*, http://www.20minutos.es/noticia/1795384/0/ajustes/recortes/gobierno/.

Maeckelbergh, Marianne. 2009. *The Will of the Many: How the Alterglobalisation Movement is Changing the Face of Democracy*. London: Pluto Press.

Maeckelbergh, Marianne. 2012. "Horizontal Democracy Now: From Alterglobalization to Occupation." *Interface* 4 (1): 207–34.

Mansbridge, Jane. 1994. "Using Power/Fighting Power." *Constellations* 1 (1): 53–73.

Marea Azul. 2014. *Más Claro Agua: El Plan de Saqueo Del Canal de Isabel II*. Madrid: Traficantes de Sueños. https://www.traficantes.net/libros/mas-claro-agua.

Mateo Regueiro, Estela (dir.), Rafael Cid, Colectivo Utopía Contagiosa, Álex Corrons, Ángeles Diez, Mario Domínguez, Desiderio Martín, et al. 2015. *Hasta Luego, Pablo: Once Ensayos Críticos Sobre Podemos*. Madrid: Catarata. http://www.catarata.org/libro/mostrar/id/1018.

Martinez, Guillem (coord.). 2012. *CT o La Cultura de La Transición. Crítica a 35 Años de Cultura Española*. Barcelona: Debolsillo.

Martínez, Miguel A. 2016. "Between Autonomy and Hybridity: Urban Struggles within the 15M Movement in Spain." In *Urban Uprisings*, edited by Hakan Thorn, Margit Meyer, and Katarina Thorn, 253–81. London: Palgrave.

Martinez, Miguel, and Ángela García. 2015. "Ocupar Las Plazas, Liberar Edificios (The Occupation of Squares and the Squatting of Buildings)." *ACME: An International Journal for Critical Geographies* 14 (1): 157–84.

McAdam, Doug. 1982. *Political Process and the Development of Black Insurgency, 1930–1970*. Chicago: University of Chicago Press.

McAdam, Doug. 1988. *Freedom Summer*. Oxford: Oxford University Press.

McAdam, Doug, 2013. "Cognitive Liberation." In *The Wiley-Blackwell Encyclopedia of Social and Political Movements*, edited by David A. Snow, et al., n.p. Oxford: Blackwell. https://onlinelibrary.wiley.com/doi/book/10.1002/9780470674871.

McAdam, Doug, Sidney Tarrow, and Charles Tilly. 2003. "Dynamics of Contention." *Social Movement Studies* 2 (1): 99–102.

McCarthy, John D., Jackie Smith, and Mayer N. Zald. 1996. "Accessing Public, Media, Electoral, and Governmental Agendas." In *Comparative Perspectives on Social Movements: Political Opportunities, Mobilizing Structures, and Cultural Framings*, edited by Doug McAdam, John D McCarthy, and Mayer N Zald, 291–311. Cambridge: Cambridge University Press.

McCarthy, John D., and Mayer N. Zald. 1977. "Resource Mobilization and Social Movements: A Partial Theory." *American Journal of Sociology* 82 (6) 1212–41.

McKay, George. 1998. *DiY Culture: Party and Protest in Nineties Britain*. London: Verso.

McVeigh, Rory. 1995. "Social Structure, Political Institutions, and Mobilization Potential." *Social Forces* 74 (2): 461–85.

Melucci, Alberto. 1989. *Nomads of the Present*. Philadelphia: Temple University Press.

Melucci, Alberto. 1994. "A Strange Kind of Newness: What's 'New' in New Social Movements?" In *New Social Movements: From Ideology to Identity*, edited by Enrique Laraña, Hank Johnston, and Joseph R. Gusfield, 103–30. Philadelphia, PA: Temple University Press.

Melucci, Alberto. 1996. *Challenging Codes: Collective Action in the Information Age*. Cambridge: Cambridge University Press.

Melucci, Alberto. 2003. "The Process of Collective Identity." In *Social Movements and Culture*, edited by Hank Johnston and Bert Klandermans, 41–63. London: Routledge.

Mercea, Dan, Laura Iannelli, and Brian D. Loader. 2016. "Protest Communication Ecologies." *Information, Communication & Society* 19 (3): 279–89.

Metroscopia. 2015. "¿Hombre o Mujer?, ¿edad? Así Son Los Votantes de PP, PSOE, C's y Podemos—Metroscopia." Metroscopia, October 11, http://metroscopia.org/recurso/pp-psoe-podemos-ciudadanos-edad-genero/.

Meyer, David S. 2003. "Social Movements and Public Policy: Eggs, Chicken, and Theory." UC Irvine Working Papers. https://escholarship.org/uc/item/2m62b74d.

Meyer, David S. 2007. *The Politics of Protest: Social Movements in America.* Oxford: Oxford University Press.

Meyer, David S., and Suzanne Staggenborg. 1996. "Movements, Countermovements, and the Structure of Political Opportunity." *American Journal of Sociology* 101 (6): 1628–60.

Milan, Stefania. 2015. "From Social Movements to Cloud Protesting: The Evolution of Collective Identity." *Information, Communication & Society* 18 (8): 887–900.

MLGM, and MLGB. 2017. *Y Al Final Ganamos Las Elecciones.* Barcelona: MLGM.

Monterde, A. 2015. "Emergencia, Evolución y Efectos Del Movimiento-Red 15M (2011–2015). Una Aproximación Tecnopolítica." PhD Thesis, Universitat Oberta de Catalunya.

Monterde, A., and J. Postill. 2014. "Mobile Ensembles: The Uses of Mobile Phones for Social Protest by Spain's Indignados." In *The Routledge Companion to Mobile Media*, edited by Gerard Goggin and Larissa Hjorth, 429–438. London: Routledge.

Moreno Caballud, Luis. 2015. *Cultures of Anyone: Studies on Cultural Democratization in the Spanish Neoliberal Crisis*, translated by Linda L. Grabner-Coronel. Liverpool: Liverpool University Press.

Morris, Aldon D. 1984. *The Origins of the Civil Rights Movement: Black Communities Organizing for Change.* New York: Free Press.

Morris, Aldon, and Suzanne Staggenborg. 2004. "Leadership in Social Movements." In *The Blackwell Companion to Social Movements*, edited by David A. Snow, Sarah Anne Soule, and Hanspeter Kriesi, 171–95. London: Blackwell.

Mosca, Lorenzo. 2014. "The Five Star Movement: Exception or Vanguard in Europe? *International Spectator* 49 (1) 36–52.

Mouffe, Chantal. 2005. *On the Political.* London: Routledge.

Mucha, Martín. 2015. "#15MpaRATO: 'La Caída de Rodrigo Rato Es Nuestra Mayor Obra de Arte.'" *El Mundo*, April 26, http://www.elmundo.es/cronica/2015/04/26/553b3e37e2704e65238b4571.html.

Muller, Edward N., and Karl Dieter Opp. 1986. "Rational Choice and Rebellious Collective Action." *American Political Science Review* 80 (2): 471–88.

Munson, Ziad W. 2008. *The Making of Pro-Life Activists: How Social Movement Mobilization Works.* Chicago: University of Chicago Press.

Negri, Toni. 1980. "Domination and Sabotage." In *Italy: Autonomia Post-political Politics*, edited by Semiotexte, 62–71. New York: Semiotexte.

Néz, Heloise. 2012. "Entre los militantes y los laboratorios deliberativos: el 15-M." In *From Social to Political*, edited by B. Tejerina and I. Perugorria, 123–40. Bilbao: University of the Basque Country.

Norris, Pippa. 2014. *Democratic Deficit: Critical Citizens Revisited*. Cambridge: Cambridge University Press.

Oliver, Pamela E. 1989. "Bringing the Crowd Back In: The Nonorganizational Elements of Social Movements." *Research in Social Movements, Conflict and Change* 11: 1–30.

Otero, Jorge. 2014. "Lo de Bankia Fue un Fraude Masivo: Rato lo Sabía y lo Ocultó." *Público*, June 12, http://www.publico.es/actualidad/bankia-fraude-masivo-rato-sabia.html.

PAH (Plataforma de Afectados por la Hipoteca). 2012. "2012 Annus horribilis: Nuevo record de desahucios en España." https://afectadosporlahipoteca.com/2012/12/27/nuevo-record-de-desahucios-en-espana-datos-cgpj/.

PAH (Plataforma de Afectados por la Hipoteca). 2013a. "De Afectado a Diputado." http://afectadosporlahipoteca.com/2013/03/12/de-afectado-a-diputado/.

PAH (Plataforma de Afectados por la Hipoteca). 2013b. "Nueva Campaña de La PAH: Escraches. Pongámosle Nombre y Apellido a Los Responsables Del #genocidioFinanciero." http://afectadosporlahipoteca.com/2013/02/04/final-ilp-campanya-escraches/.

PAH (Plataforma de Afectados por la Hipoteca). 2016. "Campaña Obra Social La PAH." http://afectadosporlahipoteca.com/category/propuestas-pah/obra_social_la_pah/.

Pateman, Caroline. 1970. *Participation and Democratic Theory*. Cambridge: Cambridge University Press.

Partido X. 2014. "2014, Viaje a las tripas del sistema electoral." https://partidox.org/2014-viaje-tripas-sistema-electoral/#conclusiones.

Peña-López, Ismael, Mariluz Congosto, and Pablo Aragón. 2014. "Spanish *Indignados* and the Evolution of the 15M Movement on Twitter: Towards Networked Para-Institutions." *Journal of Spanish Cultural Studies* 15: 1–2, 189–216. https://doi.org/10.1080/14636204.2014.931678.

Pérez, Fernando. 2018. "El Juez Archiva La Causa Por Estafa En Las Preferentes de Caja Madrid y Bancaja" *El País*, May 18, https://elpais.com/economia/2018/05/18/actualidad/1526646820_844171.html.

Peschard, Jacqueline. P. 1997. *La cultura política democrática*. Instituto Federal Electoral.

Picazo, Sergi, and Marià de Delás. 2015. "Pablo Iglesias: Que Se Queden Con La Bandera Roja y Nos Dejen En Paz. Yo Quiero Ganar," *Público*, June 24, http://www.publico.es/politica/iglesias-quiero-ganar-dejen-paz.html.

Pickerill, Jenny. 2004. "Rethinking Political Participation: Experiments in Internet Activism in Australia and Britain." In *Electronic Democracy: Mobilisation, Organisation and Participation Via New ICTs*, edited by Rachel Gibson, Andrea Rommele and Steven Ward, 170–93. London: Routledge.

Piven, Frances, and Richard A. Cloward. 1979. *Poor People's Movements: Why They Succeed, How They Fail*. New York: Vintage.

Piven, Frances Fox, and Richard A. Cloward. 1991. "Collective Protest: A Critique of Resource Mobilization Theory." *International Journal of Politics Culture and Society* 4 (4): 435–58.

Plows, Alex. 1998. "Earth First! Defending Mother Earth, Direct-Style." In *DiY Culture: Party & Protest in Nineties Britain*, edited by George McKay, 310–328. London: Verso.

Podemos. 2014. "Pablo Iglesias Presenta La Iniciativa PODEMOS." https://www.youtube.com/watch?v=R16QC4eBnj8.

Polletta, Francesca. 1998a. "Contending Stories: Narrative in Social Movements." *Qualitative Sociology* 21 (4): 419–46.

Polletta, Francesca.1998b. "It Was like a Fever . . .; Narrative and Identity in Social Protest." *Social Problems* 45 (2): 137–59.

Polletta, F. (2002). Freedom is an endless meeting: Democracy in American social movements. Chicago: University of Chicago Press.

Polletta, Francesca. 2006. *It was like a Fever*. Chicago: University of Chicago Press.

Polletta, Francesca. 2012. *Freedom Is an Endless Meeting: Democracy in American Social Movements*. Chicago: University of Chicago Press.

Postill, John. 2014a. "Freedom Technologists and the New Protest Movements: A Theory of Protest Formulas." *Convergence: The International Journal of Research into New Media Technologies* 20 (4): 402–18.

Postill, John. 2014b. "How Spain's Indignados Movement Was Born: Daniel Váquez´s Interview with Stéphane M. Grueso, Translated by John Postill." *johnpostill.wordpress.com*, https://johnpostill.wordpress.com/2014/08/01/how-spains-indignados-movement-was-born/.

Power, Séamus A. 2016. "A Violent Past but a Peaceful Present: The Cultural Psychology of an Irish Recession." *Peace and Conflict: Journal of Peace Psychology* 22 (1): 60–66.

Precarias a la Deriva. 2004. *A La Deriva: Por Los Circuitos de La Precariedad Femenina*. Madrid: Traficantes De Sueños.

Público.es. 2011. "Cronología de La Acampada 'indignada' En La Puerta Del Sol." *Público*, May 31, http://www.publico.es/actualidad/cronologia-acampada-indignada-puerta-del.html.

Público.es. 2017. "El Coste de La Crisis Financiera: El Banco de España Calcula Que No Se Recuperarán 60.600 Millones de Las Ayudas a La Banca." *Público*, June 16, http://www.publico.es/economia/banco-espana-calcula-no-recuperar-60600-millones-ayuda-banca.html.

Público.es. 2019. "El saldo de cuatro años de Carmena" *Público*, June 6, https://www.publico.es/politica/saldo-cuatro-anos-carmena-madrid-54-menos-deuda-y-superavit-1-072-millones.html.

Rancière, Jacques.2004. "Introducing Disagreement." *Angelaki: Journal of the Theoretical Humanities* 9 (3): 3–9.

Rancière, Jacques. 2011. "Democracies against Democracy." In *Democracy in What State?*, edited by Giorgio Agamben, 76–81. New York: Columbia University Press.

Rancière, Jacques. 2014. *Hatred of Democracy*. London: Verso.

Revilla, Marisa, Anabel Garrido, Ignacio Martínez, Carlos Molina Herico More, and Karen Rodríguez. 2015. "Consecuencias Inesperadas de Las Acciones de Protesta: Reconfiguración Ideológica y Electoral En España (2010–2014)." Unpublished paper.

Rivero, Jacobo. 2015. *Podemos. Objetivo: Asaltar Los Cielos*. Barcelona: Planeta.

Roberts, Alasdair. 2012. "Why the Occupy Movement Failed." *Public Administration Review* 72 (5): 754–62.

Rodon, Toni, and María José Hierro. 2016. "Podemos and Ciudadanos Shake Up the Spanish Party System: The 2015 Local and Regional Elections." *South European Society and Politics* 21 (3): 339–57.

Romanos, Eduardo. 2013. "Collective Learning Processes within Social Movements: Some Insights into the Spanish 15M/Indignados Movement." In *Understanding European Movements: New Social Movements, Global Justice Struggles, Anti-Austerity Protest*, edited by Cristina Flesher Fominaya and Laurence Cox, 203–19. London: Routledge.

Romanos, Eduardo. 2016. "Immigrants as Brokers: Dialogical Diffusion from Spanish Indignados to Occupy Wall Street." *Social Movement Studies* 15 (3): 247–62.

Romanos, Eduardo, and Igor Sádaba. 2015. "La Evolución de Los Marcos (Tecno) Discursivos Del Movimiento 15M y Sus Consecuencias." *Empiria: Revista de Metodología de Ciencias Sociales* 32: 15–36.

Roos, Jérôme E, and Leonidas Oikonomakis. 2014. "They Don't Represent Us!: The Global Resonance of the Real Democracy Movement from the Indignados to Occupy." In *Spreading Protest: Social Movements in Times of Crisis*, edited by Donatella della Porta and Alice Mattoni, 117–36. Colchester: ECPR Press.

Rusiñol, Pere. 2011. "España Vota Hoy Pendiente de Los Indignados y Los Indecisos." *Público*, May 22, http://www.publico.es/espana/espana-vota-hoy-pendiente-indignados.html.

Sahuquillo, María R. 2013. "2008–2013: Balance de Daños." *El País*, December 27, http://politica.elpais.com/politica/2013/12/27/actualidad/1388176018_072390.html.

Sainz, Jorge. 2014. "Xnet Revoluciona Lucha Contra Corrupción En España." *Telemetro.Com*, December 12, 2014. http://www.telemetro.com/internacionales/Xnet-revoluciona-lucha-corrupcion-Espana_0_761024022.html.

Sampedro, Víctor, and Josep Lobera. 2014. "The Spanish 15-M Movement: A Consensual Dissent?" *Journal of Spanish Cultural Studies* 15 (1–2): 61–80.

Sánchez, Juan Luis. 2011. "Vista Aérea de La Concentración En Sol 17M #acampadasol." https://www.youtube.com/watch?v=ar2nmOQZEjw.

Sánchez, Juan Luís. 2014. "Pablo Iglesias Prepara Su Candidatura a Las Europeas." *eldiario.es*, January 14, http://www.eldiario.es/politica/Pablo-Iglesias-Juan-Carlos-Monedero-candidato-europeas-podemos_0_216278861.html.

Sánchez, María F. 2017. "Espinar: 'Podemos Debe Liderar En Madrid y En España La Construcción de Un Espacio de Cambio.'" *Cuarto Poder*, April 30, www.cuartopoder.es/invitados/2017/04/30/espinar-podemos-debe-liderar-en-madrid-y-en-espana-la-construccion-de-un-espacio-de-cambio/12954.

Schumpeter, Joseph. 1943. *Capitalism, Socialism, and Democracy.* London: Allen and Unwin.

Segovia, Eduardo. 2015. "A Bankia le Sobraban 1.700 Millones Cuando Salió a Bolsa, Según los Cálculos del FROB." *El Confidencial*, January 14, http://www.elconfidencial.com/empresas/2015-01-14/a-bankia-le-sobraban-1-700-milones-cuando-salio-a-bolsa-segun-los-calculos-del-frob_621361/.

Shihade, Magid, Cristina Flesher Fominaya, and Laurence Cox. 2012. "The Season of Revolution: The Arab Spring and European Mobilizations." 4 (1): 1–16.

Snow, David, and Robert Benford. 1992. "Master Frames and Cycles of Protest." In *Frontiers in Social Movement Theory*, edited by Aldon D. Morris and Carol McClurg Mueller, 133–55. New Haven: Yale University Press.

Snow, David A., E. Burke Rochford, Steven K. Worden, and Robert D. Benford. 1986. "Frame Alignment Processes, Micromobilization, and Movement Participation." *American Sociological Review* 51 (4): 464–81.

Staggenborg, Suzanne. 1988. "The Consequences of Professionalization and Formalization in the Pro-Choice Movement." *American Sociological Review* 53 (4): 585–605.

Stuckler, David., and Sanjay Basu. 2013. *The Body Economic: Why Austerity Kills.* New York: Basic Books.

Taibo, Carlos. 2011. *Nada Será Como Antes : Sobre El Movimiento 15-M.* Los Libros de la Catarata. http://www.marcialpons.es/libros/nada-sera-como-antes/9788483196045/.

Tarrow, Sidney. 1993. "Cycles of Collective Action: Between Moments of Madness and the Repertoire of Contention." *Social Science History* 17 (2) 281–307.

Tarrow, Sidney. (1998) [1994]. *Power in Movements. Social Movements, Collective Action and Politics.* New York: Cambridge University Press.

Tarrow, Sidney. 2011. *Power in Movement: Social Movements and Contentious Politics.* Cambridge: Cambridge University Press.

Tarrow, Sidney. 2013. *The Language of Contention: Revolutions in Words, 1688–2012.* Cambridge: Cambridge University Press.

Taylor, V. 1989. "Social Movement Continuity: The Women's Movement in Abeyance." *American Sociological Review* 54: 761–75.

Thompson, E. P. 1963. *The Making of the English Working Class.* London: Pantheon.

Tilly, Charles. 1978. *From Mobilization to Revolution.* Reading: Addison-Wesley.

Tilly, Charles. 1999. "From Interactions to Outcomes." In *How Social Movements Matter*, edited by Marco Giugni, Doug McAdam, and Charles Tilly, 253–70. Minneapolis: University of Minnesota Press.

Toharia, José Juan. 2013a. "Escraches: Derecho, No Delito." Metroscopia Blog. *El País,* April 11, http://blogs.elpais.com/metroscopia/2013/04/el-78-de-los-españoles-68-entre-los-votantes-del-pp-85-entre-los-del-psoe-se-muestra-de-acuerdo-con-la-campaña-de.html.

Toharia, José Juan. 2013b. "Sentencia, Escraches y Burbuja." Metroscopia Blog. *El País,* March 19, http://blogs.elpais.com/metroscopia/2013/03/sentencia-escraches-y-burbuja.html.

Torcal, Mariano, Toni Rodon, and María José Hierro. 2015. "Word on the Street: The Persistence of Leftist-Dominated Protest in Europe." *West European Politics* 39 (2) 326–50.

Tormey, Simon. 2015a. "Democracy Will Never Be the Same Again: 21st Century Protest and the Transformation of Politics." *Recerca: Revista de Pensament y Anàlisi* 17: 107–28.

Tormey, Simon. 2015b. *The End of Representative Democracy.* Cambridge: Polity Press.

Tormey, Simon, and Ramón A. Feenstra. 2015. "Reinventing the Political Party in Spain: The Case of 15M and the Spanish Mobilisations." *Policy Studies* 36 (6): 590–606.

Touraine, Alain. 1997. *What Is Democracy?* Boulder: Westview Press.

Touraine, Alain. 1988. *Return of the Actor: Social Theory in Postindustrial Society.* Minneapolis: University of Minnesota Press.

Treré, Emiliano, and Veronica Barassi. 2015. "Net-Authoritarianism? How Web Ideologies Reinforce Political Hierarchies in the Italian 5 Star Movement." *Journal of Italian Cinema & Media Studies* 3 (3): 287–304.

Treré, Emiliano, and Alice Mattoni. 2016. "Media Ecologies and Protest Movements: Main Perspectives and Key Lessons." *Information, Communication & Society* 19 (3): 290–306.

Tufekci, Zeynep. 2014. "Social Movements and Governments in the Digital Age: Evaluating a Complex Landscape." *Journal of International Affairs* 68: 1–18.

Tufekci, Zeynep. 2017. *Twitter and Tear Gas: The Power and Fragility of Networked Protest.* New Haven: Yale University Press.

Uitermark, Justus, and Walter Nicholls. 2012. "How Local Networks Shape a Global Movement: Comparing Occupy in Amsterdam and Los Angeles." *Social Movement Studies* 11 (3–4): 295–301.

ULEX. 2008. *Autonomía y Metrópolis: Del Movimiento Okupa a Los Centros Sociales de Segunda Generación.* Málaga: Cedma.

United Nations. 2012. "'El Derecho a una Vivienda Digna,' Informe Relatora Especial A/67/286." https://www.ohchr.org/Documents/Issues/Housing/A-67-286_sp.pdf.

United Nations Document A/67/286. 2012. *The Right to Adequate Housing.* Note by the Secretary-General: Special Rapporteur on adequate housing as a component of the right to an adequate standard of living A/67/286, August 10. Wall, Derek.

1999. *Earth First! and the Anti-Roads Movement: Radical Environmentalism and Comparative Social Movements*. London: Routledge.

Xnet. 2012. "Un Mensaje Para El #12M15M Desde El Barrio de Internet." https://xnet-x.net/para-12m15m/.

Xnet. 2015. "15MpaRATO." https://xnet-x.net/docs/15MpaRato-dossier-english.pdf.

Xnet and 15MpaRato. 2016. "Hazte Banquero." https://xnet-x.net/hazte-banquero/.

Zald, Mayer, and John McCarthy. 2017. *Social Movements in an Organizational Society: Collected Essays*. London: Routledge.

Zamponi, Lorenzo, and Joseba Fernández González. 2017. "Dissenting Youth: How Student and Youth Struggles Helped Shape Anti-Austerity Mobilisations in Southern Europe." *Social Movement Studies* 16 (1): 64–81.

Žižek, Slavoj. 2000. *The Ticklish Subject: The Absent Centre of Political Ontology*. London: Verso.

Žižek, Slavoj. 2012. *The Year of Dreaming Dangerously*. London: Verso.

Zolberg, Aristide. R. 1972. "Moments of Madness." *Politics and Society* 2 (2): 183–207.

Index